Math in Focus®

2B

Singapore Math
by Marshall Cavendish

Consultant and Author
Dr. Fong Ho Kheong

Authors
Chelvi Ramakrishnan and Michelle Choo

U.S. Consultants
Dr. Richard Bisk
Andy Clark
Patsy F. Kanter

Marshall Cavendish Education

US Distributor

HOUGHTON MIFFLIN HARCOURT

COMMON CORE

Published by Marshall Cavendish Education
An imprint of Marshall Cavendish International (Singapore) Private Limited
Times Centre, 1 New Industrial Road, Singapore 536196
Customer Service Hotline: (65) 6411 0820
E-mail: tmesales@sg.marshallcavendish.com
Website: www.marshallcavendish.com/education

Distributed by
Houghton Mifflin Harcourt
222 Berkeley Street
Boston, MA 02116
Tel: 617-351-5000
Website: www.hmheducation.com/mathinfocus

First published 2013

Math in Focus® Grade 2 Student Book B
ISBN 978-0-547-87583-5

Printed in United States of America

2 3 4 5 6 7 8 1897 18 17 16 15 14 13
4500360944 A B C D E

Contents

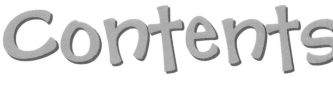

CHAPTER 10 Mental Math and Estimation

Look for **Practice and Problem Solving**

Student Book A and Student Book B	Workbook A and Workbook B
• **Let's Practice** in every lesson • **Put on Your Thinking Cap!** in every chapter	• **Independent Practice** for every lesson • **Put on Your Thinking Cap!** where applicable

Look for **Assessment Opportunities**

Student Book A and Student Book B	Workbook A and Workbook B
• Quick Check at the beginning of every chapter to assess chapter readiness • Guided Practice after every example or two to assess readiness to continue lesson	• Chapter Review/Test in every chapter to review or test chapter material • Cumulative Reviews seven times during the year • Mid-Year and End-of-Year Reviews to assess test readiness

CHAPTER 11
Money

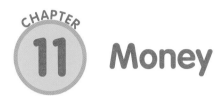

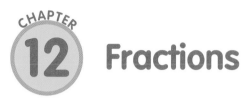

CHAPTER 12 Fractions

CHAPTER 13

Customary Measurement of Length

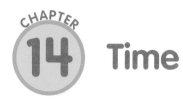

CHAPTER 14 Time

CHAPTER 15

Multiplication Tables of 3 and 4

E
U
C
S
O
N
R
M
A
D
1
2
3
4
5
6
7
8
9
10
× 4

CHAPTER 16 Using Bar Models: Multiplication and Division

CHAPTER 17

Picture Graphs

CHAPTER 18 Lines and Surfaces

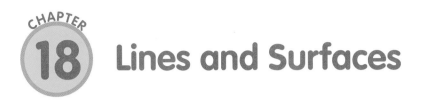

Chapter Opener 248

Recall Prior Knowledge Identifying plane shapes • Recognizing plane shapes in objects • Identifying sides and corners in plane shapes • Identifying solid shapes • Recognizing solid shapes in objects

Quick Check

1 Parts of Lines and Curves 253

Learn Recognize and identify parts of lines and curves • Combine parts of lines and curves

Hands-On Activity Trace parts of lines and curves • Trace outlines of solids to find plane shapes

2 Flat and Curved Surfaces 258

Learn See and feel flat surfaces • See and feel surfaces that are not flat • Move objects with flat or curved surfaces

Hands-On Activity Name solids shown and count the flat and curved surfaces on solid shapes, then mark whether they stack, slide or roll

Put on Your Thinking Cap! Problem Solving 265

Chapter Wrap Up 266

Chapter 19 Shapes and Patterns

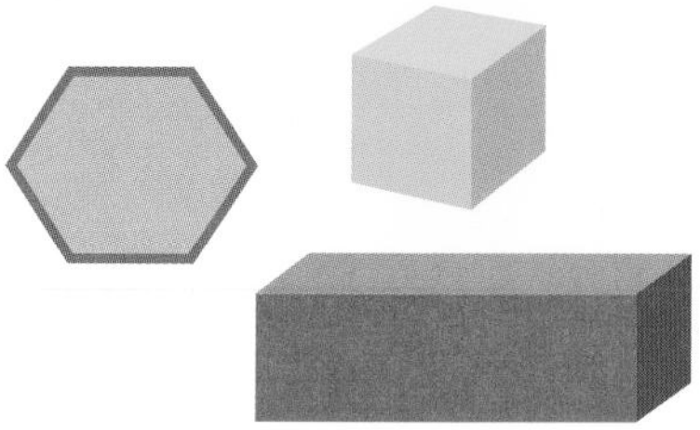

Welcome to

Math in Focus®

This exciting math program comes to you all the way from the country of Singapore. We are sure you will like all the different ways to learn math.

What makes *Math in Focus*® different?

- **Two books** You don't write in the in this textbook. This book has a matching **Workbook.** When you see ON YOUR OWN you will write in the **Workbook.**
- **Longer lessons** Some lessons may last more than a day, so you can really understand the math.
- **Math will make sense** Learn to use number bonds to understand better how numbers work.

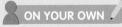

In this book, look for

Learn This means you learn something new.

Guided Practice Your teacher helps you try some problems.

Let's Practice Practice. Make sure you really understand.

ON YOUR OWN Now try some problems in your own **Workbook.**

Also look forward to *Games, Hands-On Activities, Put on Your Thinking Cap!*, and more. Enjoy some real math challenges!

What's in the Workbook?

Math in Focus® will give you time to learn important math ideas and do math problems. The **Workbook** will give you different types of practice.

- *Practice* problems will help you remember the new math idea you are learning. Watch for this ON YOUR OWN in your book. That will tell you which pages to use for practice.
- *Put on Your Thinking Cap!*

  Challenging Practice problems invite you to think in new ways to solve harder problems.

  Problem Solving gives you opportunities to solve questions in different ways.
- *Math Journal* activities ask you to think about thinking, and then write about that!

Students in Singapore have been using this kind of math program for many years. Now you can too — are you ready?

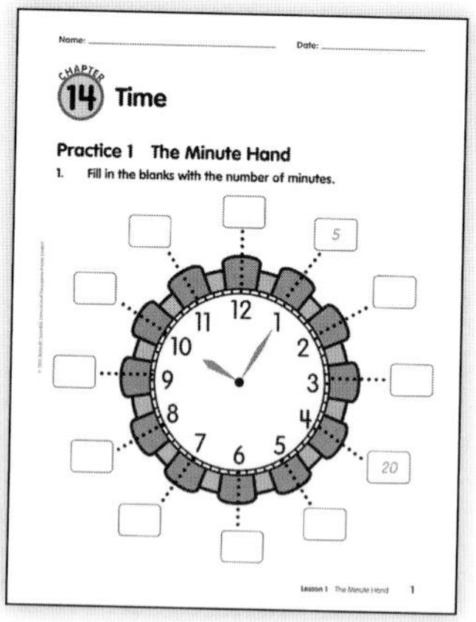

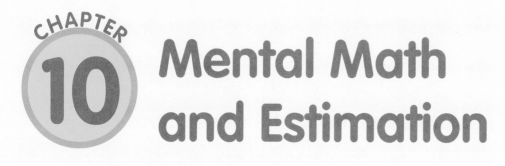

CHAPTER 10

Mental Math and Estimation

Tania and Mona take a math quiz.

Lesson 1	Meaning of Sum
Lesson 2	Mental Addition
Lesson 3	Meaning of Difference
Lesson 4	Mental Subtraction
Lesson 5	Rounding Numbers to Estimate

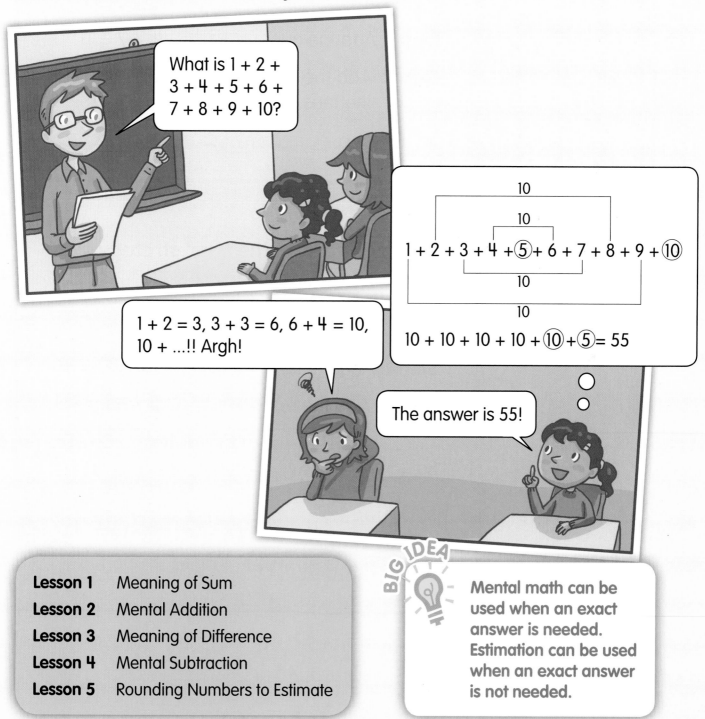

BIG IDEA

Mental math can be used when an exact answer is needed. Estimation can be used when an exact answer is not needed.

Recall Prior Knowledge

Adding ones mentally using the 'add the ones' strategy

Find 14 + 7.
Group 14 into tens and ones.

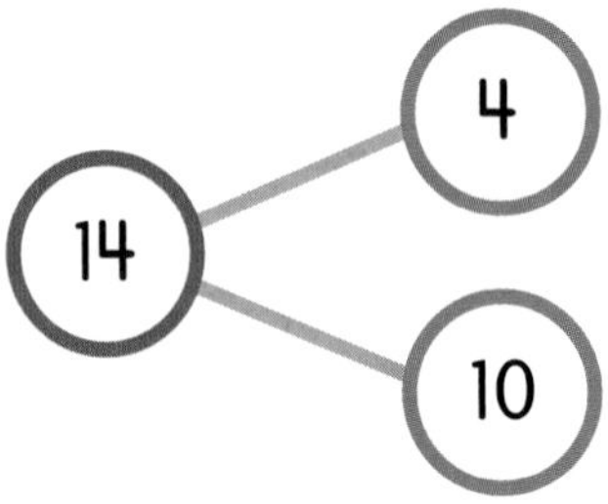

Step 1 Add the ones. $4 + 7 = 11$

Step 2 Add the result to the tens. $10 + 11 = 21$

So, 14 + 7 = 21.

Adding tens mentally using the 'add the tens' strategy

Find 15 + 30.
Group 15 into tens and ones.

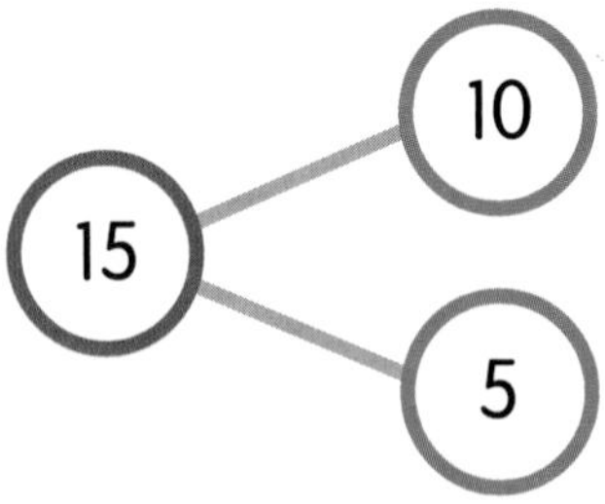

Step 1 Add the tens. $10 + 30 = 40$

Step 2 Add the result to the ones. $5 + 40 = 45$

So, 15 + 30 = 45.

Subtracting ones mentally using the 'subtract the ones' strategy

Find 27 – 4.
Group 27 into tens and ones.

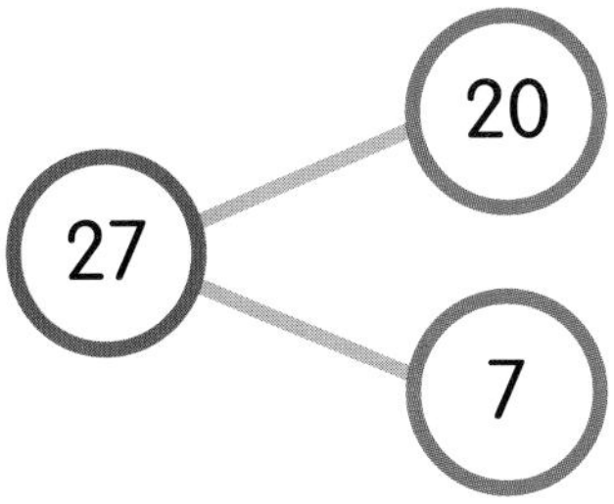

Step 1 Subtract the ones. 7 – 4 = 3

Step 2 Add the result to the tens. 20 + 3 = 23

So, 27 – 4 = 23.

Subtracting ones mentally by recalling number bonds

Find 15 – 8.

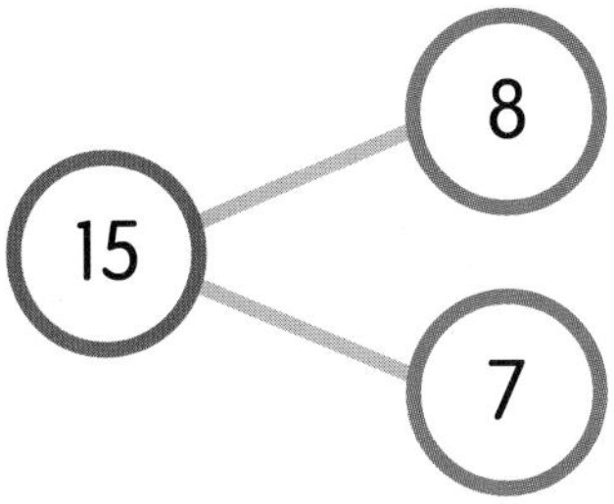

Think of addition.
8 and 7 make 15.

So, 15 – 8 = 7.

Subtracting tens mentally using the 'subtract the tens' strategy

Find 39 – 20.
Group 39 into tens and ones.

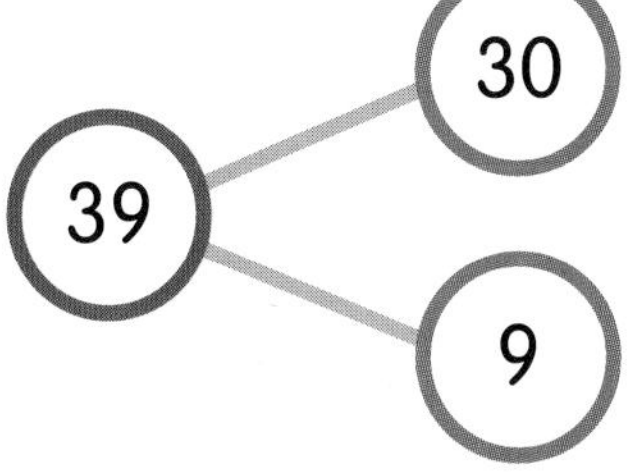

Step 1 Subtract the tens. 30 – 20 = 10

Step 2 Add the result to the ones. 9 + 10 = 19

So, 39 – 20 = 19.

Using a number line to count on to find how many more and count back to find how many less

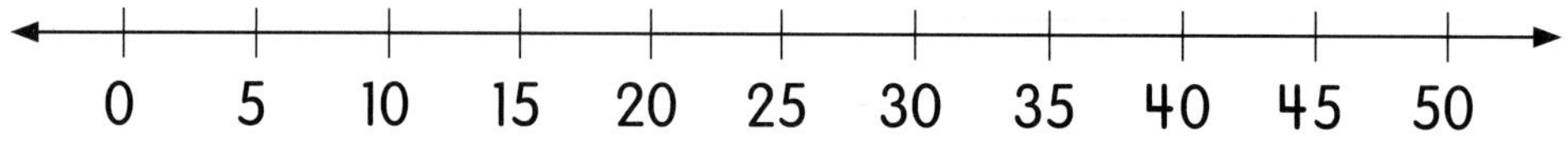

On a number line, numbers are arranged in order to form a regular pattern.

Hundreds, tens and ones

174 = 170 + 4

238 = 208 + 30

320 = 300 + 20

678 = 600 + 78

Adding using bar models

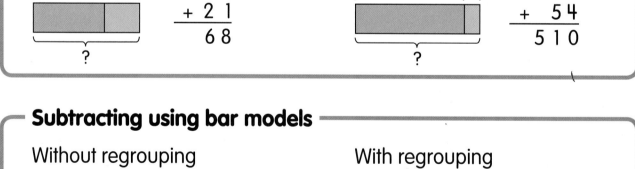

Without regrouping

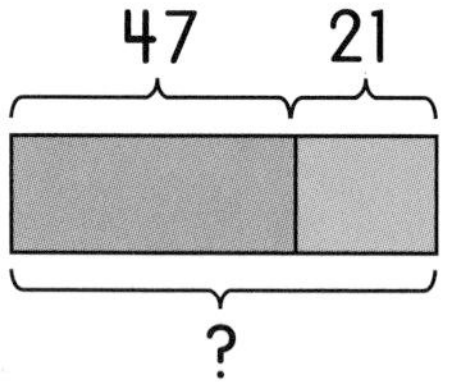

$$\begin{array}{r} 47 \\ +\ 21 \\ \hline 68 \end{array}$$

With regrouping

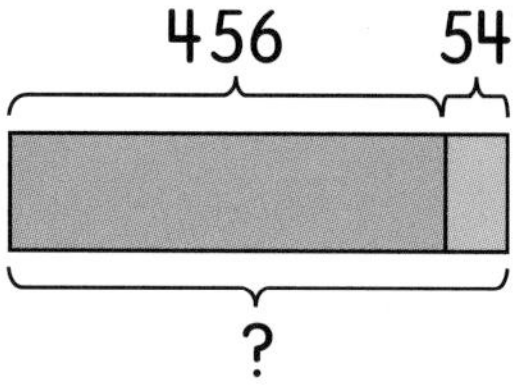

$$\begin{array}{r} \scriptsize{1\ 1} \quad \\ 456 \\ +\ \ 54 \\ \hline 510 \end{array}$$

Subtracting using bar models

Without regrouping

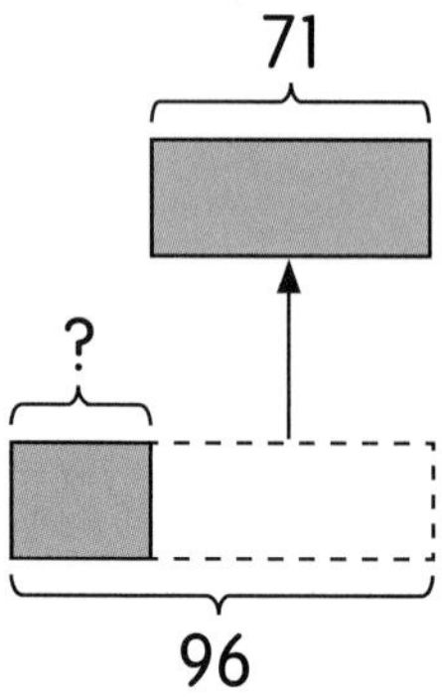

$$\begin{array}{r} 96 \\ -\ 71 \\ \hline 25 \end{array}$$

With regrouping

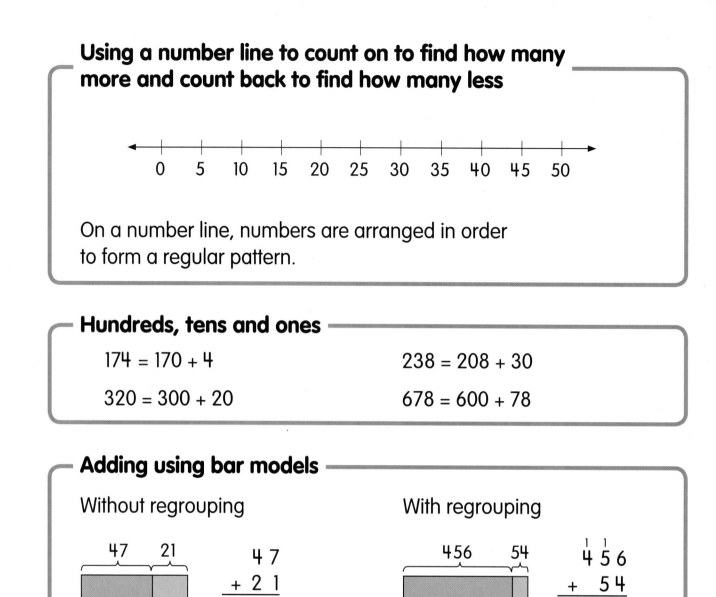

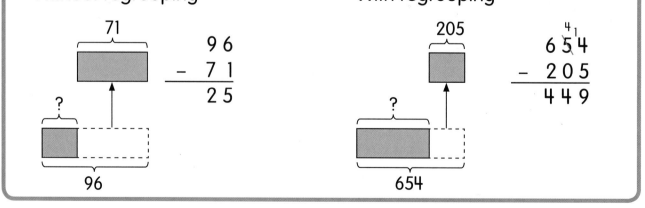

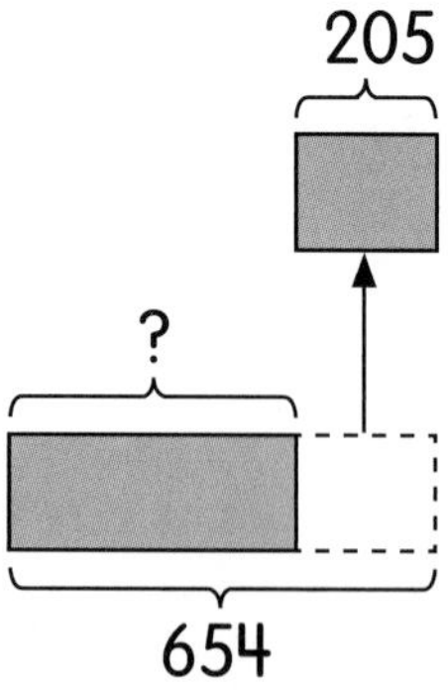

$$\begin{array}{r} \scriptsize{4\ 1} \ \\ 6\not{5}4 \\ -\ 205 \\ \hline 449 \end{array}$$

✔Quick Check

Add mentally.
Use number bonds to help you.

1. 16 + 8 = ____
2. 23 + 7 = ____
3. 17 + 10 = ____
4. 13 + 20 = ____

Subtract mentally.
Use number bonds to help you.

5. 28 – 5 = ____
6. 13 – 9 = ____
7. 26 – 10 = ____
8. 33 – 20 = ____

Find the missing numbers on the number line.

9. 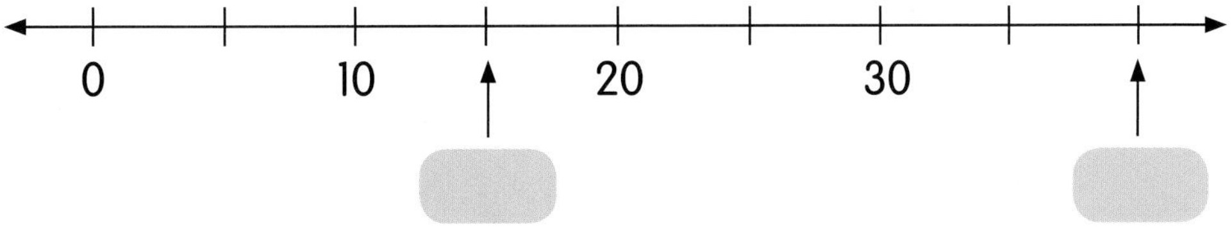

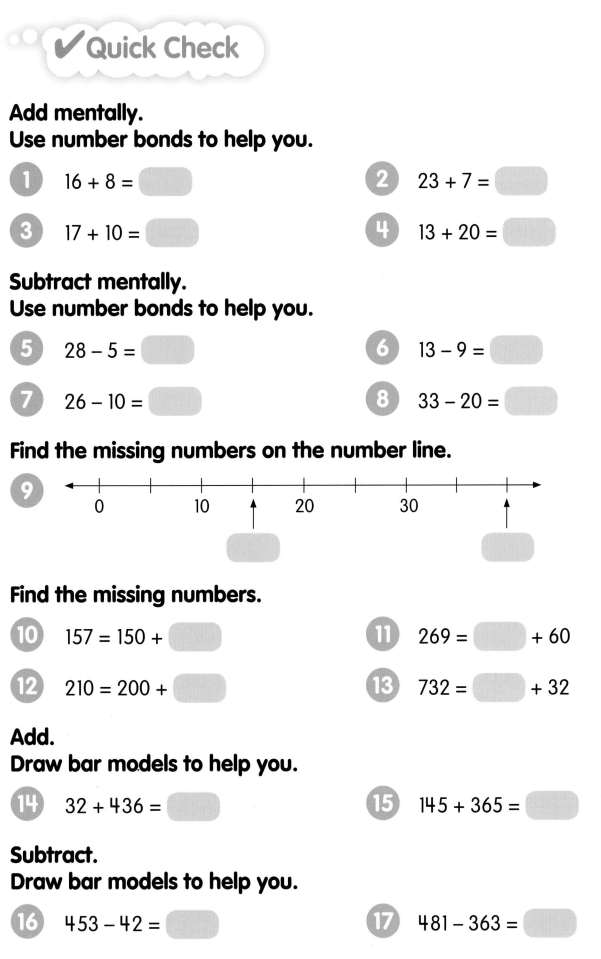

Find the missing numbers.

10. 157 = 150 + ____
11. 269 = ____ + 60
12. 210 = 200 + ____
13. 732 = ____ + 32

Add.
Draw bar models to help you.

14. 32 + 436 = ____
15. 145 + 365 = ____

Subtract.
Draw bar models to help you.

16. 453 – 42 = ____
17. 481 – 363 = ____

LESSON 1 Meaning of Sum

Lesson Objective

- Relate 'sum' to the addition operation.

Vocabulary
sum

Learn — Meaning of sum

Find the **sum** of the numbers 31 and 45.

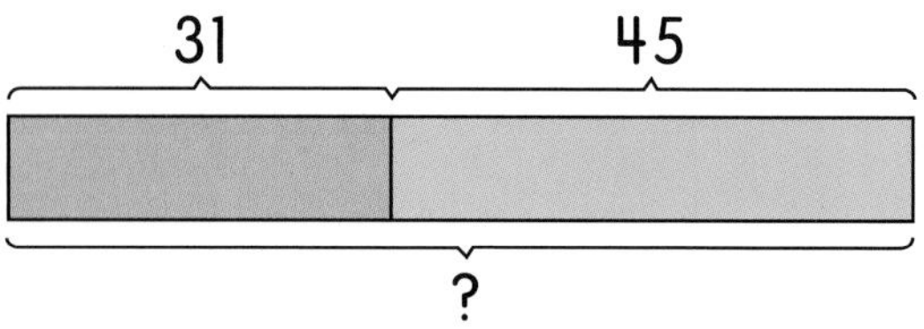

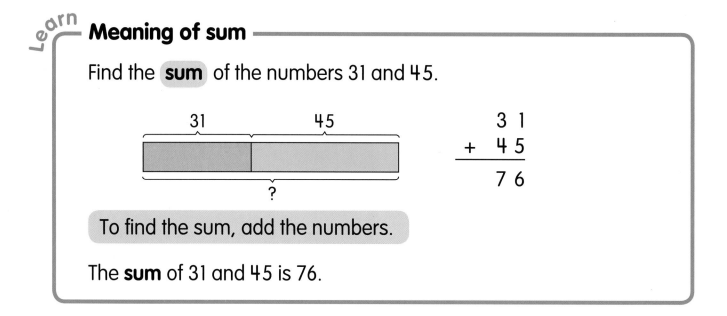

$$\begin{array}{r} 31 \\ +\ 45 \\ \hline 76 \end{array}$$

To find the sum, add the numbers.

The **sum** of 31 and 45 is 76.

Guided Practice

Find the sum of these numbers.

1. 35 and 59 ____
2. 220 and 48 ____
3. 715 and 160 ____
4. 814 and 126 ____

Solve. Use bar models to help you.

5. Ben has 425 stamps.
   Peter has 275 stamps.
   Find the sum of the numbers of stamps they have.

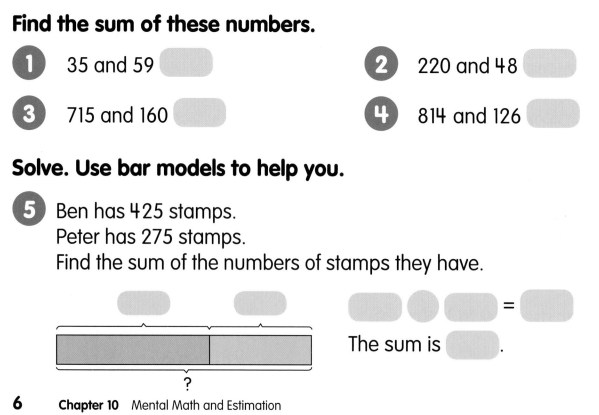

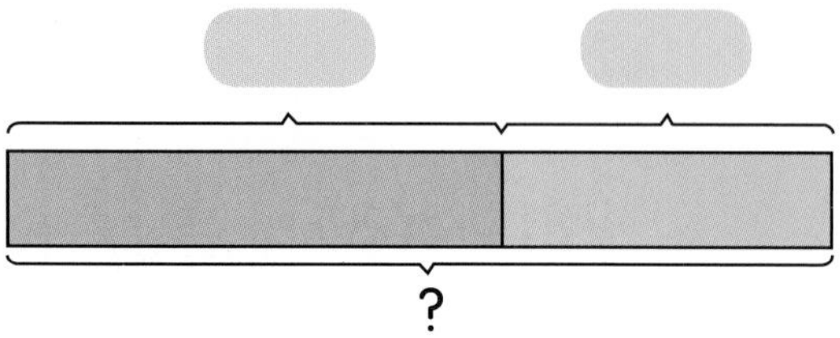

____ ____ ____ = ____

The sum is ____.

Let's Practice

Find the sum of these numbers.

1. 53 and 19 ☐

2. 48 and 167 ☐

Solve.
Draw bar models to help you.

3. Andy has 43 stickers.
Claire has 102 stickers.
Find the sum of the numbers of stickers they have.

4. José has 250 baseball cards of the Phoenix team.
He has 182 baseball cards of the Lions team.
Find the sum of the numbers of cards he has.

5. Alma has collected 125 popsicle sticks.
Bert has collected 187.
Find the sum of the numbers of popsicle sticks.

ON YOUR OWN

Go to Workbook B:
Practice 1, pages 1–2

LESSON 2

Mental Addition

Lesson Objective

- Add numbers with up to 3 digits mentally with with and without regrouping.

Vocabulary
add mentally

Learn

You can add ones to a 2-digit number mentally using the 'add 10 then subtract the extra ones' strategy.

What is 58 + 8?

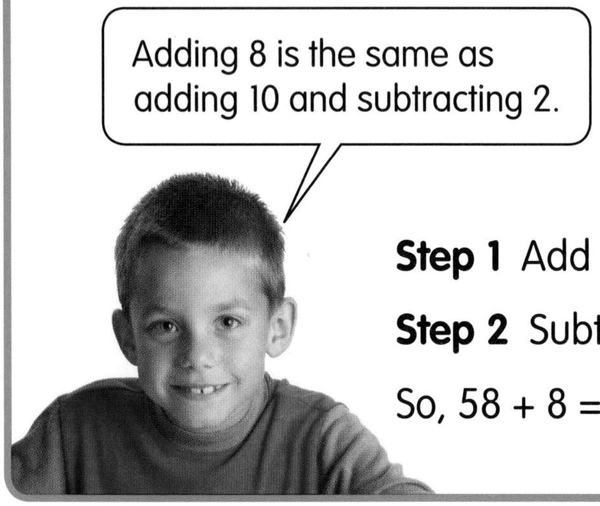

Adding 8 is the same as adding 10 and subtracting 2.

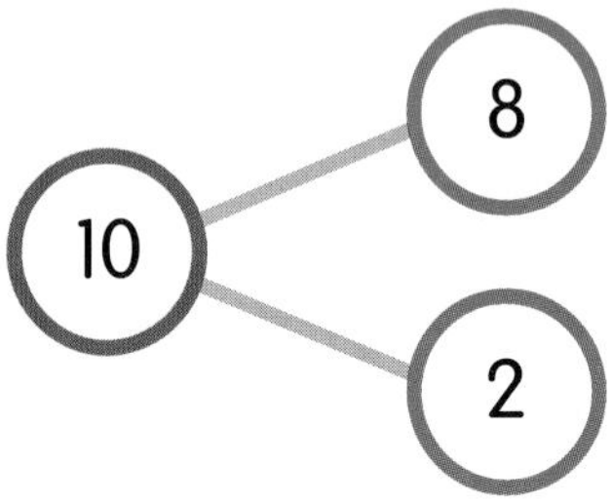

Step 1 Add 10 to 58. 58 + 10 = 68

Step 2 Subtract 2 from the result. 68 – 2 = 66

So, 58 + 8 = 66.

Guided Practice

Add mentally.
Use number bonds to help you.

1 Find 76 + 9.

9 = 10 – ____

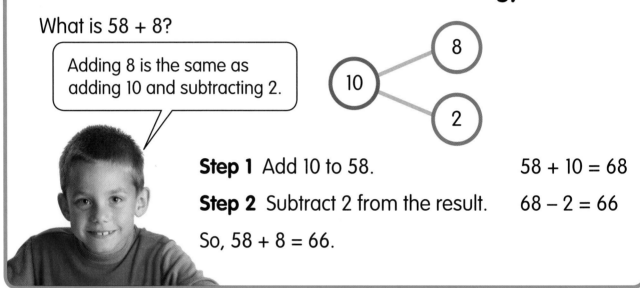

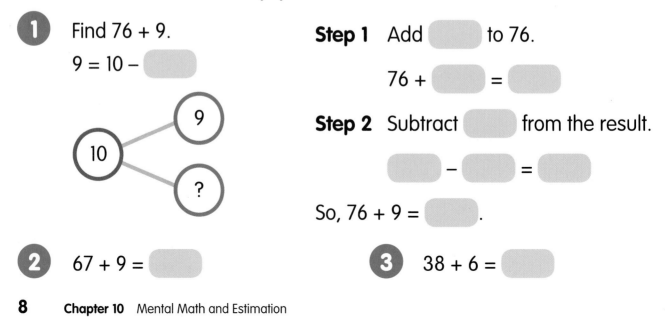

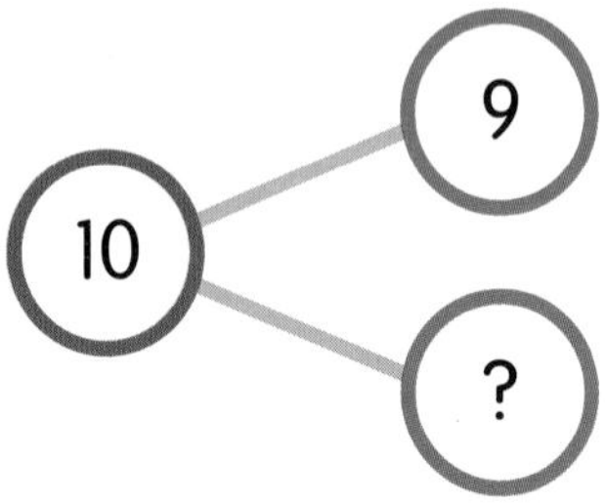

Step 1 Add ____ to 76.

76 + ____ = ____

Step 2 Subtract ____ from the result.

____ – ____ = ____

So, 76 + 9 = ____.

2 67 + 9 = ____

3 38 + 6 = ____

WORKING TOGETHER **Game**

Add Mentally!

Players: 2 to 4

You need:

- a number cube
- cards with numbers 6, 7, 8, and 9

How to play:

STEP 1 Player 1 rolls the number cube two times to make a two-digit number.

STEP 2 Player 1 picks a card to get another number.

STEP 3 Player 1 adds the two numbers mentally.

STEP 4 Players check the answer. Player 1 gets 1 point for a correct answer.

STEP 5 The other players take turns following STEP 1 to STEP 4. Stop after eight rounds.

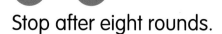

The player with the most points wins!

Learn: You can add ones to a 3-digit number mentally using the 'add the ones' strategy.

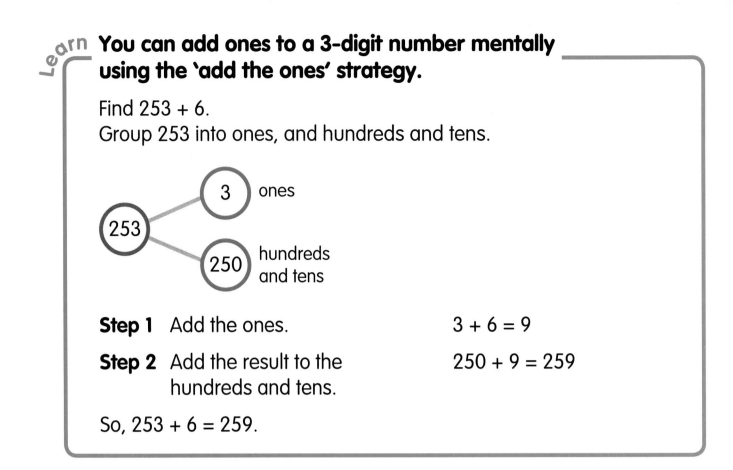

Find 253 + 6.
Group 253 into ones, and hundreds and tens.

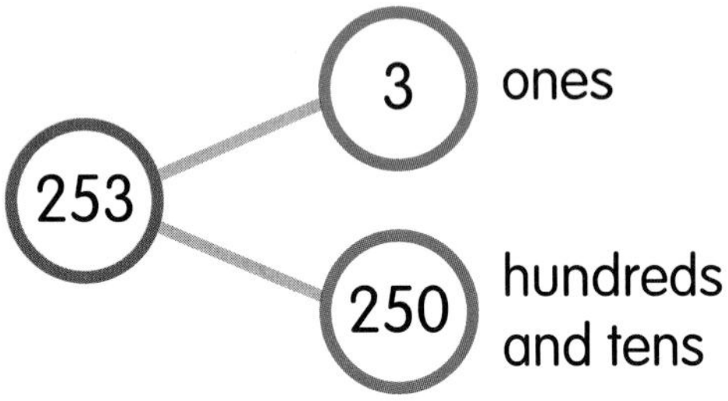

Step 1 Add the ones. 3 + 6 = 9

Step 2 Add the result to the hundreds and tens. 250 + 9 = 259

So, 253 + 6 = 259.

Guided Practice

Add mentally.
Use number bonds to help you.

4 Find 472 + 5.
Group 472 into ones, and hundreds and tens.

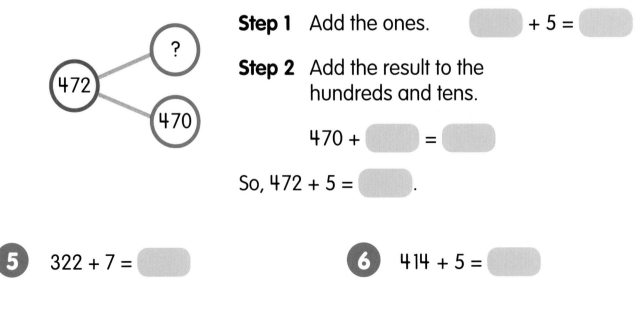

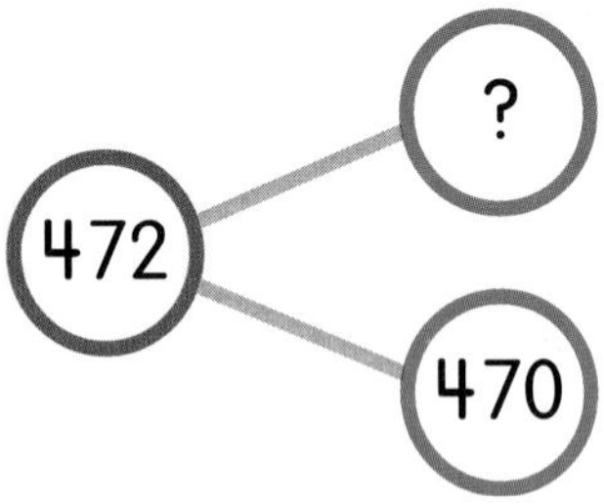

Step 1 Add the ones. ____ + 5 = ____

Step 2 Add the result to the hundreds and tens.

470 + ____ = ____

So, 472 + 5 = ____.

5 322 + 7 = ____

6 414 + 5 = ____

Learn You can add ones to a 3-digit number mentally using the 'add 10 then subtract the extra ones' strategy.

Find 128 + 4.

Adding 4 is the same as adding 10 and subtracting 6.

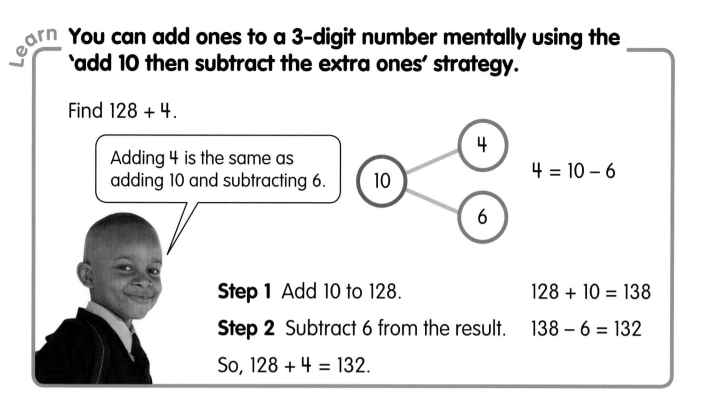

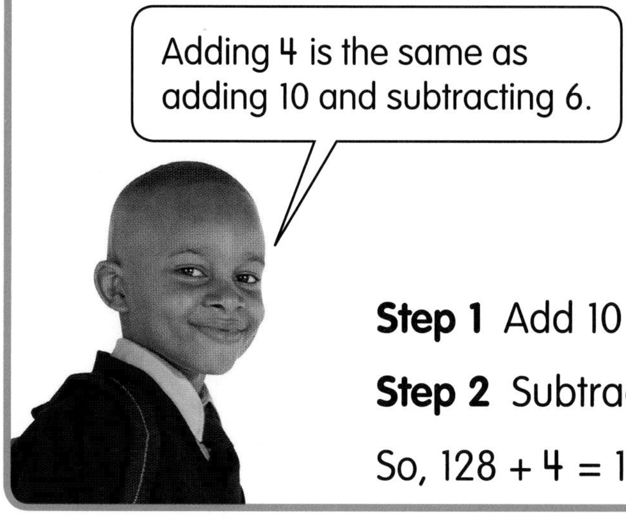

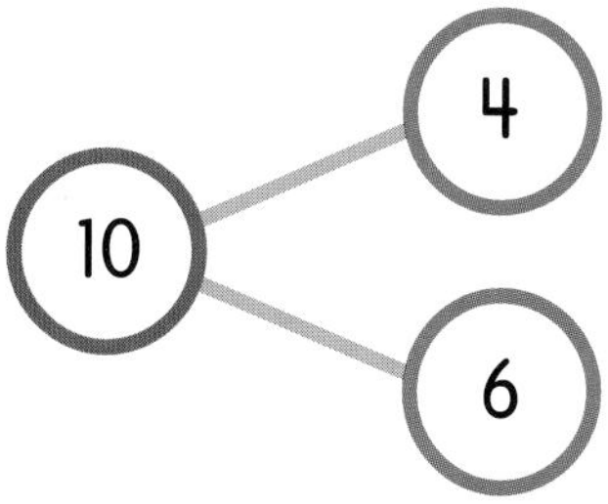

$4 = 10 - 6$

Step 1 Add 10 to 128. $128 + 10 = 138$

Step 2 Subtract 6 from the result. $138 - 6 = 132$

So, $128 + 4 = 132$.

Guided Practice

Add mentally.
Use number bonds to help you.

7 Find 347 + 8.

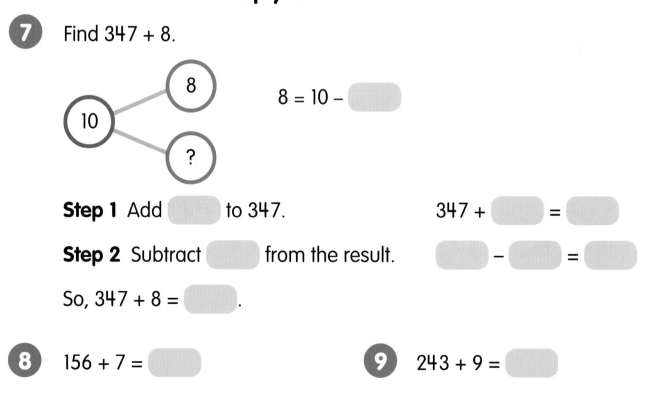

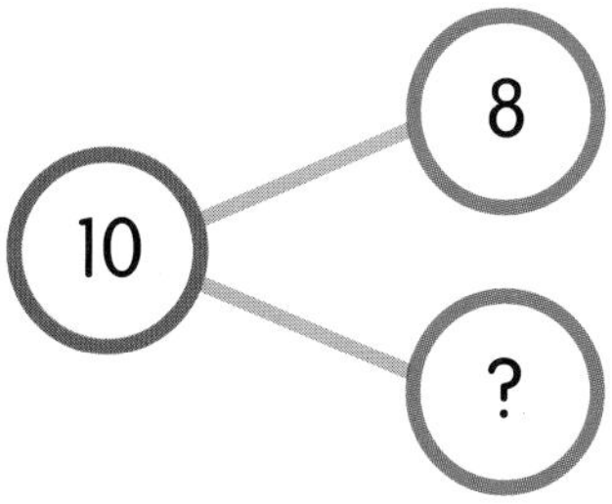

$8 = 10 - \boxed{}$

Step 1 Add $\boxed{}$ to 347. $347 + \boxed{} = \boxed{}$

Step 2 Subtract $\boxed{}$ from the result. $\boxed{} - \boxed{} = \boxed{}$

So, $347 + 8 = \boxed{}$.

8 $156 + 7 = \boxed{}$

9 $243 + 9 = \boxed{}$

Learn

You can add tens to a 3-digit number mentally using the 'add the tens' strategy.

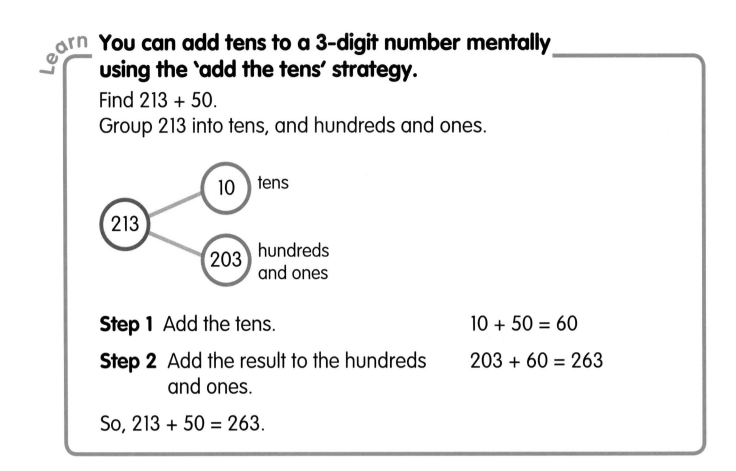

Find 213 + 50.
Group 213 into tens, and hundreds and ones.

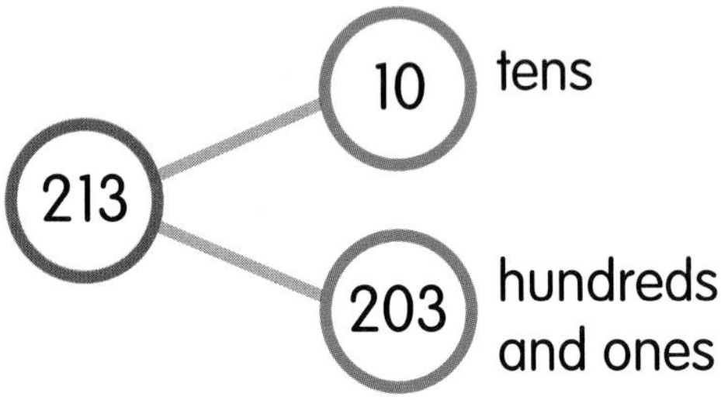

Step 1 Add the tens. 10 + 50 = 60

Step 2 Add the result to the hundreds and ones. 203 + 60 = 263

So, 213 + 50 = 263.

Guided Practice

Add mentally.
Use number bonds to help you.

10 Find 351 + 40.
Group 351 into tens, and hundreds and ones.

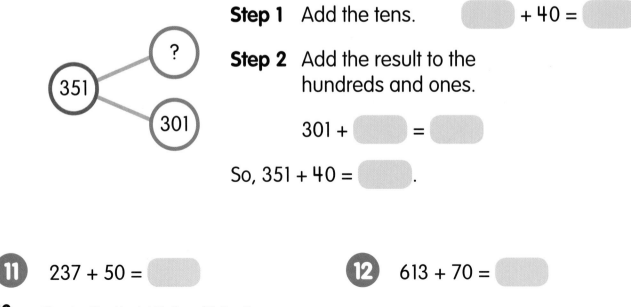

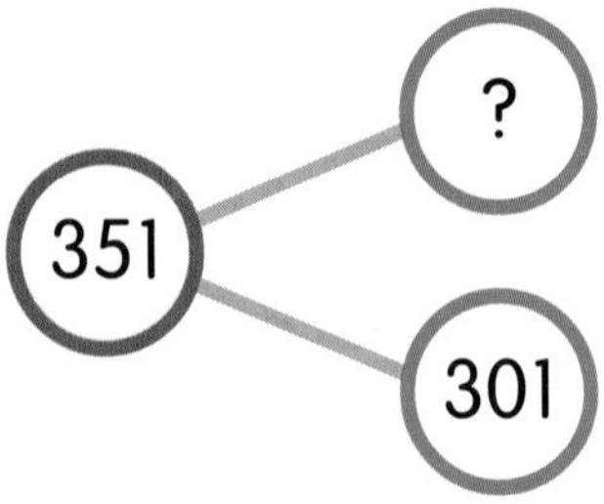

Step 1 Add the tens. ____ + 40 = ____

Step 2 Add the result to the hundreds and ones.

301 + ____ = ____

So, 351 + 40 = ____.

11 237 + 50 = ____

12 613 + 70 = ____

Learn

You can add tens to a 3-digit number mentally using the 'add 100 then subtract the extra tens' strategy.

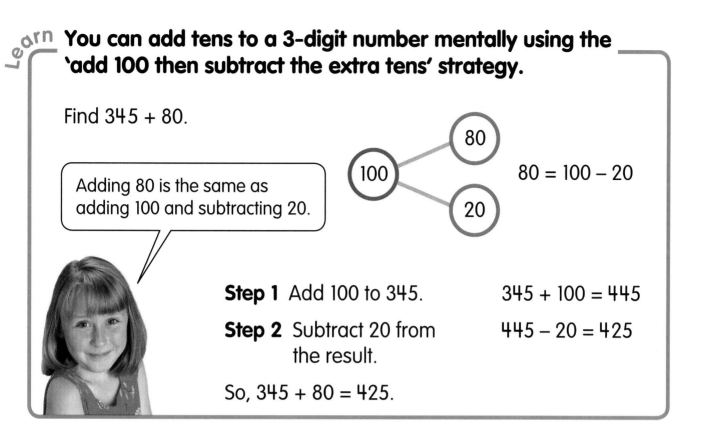

Find 345 + 80.

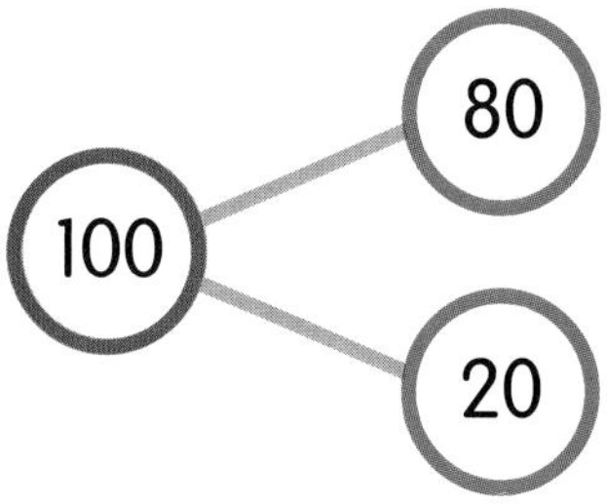

80 = 100 – 20

Adding 80 is the same as adding 100 and subtracting 20.

Step 1 Add 100 to 345. 345 + 100 = 445

Step 2 Subtract 20 from the result. 445 – 20 = 425

So, 345 + 80 = 425.

Guided Practice

Add mentally.
Use number bonds to help you.

13 Find 568 + 90.

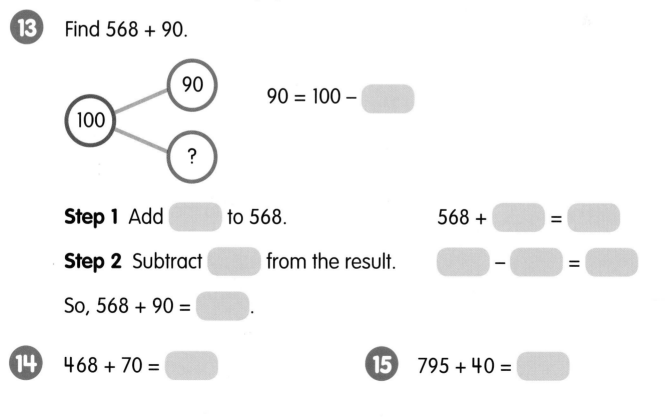

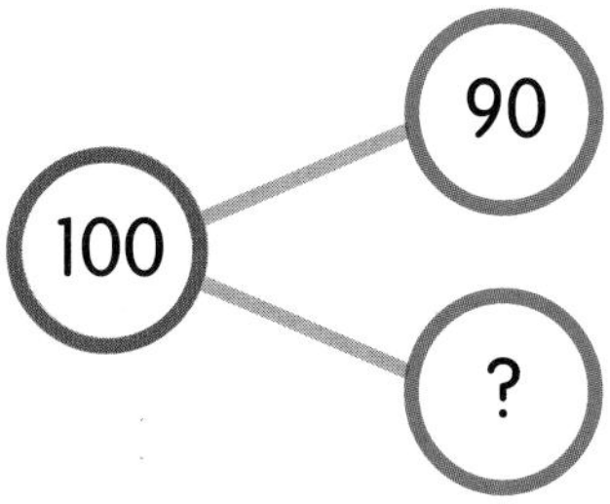

90 = 100 – ____

Step 1 Add ____ to 568. 568 + ____ = ____

Step 2 Subtract ____ from the result. ____ – ____ = ____

So, 568 + 90 = ____.

14 468 + 70 = ____

15 795 + 40 = ____

Learn You can add hundreds to a 3-digit number mentally using the 'add the hundreds' strategy.

Find 172 + 300.

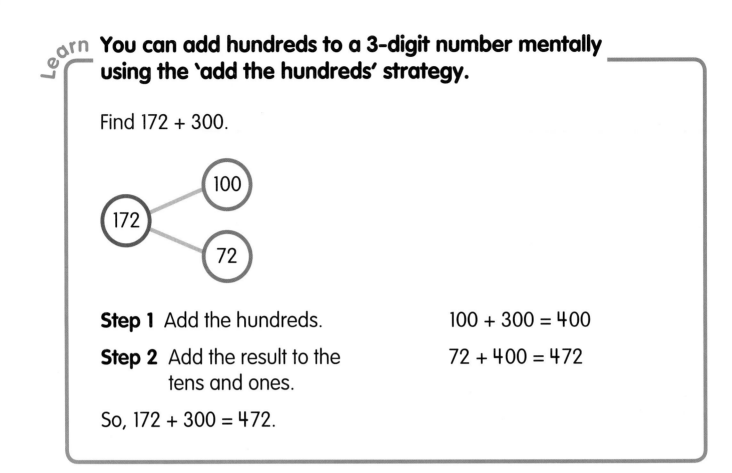

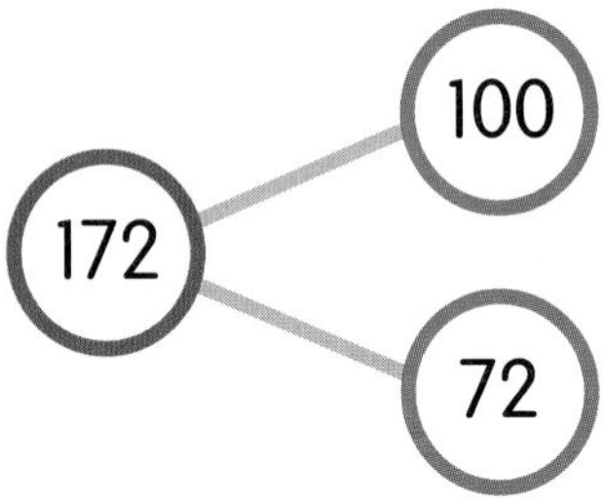

Step 1 Add the hundreds. 100 + 300 = 400

Step 2 Add the result to the tens and ones. 72 + 400 = 472

So, 172 + 300 = 472.

Guided Practice

Add mentally.
Use number bonds to help you.

16 Find 469 + 200.

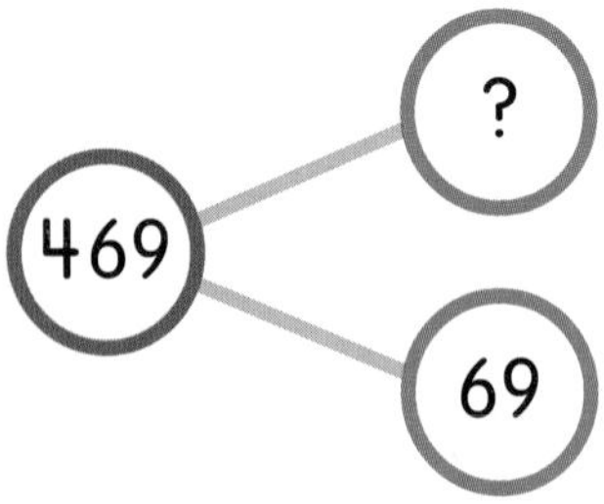

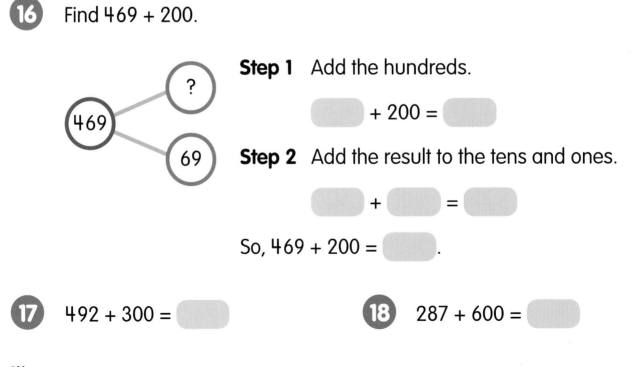

Step 1 Add the hundreds.

____ + 200 = ____

Step 2 Add the result to the tens and ones.

____ + ____ = ____

So, 469 + 200 = ____.

17 492 + 300 = ____

18 287 + 600 = ____

Let's Practice

Find each missing number.

1. 5 = 10 − ___
2. 7 = 10 − ___

Add mentally.
Use number bonds to help you.

3. 79 + 8 = ___
4. 45 + 7 = ___
5. 6 + 88 = ___
6. 9 + 65 = ___

Add mentally.
Use number bonds to help you.

7. 325 + 4 = ___
8. 734 + 3 = ___
9. 247 + 5 = ___
10. 8 + 339 = ___

Find each missing number.

11. 40 = 100 − ___
12. 70 = 100 − ___
13. 446 + 30 = ___
14. 628 + 20 = ___
15. 357 + 80 = ___
16. 498 + 60 = ___

Find each missing number.

17. 248 + 500 = ___
18. 397 + 600 = ___
19. 199 + 800 = ___
20. 578 + 200 = ___

ON YOUR OWN

Go to Workbook B:
Practice 2, pages 3–6

Let's Explore!

WORKING TOGETHER

Think of new and different ways to add these numbers mentally. Describe your steps.

1. 46 + 8

2. 34 + 57

3. 527 + 28

READING AND WRITING MATH

Math Journal

Which strategy would you choose to add 527 and 8 mentally? Why? Explain your steps.

STEP 1 : ____________________

STEP 2 : ____________________

LESSON 3 Meaning of Difference

Lesson Objective

- Relate 'difference' to the subtraction operation.

Vocabulary
difference

Learn: Meaning of difference

Hi, Sam! Miss Tanner asked me to find the difference between 67 and 80. Is this the same as finding the sum?

No! To find the sum, you add. To find the difference, you subtract.

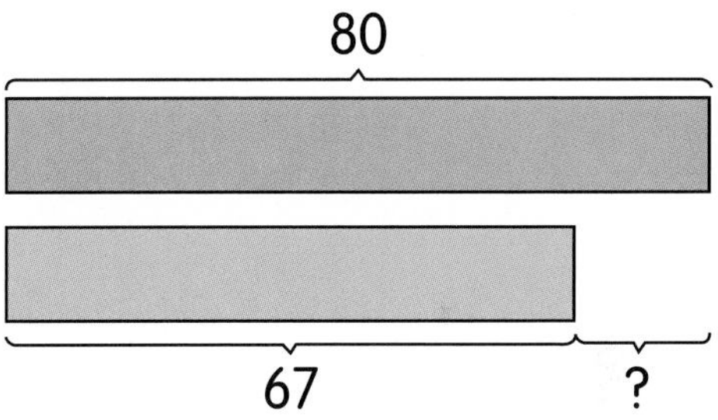

The **difference** between 67 and 80 is 13.

$$\begin{array}{r} \overset{7}{\cancel{8}}\ {}^{1}0 \\ -\ 6\ \ 7 \\ \hline 1\ \ 3 \end{array}$$

To find the difference, subtract the number that is less from the greater number.

Remember to subtract the number that is less from the greater number.

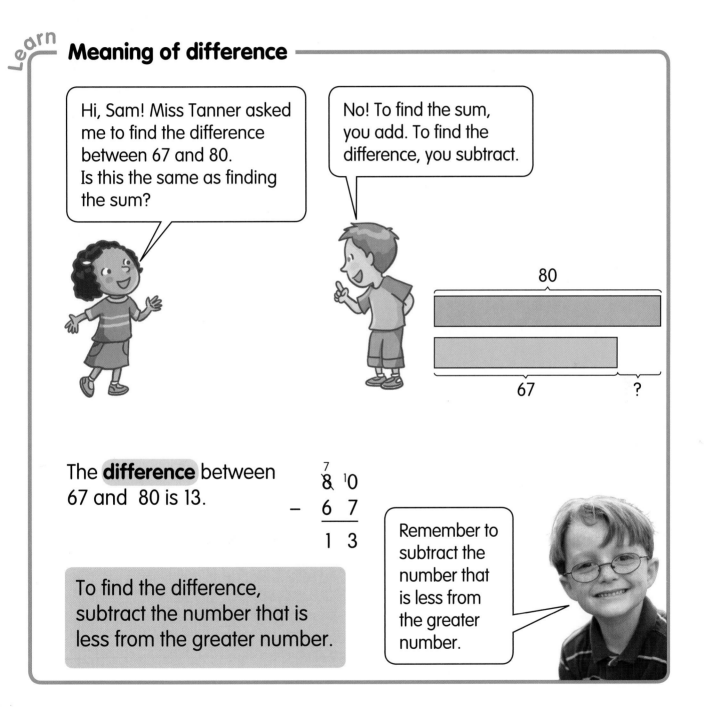

Guided Practice

Find the difference between these numbers.

1. 23 and 19 ____
2. 68 and 76 ____
3. 791 and 368 ____
4. 437 and 682 ____

Solve.
Use bar models to help you.

5. Grace has 34 apples in her basket.
Nina has 16 apples in her basket.
Find the difference between the numbers of apples.

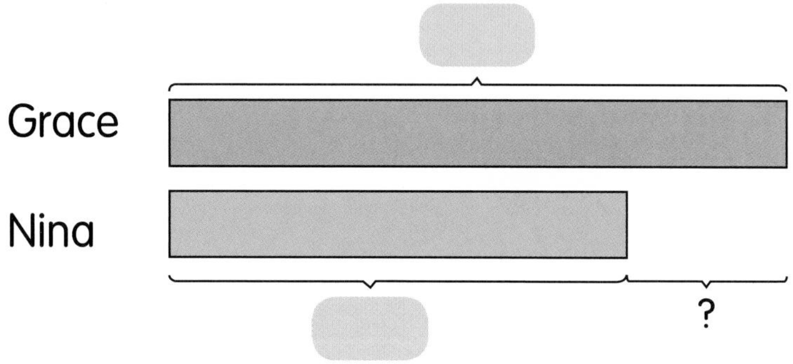

____ ____ ____ = ____

The difference is ____.

6. Lucy read 84 pages.
Mariah read 56 pages.
Find the difference between the numbers of pages.

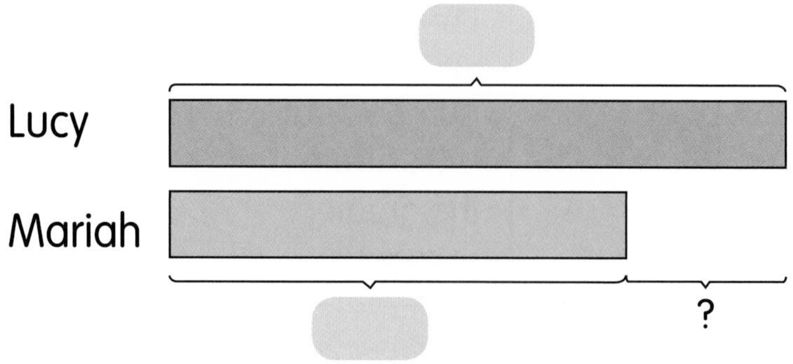

____ ____ ____ = ____

The difference is ____.

Let's Practice

Find the difference between these numbers.

1. 62 and 38 ▭
2. 90 and 74 ▭
3. 458 and 724 ▭
4. 213 and 800 ▭

Solve.
Draw bar models to help you.

5. Min made 108 paper cranes.
   Eric made 79 paper cranes.
   Find the difference between the numbers of paper cranes.

6. Juliana picked 307 strawberries.
   Rica picked 258 strawberries.
   Find the difference between the numbers of strawberries.

ON YOUR OWN

Go to Workbook B:
Practice 3, pages 7–10

Mental Subtraction

LESSON 4

Lesson Objective

- Subtract up to 3-digit numbers mentally with and without regrouping.

Vocabulary
subtract mentally

Learn **You can subtract ones from a 2-digit number mentally using the 'subtract 10 then add the extra ones' strategy.**

Find 62 – 8.

Subtracting 8 is the same as subtracting 10 and adding 2.

10 — 8 / 2

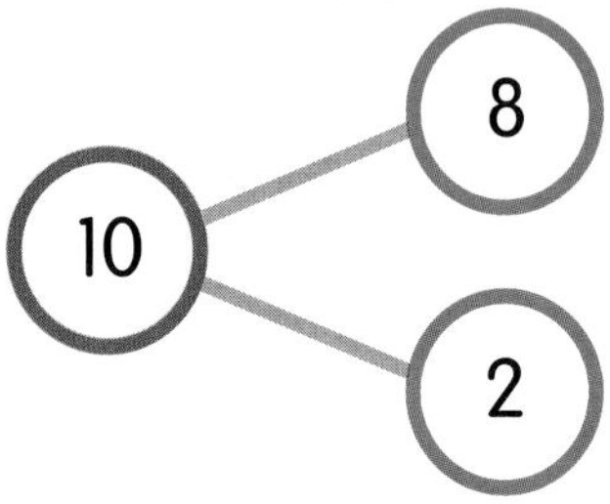

Step 1 Subtract 10 from 62. $62 - 10 = 52$

Step 2 Add 2 to the result. $52 + 2 = 54$

So, $62 - 8 = 54$.

Guided Practice

Subtract mentally.
Use number bonds to help you.

1 Find 84 – 7.

10 — 7 / ?

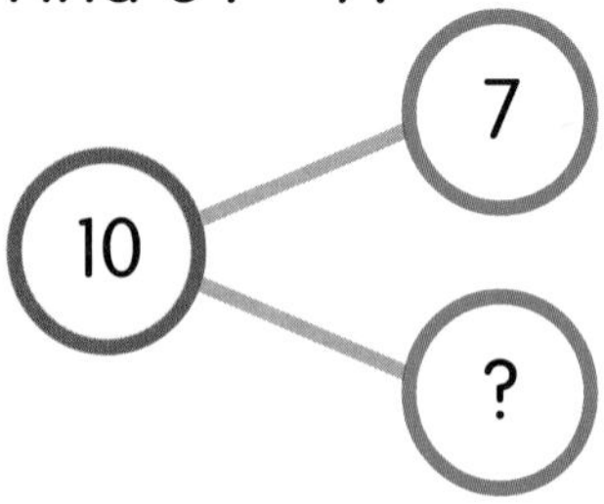

Step 1 Subtract [] from 84.

$84 - \boxed{} = \boxed{}$

Step 2 Add [] to the result.

$\boxed{} + \boxed{} = \boxed{}$

So, $84 - 7 = \boxed{}$.

2 $72 - 9 = \boxed{}$

3 $62 - 6 = \boxed{}$

Learn You can subtract ones from a 3-digit number mentally using the 'subtract the ones' strategy.

Find 429 – 4.
Group 429 into ones, and hundreds and tens.

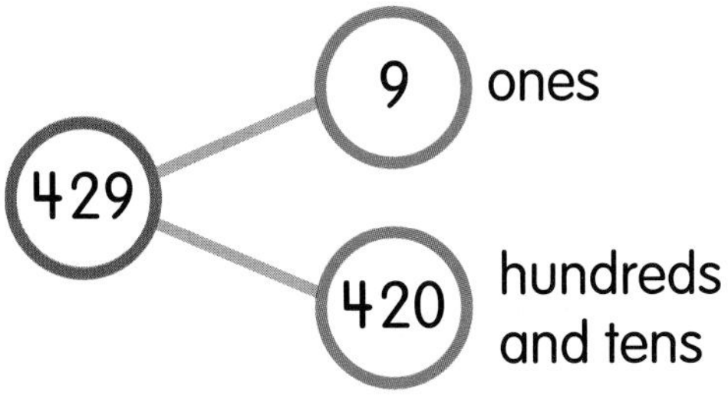

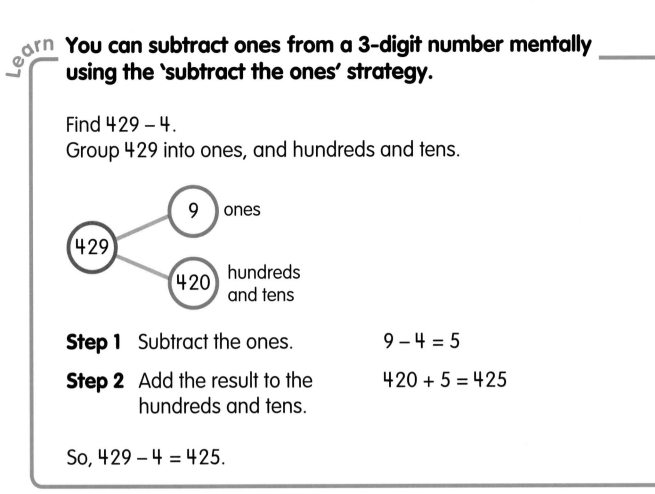

Step 1 Subtract the ones. $9 - 4 = 5$

Step 2 Add the result to the hundreds and tens. $420 + 5 = 425$

So, 429 – 4 = 425.

Guided Practice

Subtract mentally.
Use number bonds to help you.

4 Find 748 – 5.
Group 748 into ones, and hundreds and tens.

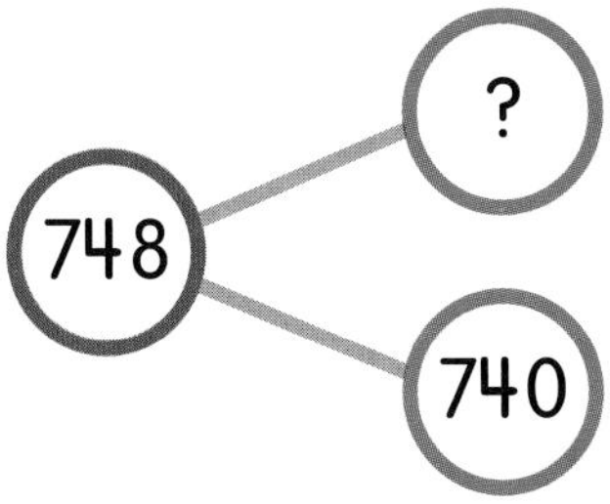

Step 1 Subtract the ones.

____ – 5 = ____

Step 2 Add the result to the hundreds and tens.

740 + ____ = ____

So, 748 – 5 = ____.

5 437 – 3 = ____

6 628 – 4 = ____

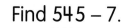

Learn: You can subtract ones from a 3-digit number mentally using the 'subtract 10 then add the extra ones' strategy.

Find 545 – 7.

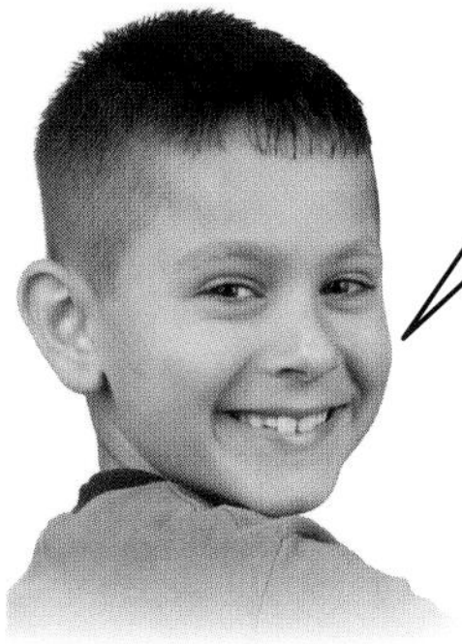

Subtracting 7 is the same as subtracting 10 and adding 3.

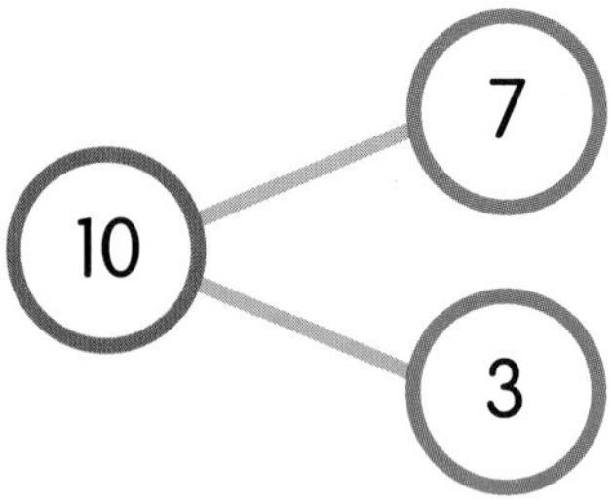

Step 1 Subtract 10 from 545. 545 – 10 = 535

Step 2 Add 3 to the result. 535 + 3 = 538

So, 545 – 7 = 538.

Guided Practice

Subtract mentally.
Use number bonds to help you.

7 Find 872 – 6.

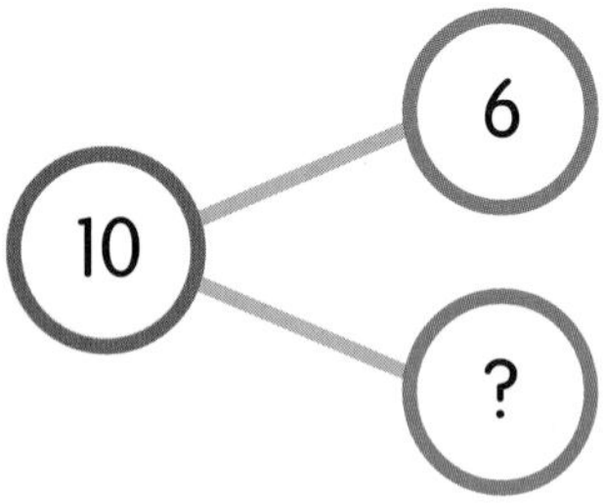

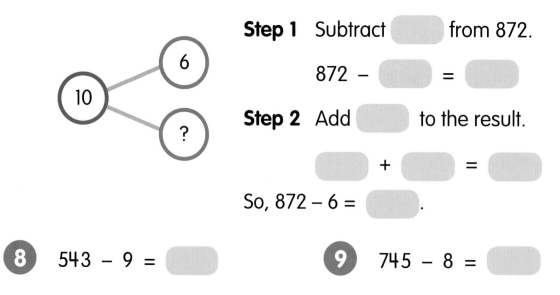

Step 1 Subtract ___ from 872.

872 – ___ = ___

Step 2 Add ___ to the result.

___ + ___ = ___

So, 872 – 6 = ___.

8 543 – 9 = ___

9 745 – 8 = ___

Learn

You can subtract tens from a 3-digit number mentally using the 'subtract the tens' strategy.

Find 753 – 30.
Group 753 into tens, and hundreds and ones.

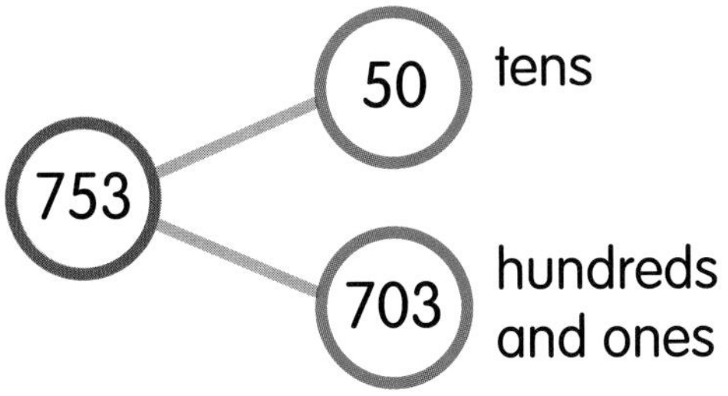

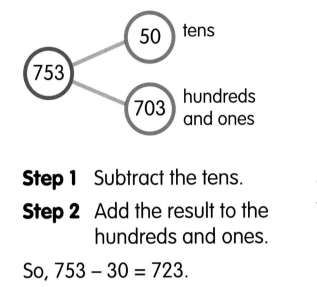

Step 1 Subtract the tens. 50 – 30 = 20

Step 2 Add the result to the hundreds and ones. 703 + 20 = 723

So, 753 – 30 = 723.

Guided Practice

Subtract mentally.
Use number bonds to help you.

10 Find 692 – 40.
Group 692 into tens, and hundreds and ones.

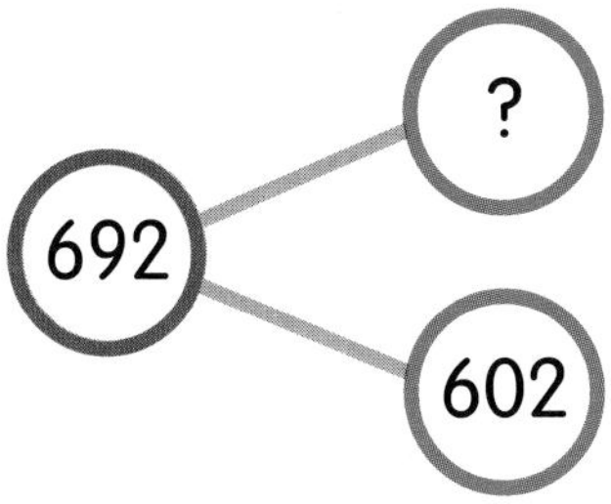

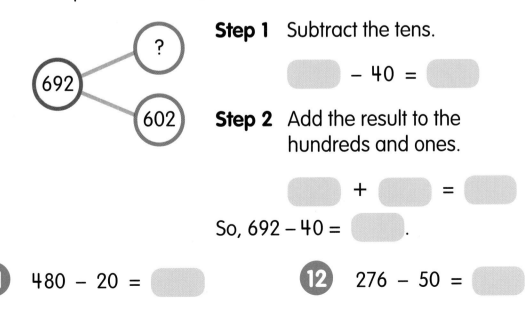

Step 1 Subtract the tens.

___ – 40 = ___

Step 2 Add the result to the hundreds and ones.

___ + ___ = ___

So, 692 – 40 = ___.

11 480 – 20 = ___

12 276 – 50 = ___

Learn You can subtract tens from a 3-digit number mentally using the 'subtract 100 then add the extra tens' strategy.

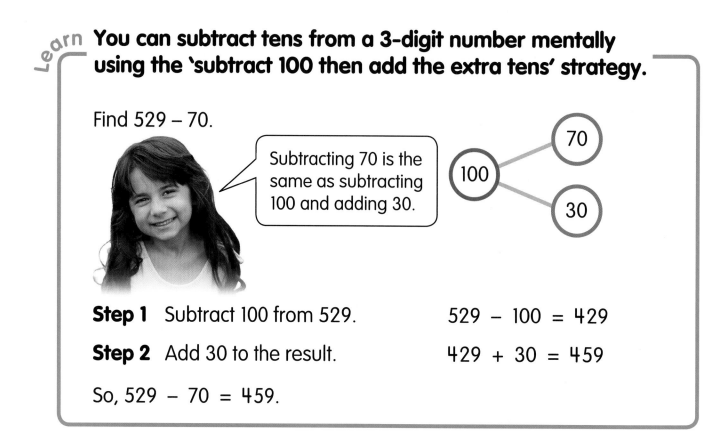

Find 529 – 70.

Subtracting 70 is the same as subtracting 100 and adding 30.

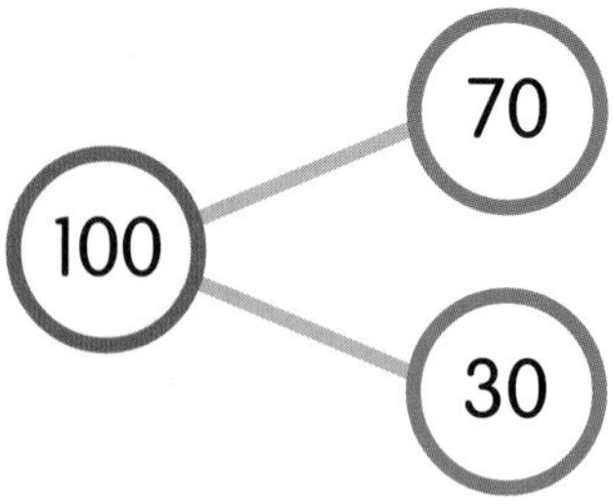

Step 1 Subtract 100 from 529. 529 – 100 = 429

Step 2 Add 30 to the result. 429 + 30 = 459

So, 529 – 70 = 459.

Guided Practice

Subtract mentally.
Use number bonds to help you.

13 Find 936 – 80.

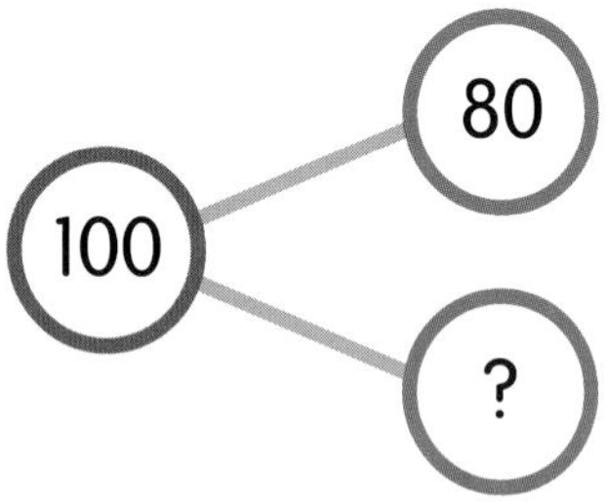

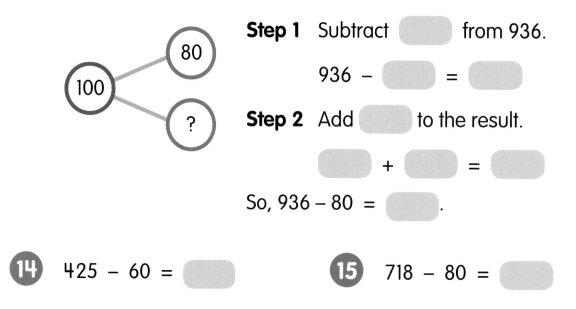

Step 1 Subtract ____ from 936.

936 – ____ = ____

Step 2 Add ____ to the result.

____ + ____ = ____

So, 936 – 80 = ____.

14 425 – 60 = ____

15 718 – 80 = ____

Learn

You can subtract hundreds from a 3-digit number mentally using the 'subtract the hundreds' strategy.

Find 827 – 400.

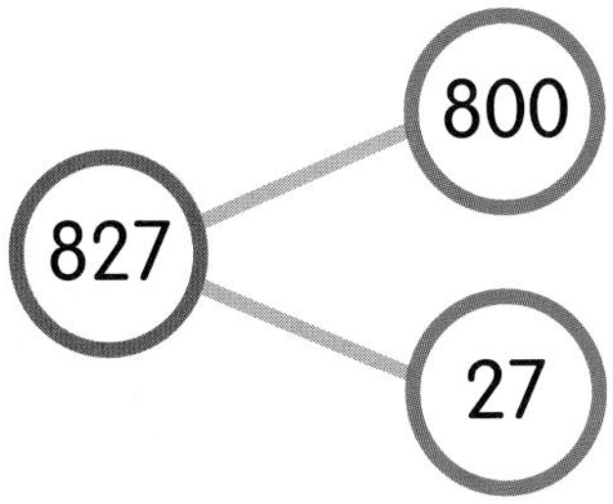

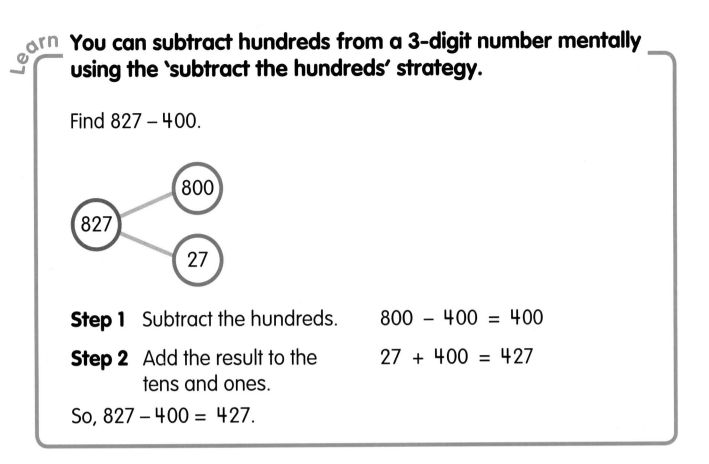

Step 1 Subtract the hundreds. 800 – 400 = 400

Step 2 Add the result to the tens and ones. 27 + 400 = 427

So, 827 – 400 = 427.

Guided Practice

Subtract mentally.
Use number bonds to help you.

16 Find 749 – 500.

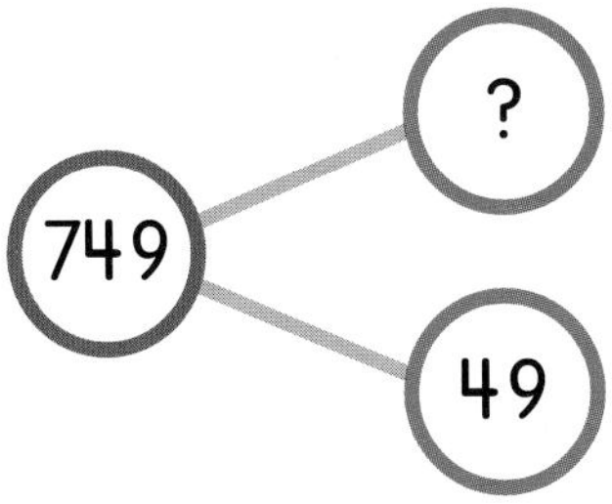

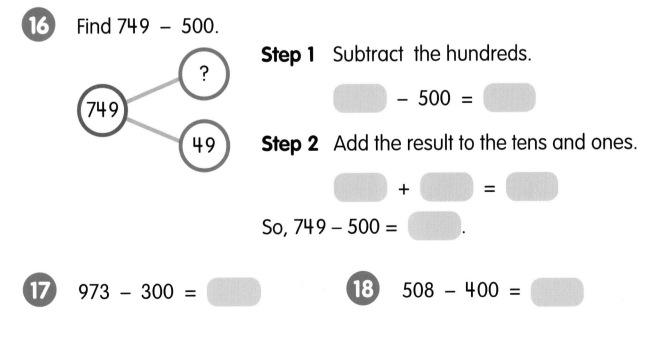

Step 1 Subtract the hundreds.

___ – 500 = ___

Step 2 Add the result to the tens and ones.

___ + ___ = ___

So, 749 – 500 = ___.

17 973 – 300 = ___

18 508 – 400 = ___

Let's Practice

Subtract mentally.
Use number bonds to help you.

1. 32 − 7 = ▢
2. 81 − 9 = ▢

Subtract mentally.
Use number bonds to help you.

3. 378 − 6 = ▢
4. 749 − 5 = ▢

Subtract mentally.
Use number bonds to help you.

5. 452 − 8 = ▢
6. 581 − 6 = ▢
7. 743 − 7 = ▢
8. 267 − 9 = ▢

Subtract mentally.
Use number bonds to help you.

9. 275 − 30 = ▢
10. 491 − 60 = ▢
11. 578 − 80 = ▢
12. 372 − 90 = ▢
13. 729 − 70 = ▢
14. 186 − 20 = ▢

Subtract mentally.
Use number bonds to help you.

15. 647 − 300 = ▢
16. 928 − 600 = ▢

ON YOUR OWN

Go to Workbook B: Practice 4, pages 11–14

Let's Explore!

WORKING TOGETHER

Think of new and different ways to subtract these numbers mentally. Describe your steps.

1. 63 − 7

2. 82 − 38

3. 615 − 37

READING AND WRITING MATH

Math Journal

Which strategy would you use to subtract 70 from 615 mentally? Why? Explain your steps.

STEP 1 : ______________________________

STEP 2 : ______________________________

LESSON 5

Rounding Numbers to Estimate

Lesson Objectives

- Use a number line to round numbers to the nearest ten.
- Use rounding to estimate sums and differences.
- Estimate to check reasonableness of answers.

Vocabulary

number line
about
round
nearest ten
estimate
reasonable

Learn

Round a 2-digit number down to the nearest ten.

Ribbon A is 82 centimeters long.

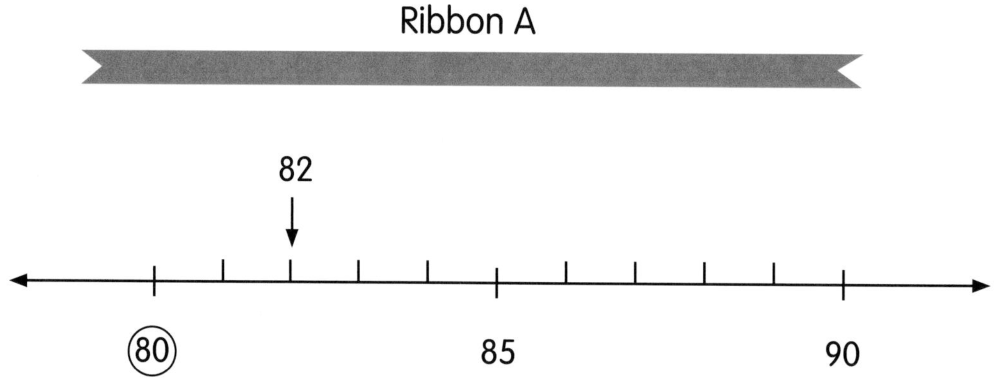

The **number line** shows that
82 is between 80 and 90.
82 is nearer to 80 than to 90 on the number line.
82 is 80 when rounded to the **nearest ten**.
You can say 82 is **about** 80.

The length of Ribbon A is about 80 centimeters, rounded to the nearest 10 centimeters.

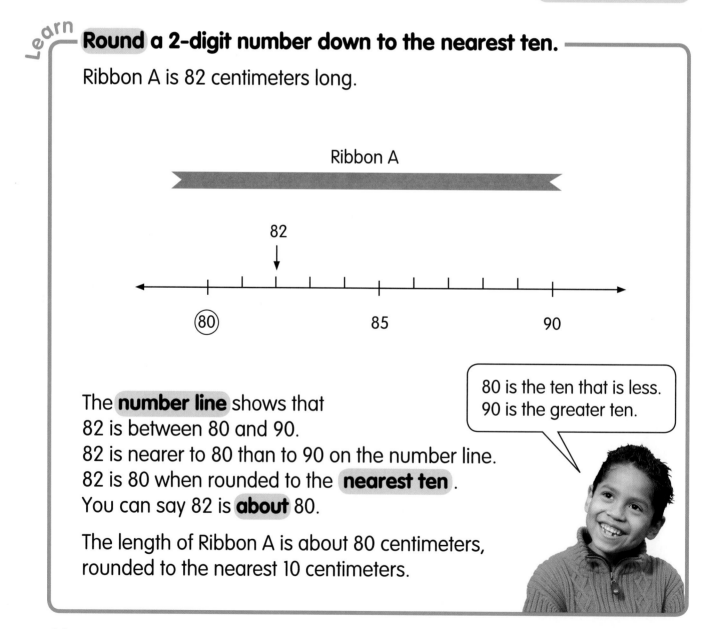

80 is the ten that is less.
90 is the greater ten.

Learn Round a 2-digit number up to the nearest ten.

Ribbon B is 17 centimeters long.

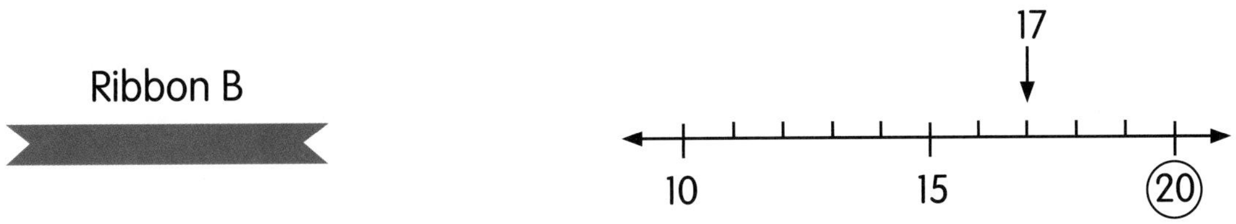

The **number line** shows that 17 is between 10 and 20.
It is nearer to 20 than to 10.
17 is about 20 when rounded to the nearest ten.

The length of Ribbon B is about 20 centimeters, rounded to the nearest 10 centimeters.

Ribbon C is 95 centimeters long.

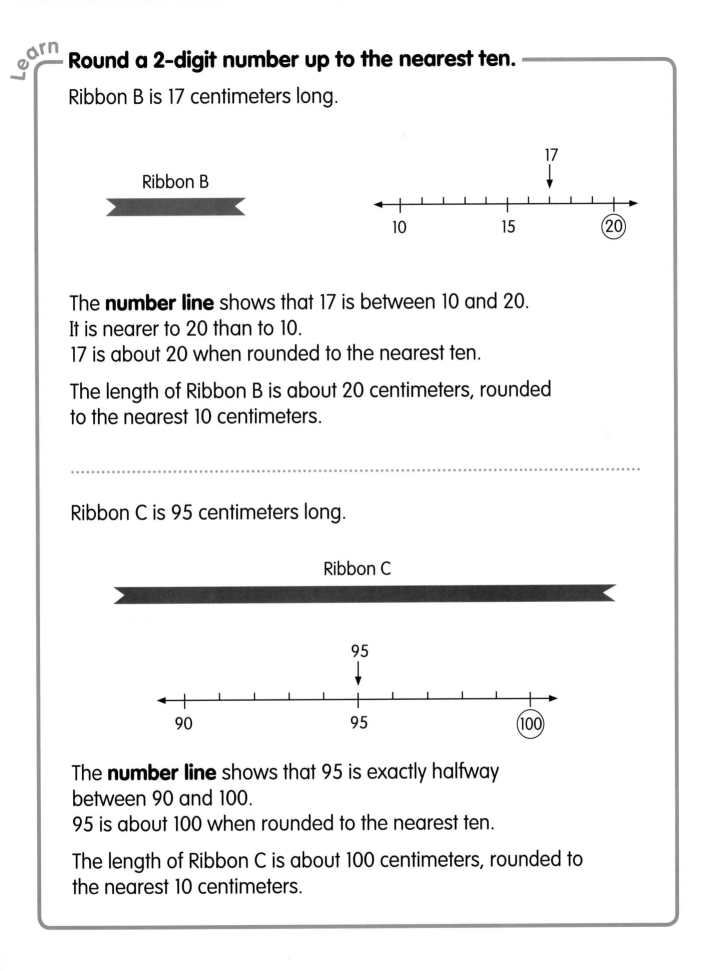

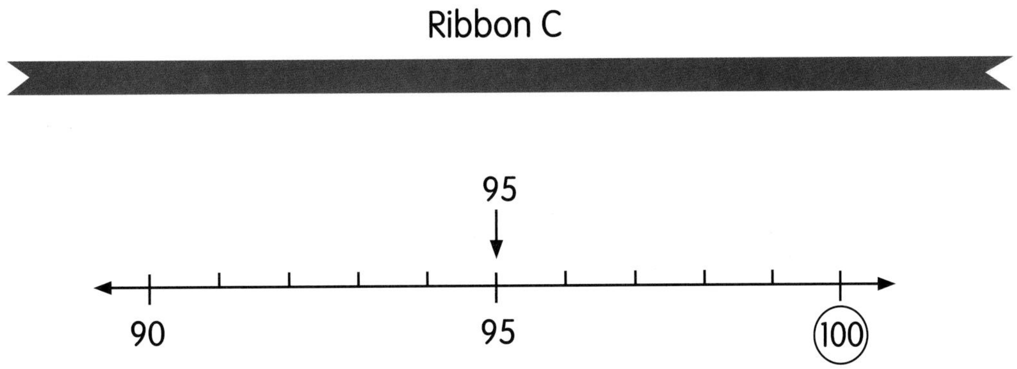

The **number line** shows that 95 is exactly halfway between 90 and 100.
95 is about 100 when rounded to the nearest ten.

The length of Ribbon C is about 100 centimeters, rounded to the nearest 10 centimeters.

Rounding to the nearest 10
Look at the digit in the ones place.
If it is 1, 2, 3, or 4, round to the ten that is less.
If it is 5, 6, 7, 8, or 9, round to the greater ten.

Guided Practice

Mark each number with an *X* on a copy of the number line. Round each number to the nearest ten and circle it.

Example

13

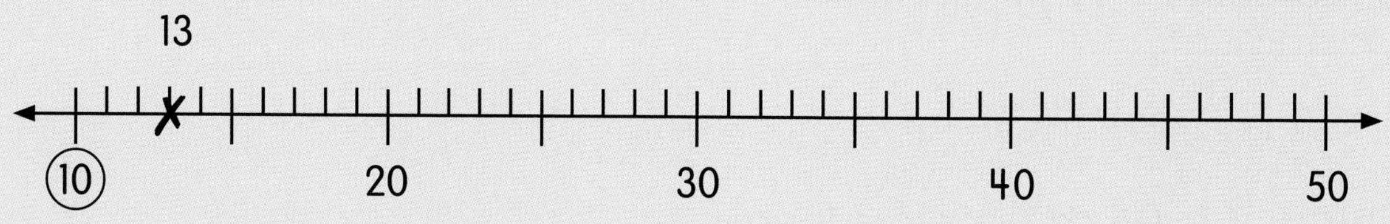

13 is 10 when rounded to the nearest ten.

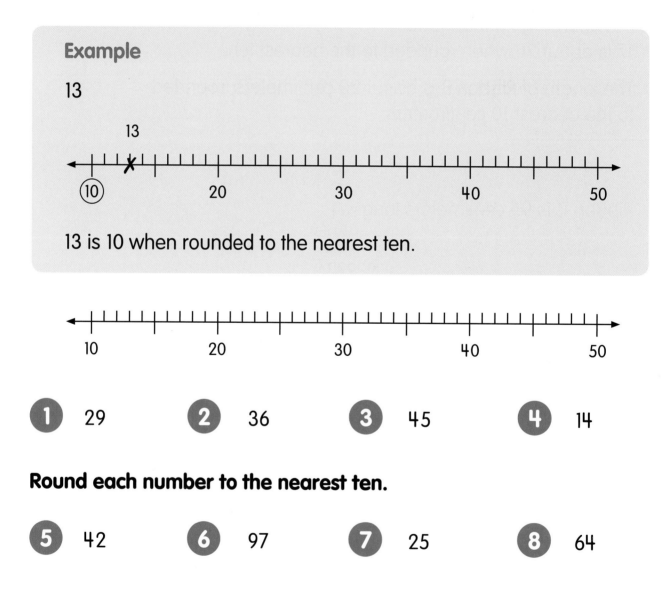

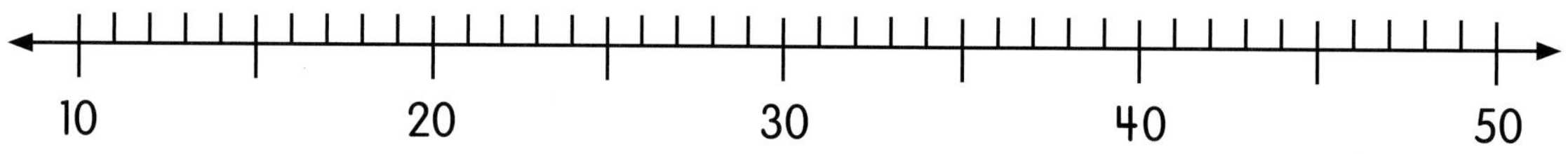

1. 29
2. 36
3. 45
4. 14

Round each number to the nearest ten.

5. 42
6. 97
7. 25
8. 64

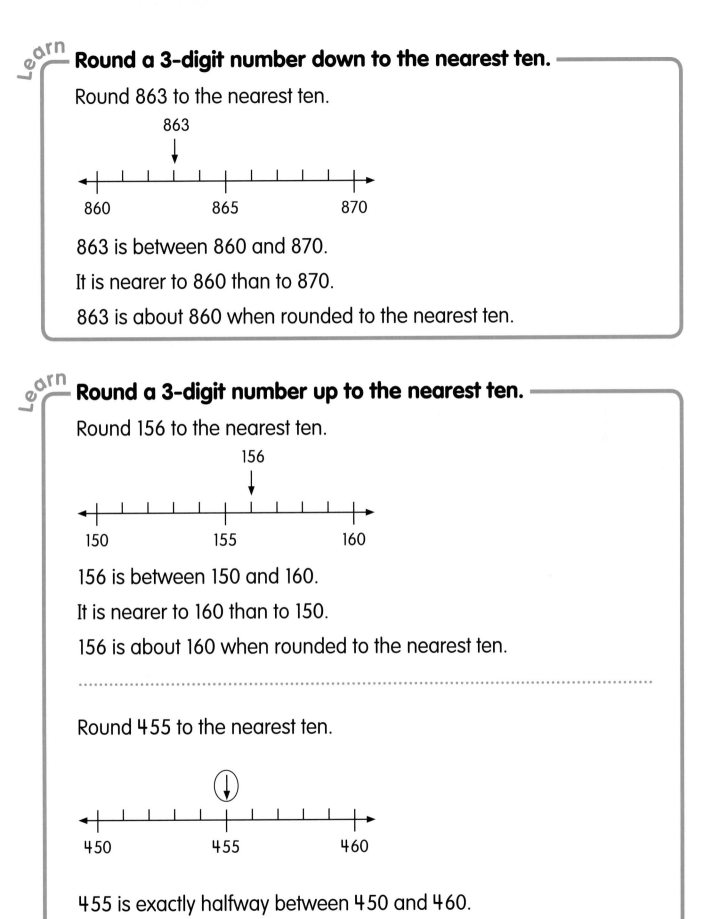

Learn

Round a 3-digit number down to the nearest ten.

Round 863 to the nearest ten.

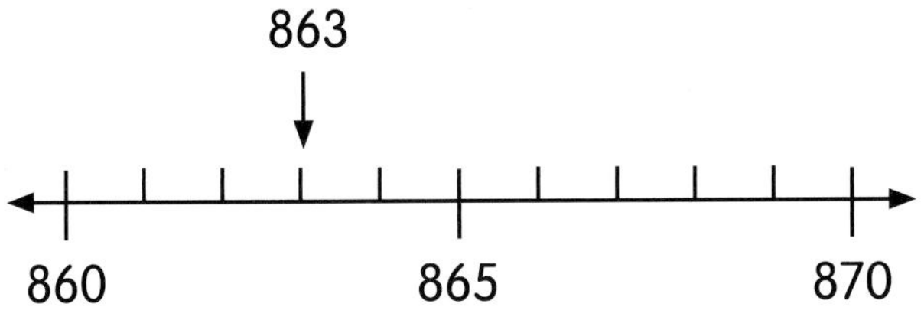

863 is between 860 and 870.

It is nearer to 860 than to 870.

863 is about 860 when rounded to the nearest ten.

Learn

Round a 3-digit number up to the nearest ten.

Round 156 to the nearest ten.

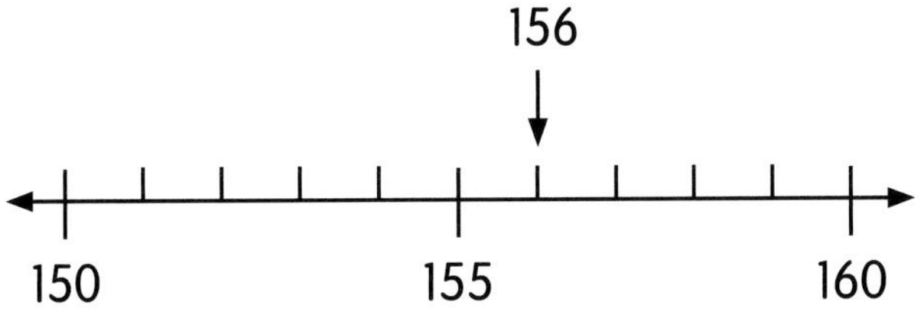

156 is between 150 and 160.

It is nearer to 160 than to 150.

156 is about 160 when rounded to the nearest ten.

Round 455 to the nearest ten.

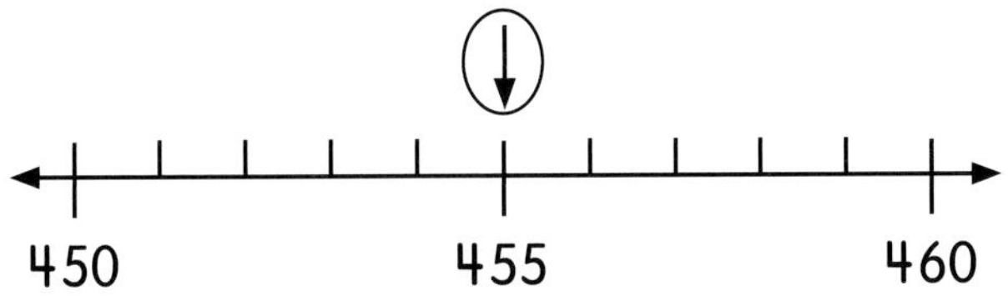

455 is exactly halfway between 450 and 460.

455 is about 460 when rounded to the nearest ten.

Guided Practice

Mark each number with an *X* on a copy of the number line. Round the number to the nearest ten and circle it.

Example

306

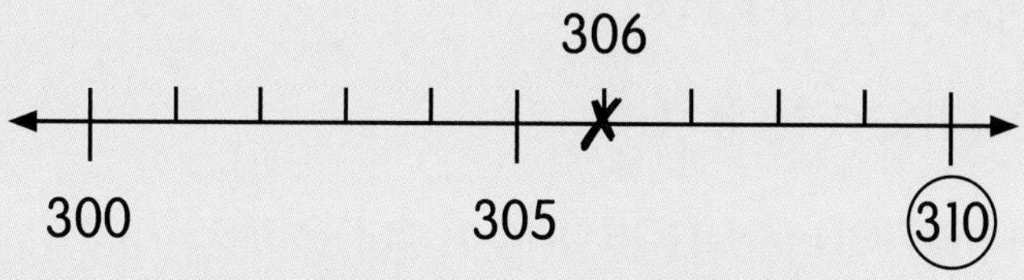

306 is 310 when rounded to the nearest ten.

Look at each number and find the ten before and after it.
In the example, the number 306 lies between these two nearest tens.

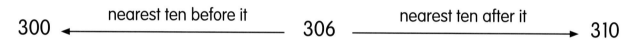

300 ← nearest ten before it — 306 — nearest ten after it → 310

So, the number line for 306 starts at 300 and ends at 310.

For each number, where do I start and end the number line?

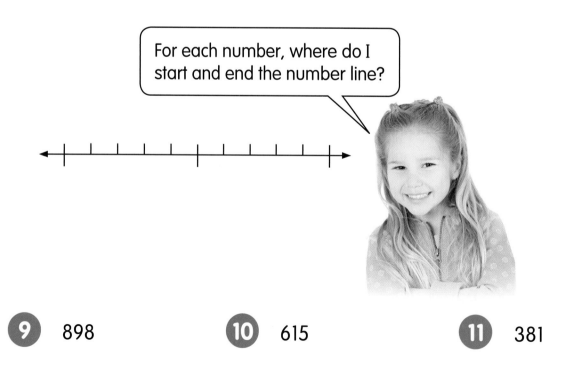

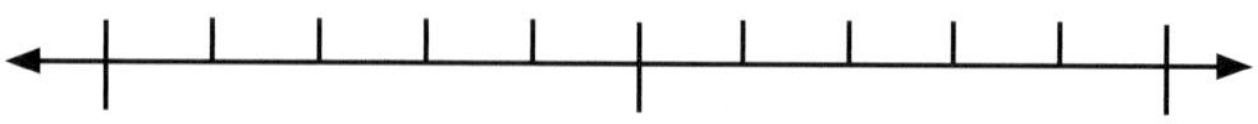

9 898 **10** 615 **11** 381

Let's Explore!

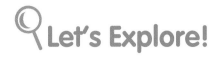

WORK IN PAIRS

Find all the numbers that give these answers when rounded to the nearest ten. Use the number line to help you.

1. 50

2. 500

3. For each set of answers in 1 and 2, which is

   a. the least number?

   b. the greatest number?

Example

60

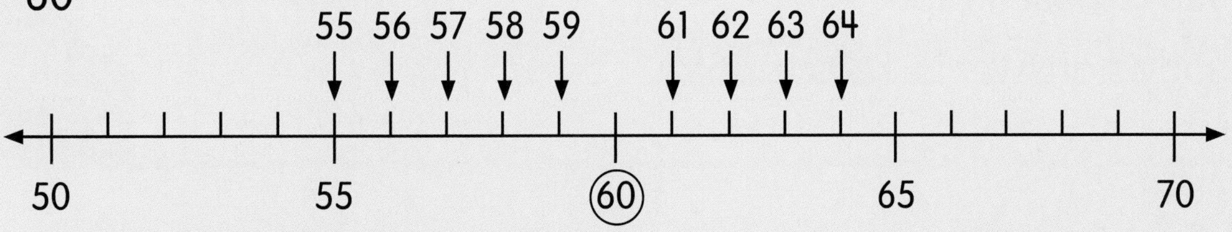

55, 56, 57, 58, 59, 61, 62, 63, and 64 give the answer 60 when rounded to the nearest ten.

55 is the least number.

64 is the greatest number.

4. Find

   a. the least number

   b. the greatest number

   that is 470 when rounded to the nearest ten.

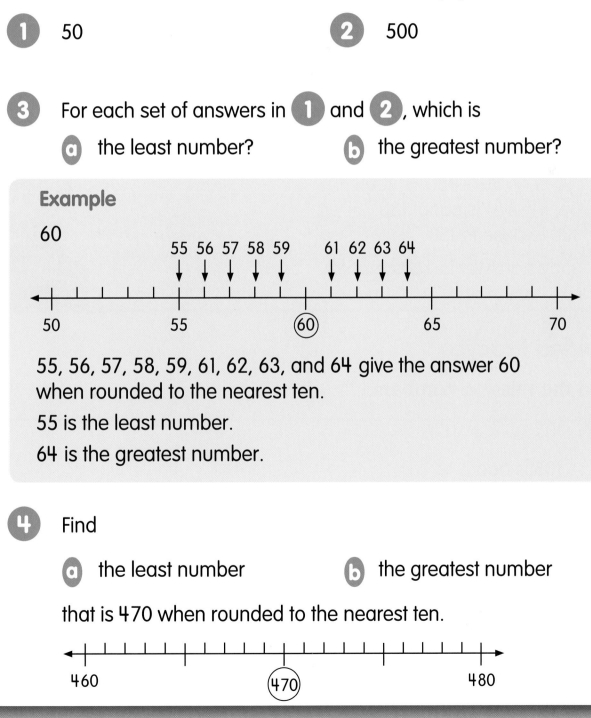

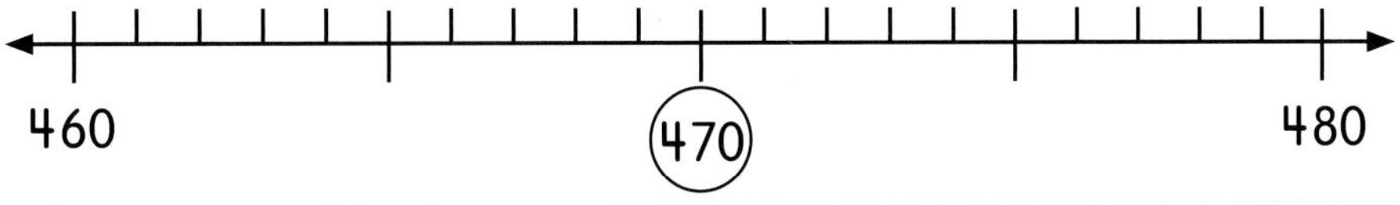

Learn

You can use rounding to estimate sums and check that the answers are reasonable.

Let's estimate the sum of 47 and 81 to check if Judy's answer is reasonable.

Step 1 Round each number to the nearest ten.
47 is 50 when rounded to the nearest ten.
81 is 80 when rounded to the nearest ten.

47 is about 50.
81 is about 80.

Step 2 Add.
50 + 80 = 130.

So, 47 + 81 is about 130.
128 is close to 130.

Judy's answer is **reasonable**.

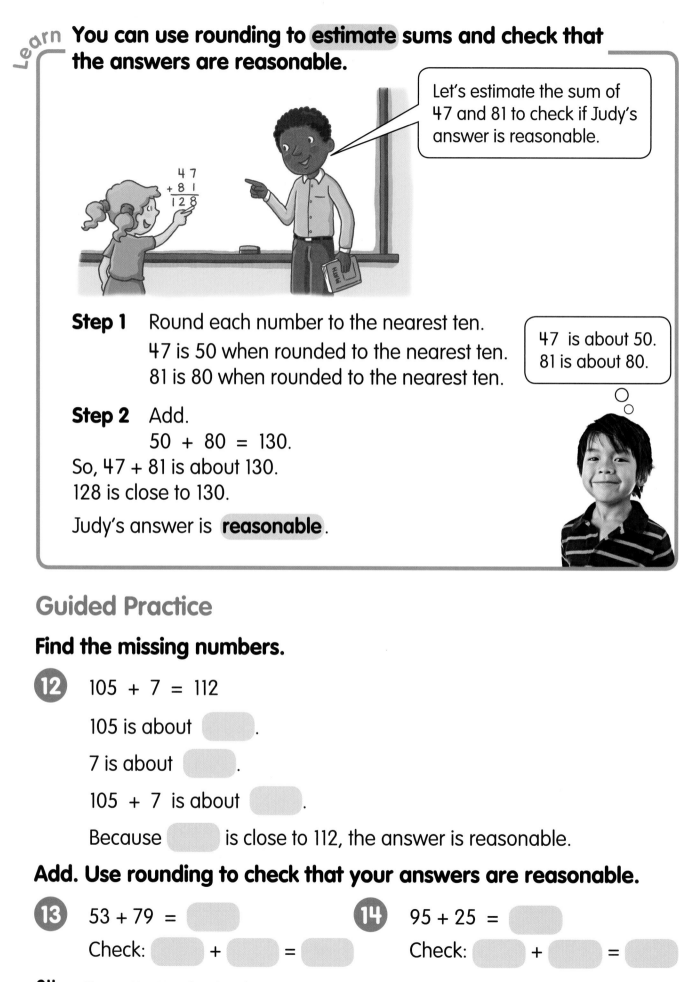

Guided Practice

Find the missing numbers.

12 105 + 7 = 112

105 is about ____.

7 is about ____.

105 + 7 is about ____.

Because ____ is close to 112, the answer is reasonable.

Add. Use rounding to check that your answers are reasonable.

13 53 + 79 = ____

Check: ____ + ____ = ____

14 95 + 25 = ____

Check: ____ + ____ = ____

Learn You can use rounding to estimate differences and check that the answers are reasonable.

Estimate the difference between 83 and 42.

$$\begin{array}{r} 83 \\ -42 \\ \hline 41 \end{array}$$

Step 1 Round each number to the nearest ten.
83 is 80 when rounded to the nearest ten.
42 is 40 when rounded to the nearest ten.

Step 2 Subtract.
80 − 40 = 40

So, 83 − 42 is about 40.
41 is close to 40.

The answer is **reasonable**.

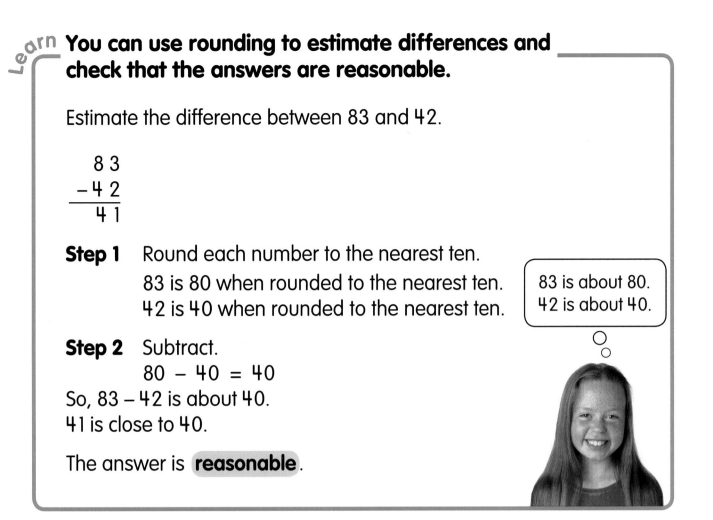

83 is about 80.
42 is about 40.

Guided Practice

Find the missing numbers.

15 176 − 12 = 164

176 is about ____.

12 is about ____.

176 − 12 is about ____.

Because ____ is close to 164, the answer is reasonable.

Subtract.
Use rounding to check that your answers are reasonable.

16 456 − 25 = ____

Check: ____ − ____ = ____

17 681 − 208 = ____

Check: ____ − ____ = ____

Let's Practice

Mark each number with an ✗ on a copy of the number line. Round each number to the nearest ten and circle it.

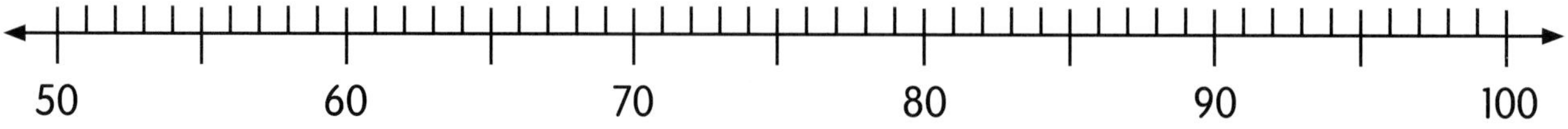

1. 83
2. 97
3. 65

Round each number to the nearest ten.

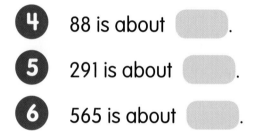

4. 88 is about ____.
5. 291 is about ____.
6. 565 is about ____.

Trace the number line and answer the questions.

7.

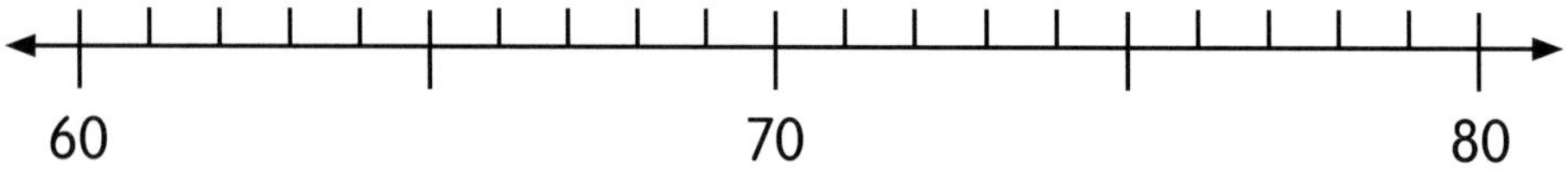

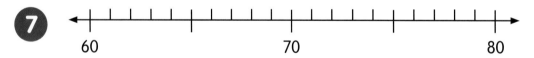

A number when rounded to the nearest 10 is 70.

a. Find all the numbers that give 70 when rounded to the nearest ten. Mark each number with a ✗ on the number line.

b. Which number is the least?

c. Which number is the greatest?

8 147 + 82 = 229

Round 147 and 82 to the nearest ten.
Then estimate the sum of 147 and 82.
Check that the sum is reasonable. Explain.

147 is about ___.

82 is about ___.

147 + 82 is about ___ + ___.

Is the answer reasonable?

9 495 − 336 = 159

Round 495 and 336 to the nearest ten.
Then estimate the difference between 495 and 336.
Check that the difference is reasonable. Explain.

495 is about ___.

336 is about ___.

495 − 336 is about ___ − ___.

Is the answer reasonable?

Find the sum or difference.
Then round each given number to the nearest ten.
Estimate the sum or difference to check that the answers are reasonable.

10 38 + 72 = ___

___ + ___ = ___

11 96 − 28 = ___

___ − ___ = ___

12 289 − 134 = ___

___ − ___ = ___

13 573 + 209 = ___

___ + ___ = ___

ON YOUR OWN

Go to Workbook B:
Practice 5, pages 15–20

READING AND WRITING MATH

Math Journal

How would you check that the sum or difference is reasonable?

1 479 + 312

STEP 1 : Find the sum of 479 and 312.

STEP 2 : ____________________

STEP 3 : ____________________

STEP 4 : ____________________

2 685 – 425

STEP 1 : ____________________

STEP 2 : ____________________

STEP 3 : ____________________

STEP 4 : ____________________

CRITICAL THINKING SKILLS

Put On Your Thinking Cap!

PROBLEM SOLVING

Two of these numbers are rounded to the nearest ten.
70 is their estimated sum.
Which two numbers might they be?

70 140 35 45

25 71 48

58 22

Make a list of the possible answers.

Chapter Wrap Up

You have learned...

Mental Math and Estimation

Mental Math

Addition

A sum is the answer when adding two numbers.

- 3-digit numbers and ones
  $462 + 6 = ?$

  Step 1 $2 + 6 = 8$
  Step 2 $460 + 8 = 468$
  $462 + 6 = 468$

  $357 + 8 = ?$

  Step 1 $357 + 10 = 367$
  Step 2 $367 - 2 = 365$
  $357 + 8 = 365$

- 3-digit numbers and tens
  $231 + 40 = ?$

  Step 1 $30 + 40 = 70$
  Step 2 $201 + 70 = 271$
  $231 + 40 = 271$

  $574 + 60 = ?$

  Step 1 $574 + 100 = 674$
  Step 2 $674 - 40 = 634$
  $574 + 60 = 634$

- 3-digit numbers and hundreds
  $238 + 400 = ?$

  Step 1 $200 + 400 = 600$
  Step 2 $38 + 600 = 638$
  $238 + 400 = 638$

Subtraction

A difference is the answer when subtracting two numbers.

- 3-digit numbers and ones
  $679 - 3 = ?$

  Step 1 $9 - 3 = 6$
  Step 2 $670 + 6 = 676$
  $679 - 3 = 676$

  $457 - 9 = ?$

  Step 1 $457 - 10 = 447$
  Step 2 $447 + 1 = 448$
  $457 - 9 = 448$

- 3-digit numbers and tens
  $388 - 30 = ?$

  Step 1 $80 - 30 = 50$
  Step 2 $308 + 50 = 358$
  $388 - 30 = 358$

  $767 - 90 = ?$

  Step 1 $767 - 100 = 667$
  Step 2 $667 + 10 = 677$
  $767 - 90 = 677$

- 3-digit numbers and hundreds
  $547 - 200 = ?$

  Step 1 $500 - 200 = 300$
  Step 2 $47 + 300 = 347$
  $547 - 200 = 347$

BIG IDEA

Mental math can be used when an exact answer is needed.
Estimation can be used when an exact answer is not needed.

Rounding Numbers to Estimate

Round to the nearest ten
Look at the digit in the ones place.
If it is 1, 2, 3, or 4, round to the ten that is less.
If it is 5, 6, 7, 8, or 9, round to the greater ten.

23 is about 20.
25 is about 30.
27 is about 30.

Estimate to check that an answer is reasonable

Addition

Find the sum of 123 and 456.

$123 + 456 = 579$

Check that the answer is reasonable. Round 123 and 456 to the nearest ten.

123 is about 120.
456 is about 460.
$120 + 460 = 580$
579 is about 580.

The answer is reasonable.

Subtraction

Find the difference between 678 and 345.

$678 - 345 = 333$

Check that the answer is reasonable. Round 678 and 345 to the nearest ten.

678 is about 680.
345 is about 350.
$680 - 350 = 330$
333 is about 330.

The answer is reasonable.

ON YOUR OWN

Go to Workbook B: Chapter Review/Test, pages 21–22

CHAPTER 11 Money

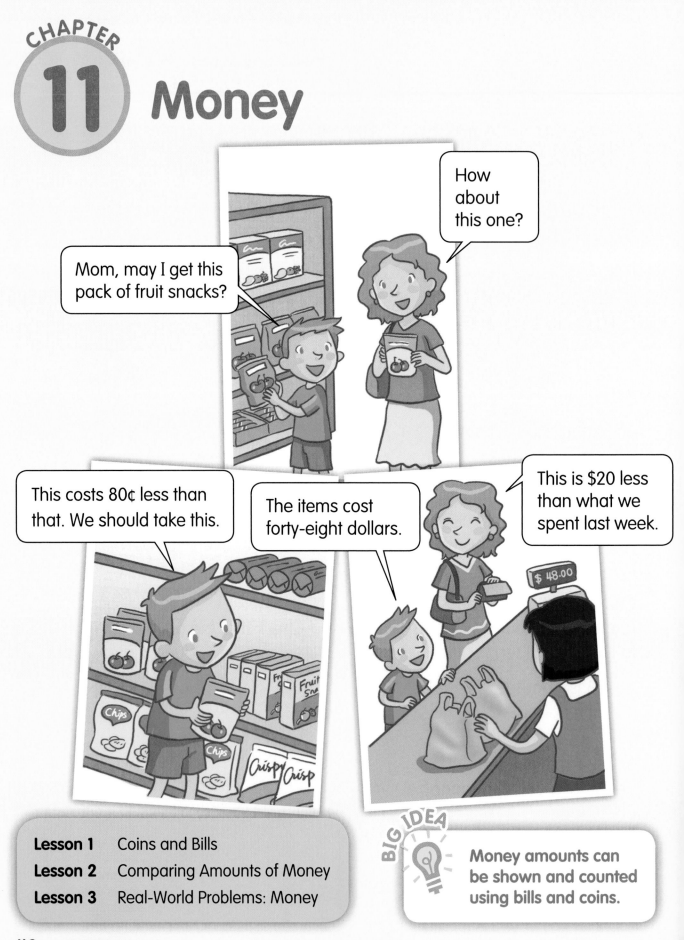

BIG IDEA

Money amounts can be shown and counted using bills and coins.

Recall Prior Knowledge

Types of coins

These are the two faces of a penny.
A penny has a value of 1 cent.

These are the two faces of a nickel.
A nickel has a value of 5 cents.

These are the two faces of a dime.
A dime has a value of 10 cents.

These are the two faces of a quarter.
A quarter has a value of 25 cents.

Exchanging coins

 = 

 =  OR 

 =  OR 

OR

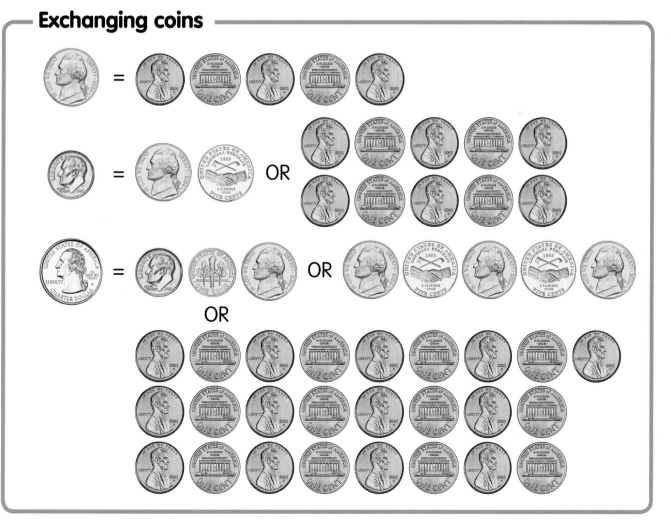

Combining coins to show a given amount

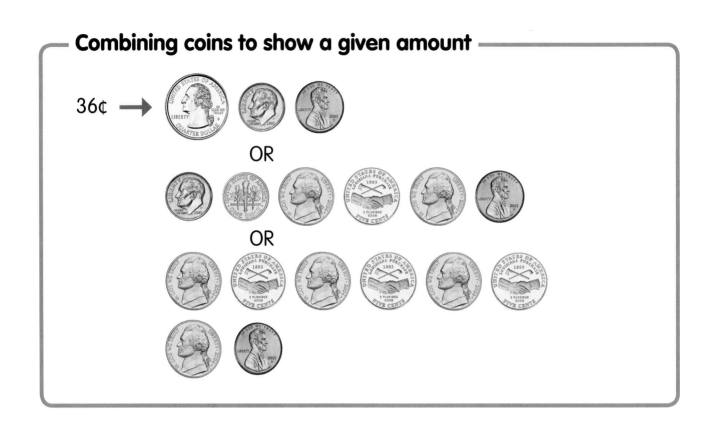

36¢ → 

OR

OR

✔ Quick Check

Look at the coins.
How many of each coin are there?

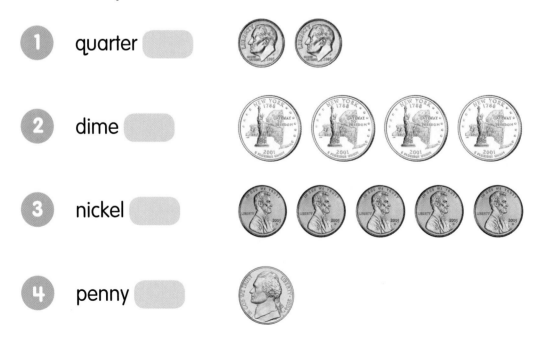

1. quarter ____ 

2. dime ____ 

3. nickel ____ 

4. penny ____ 

Write the value of each coin.

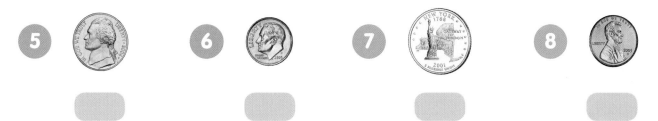

5 

6 

7 

8 

Find the amount.

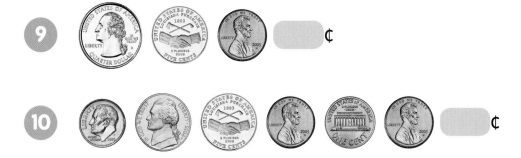

9  ¢

10  ¢

Circle the coins that make the given value.

11 55¢

12 85¢

LESSON

1 Coins and Bills

Lesson Objectives

- Recognize \$1, \$5, \$10, and \$20 bills.
- Show and count money using coins and bills to \$20.
- Write money amounts using \$ and ¢.
- Write dollars as cents and cents as dollars.

Vocabulary

\$1 bill	cent sign (¢)
\$5 bill	dollar sign (\$)
\$10 bill	decimal point
\$20 bill	

Learn Bills have different values.

This is a one-dollar bill. It has a value of \$1 or 100¢.

This is a five-dollar bill. It has a value of \$5.

This is a ten-dollar bill. It has a value of \$10.

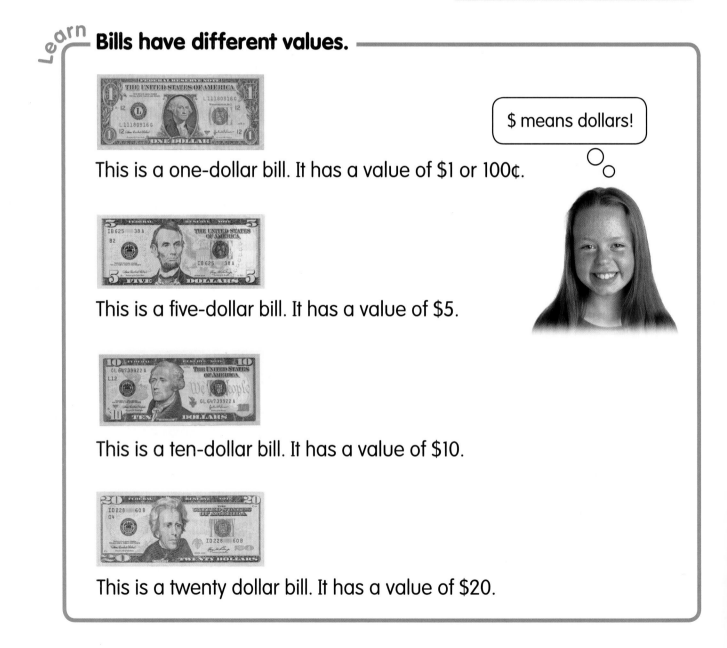

This is a twenty dollar bill. It has a value of \$20.

Guided Practice

Look at the bills. Then answer the questions.

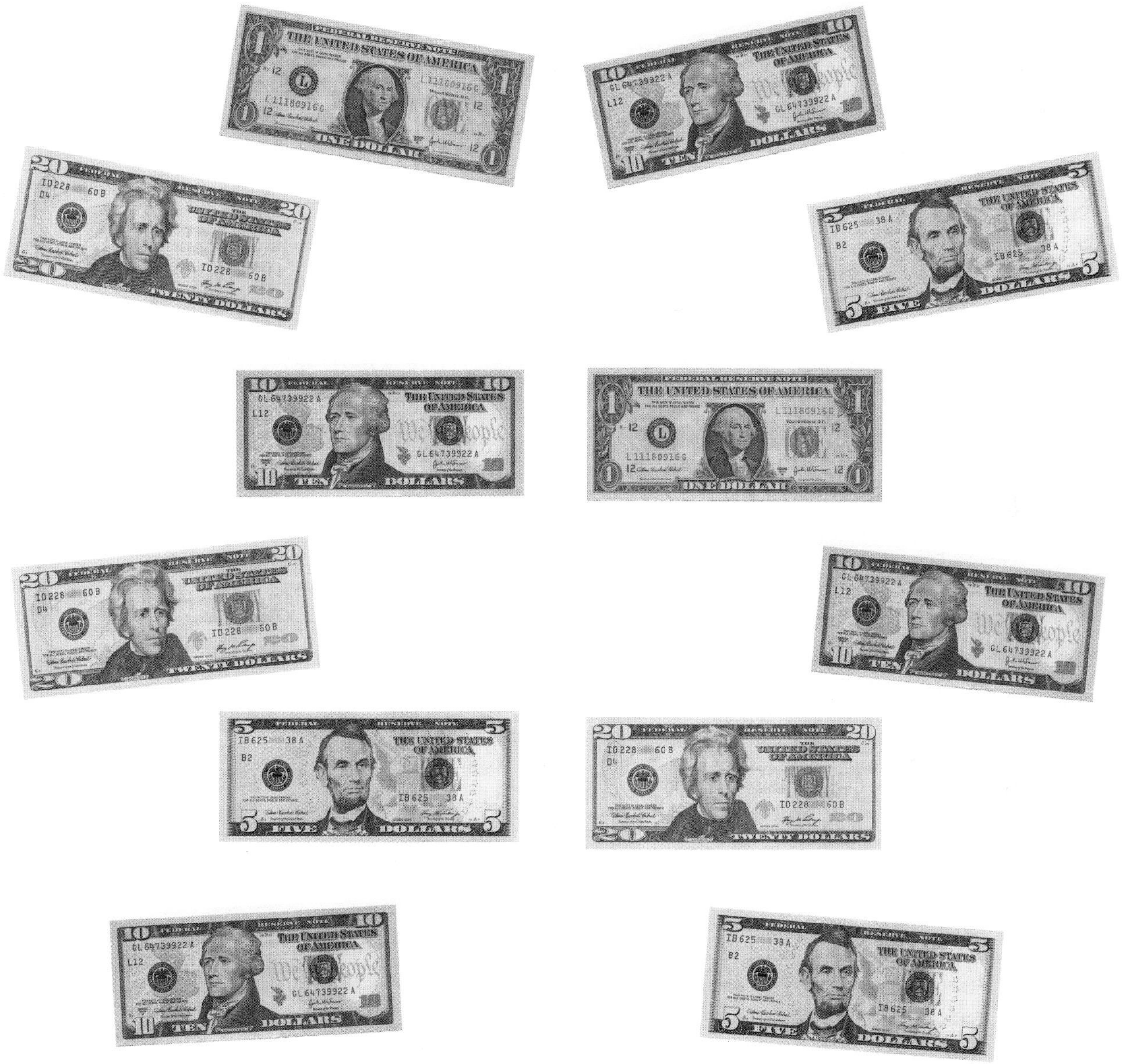

How many are there?

1. ______ \$1 bills
2. ______ \$5 bills
3. ______ \$10 bills
4. ______ \$20 bills

Learn

You can exchange bills.

1 five-dollar bill

=

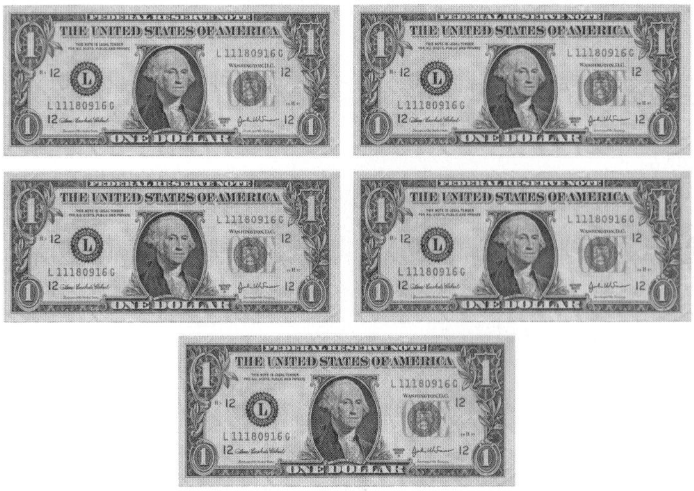

5 one-dollar bills

1 ten-dollar bill

=

2 five-dollar bills

Guided Practice

Fill in the blanks.

5

=

1 twenty-dollar bill 2 ______ bills

6 List other ways of exchanging a $20 bill for $1, $5, and $10 bills.

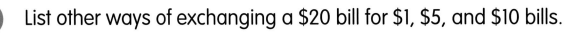

Learn You can combine bills to show a given amount.

Ben has some bills.
How much money does Ben have?
Count on from the greatest value.

20, 30, 40, 50,
60, 65, 66 dollars.

Ben has $66.

Guided Practice

Find the missing numbers.

7 John pays  for a car model.

The car model costs $____.

8 Sue pays 

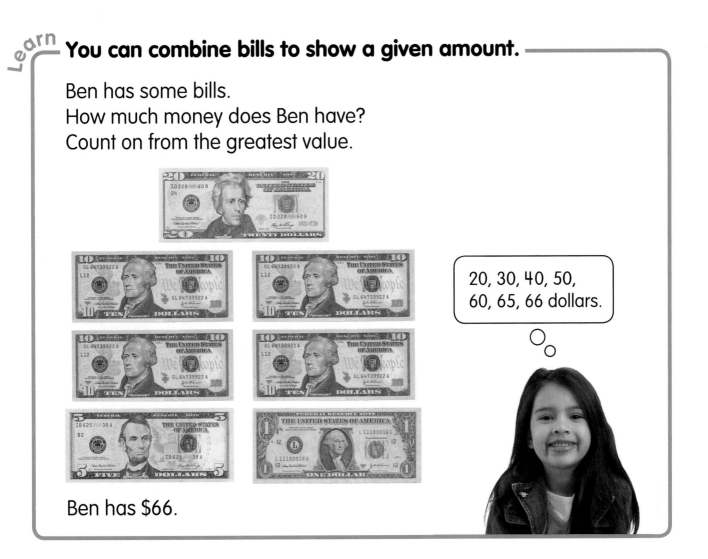

for a musical box.

The musical box costs $____.

Learn You can exchange a one-dollar bill for coins.

=

1 one-dollar bill

4 quarters

Count on in 25s.

25 50 75 100

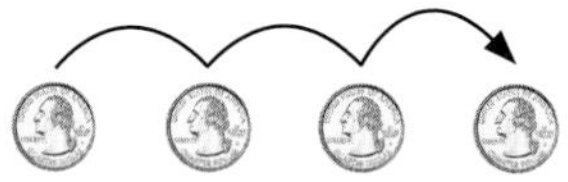

100¢

Four quarters have a value of 100¢.

=

1 one-dollar bill

10 dimes

Count on in 10s.
10, 20, 30 ,40, 50, 60, 70, 80, 90, 100.
Ten dimes have a value of 100¢.

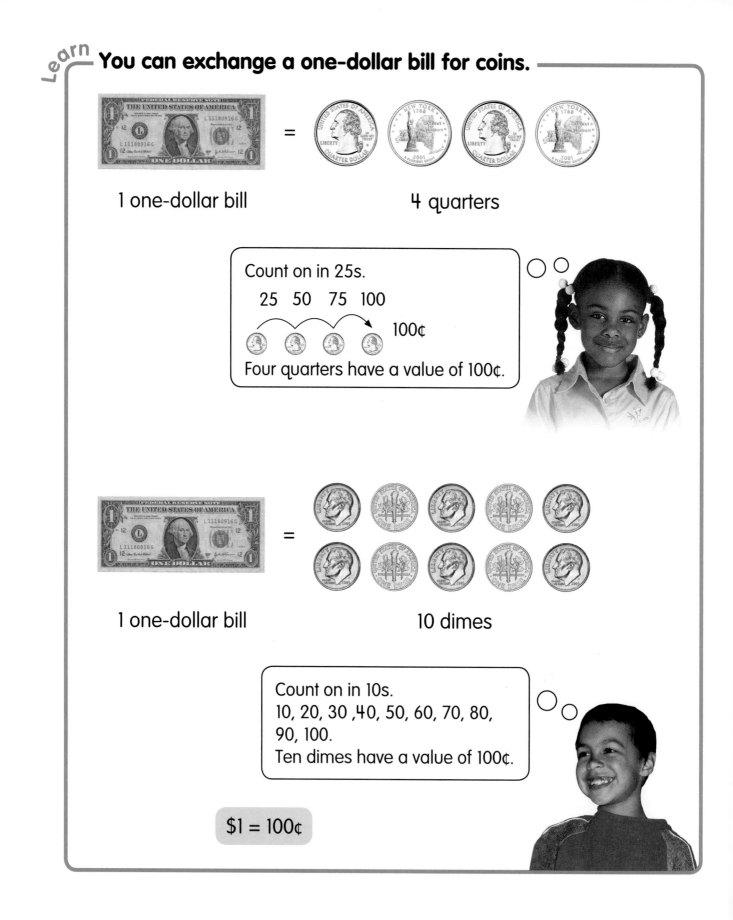

$1 = 100¢

Guided Practice

Fill in the blanks.

9  = 

1-dollar   2 ____ and 5 ____.

2 ____ have a value of 50¢.

5 ____ have a value of ____¢.

2 ____ and 5 ____ have a value of ____¢.

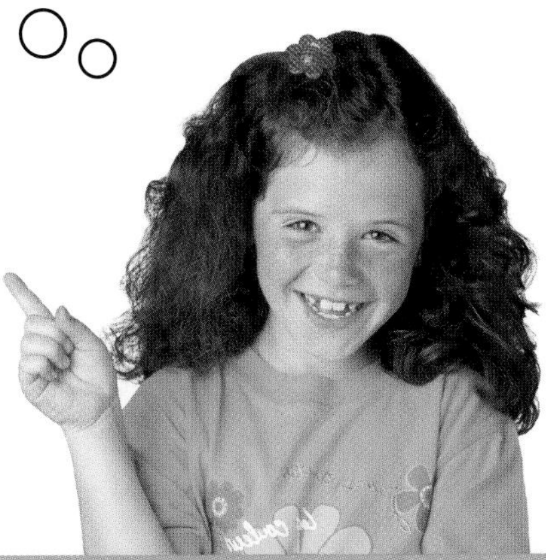

Let's Explore!

10,... 20, ...100!

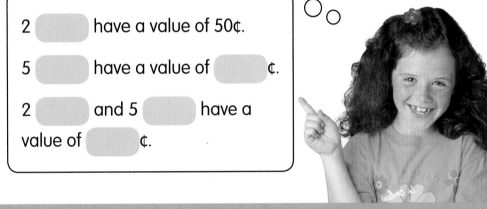

Rick has collected 100 pennies.
He stacks them in piles of 10.

He wants to change the pennies for other coins.
Make a table to show the different types of coins he can get.

Can he get a bill for the pennies?
What is the value of this bill in cents?

Complete $____ = ____¢

Learn Count the coins.

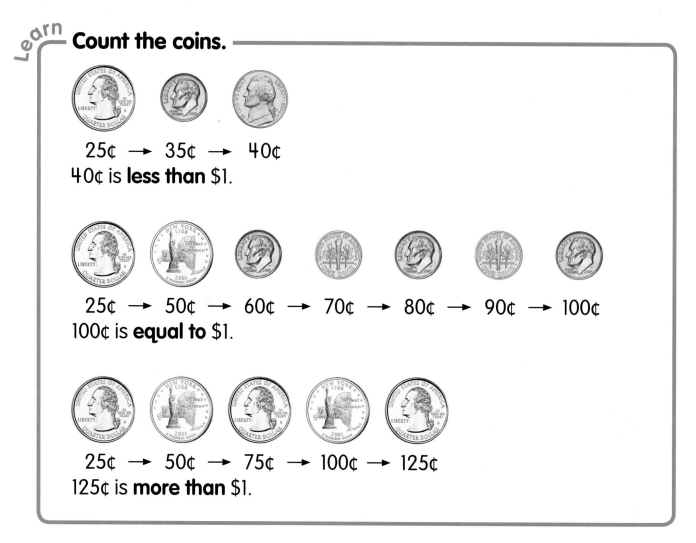

25¢ → 35¢ → 40¢

40¢ is **less than** $1.

25¢ → 50¢ → 60¢ → 70¢ → 80¢ → 90¢ → 100¢

100¢ is **equal to** $1.

25¢ → 50¢ → 75¢ → 100¢ → 125¢

125¢ is **more than** $1.

Guided Practice

Complete. Write *less than, equal to,* or *more than.*

10  ______ $1.00

11  ______ $1.00

12  ______ $1.00

13  ______ $1.00

Let's Explore!

WORKING TOGETHER

Here are some ways to show $10.

a

b

c

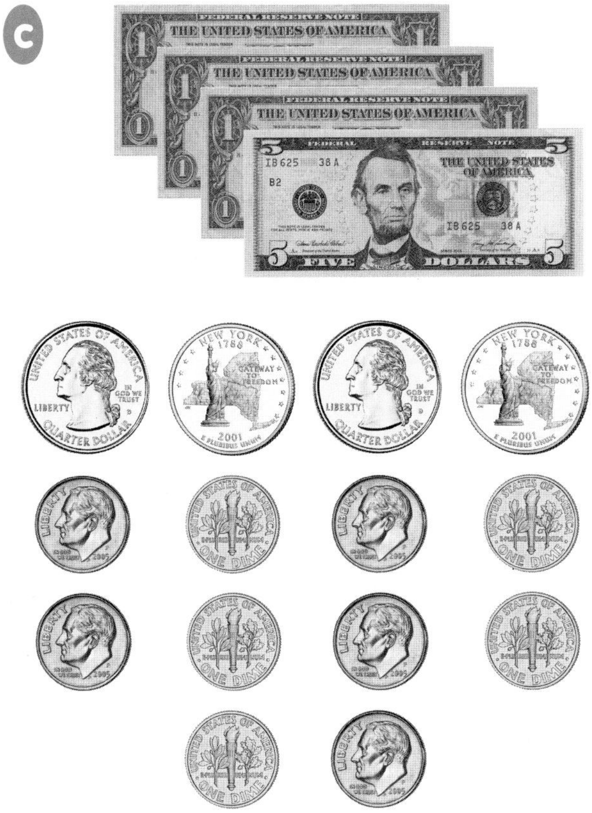

d

Work in groups of 2 or 4. Use bills and coins. Show different ways to make each amount.

1. 90¢
2. $6
3. $9

Learn You can put bills and coins together to find out how much money there is in all.

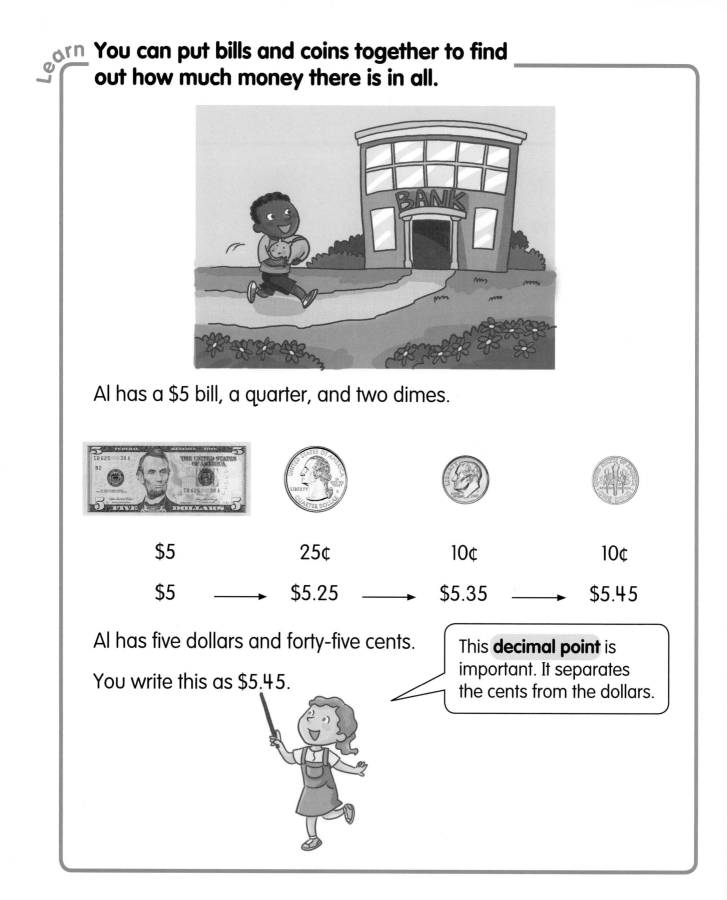

Al has a $5 bill, a quarter, and two dimes.

$5		25¢		10¢		10¢
$5	→	$5.25	→	$5.35	→	$5.45

Al has five dollars and forty-five cents.

You write this as $5.45.

This **decimal point** is important. It separates the cents from the dollars.

Learn

You can write an amount of money in different ways.

Ryan has two $10 bills and a $5 bill.

He has twenty-five dollars.
Write this amount as $25
or $25.00.

There are no cents.
So you can write two
zeros after the decimal point.

Luke also has some money.

He has twenty-five cents.
Write this amount as 25¢
or $0.25.

There are no dollars.
So you can write a zero
before the decimal point.

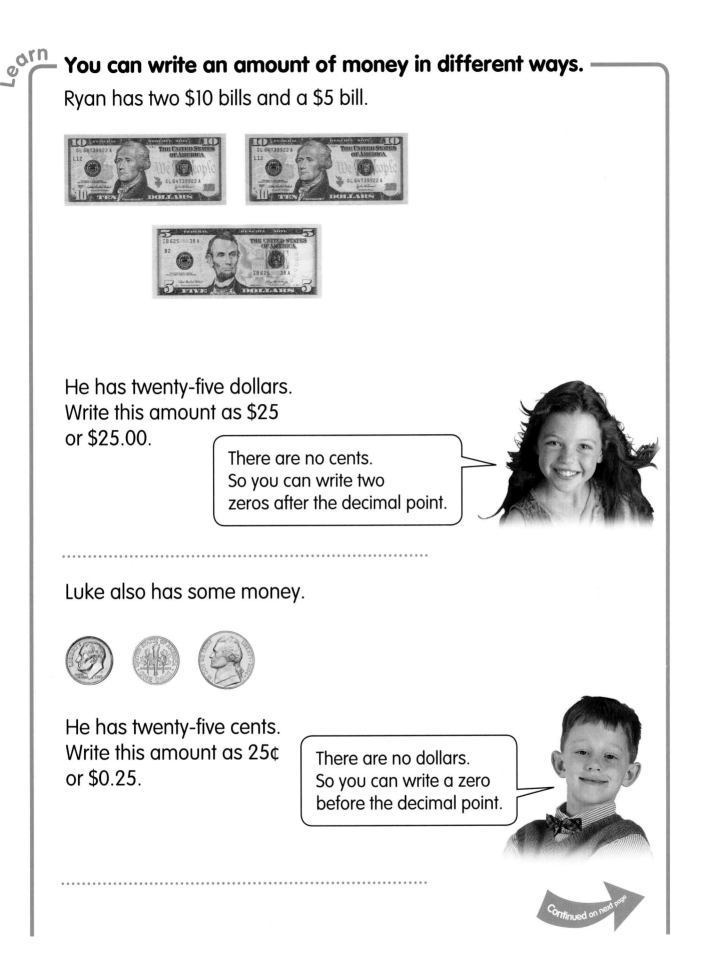

Continued on next page

John has some money.

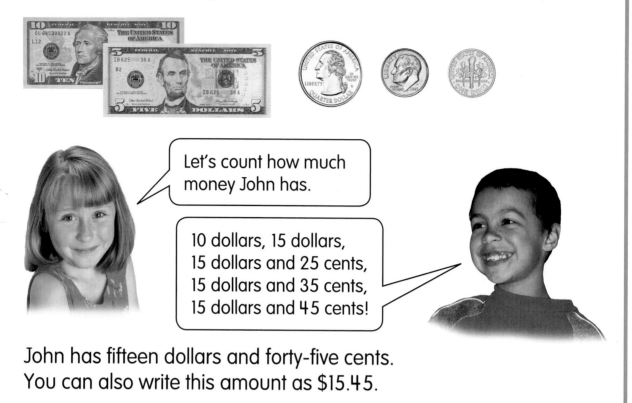

Let's count how much money John has.

10 dollars, 15 dollars,
15 dollars and 25 cents,
15 dollars and 35 cents,
15 dollars and 45 cents!

John has fifteen dollars and forty-five cents.
You can also write this amount as $15.45.

Guided Practice

Count the money.
Then write the amount in two ways.

14 

$ ____ or $ ____

15 

____ ¢ or $ ____ .

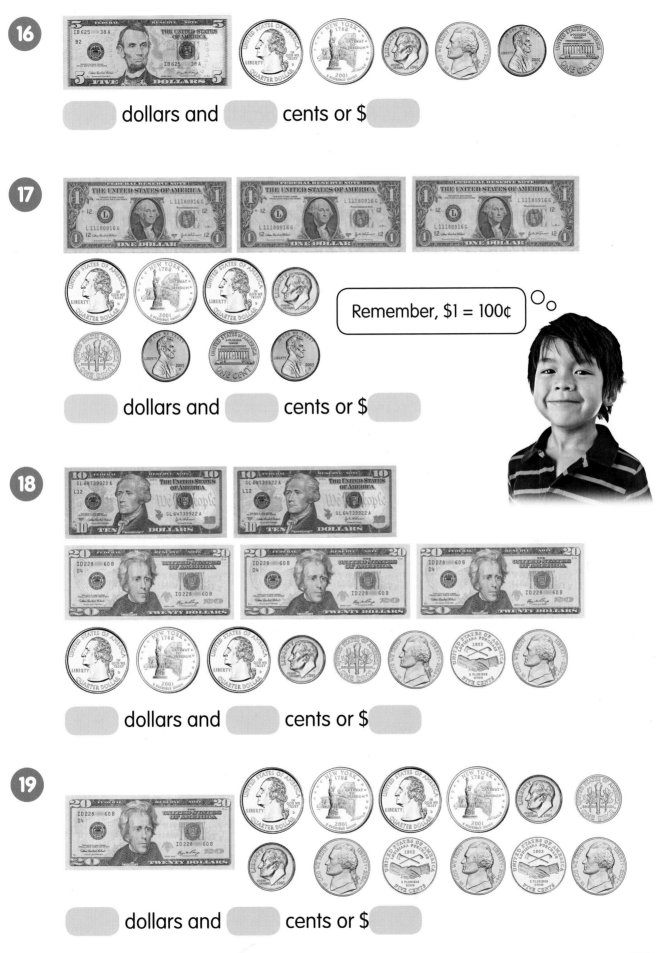

16

dollars and cents or $

17

Remember, $1 = 100¢

dollars and cents or $

18

dollars and cents or $

19

dollars and cents or $

Learn: You can exchange cents for dollars.

100¢ = $1.00 200¢ = $2.00

203¢ = $2.03

Two hundred three cents is two dollars and three cents.

1¢ is written as $0.01

14¢ is written as $0.14

520¢ is written as $5.20

1,000¢ is written as $10.00

Learn: You can exchange dollars for cents.

$1.50 = 150¢

One dollar and fifty cents is one hundred fifty cents.

$7.95 is written as 795¢

$9 is written as 900¢

$0.08 is written as 8¢

$0.50 is written as 50¢

Guided Practice

Find each missing amount.

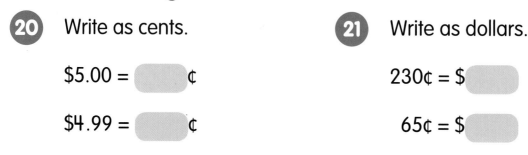

20 Write as cents.

$5.00 = ___ ¢

$4.99 = ___ ¢

21 Write as dollars.

230¢ = $ ___

65¢ = $ ___

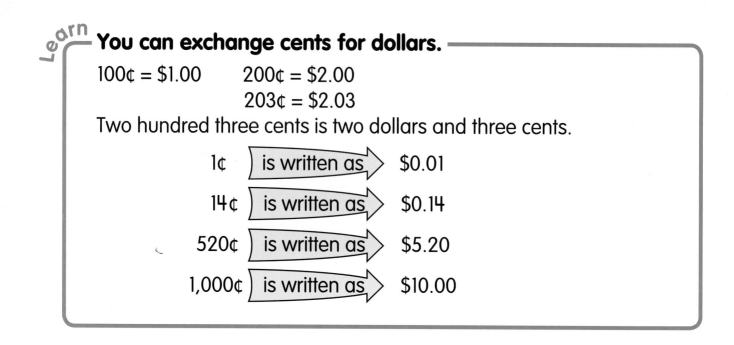

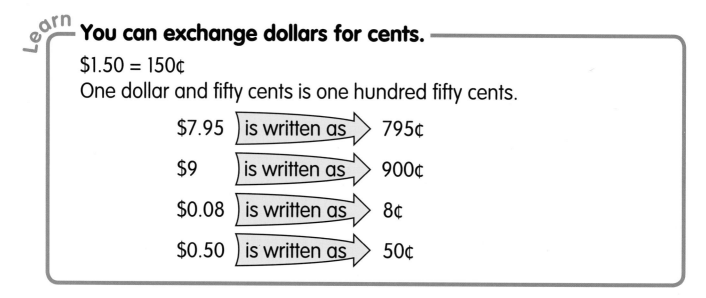

Hands-On Activity

WORKING TOGETHER

It's maze time!
Count. The children must keep to their color paths.
Write the total amount each child has.

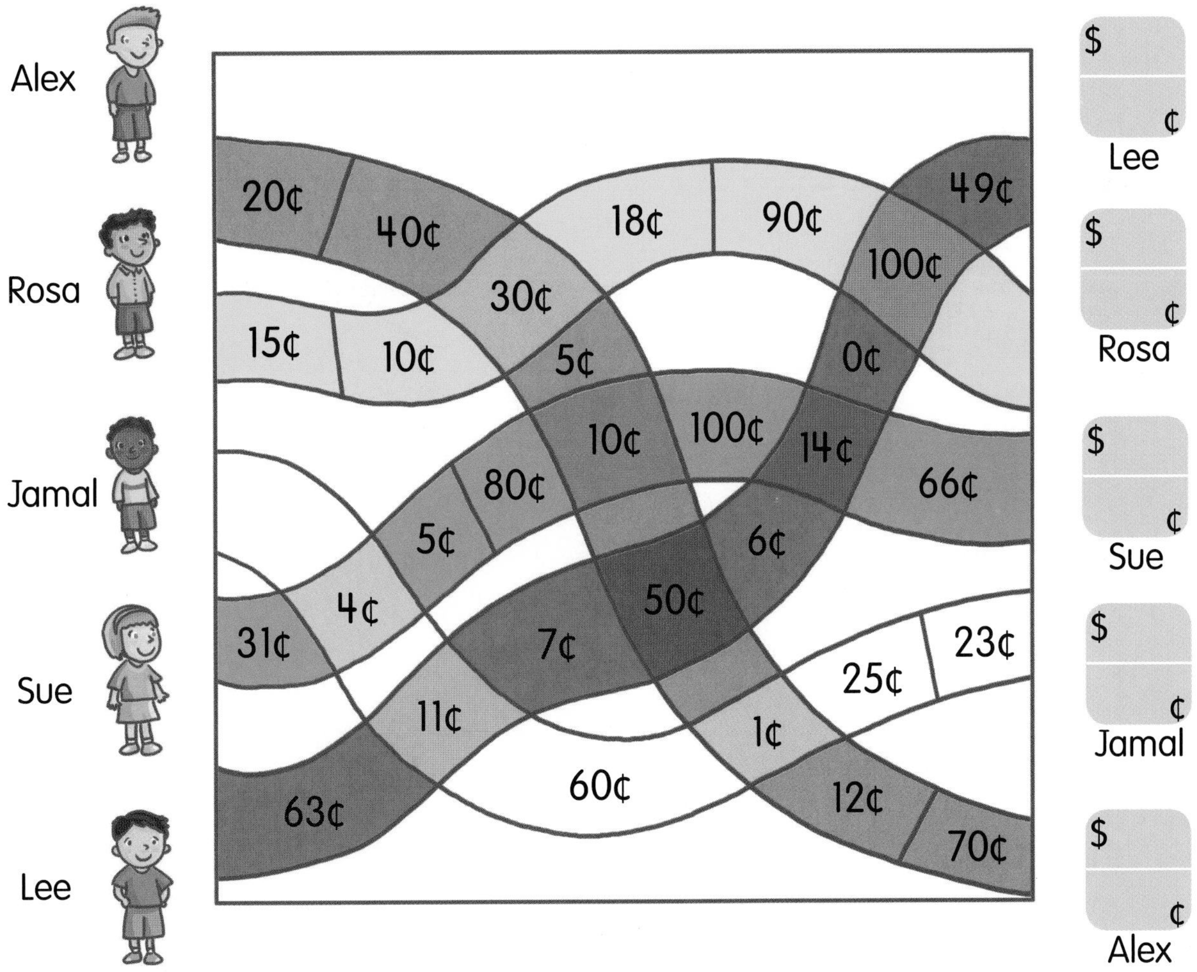

Use your answers in the maze. Answer each question.
Who has the greatest amount of money?
Who has the least amount of money?

Let's Practice

Look at each picture.
Write the price.

Example

$2.20

two dollars and twenty cents

1. 

$ ____

four dollars and sixty-five cents

2. 

$ ____

ninety-nine cents

3. 

$ ____

three dollars

4. 

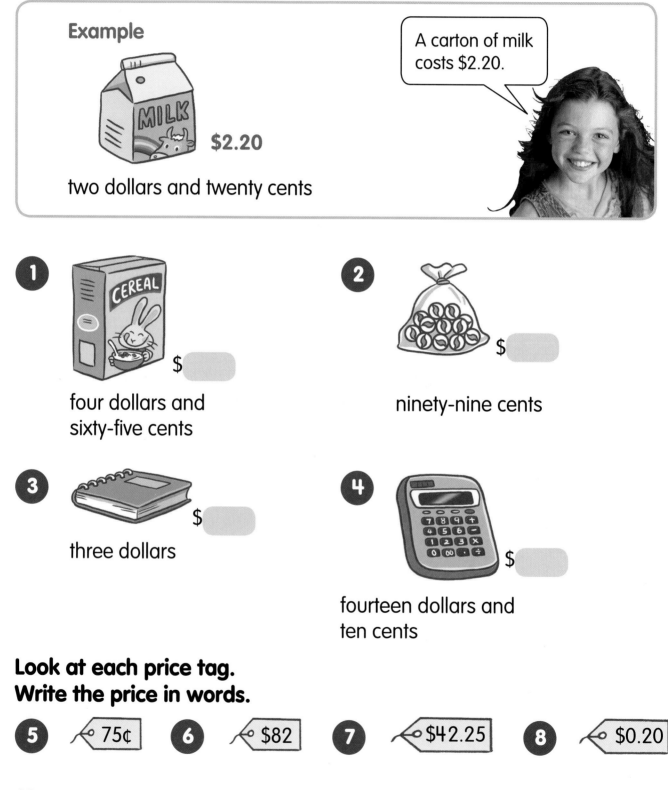

$ ____

fourteen dollars and ten cents

Look at each price tag.
Write the price in words.

5. 75¢
6. $82
7. $42.25
8. $0.20

Find each missing number.

9 $10.00 = ___ dollars and ___ cents

10 $0.80 = ___ dollars and ___ cents

11 $75.02 = ___ dollars and ___ cents

Count. Write each amount in two ways.

12

___ dollars and ___ cents = $___

13

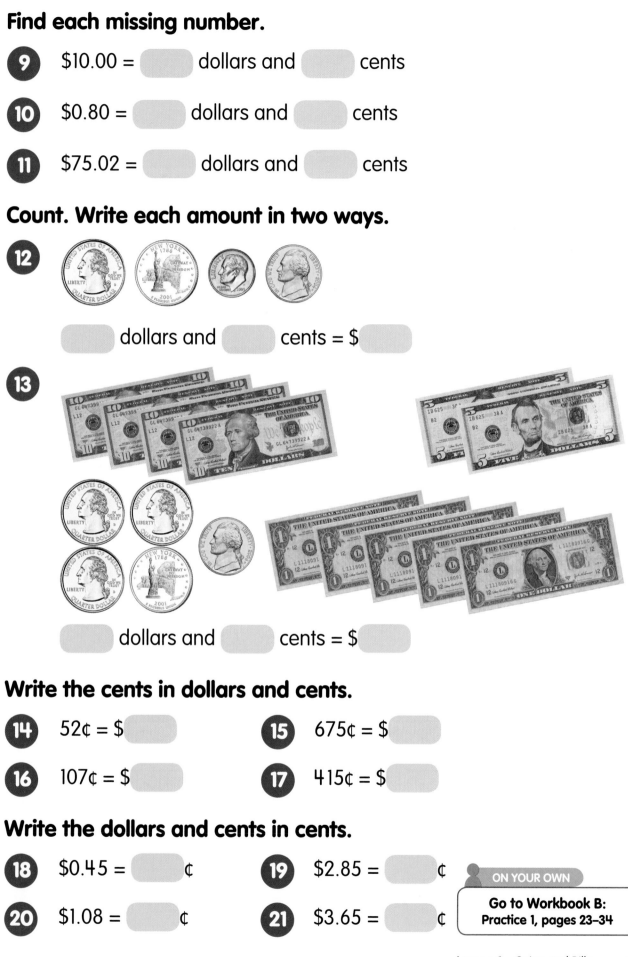

___ dollars and ___ cents = $___

Write the cents in dollars and cents.

14 52¢ = $___

15 675¢ = $___

16 107¢ = $___

17 415¢ = $___

Write the dollars and cents in cents.

18 $0.45 = ___¢

19 $2.85 = ___¢

20 $1.08 = ___¢

21 $3.65 = ___¢

ON YOUR OWN

Go to Workbook B: Practice 1, pages 23–34

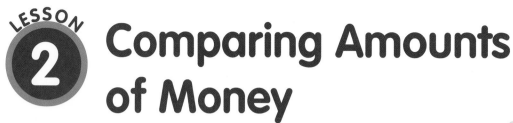

LESSON 2

Comparing Amounts of Money

Lesson Objective

- Compare amounts of money using tables.

Vocabulary
table

Learn You can use dollars and cents tables to compare amounts of money.

Who has more?

Susan has $29.50.

Dollars	Cents
29	50

Mike has $32.20.

Dollars	Cents
32	20

$32.20 is more than $29.50.
$29.50 is less than $32.20.

So, Mike has more.

First, compare the dollars.
32 is greater than 29.

Who has less?

Caiden has $63.25.

Dollars	Cents
63	25

Lily has $63.70.

Dollars	Cents
63	70

$63.70 is more than $63.25.
$63.25 is less than $63.70.

So, Caiden has less.

First, compare the dollars.
They are the same.

Then, compare the cents.
70 is greater than 25.

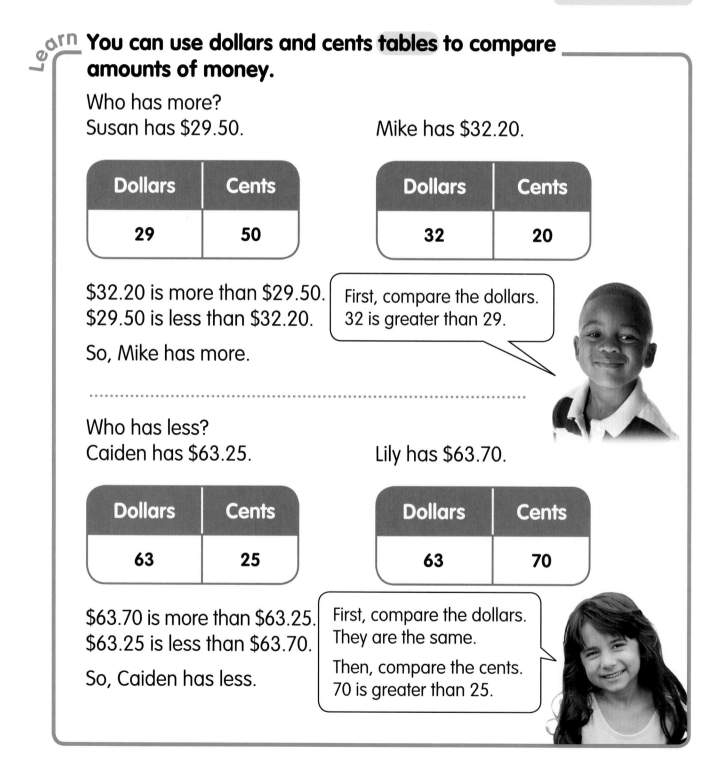

Guided Practice

Compare.
Who has less?

1 Cherice $20.40

Dollars	Cents
20	40

$ ____ > $ ____

Noah $20.25

Dollars	Cents
20	25

$ ____ < $ ____

So, ____ has less.

> more than
< less than

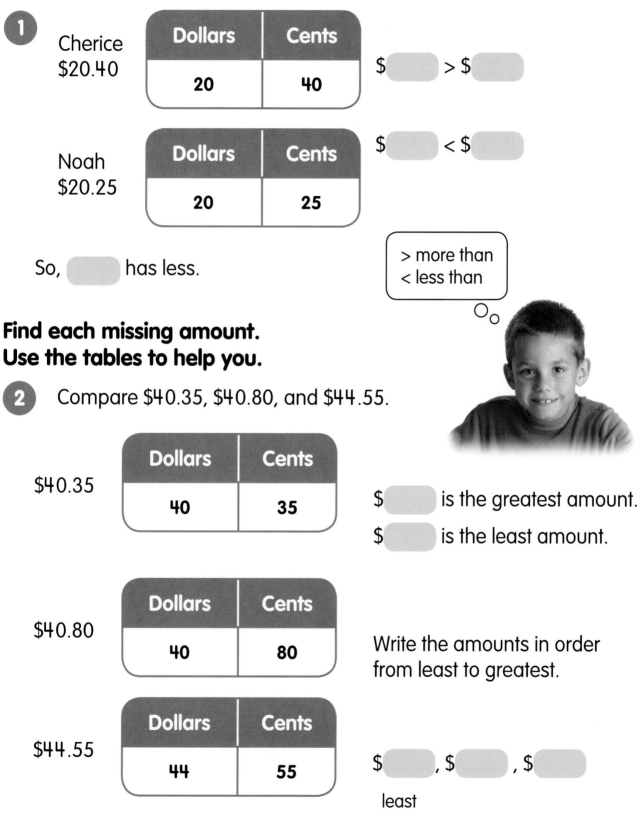

Find each missing amount.
Use the tables to help you.

2 Compare $40.35, $40.80, and $44.55.

$40.35

Dollars	Cents
40	35

$ ____ is the greatest amount.

$ ____ is the least amount.

$40.80

Dollars	Cents
40	80

Write the amounts in order from least to greatest.

$44.55

Dollars	Cents
44	55

$ ____, $ ____, $ ____
least

Let's Practice

Which set has more?

1

Set A

Set B

Which set has less?

2

Set A

Set B

Which amount is more?

3 $22 $19

4 $0.95 $1.04

Which amount is less?

5 $25.10 $30.05

6 $45.15 $38.90

Compare.

$42.35 $49.05 $55.75

7 Which amount is the least? $ ____

8 Which amount is the greatest? $ ____

Arrange the amounts in order from least to greatest.

9 $50.15 $58.45 $50.35

Arrange the amounts in order from greatest to least.

10 $34.50 $43.50 $34.85

ON YOUR OWN

Go to Workbook B: Practice 2, pages 35–38

LESSON 3 Real-World Problems: Money

Lesson Objective

- Use bar models to solve real-world problems involving addition and subtraction of money.

Learn You can use bar models to solve real-world problems.

Maggie has 27¢.
She saves 15¢ more.
She spends 19¢.
How much money does Maggie have left?

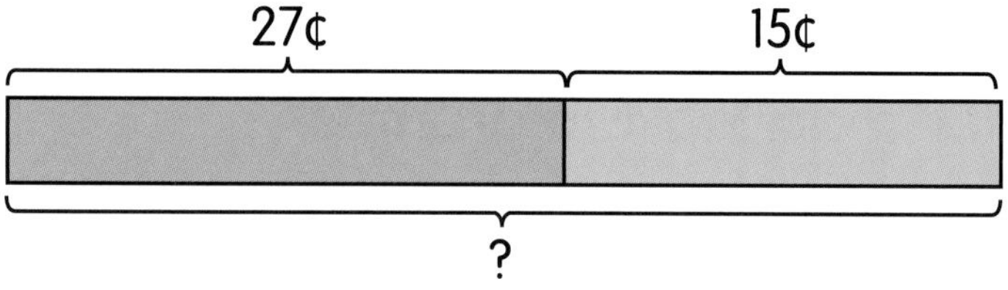

First, find out how much money Maggie has.

27¢ + 15¢ = 42¢

Maggie has 42¢ in all.

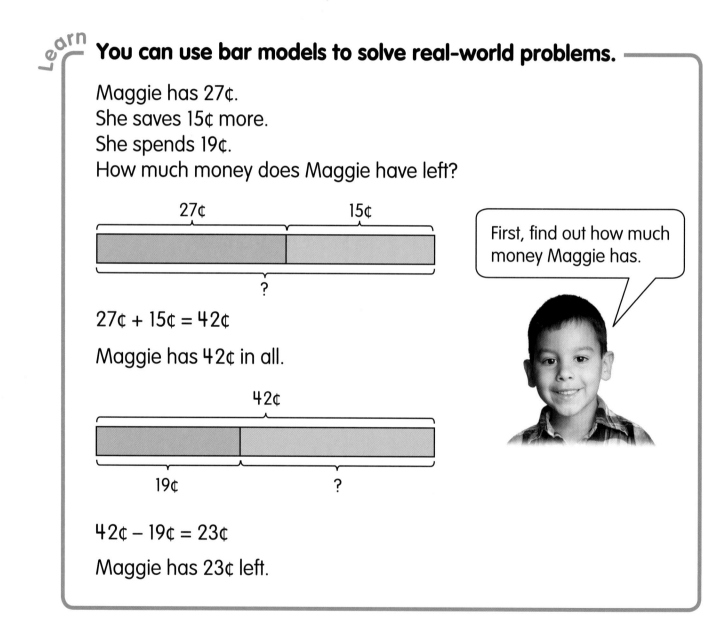

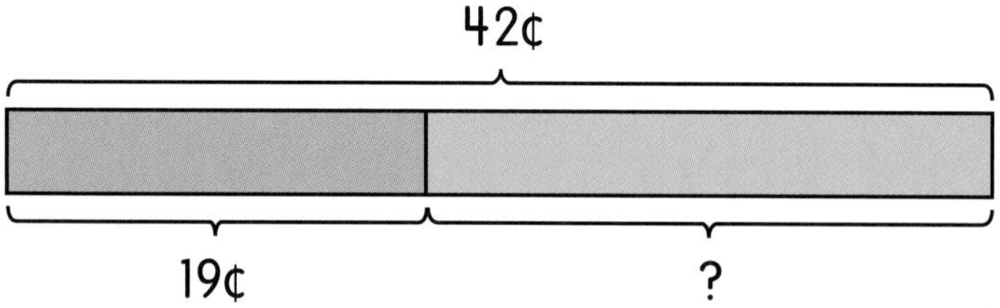

42¢ – 19¢ = 23¢

Maggie has 23¢ left.

Guided Practice

Solve.
Use bar models to help you.

1 A DVD player costs $168. A camera costs $75 more than the DVD player. A computer costs $300. How much more does the computer cost than the camera?

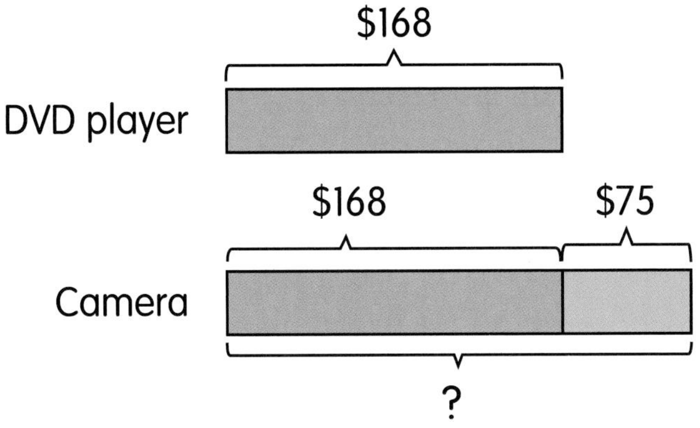

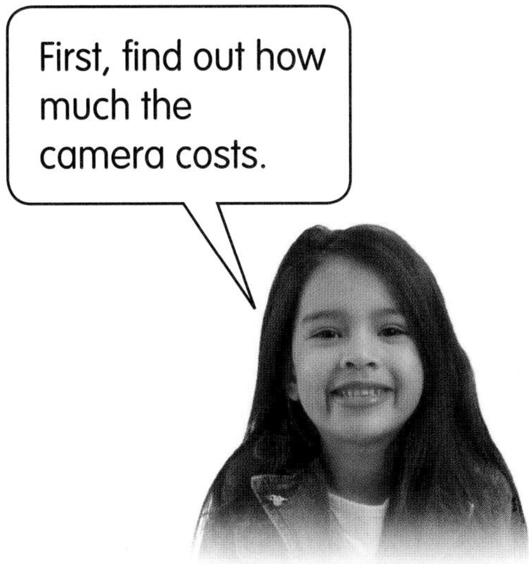

First, find out how much the camera costs.

$ ____ + $ ____ = $ ____

The camera costs $ ____.

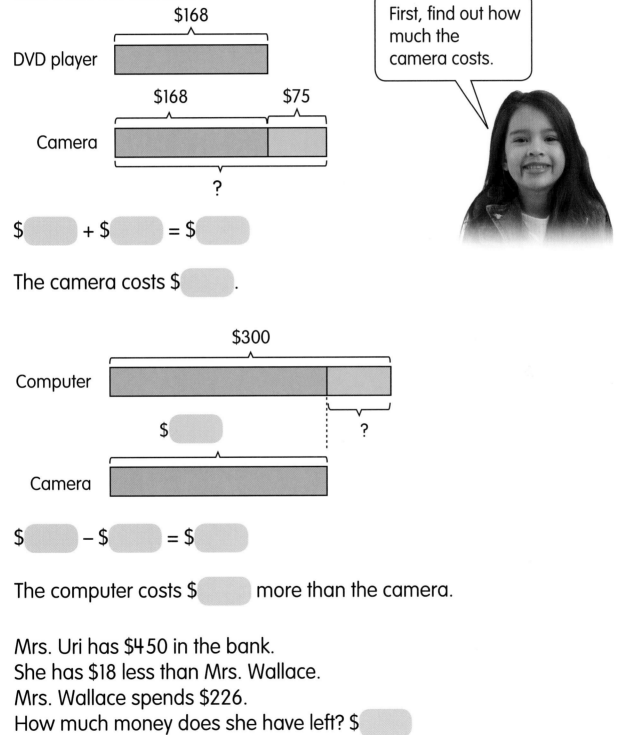

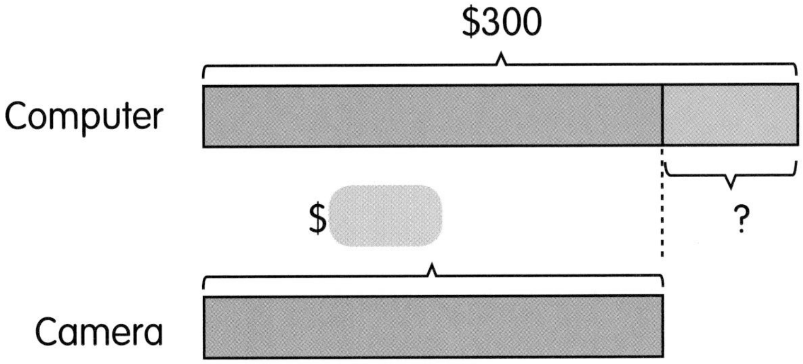

$ ____ – $ ____ = $ ____

The computer costs $ ____ more than the camera.

2 Mrs. Uri has $450 in the bank.
She has $18 less than Mrs. Wallace.
Mrs. Wallace spends $226.
How much money does she have left? $ ____

Learn: You can use bar models to solve real-world problems.

Randy bought an eraser, a pencil, and a ruler.
The eraser cost 30¢, the pencil cost 45¢, and the ruler cost 50¢.
How much did he pay in all?

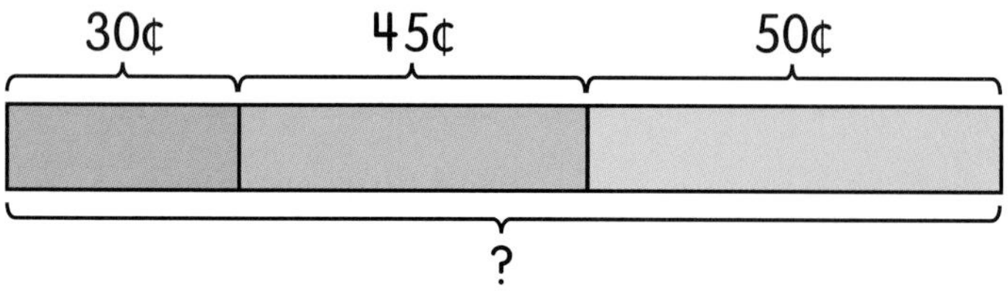

30¢ + 45¢ + 50¢ = $1.25

He paid $1.25 in all.

100¢ = $1
125¢ = $1.25

Guided Practice

Solve.
Use bar models to help you.

3 Elle buys a box of paperclips for 55¢, a marker for 85¢, and a note pad for 90¢.
How much does she pay in all?

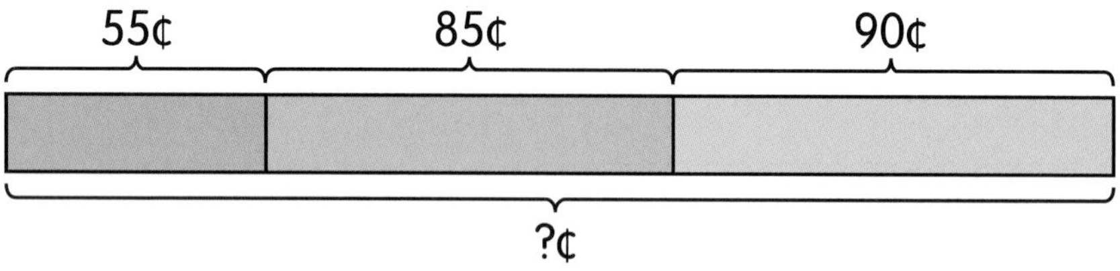

___¢ + ___¢ + ___¢ = $___

___¢ = $___

Elle pays $___ in all.

Let's Practice

Solve.
Draw bar models to help you.

1. Carrie and Neil have $230.
   Carrie has $159.
   How much money does Neil have?

2. Joe buys an apple for 35¢. Leanne buys a melon for 82¢.
   How much do they spend in all?

3. Nellie bought a pencil for 25¢ and an eraser for 15¢.
   If she had 81¢ at first, how much money did she have left?

4. A note pad costs 80¢.
   A bookmark costs 25¢.
   After buying one of each item, Jennifer had 35¢ left.
   How much money did she have at first?

5. Britney spent $65 on a coat and $18 on food.
   She has $25 left.
   How much money did she have at first?

6. Rachel orders toast and a glass of juice for breakfast.
   The toast costs 45¢ and the juice costs 40¢ more.
   How much does Rachel pay in all?

7. Patrick buys a pen for 59¢.
   Kelly buys the same pen for 14¢ less.
   How much do both pens cost?

8. A train model costs $42.
A racing car model costs $38 more.
An airplane model costs $99.
How much more does the airplane model cost than the racing car model?

9. A stool costs $18.
A table costs $66.
If Diana has $153 at first, how much has she left after buying a stool and a table?

ON YOUR OWN
Go to Workbook B:
Practice 3, pages 39–40

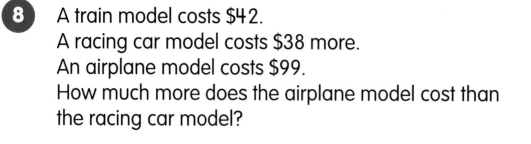

CRITICAL THINKING SKILLS

Put On Your Thinking Cap!

Peter saves his money in $1 bills and quarters.
So far he has saved $5.
He has more than 2 bills and more than 4 coins.
How many $1 bills and quarters does he have?

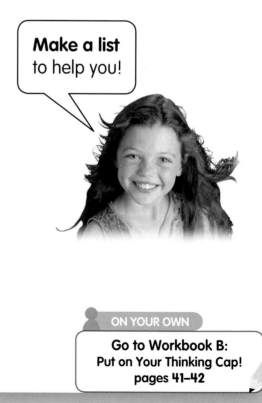

Make a list to help you!

ON YOUR OWN
Go to Workbook B:
Put on Your Thinking Cap!
pages 41–42

Chapter Wrap Up

You have learned...

BIG IDEA

Money amounts can be shown and counted using bills and coins.

identifying bills

counting money

Bills

= $36

Thirty-six dollars can be written as $36.
It can also be written as $36.00.
The decimal point separates the cents from the dollars.
There are no cents so we put two zeros after the decimal point.

100 cents is equal to one dollar.

Coins

= 125¢

= $1.25

Bills and Coins

= $15.06

Fifteen dollars and six cents can be written as $15.06.

changing money

Cents to Dollars

350¢ = \$3.50
Three hundred fifty cents is three dollars and fifty cents.

18¢ is written as \$0.18.
485¢ is written as \$4.85.
1,000¢ is written as \$10.00.

Dollars to Cents

\$2.55 = 255¢
Two dollars and fifty-five cents is two hundred fifty-five cents.

\$8.65 is written as 865¢.
\$0.07 is written as 7¢.
\$0.90 is written as 90¢.

comparing money

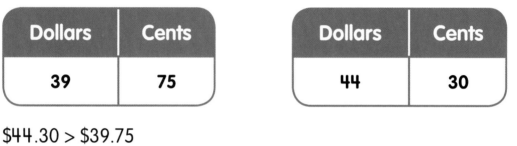

Dollars	Cents
39	75

Dollars	Cents
44	30

\$44.30 > \$39.75
\$39.75 < \$44.30

adding and subtracting money

Bar models can be used to solve word-problems.

A balloon costs 65¢.
A kite costs 95¢.
How much do both cost?

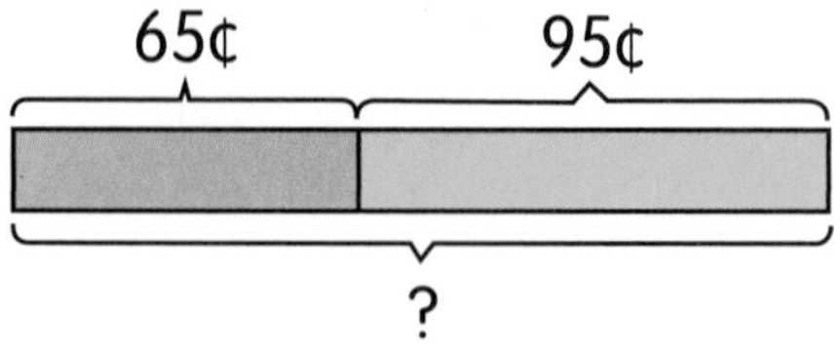

65¢ + 95¢ = \$1.60

Both cost \$1.60.

Ana has \$35.
She spends \$15.
How much money does she have left?

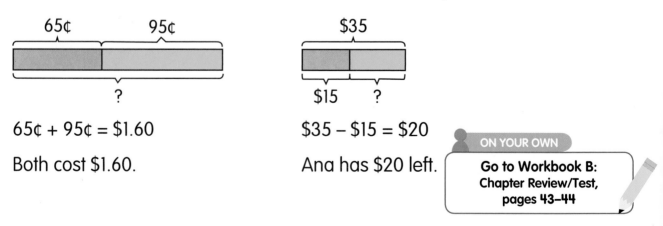

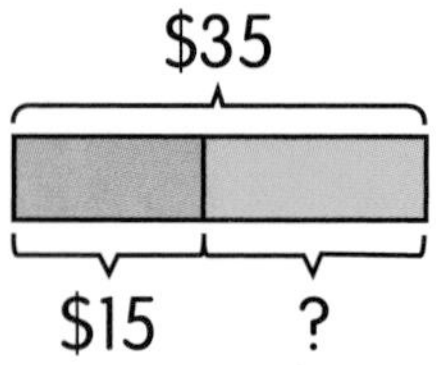

\$35 – \$15 = \$20

Ana has \$20 left.

ON YOUR OWN
Go to Workbook B: Chapter Review/Test, pages 43–44

CHAPTER 12

Fractions

Use a square piece of paper.

1 Fold it in half.
What shape do you get?

I get a rectangle!
I get a triangle!

2 Fold it in half again.
What shape do you get?

I get a square!
I get a smaller triangle!

3 Open up the paper.
Draw lines along the folds.

I get this!
I get this!

How many designs can you make?
Look at these designs.
How can you make them?

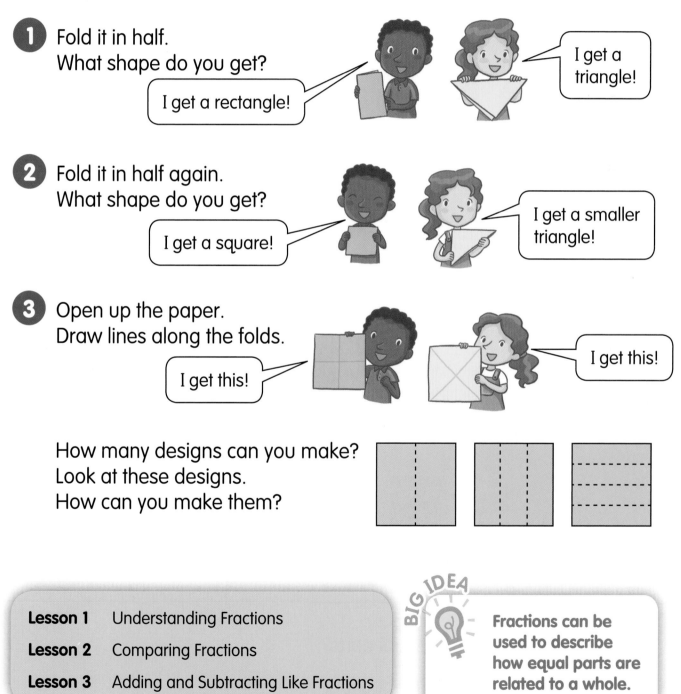

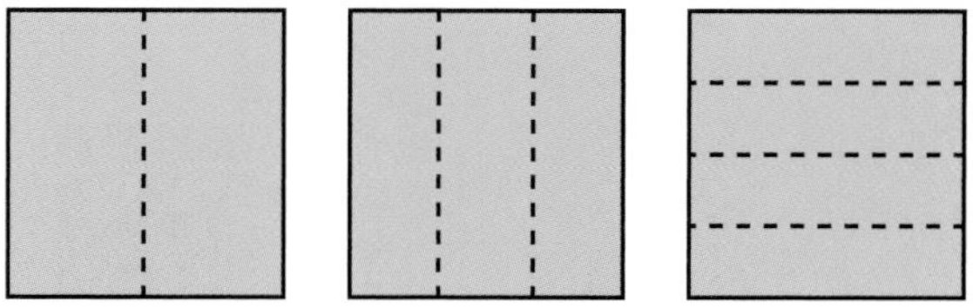

Lesson 1 Understanding Fractions

Lesson 2 Comparing Fractions

Lesson 3 Adding and Subtracting Like Fractions

BIG IDEA

Fractions can be used to describe how equal parts are related to a whole.

Recall Prior Knowledge

These shapes are divided into equal parts.

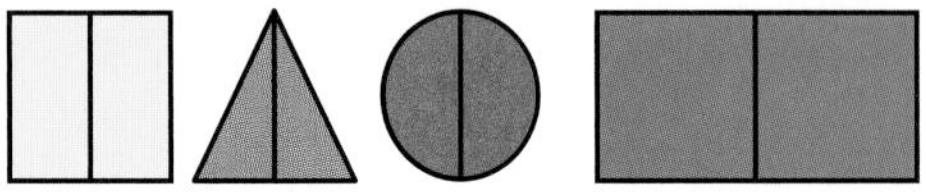

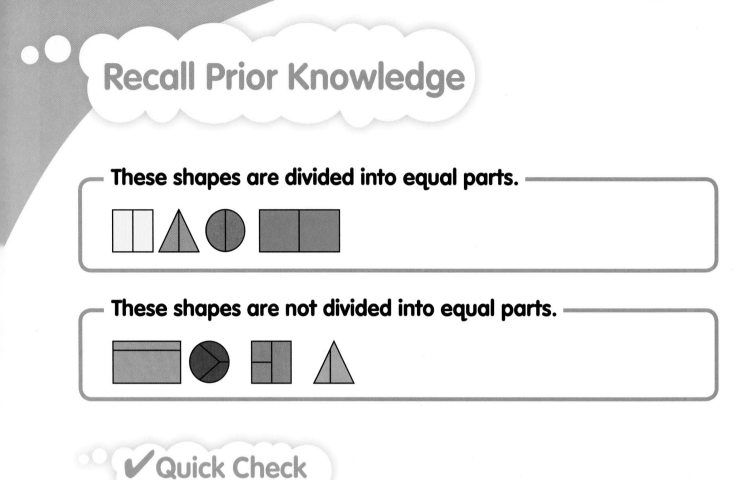

These shapes are not divided into equal parts.

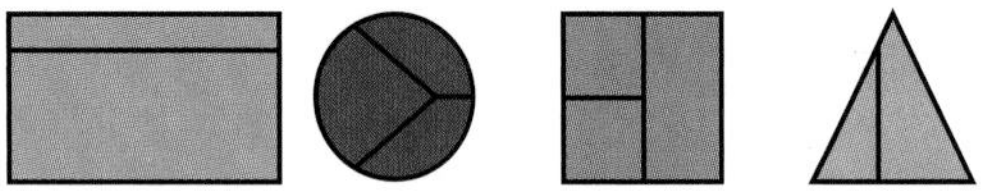

✔Quick Check

Look at the figures.
Then answer the questions.

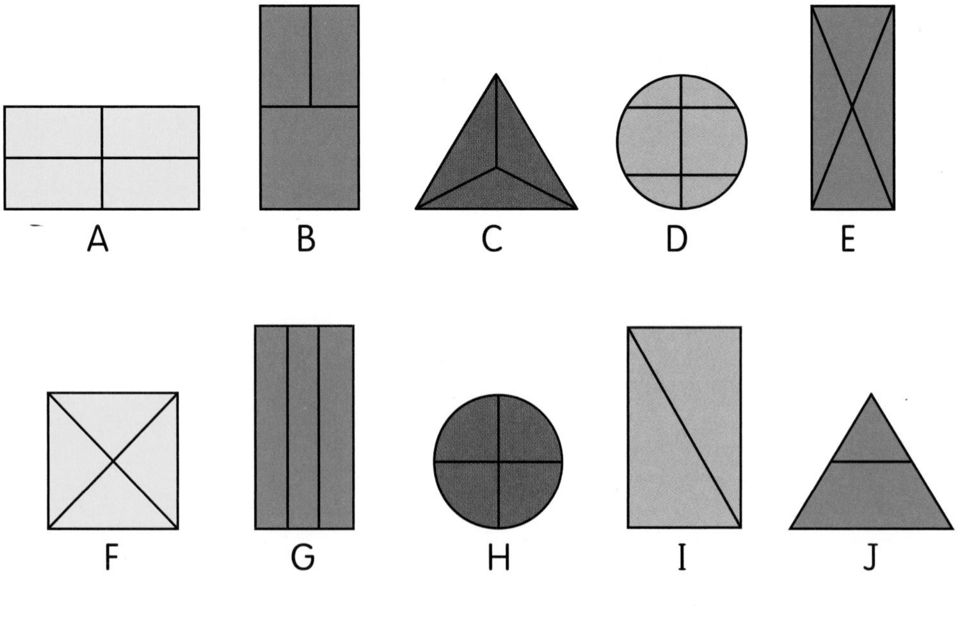

1. Which figures have equal parts? ______
2. Which figures have unequal parts? ______

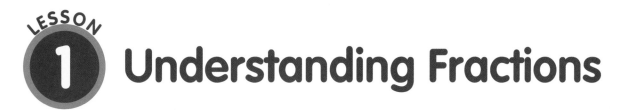

LESSON 1 Understanding Fractions

Lesson Objectives

- Identify whether a shape is divided into equal fractional parts.
- Read, write, and identify unit fractions for halves, thirds, and fourths.
- Show fractions and a whole using model drawings.

Vocabulary

equal	one-half
unequal	one-third
whole	one-fourth
fraction	unit fraction

Learn

You can make equal parts in many ways.

A square is divided into 4 parts.
Each part is the same size.
All the parts are equal.

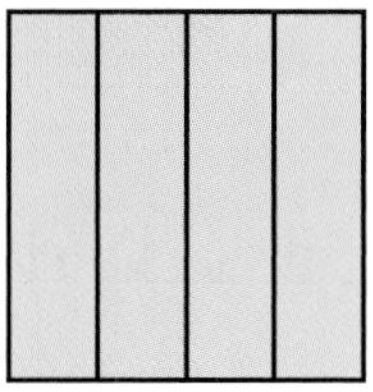

Can you think of another way to divide the square into 4 equal parts?

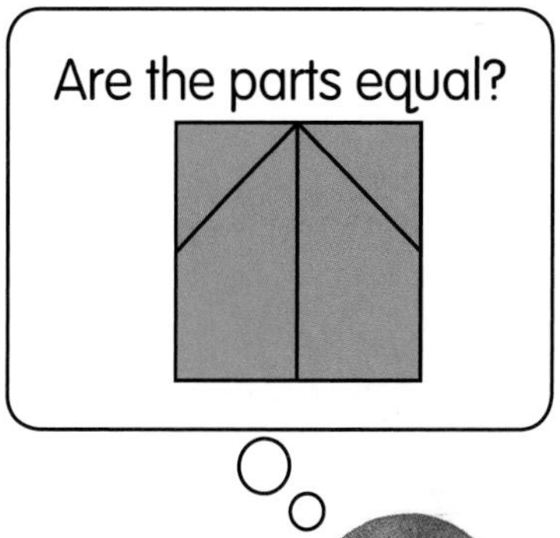

This square is not divided into 4 equal parts.

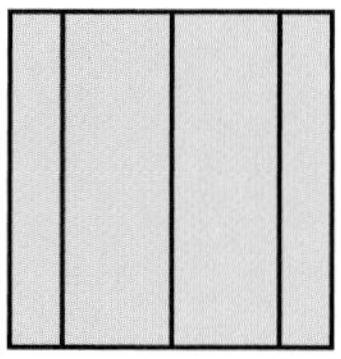

Each part is not the same size.
The parts are **unequal**.

Can you think of other ways of dividing the square into 4 unequal parts?

Guided Practice

Find the shapes that are divided into equal parts.

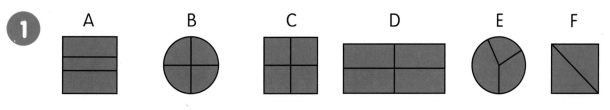

1 A B C D E F

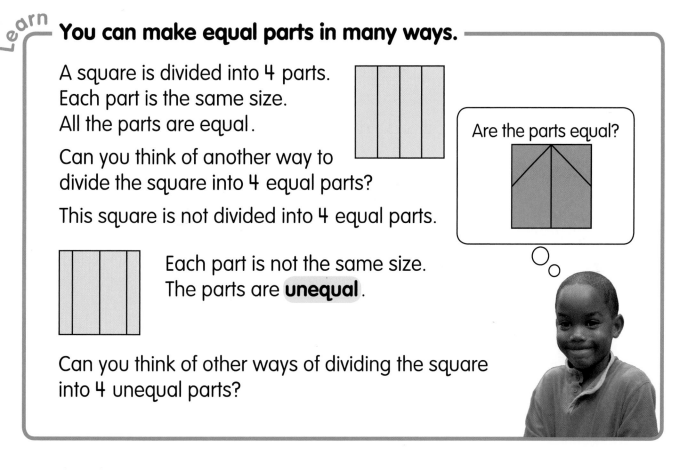

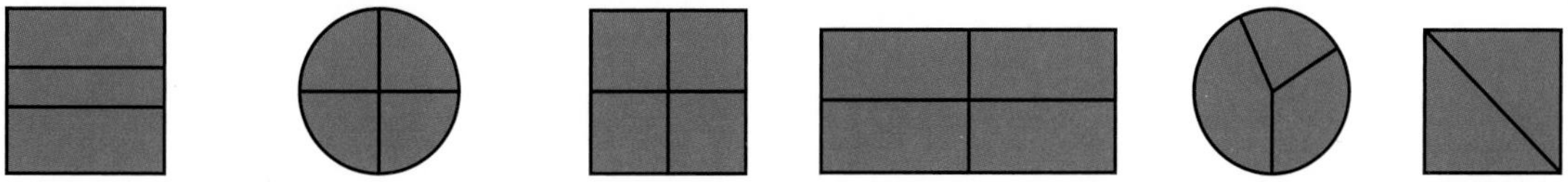

Learn — You can use fractions to describe equal parts of a whole.

This is a slice of bread.
It is one whole.

This is a whole muffin. It is divided into 2 equal parts.

If Jake eats only 1 part, he eats 1 out of 2 equal parts.

You write this as $\frac{1}{2}$.

$\frac{1}{2}$ is an example of a **fraction**.

Divide a loaf of bread into 3 equal parts.

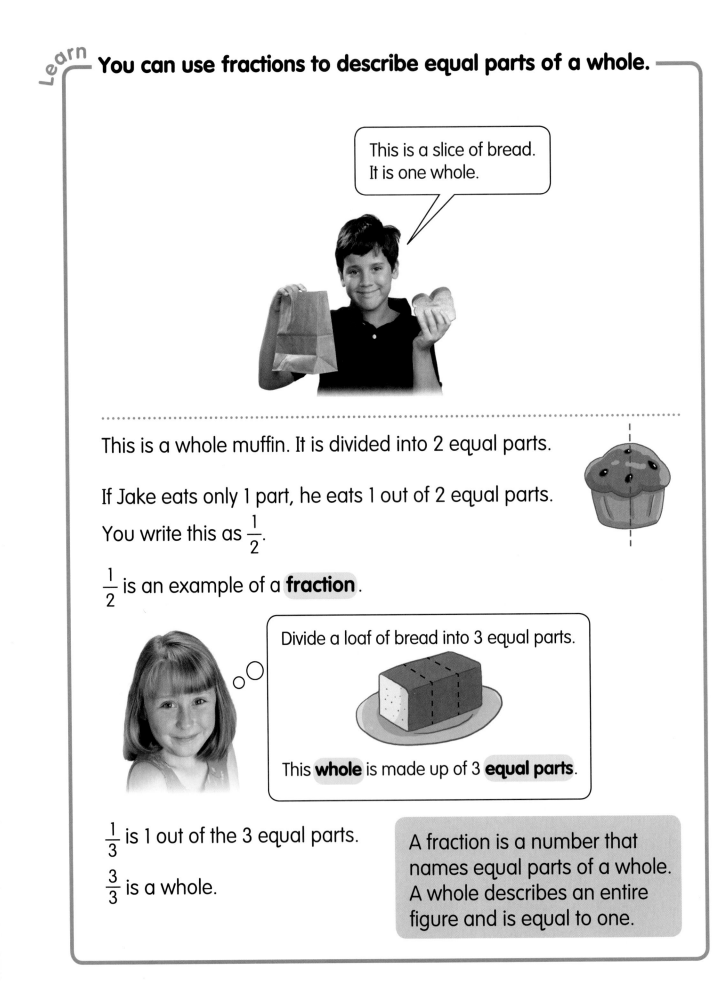

This **whole** is made up of 3 **equal parts**.

$\frac{1}{3}$ is 1 out of the 3 equal parts.

$\frac{3}{3}$ is a whole.

A fraction is a number that names equal parts of a whole. A whole describes an entire figure and is equal to one.

Guided Practice

Find the missing numbers and fractions.

2. The circle is divided into 4 equal parts.

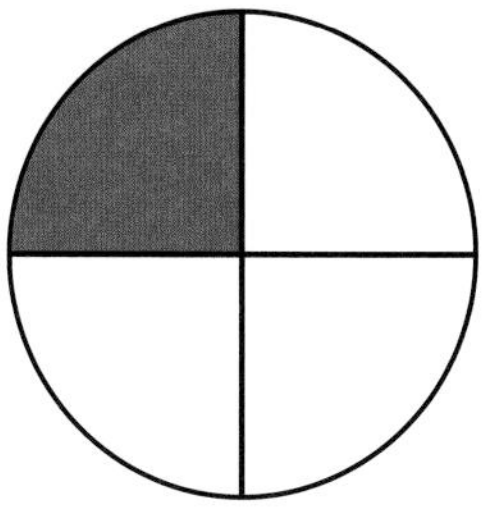

What fraction of the circle is shaded?
The whole is made up of 4 equal parts.

___ part out of the ___ equal parts is shaded.

___ of the circle is shaded.

3. Sam bought a chicken pot pie.
He cut the pie into ___ equal pieces.
He ate 1 piece.
What fraction of the pie did he eat? ___

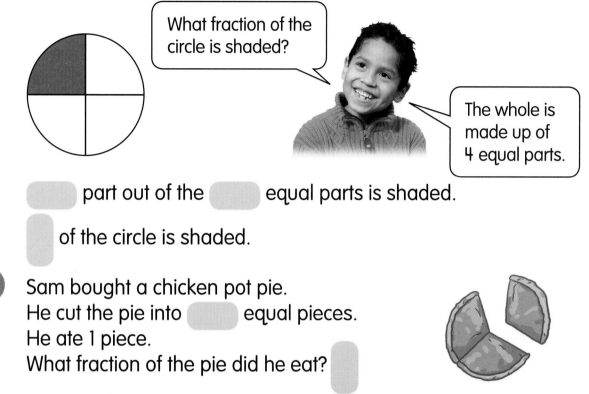

Hands-On Activity

Cut out three rectangles.

1. Show how you can fold each rectangle into

   2 equal parts
   3 equal parts
   4 equal parts

2. For each rectangle shade 1 of the equal parts.
What fraction of the whole is each equal part?

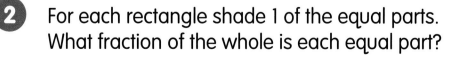

Learn Name fractional parts.

How do you read fractional parts?

Fraction		Read As
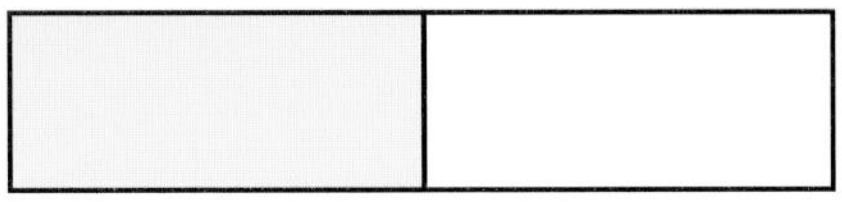	$\frac{1}{2}$	one-half
	$\frac{1}{3}$	one-third
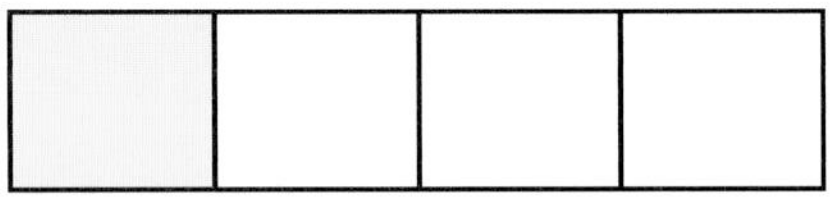	$\frac{1}{4}$	one-quarter or one-fourth

$\frac{1}{2}$, $\frac{1}{3}$, and $\frac{1}{4}$ are unit fractions.
A **unit fraction** names one of the equal parts of a whole.

Guided Practice

**What part of the figure is shaded?
Express your answer in two ways.**

4

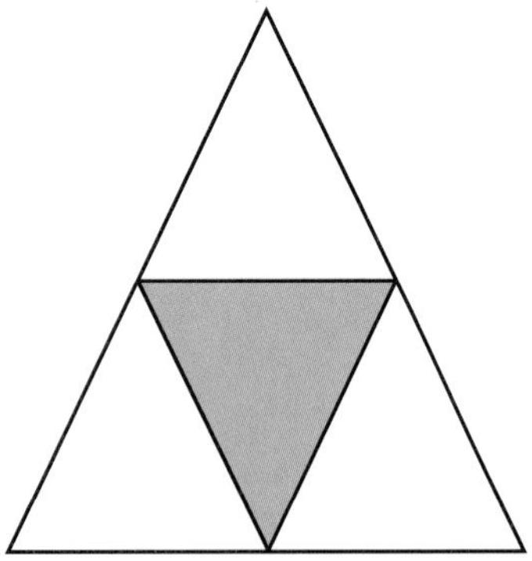

____-fourth

5

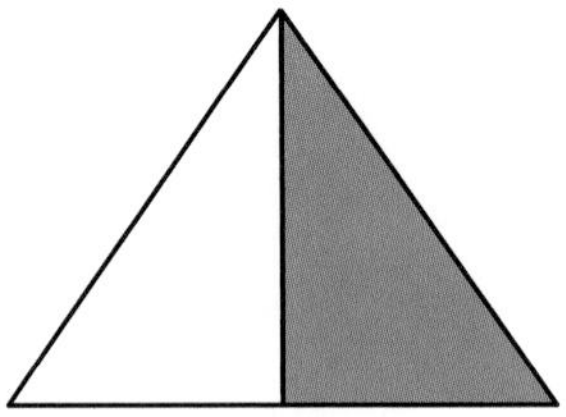

one-____

Learn

You can use model drawings to show a whole in different ways.

This model shows a whole with 2 equal parts.

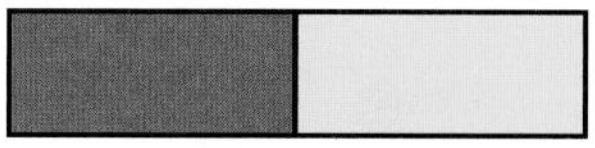

1 part is red and 1 part is yellow.

What fraction of the whole is red?

Number of red parts = 1

Number of parts in all = 2

The red part of the whole is the fraction $\frac{1}{2}$.

The yellow part of the whole is the fraction $\frac{1}{2}$.

The red part and yellow part make one whole.

$\frac{1}{2}$ and $\frac{1}{2}$ make 1 whole.

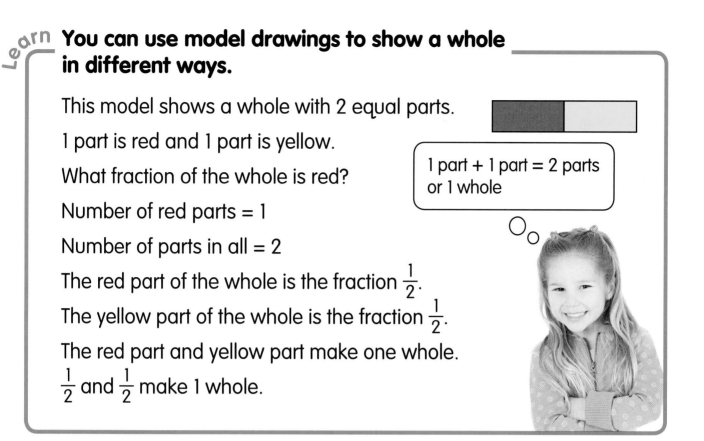

Guided Practice

The model shows one whole divided into equal parts. Name each part.

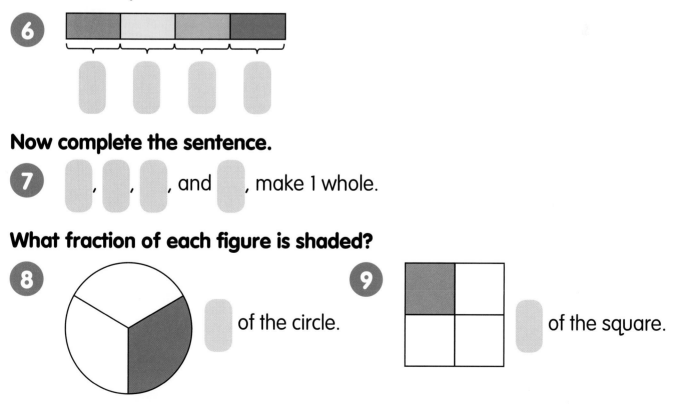

6 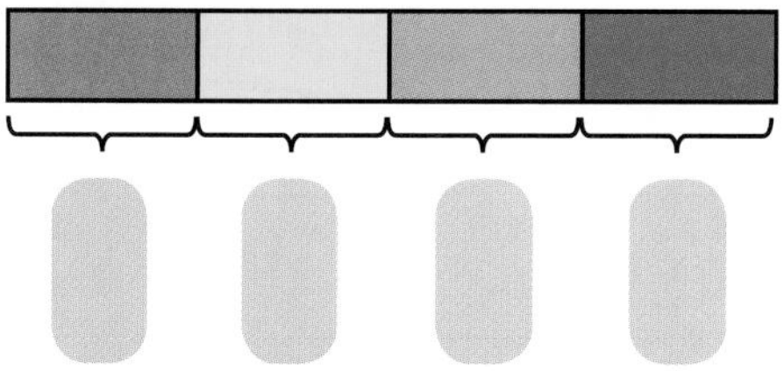

Now complete the sentence.

7 ___, ___, ___, and ___, make 1 whole.

What fraction of each figure is shaded?

8 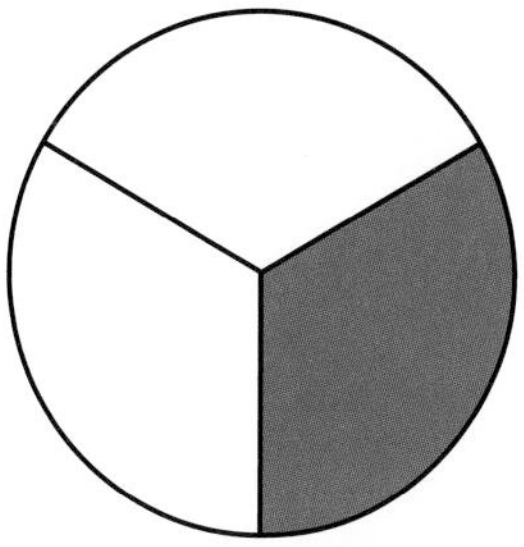

___ of the circle.

9 

___ of the square.

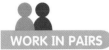

Hands-On Activity

WORK IN PAIRS

Use connecting cubes.

STEP 1 Put 6 cubes of different colors into a bag.

STEP 2 Your partner takes 2, 3, or 4 cubes from the bag and places them in a row.

STEP 3 You draw a model. Then write a number sentence for the number of parts that equal one whole.

STEP 4 Your partner checks your drawing.

STEP 5 Your partner draws a model and colors it to show the unit fraction. Then your partner writes the fraction for the colored part.

STEP 6 You check your partner's drawing.

STEP 7 Take turns to repeat STEP 2 to STEP 6 with a different number of cubes.

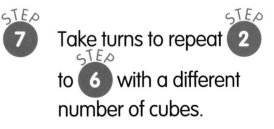

Let's Practice

Answer the questions.

1 Which shape is divided into equal parts?
Write the letter of the shape.

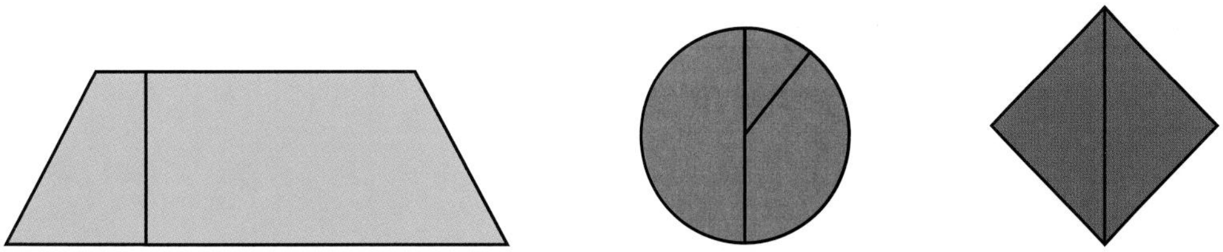

A B C

2 What fraction of each shape is shaded?

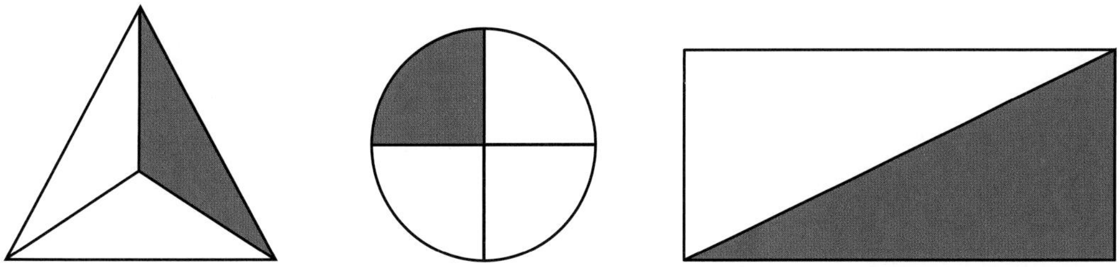

3 What fraction of each shape is shaded?
Write in words.

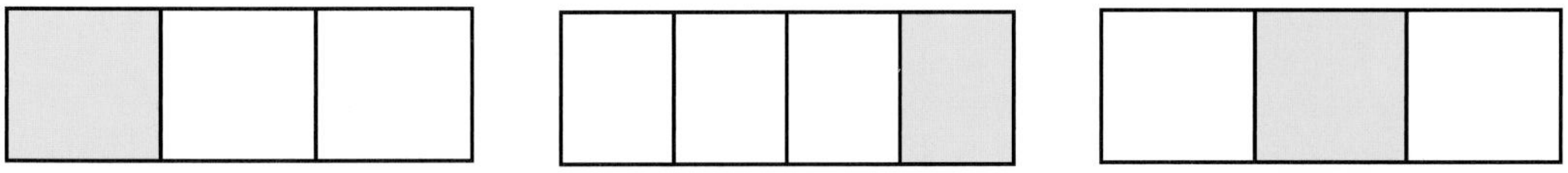

The model shows a whole divided into equal parts.
Name each part.

4

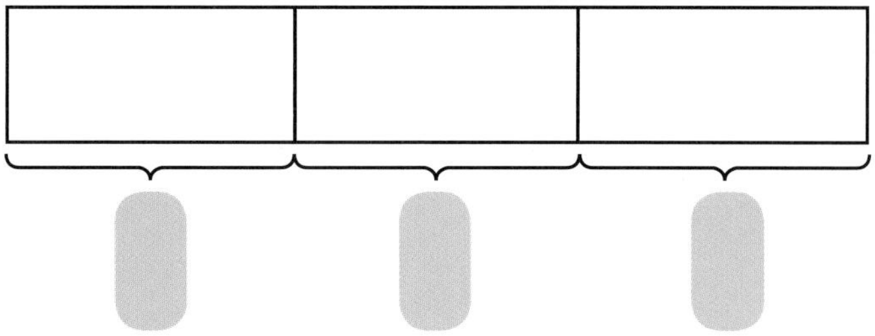

Now complete the number sentence.

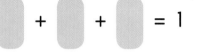

___ + ___ + ___ = 1

Look at the models.
Make a ✔ in the box if the number sentence and model match.

5

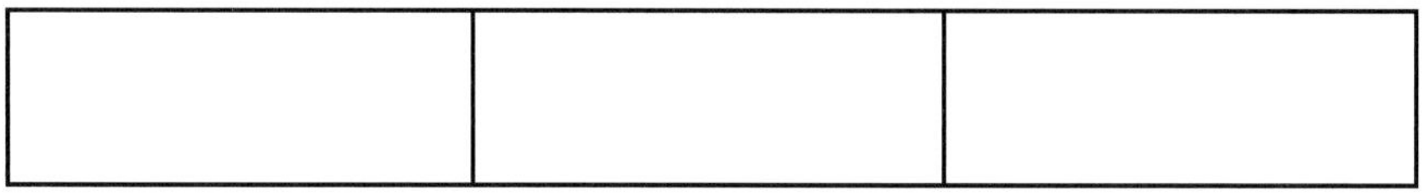

$\frac{1}{3} + \frac{1}{3} = 1$

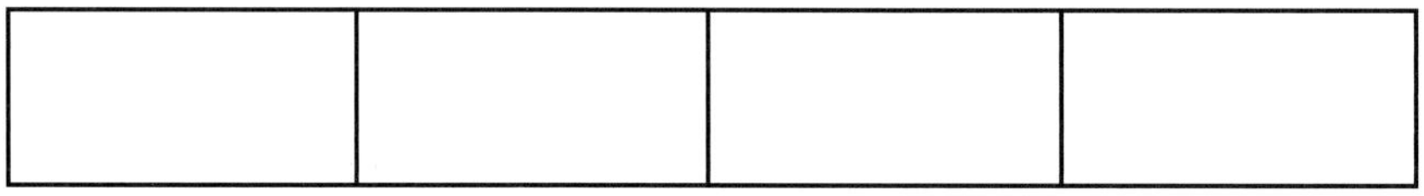

$\frac{1}{4} + \frac{1}{4} + \frac{1}{4} + \frac{1}{4} = 1$

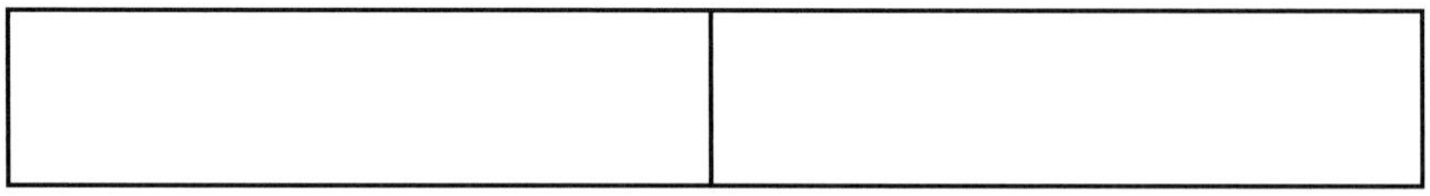

$\frac{1}{2} + \frac{1}{2} = 1$

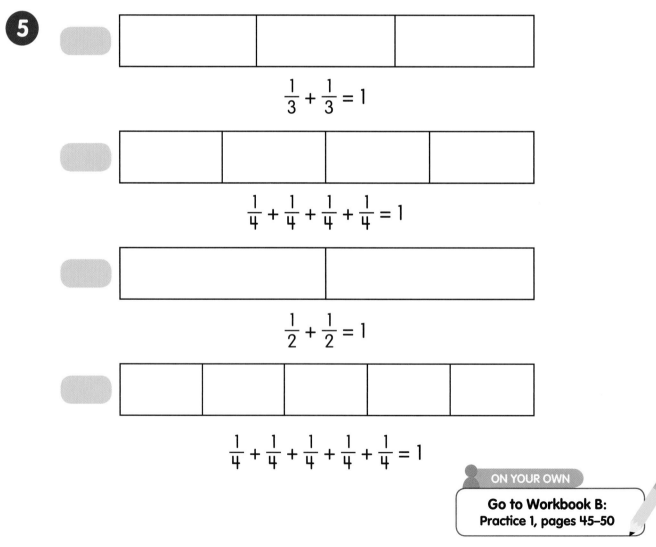

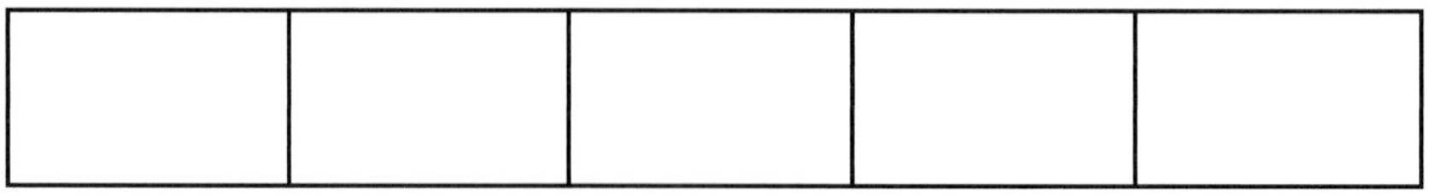

$\frac{1}{4} + \frac{1}{4} + \frac{1}{4} + \frac{1}{4} + \frac{1}{4} = 1$

ON YOUR OWN
Go to Workbook B:
Practice 1, pages 45–50

LESSON 2 Comparing Fractions

Lesson Objectives

- Compare two or more unit fractions using models of the same size.
- Order two or more unit fractions with or without the use of models of the same size.

Vocabulary
same
greater than
less than

Learn

You can use models to compare fractions.

David eats $\frac{1}{2}$ of a sandwich.

Seth eats $\frac{1}{4}$ of the **same** sandwich.

Who eats more?

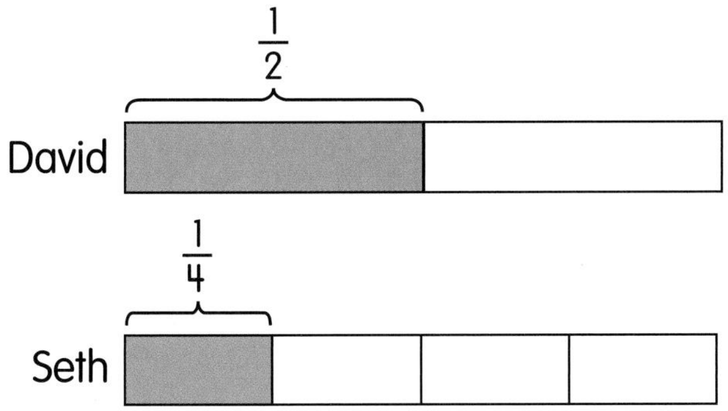

> stands for **greater than**.
< stands for **less than**.

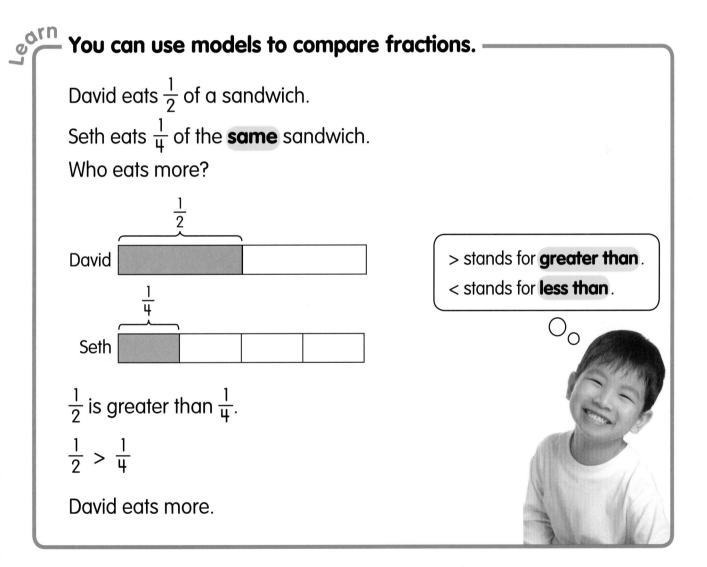

$\frac{1}{2}$ is greater than $\frac{1}{4}$.

$\frac{1}{2} > \frac{1}{4}$

David eats more.

Guided Practice

Compare.
Use > or <.
Then answer the question.
Use models to help you.

1 Louie eats $\frac{1}{4}$ of a granola bar.

Liza eats $\frac{1}{3}$ of the same granola bar.

Who eats less?

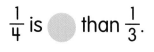

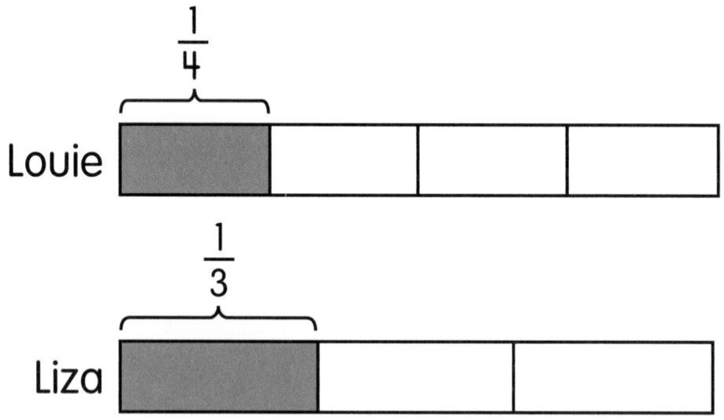

$\frac{1}{4}$ is ___ than $\frac{1}{3}$.

___ eats less.

Learn

You can use identical models to compare $\frac{1}{2}$, $\frac{1}{3}$ and $\frac{1}{4}$, and arrange them in order.

There are 3 paper strips of the **same** size.

Jamal colors $\frac{1}{2}$ of the first paper strip.

Sally colors $\frac{1}{3}$ of the second paper strip.

Edwina colors $\frac{1}{4}$ of the third paper strip.

Who colors the greatest part of a paper strip?

Who colors the least part?

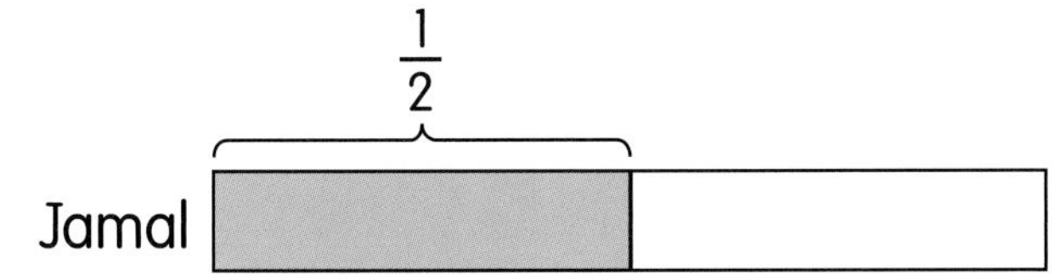

$\frac{1}{2}$ is greater than $\frac{1}{3}$.
Jamal colors more than Sally.

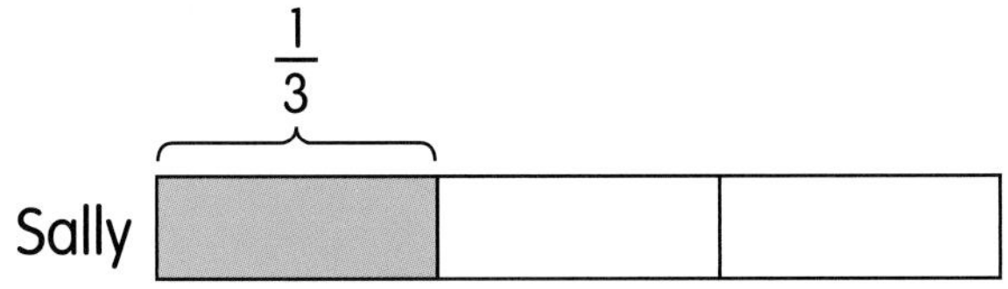

$\frac{1}{3}$ is greater than $\frac{1}{4}$.
Sally colors more than Edwina.

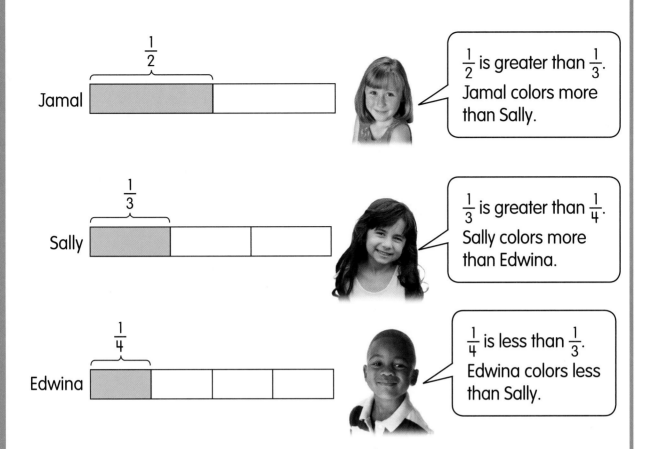

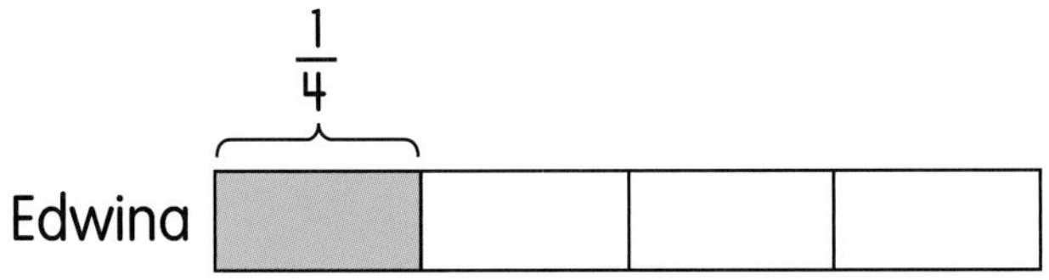

$\frac{1}{4}$ is less than $\frac{1}{3}$.
Edwina colors less than Sally.

Jamal colors the greatest part of a paper strip.
Edwina colors the least.

$\frac{1}{2} > \frac{1}{3}$

$\frac{1}{3} > \frac{1}{4}$

So, $\frac{1}{2} > \frac{1}{4}$

You can now arrange $\frac{1}{2}$, $\frac{1}{3}$, and $\frac{1}{4}$ in order from greatest to least.

$\frac{1}{2}$ $\quad \frac{1}{3}$ $\quad \frac{1}{4}$
greatest

Guided Practice

2 **Color a copy of the model to show each fraction.**

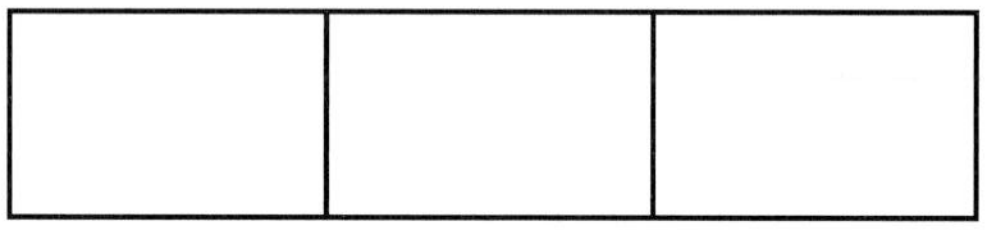

$\frac{1}{3}$

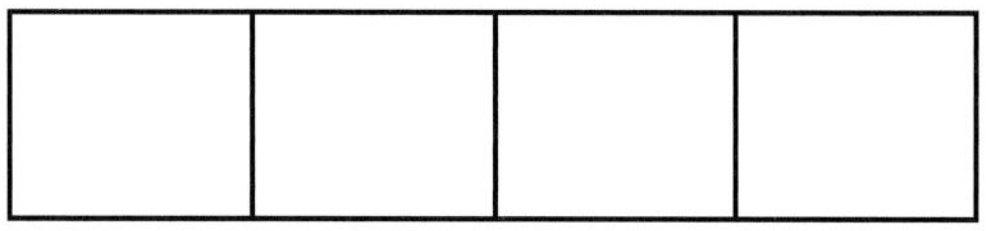

$\frac{1}{4}$

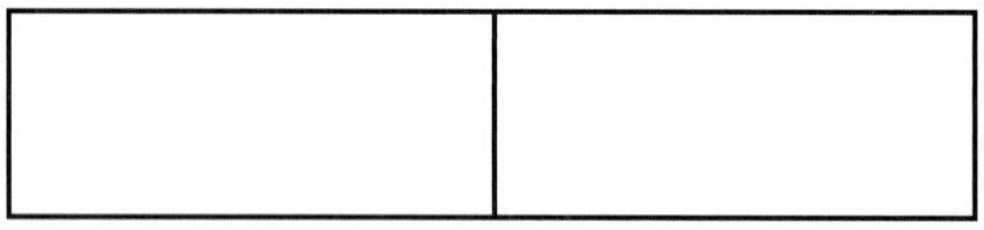

$\frac{1}{2}$

Order the fractions from least to greatest.

Hands-On Activity

WORKING TOGETHER

Use paper strips of the same size.

STEP **1** Take one strip and name it as shown.

one whole

STEP **2** Fold a second strip into 2 equal parts.
Unfold the strip. Draw a line along the fold.
Then name one of the two equal parts.

STEP **3** In the same way, make 3 equal parts with the third strip.
Make 4 equal parts with the fourth strip.

STEP **4** Shade the named parts.
Arrange the strips in order, beginning with the longest part shaded.

a Which fraction is greatest?

b Which fraction is least?

c Name a fraction that is greater than $\frac{1}{4}$.

d Name a fraction that is less than $\frac{1}{3}$.

Look at the fractions and the lengths of the shaded parts.
Do you see a pattern?
Describe what you see.

Let's Practice

Compare.
Use > or <.
Then answer the question.
Use models to help you.

1 Two muffins are the same size.
Derek eats $\frac{1}{2}$ of one muffin.
Sue eats $\frac{1}{3}$ of the other muffin.
Who eats more?

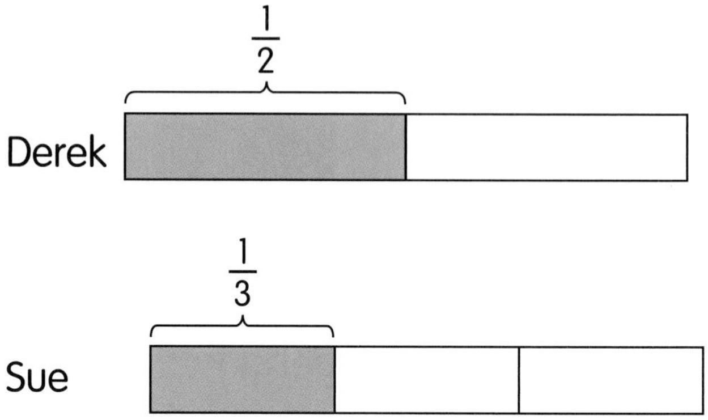

$\frac{1}{2}$ ___ $\frac{1}{3}$

$\frac{1}{3}$ ___ $\frac{1}{2}$

___ eats more.

Answer the questions.

2 The rectangles are the same size.
Which fraction is greatest?
Which fraction is least?

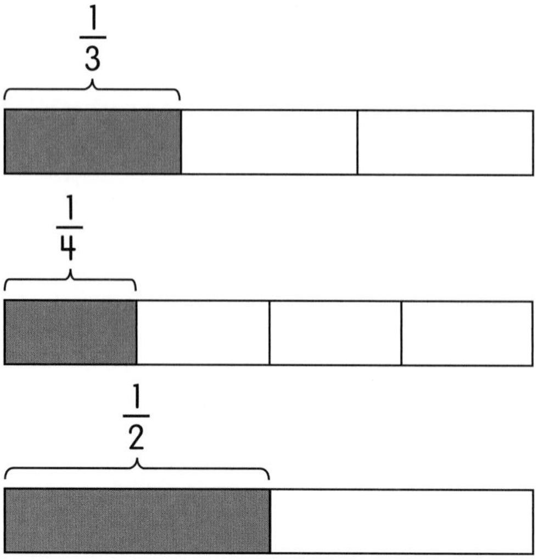

___ is greatest.

___ is least.

Copy the shapes and complete.

3 The circles are the same size.
On a copy of each circle, color one part.
Then name the unit fraction.

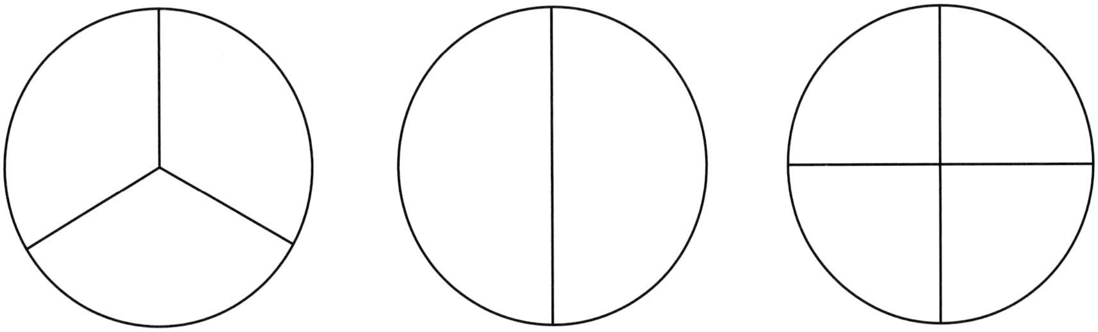

Order the fractions from greatest to least.

4 The triangles are the same size.
On a copy of each triangle, color one part.
Then name the unit fraction.

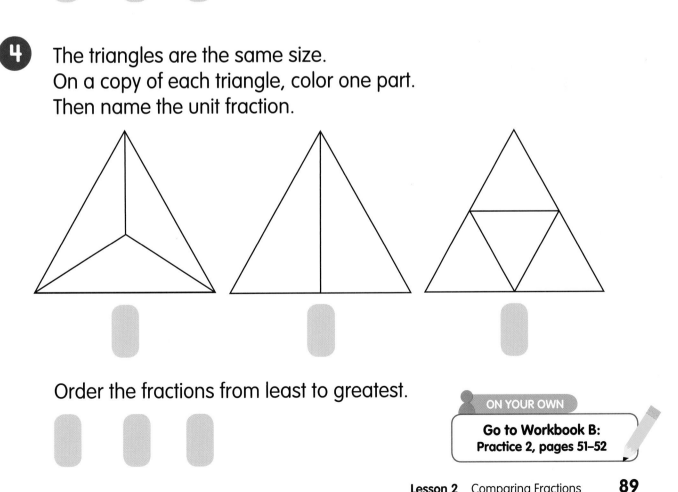

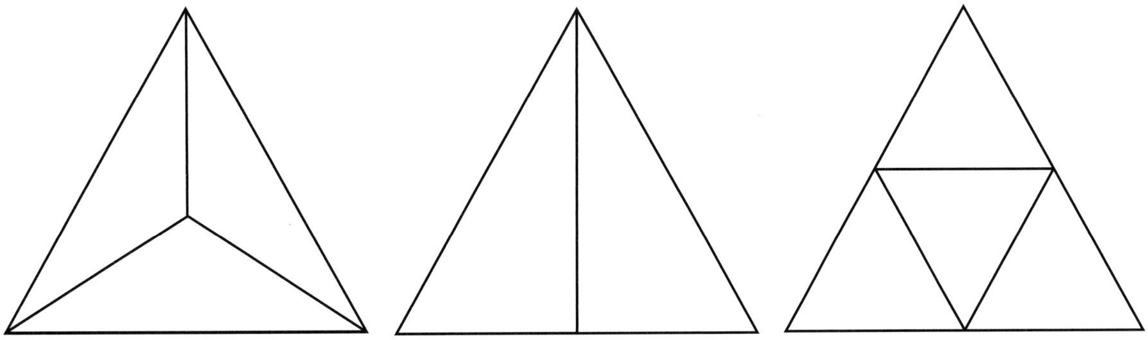

Order the fractions from least to greatest.

ON YOUR OWN

Go to Workbook B:
Practice 2, pages 51–52

LESSON 3 Adding and Subtracting Like Fractions

Lesson Objectives

- Identify fractions that name more than one equal part of a whole.
- Use models to add and subtract fractions.
- Add or subtract like fractions.

Vocabulary
like fractions

Learn

Fractions can name more than one equal part of a whole.

The pizza shows one whole.

It is divided into 4 equal parts.

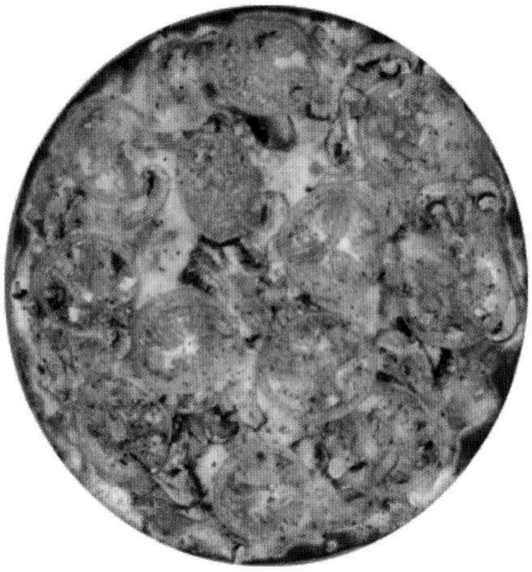

Tina eats 1 part .

She eats 1 part of 4 equal parts.

She eats $\frac{1}{4}$.

Ben eats 3 parts.

He eats 3 parts of 4 equal parts.

He eats $\frac{3}{4}$.

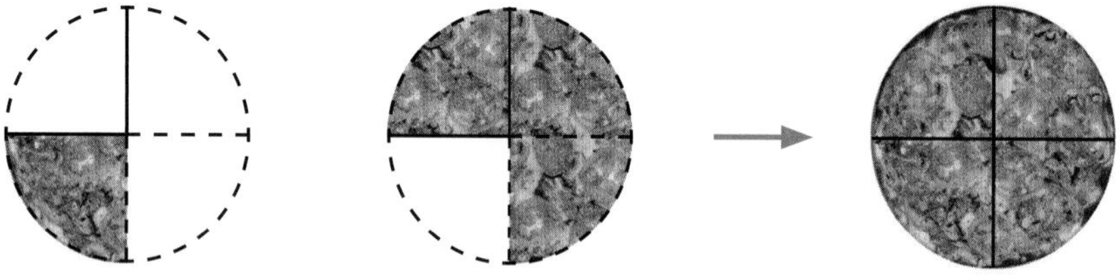

$\frac{1}{4}$ $\frac{3}{4}$ $\frac{4}{4}$

Tina and Ben eat 4 out of 4 equal parts.

They eat $\frac{4}{4}$.

They eat the whole pizza.

$\frac{1}{4}$, $\frac{3}{4}$, and $\frac{4}{4}$ are fractions.

$\frac{1}{4}$ is a unit fraction.

$\frac{3}{4}$ is a fraction that names more than one equal part of a whole.

$\frac{4}{4}$ is a fraction describing all the equal parts in one whole.

$\frac{4}{4}$ equals one whole.

Guided Practice

What fraction of each figure is shaded?

1 

2 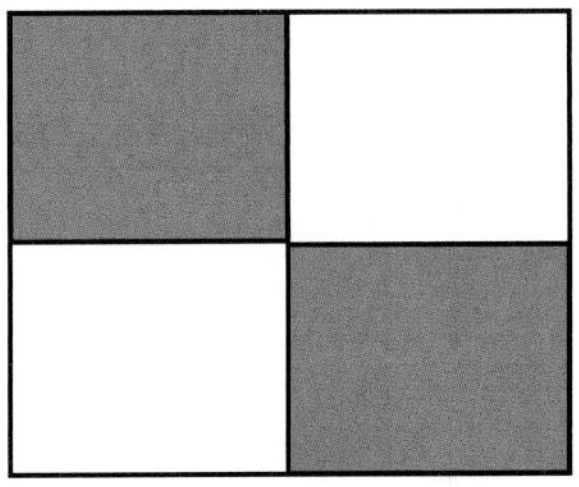

3 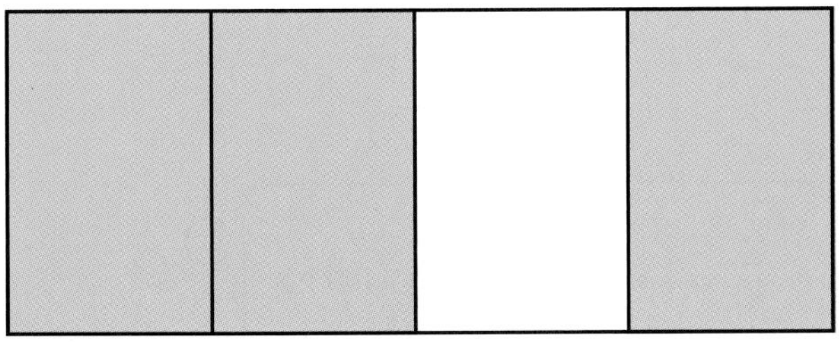

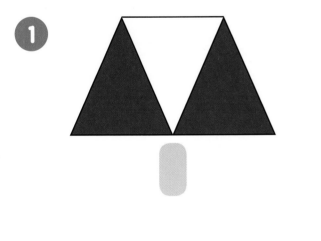

Learn

You can use fraction models to add like fractions.

Dylan ate $\frac{1}{4}$ of a waffle.

Olivia ate $\frac{2}{4}$ of it.

What fraction of the waffle did they eat in all?

$\frac{1}{4}$ and $\frac{2}{4}$ are **like fractions**.

The bottom number is the same.

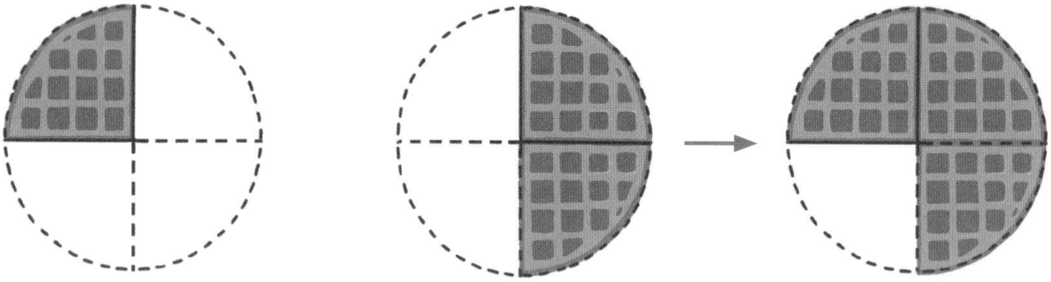

$\frac{1}{4}$ $\frac{2}{4}$

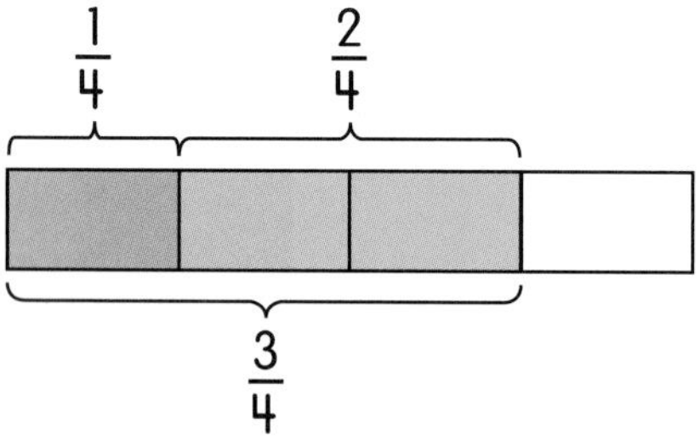

$$\frac{1}{4} + \frac{2}{4} = \frac{3}{4}$$

They ate $\frac{3}{4}$ of the waffle.

$\frac{1}{4} + \frac{2}{4}$ = 1 fourth + 2 fourths

= 3 fourths

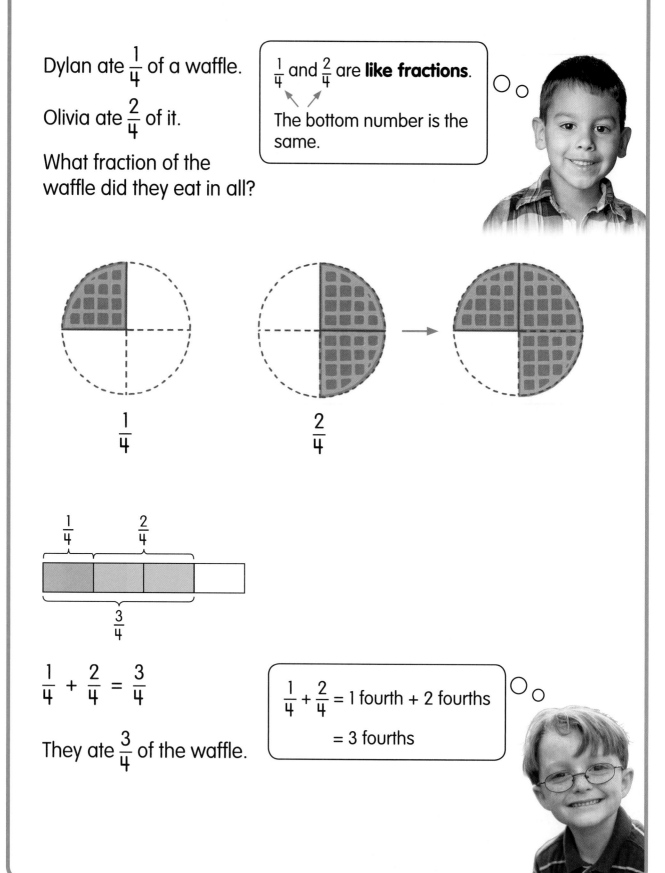

Guided Practice

Add.
Use models to help you.

4 $\frac{1}{4} + \frac{1}{4} + \frac{2}{4}$

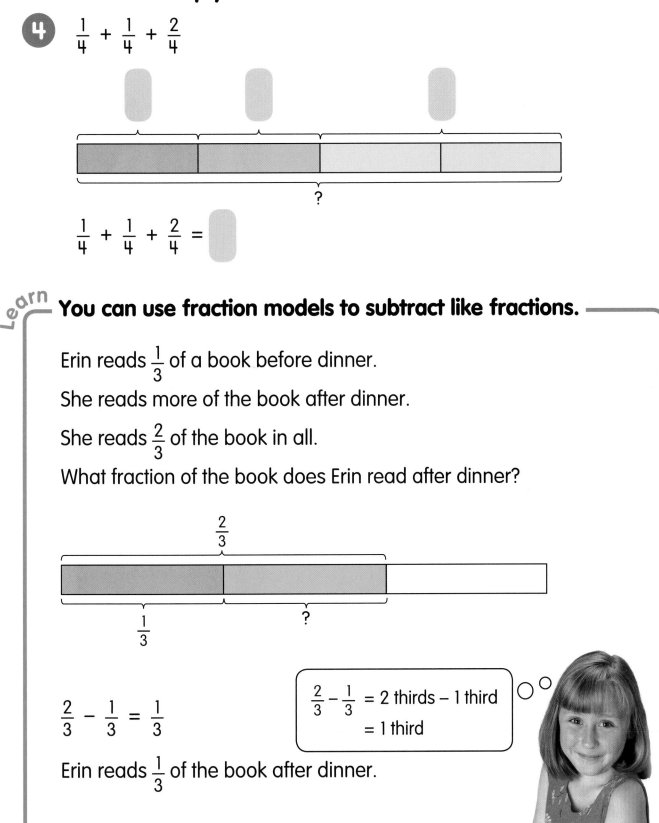

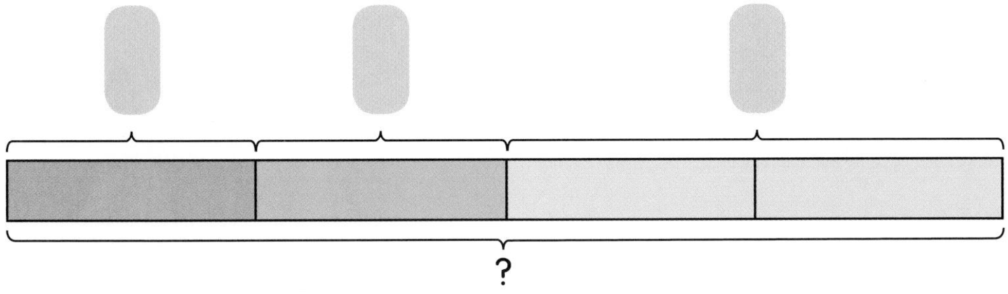

$\frac{1}{4} + \frac{1}{4} + \frac{2}{4} = \square$

Learn

You can use fraction models to subtract like fractions.

Erin reads $\frac{1}{3}$ of a book before dinner.

She reads more of the book after dinner.

She reads $\frac{2}{3}$ of the book in all.

What fraction of the book does Erin read after dinner?

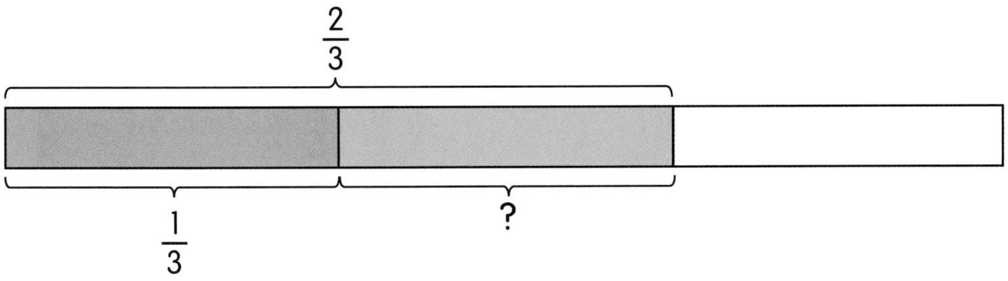

$\frac{2}{3} - \frac{1}{3} = \frac{1}{3}$

$\frac{2}{3} - \frac{1}{3}$ = 2 thirds – 1 third
= 1 third

Erin reads $\frac{1}{3}$ of the book after dinner.

Guided Practice

Subtract.
Use the model to help you.

5 $1 - \frac{1}{2}$

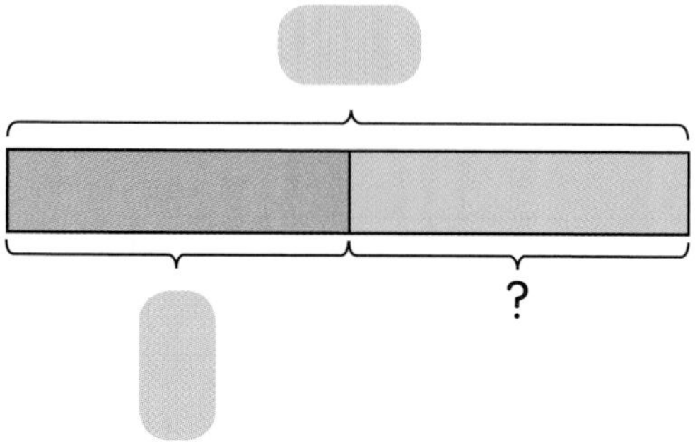

$1 - \frac{1}{2} =$

1 whole = $\frac{2}{2}$

WORKING TOGETHER **Game**

Fix and Win!

Players: 2 to 3
You need:

- 1 brown bag
- pieces of a circle (see below)

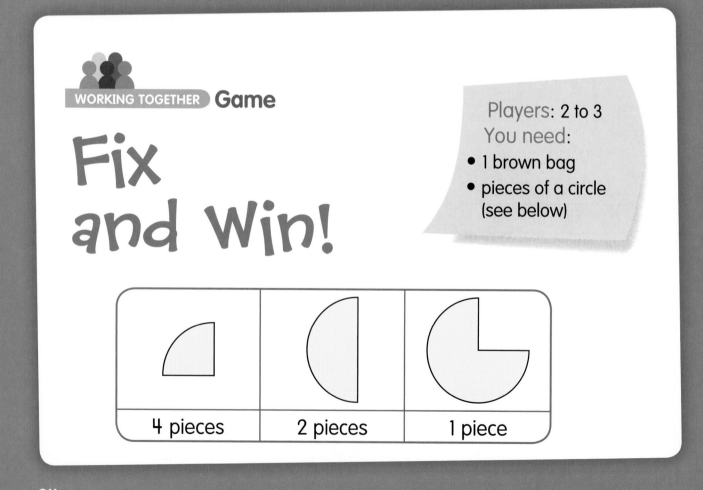

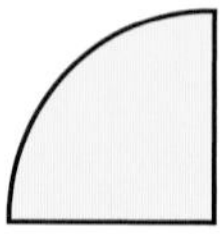	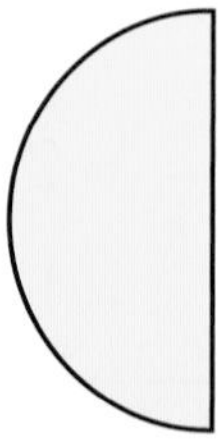	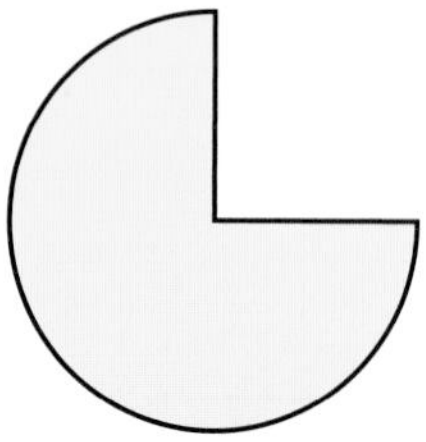
4 pieces	2 pieces	1 piece

How to play:

STEP 1 Player 1 takes a circle piece from the bag.
Player 1 places it on the table.

STEP 2 Player 2 takes another circle piece.
Player 2 joins this to the piece on the table.
Does the second piece make more than one whole?
Then put the second piece back into the bag.
Now it is Player 1's turn to take a circle piece.

The first player to complete the circle wins!

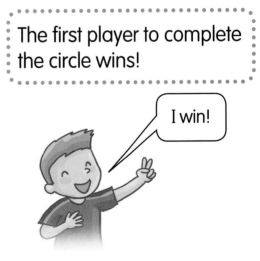

Let's Practice

Find the missing numbers.

1. 1 whole = $\frac{\square}{2}$

2. $\frac{3}{\square}$ = 1 whole

Add.
Use models to help you.

3. $\frac{1}{3} + \frac{2}{3} = \square$

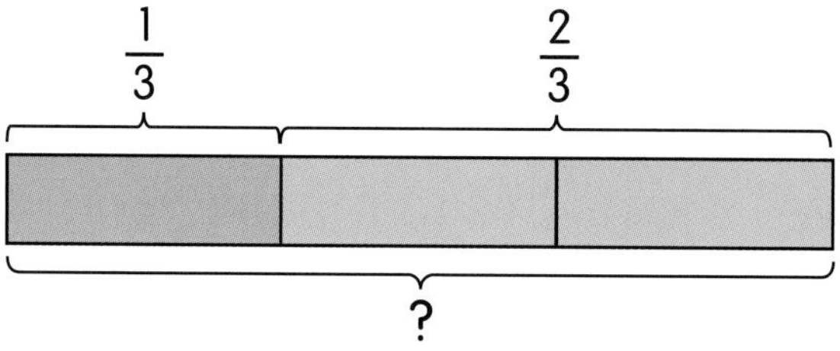

4. $\frac{1}{4} + \frac{1}{4} + \frac{1}{4} = \square$

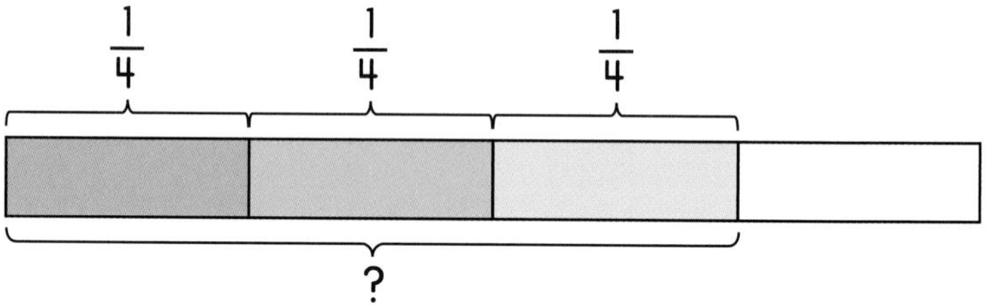

Subtract.
Use models to help you.

5. $\frac{3}{4} - \frac{1}{4} = \square$

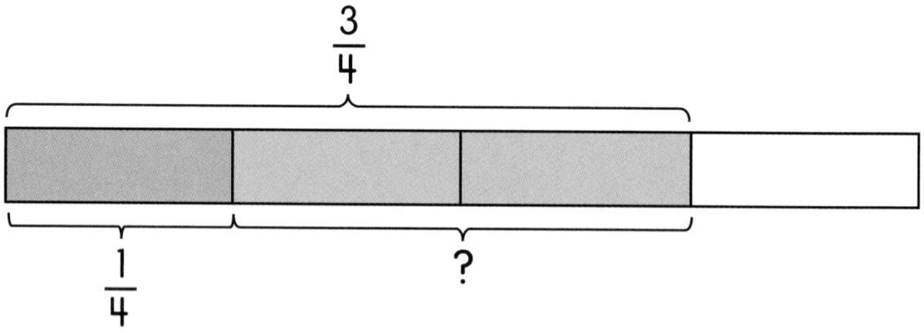

6. $1 - \frac{1}{3} = \square$

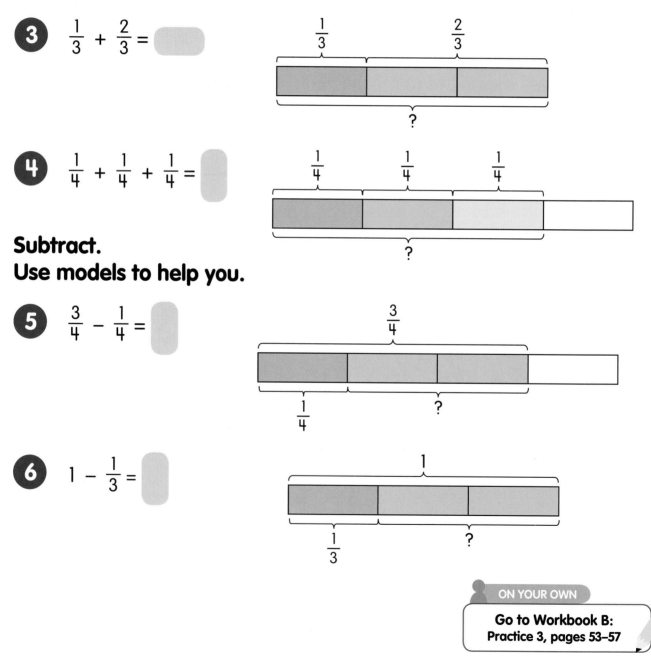

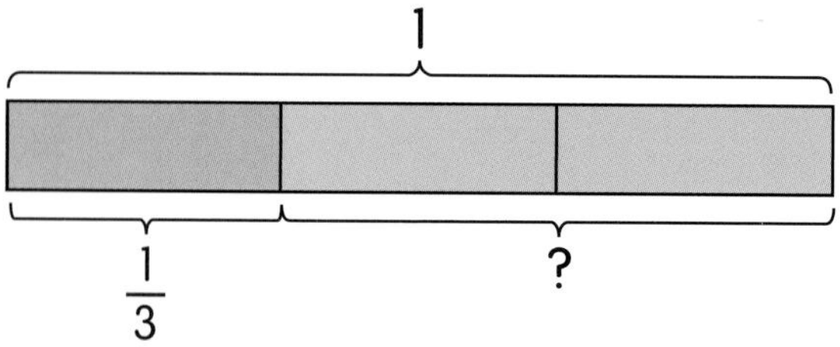

ON YOUR OWN

Go to Workbook B:
Practice 3, pages 53–57

Put On Your Thinking Cap!

PROBLEM SOLVING

Mandy eats $\frac{1}{2}$ of a sandwich.

Keisha eats $\frac{1}{2}$ of another sandwich.

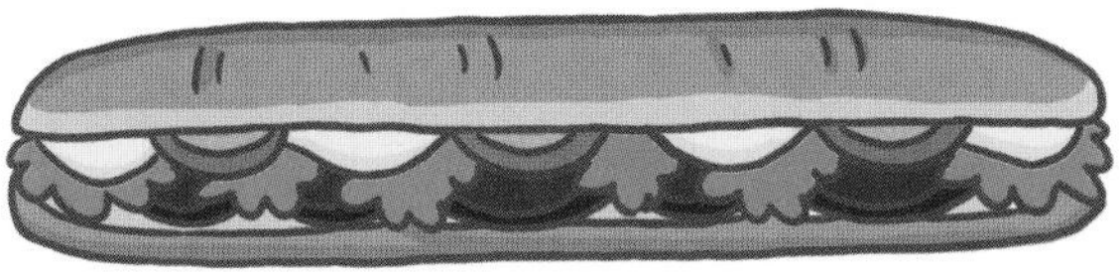

Who eats more?
Why?

ON YOUR OWN

Go to Workbook B:
Put on Your Thinking Cap!
page 58

Chapter Wrap Up

You have learned...

Fractions

What is a fraction?

A fraction names equal parts of a whole.

Unit fraction

A unit fraction names one of the equal parts of a whole.

$\frac{1}{2}, \frac{1}{3}, \frac{1}{4}$

2 equal parts

$\frac{1}{2}$ is 1 out of 2 equal parts.

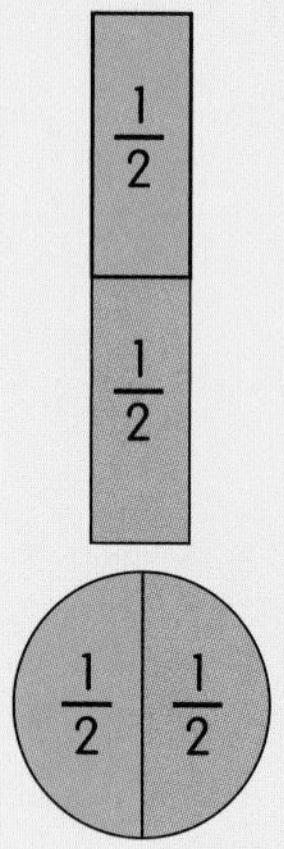

3 equal parts

$\frac{1}{3}$ is 1 out of 3 equal parts.

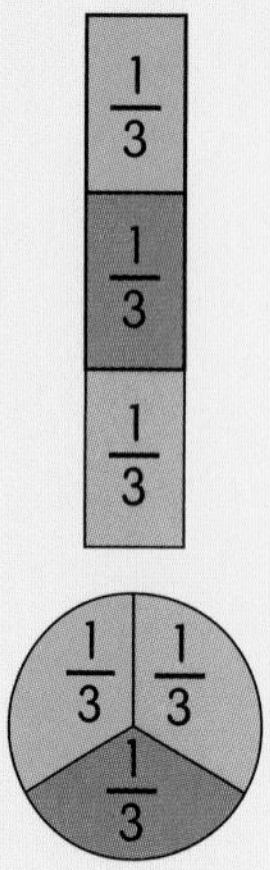

4 equal parts

$\frac{1}{4}$ is 1 out of 4 equal parts.

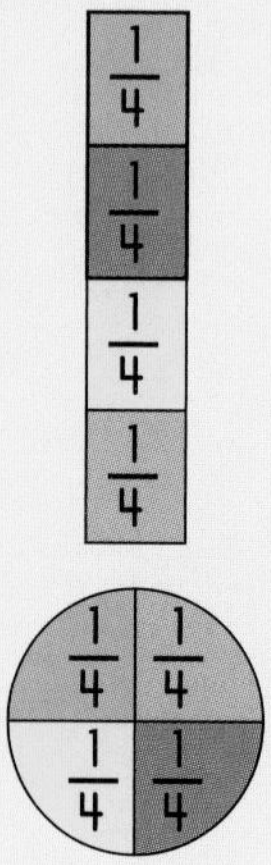

Other fractions

1 whole

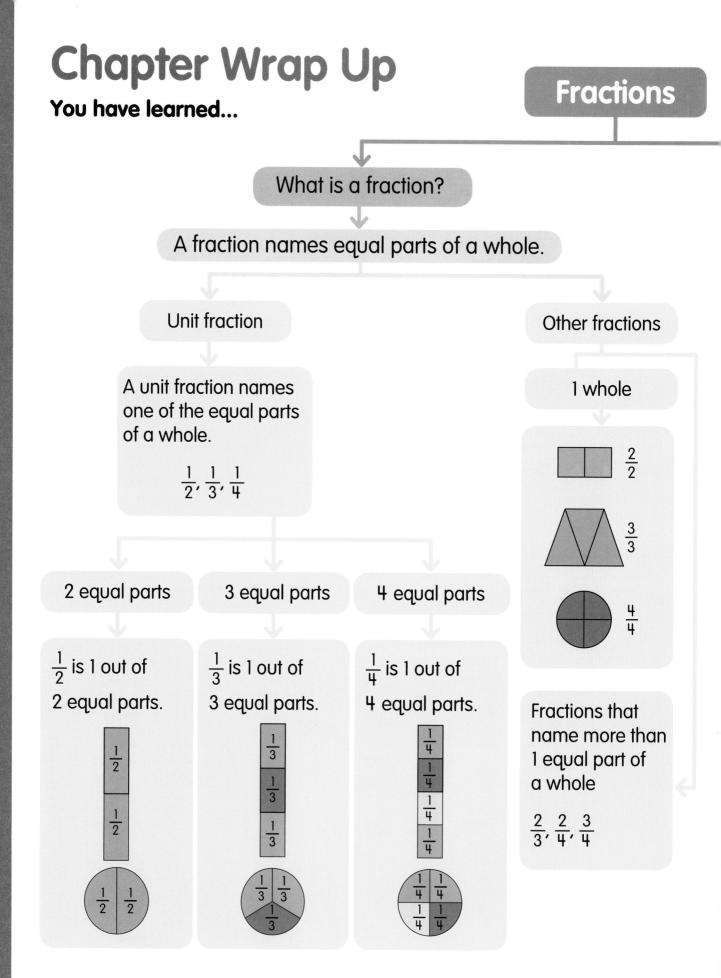

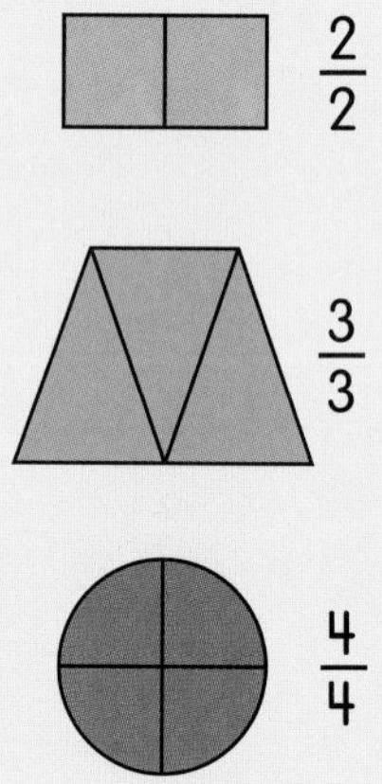

Fractions that name more than 1 equal part of a whole

$\frac{2}{3}, \frac{2}{4}, \frac{3}{4}$

BIG IDEA

Fractions can be used to describe how equal parts are related to a whole.

Comparing and Ordering Fractions

Comparing Fractions

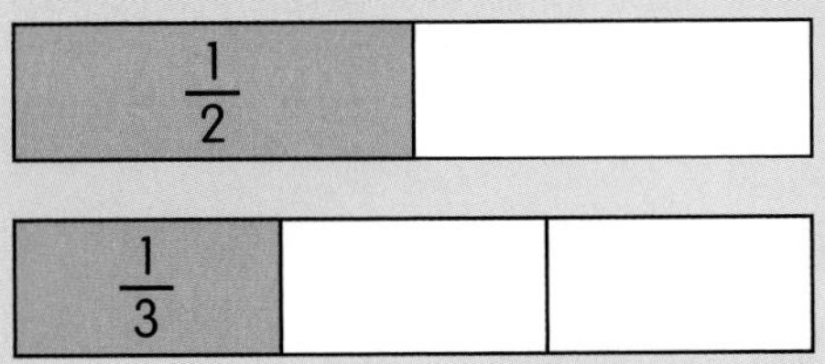

$\frac{1}{2} > \frac{1}{3}$

$\frac{1}{3} < \frac{1}{2}$

Ordering Fractions

Fractions can be arranged in order from least to greatest or from greatest to least.

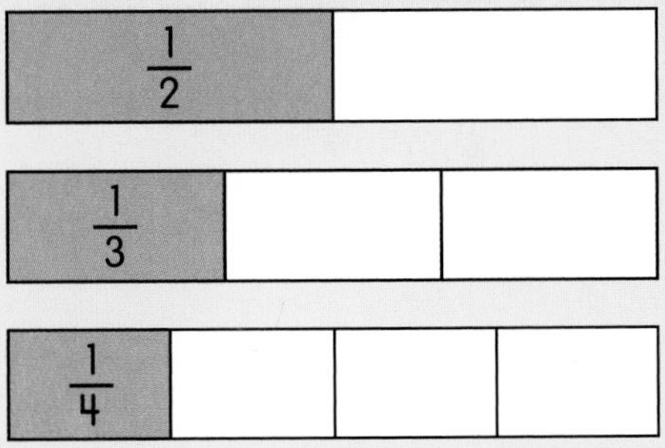

$\frac{1}{2}$ greatest $\frac{1}{3}$ $\frac{1}{4}$ least

Adding and Subtracting Like Fractions

Like fractions are fractions whose wholes are divided into the same number of equal parts.

$\frac{1}{3}, \frac{2}{3}, \frac{3}{3}$ $\frac{1}{4}, \frac{2}{4}, \frac{3}{4}, \frac{4}{4}$

Add.

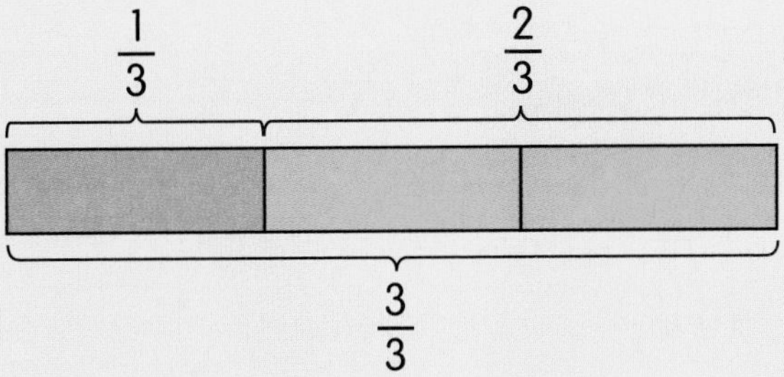

$\frac{1}{3} + \frac{2}{3} = \frac{3}{3}$

Subtract.

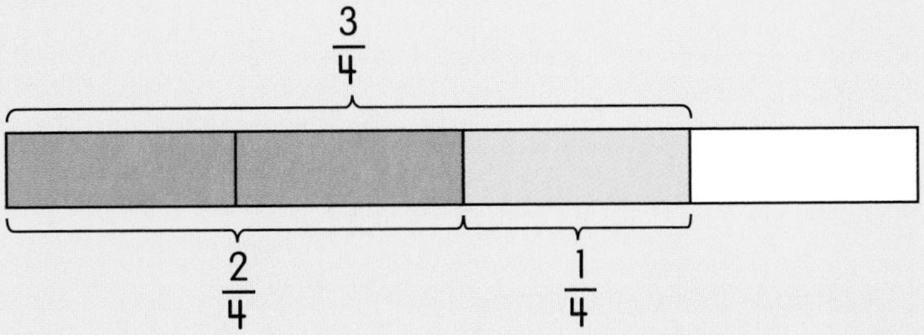

$\frac{3}{4} - \frac{2}{4} = \frac{1}{4}$

ON YOUR OWN

Go to Workbook B: Chapter Review/Test, pages 59–62

CHAPTER 13 Customary Measurement of Length

BIG IDEA

Rulers can be used to measure and compare how long and how tall things are.

Recall Prior Knowledge

Measuring length using a ruler

The length of the ribbon is 10 centimeters.

Adding and subtracting without regrouping

124 + 65 = 189

$$\begin{array}{r} 124 \\ +\ \ 65 \\ \hline 189 \end{array}$$

178 – 35 = 143

$$\begin{array}{r} 178 \\ -\ \ 35 \\ \hline 143 \end{array}$$

Adding and subtracting with regrouping

347 + 159 = 506

$$\begin{array}{r} {}^{1}\ {}^{1}\ \ \\ 347 \\ +\ 159 \\ \hline 506 \end{array}$$

200 – 157 = 43

$$\begin{array}{r} {}^{1}\ {}^{9}\ \ \\ \not{2}\,\not{0}\,{}^{1}0 \\ -\ 157 \\ \hline 43 \end{array}$$

✔Quick Check

Look at the drawing.
Then find the missing numbers.

1

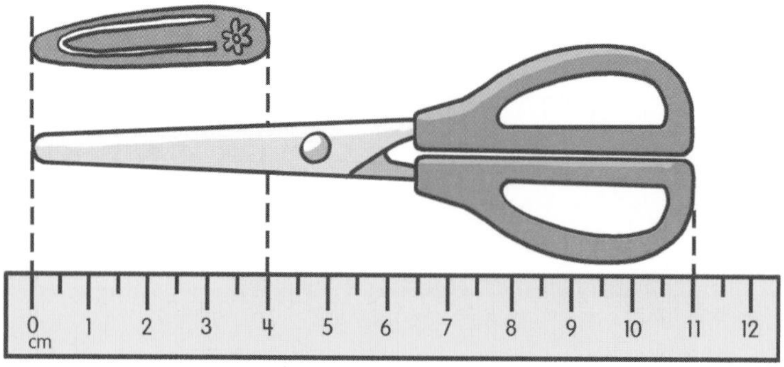

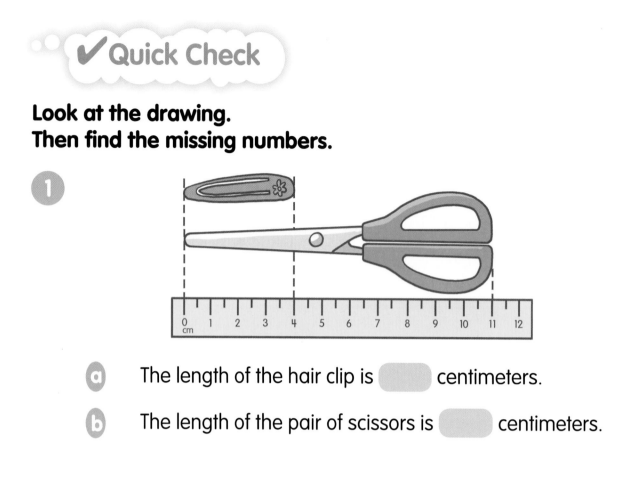

a) The length of the hair clip is ____ centimeters.

b) The length of the pair of scissors is ____ centimeters.

Add or subtract.

2) 36 + 42 = ____

3) 98 – 82 = ____

4) 364 + 123 = ____

5) 462 – 231 = ____

6) 83 + 69 = ____

7) 78 – 56 = ____

8) 174 + 545 = ____

9) 300 – 197 = ____

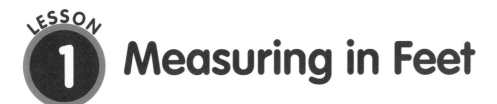

LESSON 1

Measuring in Feet

Lesson Objective

- Use a ruler to estimate and measure length.

Vocabulary

- foot/feet (ft)
- length
- ruler
- unit
- width
- height

Learn

You can use a ruler to measure length and height.

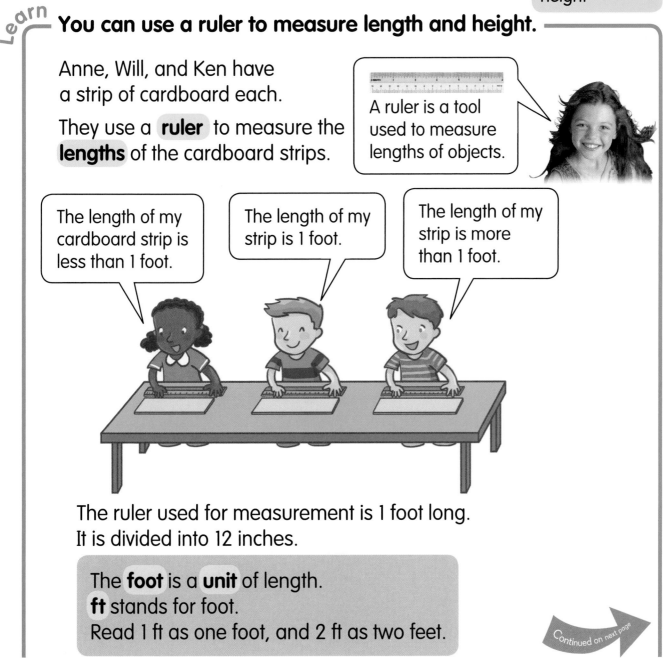

Anne, Will, and Ken have a strip of cardboard each.

They use a **ruler** to measure the **lengths** of the cardboard strips.

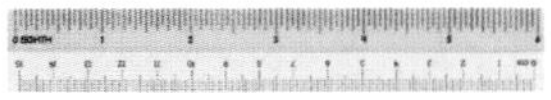

A ruler is a tool used to measure lengths of objects.

The length of my cardboard strip is less than 1 foot.
The length of my strip is 1 foot.
The length of my strip is more than 1 foot.

The ruler used for measurement is 1 foot long.
It is divided into 12 inches.

The **foot** is a **unit** of length.
ft stands for foot.
Read 1 ft as one foot, and 2 ft as two feet.

Continued on next page

Guided Practice

Look at the drawings.
Then fill in the blanks with more or less.

1 Box A

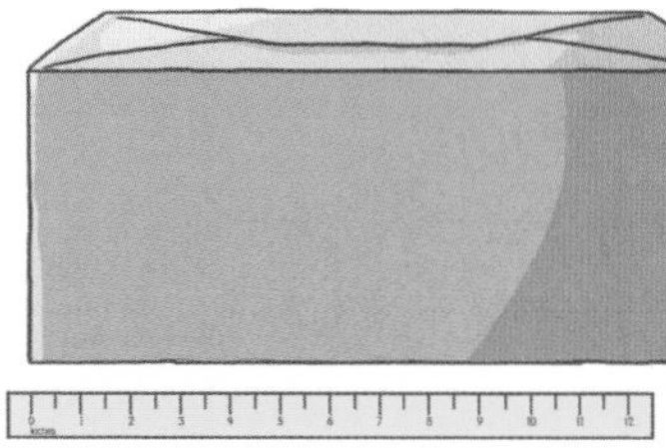
foot ruler

Box B

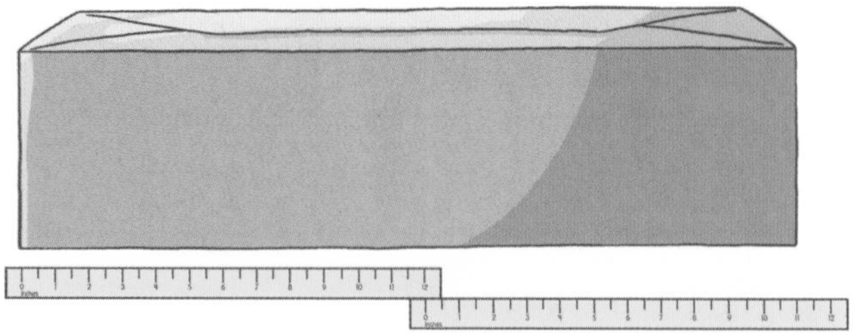

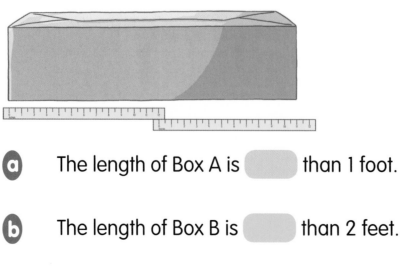

a The length of Box A is ______ than 1 foot.

b The length of Box B is ______ than 2 feet.

Use a foot ruler to measure.
Then answer the questions.

2 Is the flag pole at your school more than or less than 1 foot high?

3 Name two objects in your classroom that are about

a 1 foot long **b** 1 foot tall

4 Name two objects in your home that are

a less than 1 foot wide **b** more than 1 foot tall

Hands-On Activity

WORKING TOGETHER

Use a ruler or a string that is 1 foot long.

First, guess the length of each object in your classroom.
Then, use the ruler or string to measure.

Record your answers in a chart like this.

	My guess	The length is between
The length of your friend's arm	*about 2 feet*	*2 feet and 3 feet*
The width of your desk		
The height of your chair		
The height of your teacher's desk		
The length of your classroom bookshelf		
The width of your classroom window		
The width of your classroom		
The length of your classroom		

Let's Practice

**Use a foot ruler to measure.
Then answer the questions.**

1. Is the width of your classroom door more than or less than 1 foot?

2. Is the height of your classroom window more than or less than 1 foot?

3. Is the length of your pencil case more than or less than 1 foot?

4. List five objects in a chart like this.
Measure the lengths of the objects.
Then put a check in the correct box.

Object	Less than 1 foot	1 foot	More than 1 foot
Classroom phone	✓		

ON YOUR OWN

Go to Workbook B: Practice 1, pages 73–76

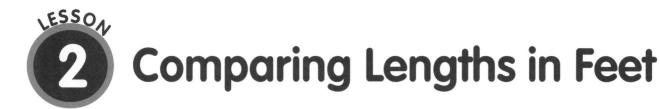

LESSON 2

Comparing Lengths in Feet

Lesson Objectives

- Compare lengths.
- Find the difference in lengths of objects.

Vocabulary
longest
shortest

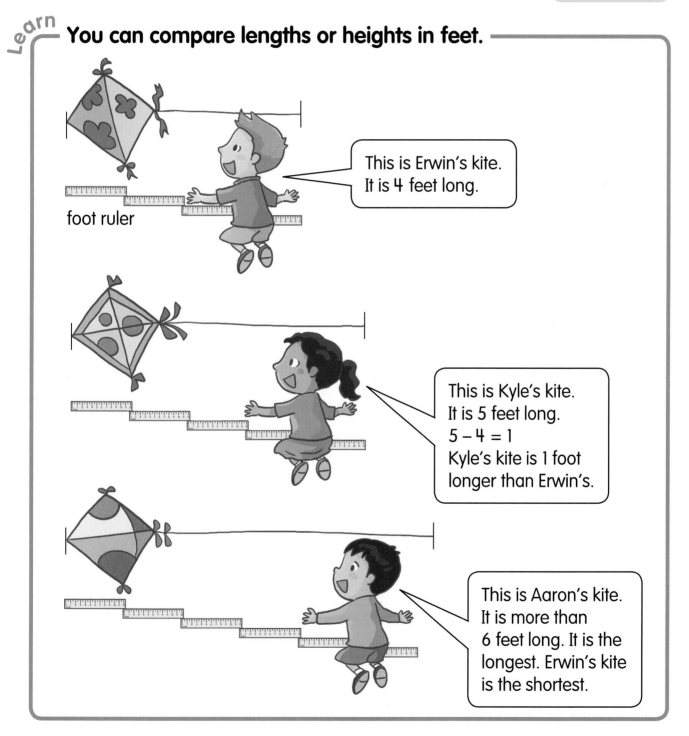

Learn — You can compare lengths or heights in feet.

foot ruler
This is Erwin's kite. It is 4 feet long.

This is Kyle's kite.
It is 5 feet long.
5 – 4 = 1
Kyle's kite is 1 foot
longer than Erwin's.

This is Aaron's kite.
It is more than
6 feet long. It is the
longest. Erwin's kite
is the shortest.

Guided Practice

Use foot rulers to answer each question.

Bookshelf A is 3 feet long.

Bookshelf B is 2 feet long.

1. Which bookshelf is longer? ______

2. How much longer is it? ______

Barry makes two strings of paper cranes for his art class.
The string of red paper cranes is 14 feet long.
The string of green paper cranes is 22 feet long.

3. Which string is shorter? ______

4. How much shorter is it? ______

Hands-On Activity

1. Use a foot ruler to measure objects on your playground. Then answer the questions.

   How high is the slide?

   How long is the swing seat?

   Which is longer, the seesaw or the slide?

2. Choose two objects that can be found in your gym. Use a ruler to find out which of the two objects is longer.

Let's Practice

Answer the questions.

1. Joel has two balls of yarn.
   The red ball of yarn is 35 feet long.
   The blue ball of yarn is 29 feet long.

   a. Which ball of yarn is shorter? ____

   b. How much shorter is it? ____

   c. What is the total length of the two balls of yarn? ____

2 The length of a toy car racetrack is 10 feet.
The length of a toy train track is 15 feet.

a Which is longer?

b How much longer is it?

3 Aldrin is 4 feet tall.
The monkey bar is 5 feet tall.
The flagpole is 8 feet tall.

a Which is the tallest?

b How much taller is the flagpole than the monkey bar?

c How much shorter is Aldrin than the monkey bar?

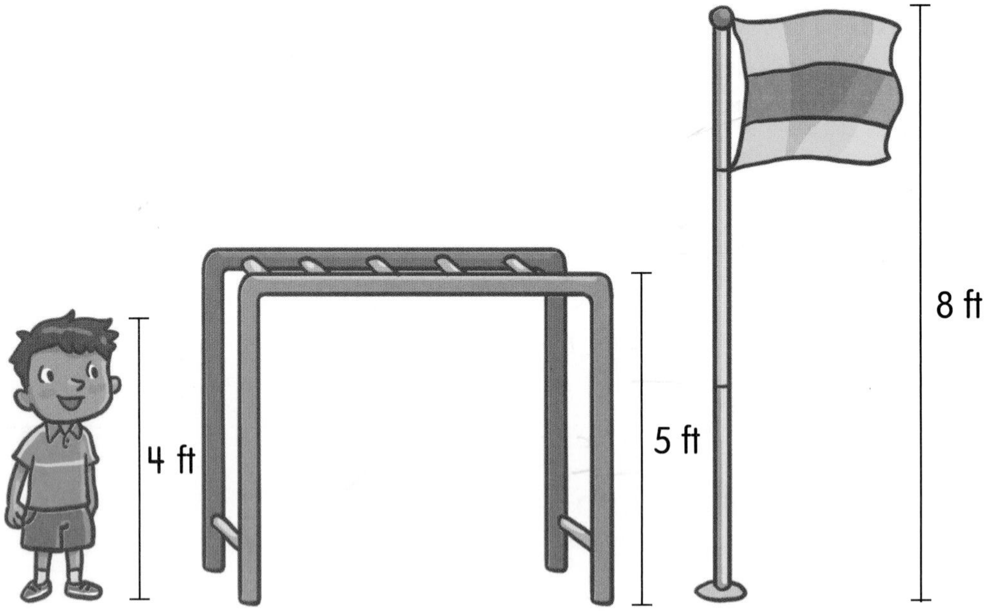

ON YOUR OWN

**Go to Workbook B:
Practice 2, pages 77–78**

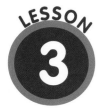

LESSON

3 Measuring in Inches

Lesson Objectives

- Use a ruler to measure length to the nearest inch.
- Draw parts of lines of given lengths.

Vocabulary
inch (in.)

Learn

You can use inches to measure the length of shorter objects.

Inches are marked on this ruler. There are 12 inches in one foot.

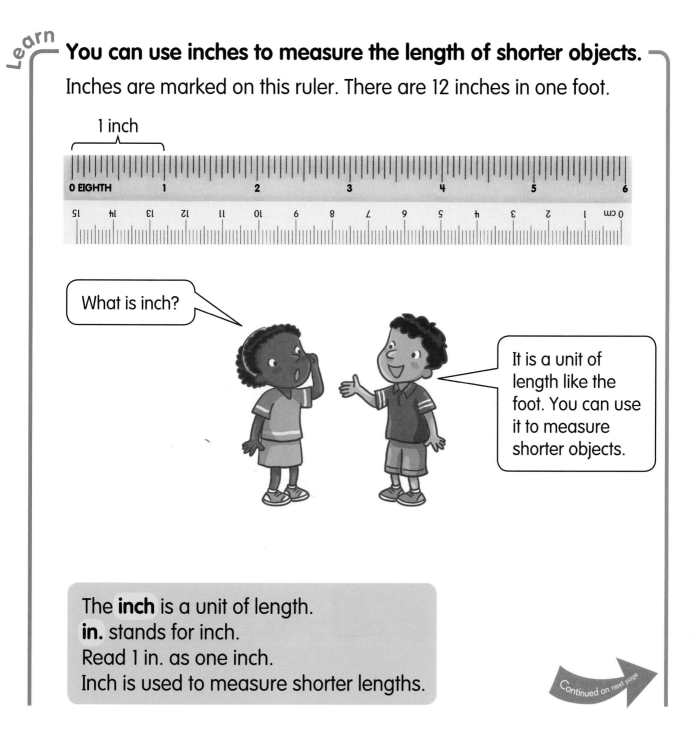

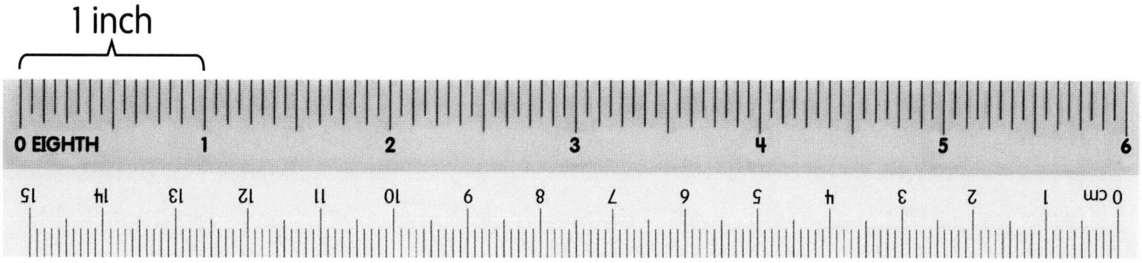

What is inch?
It is a unit of length like the foot. You can use it to measure shorter objects.

The **inch** is a unit of length.
in. stands for inch.
Read 1 in. as one inch.
Inch is used to measure shorter lengths.

Continued on next page

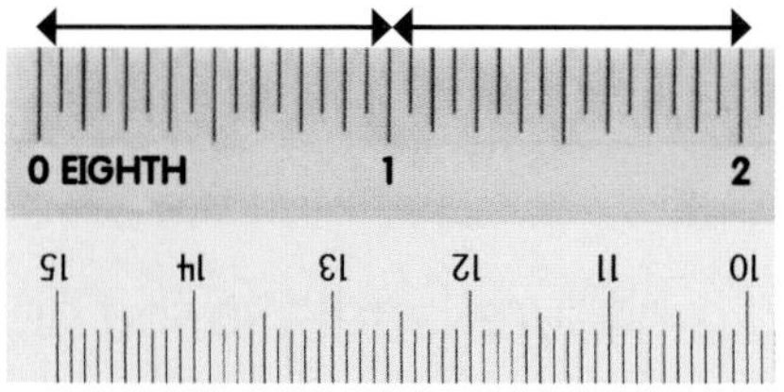

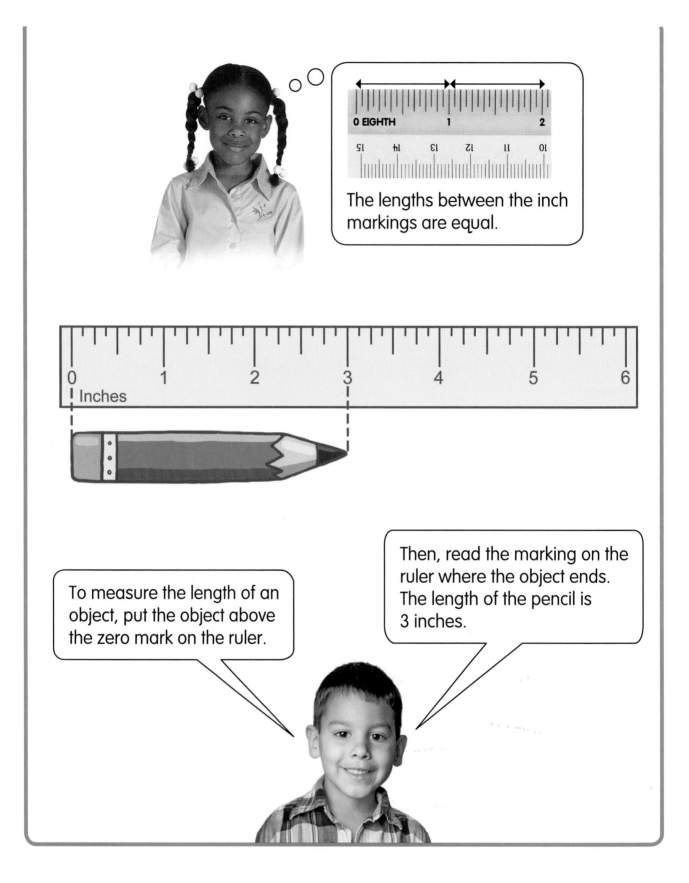

The lengths between the inch markings are equal.

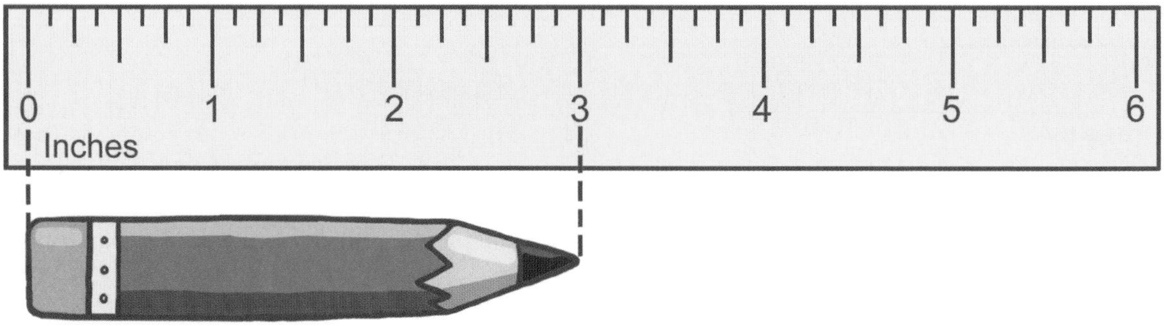

To measure the length of an object, put the object above the zero mark on the ruler.

Then, read the marking on the ruler where the object ends. The length of the pencil is 3 inches.

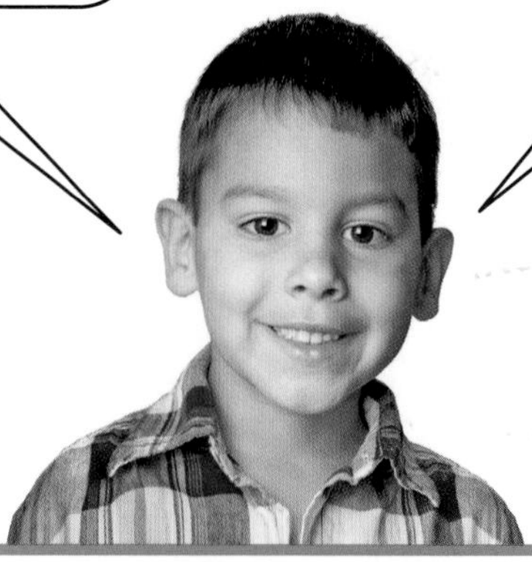

Guided Practice

Look at the pictures.

1. Which shows the correct way of measuring the paintbrush? A, B, or C?

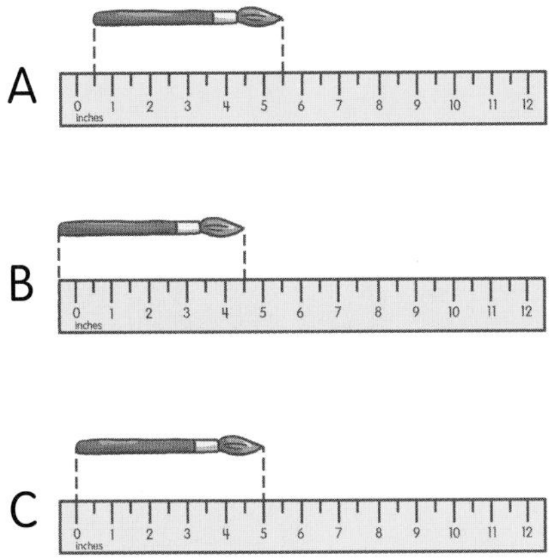

These rulers are smaller than in real life.

Use the inch ruler to find the missing numbers.

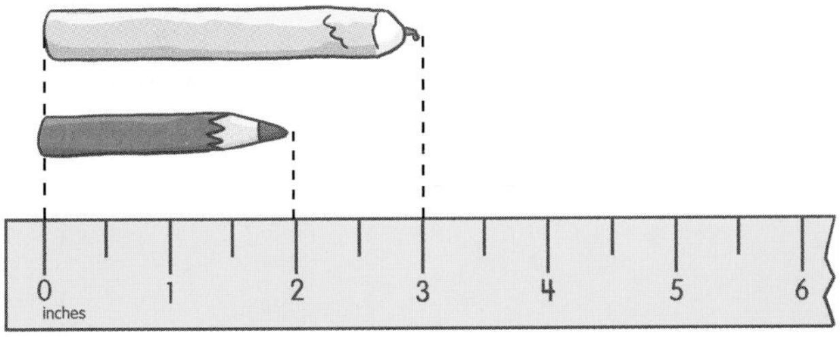

2. The length of the candle is ______ inches.

3. The length of the pencil is ______ inches.

4. Look at the curve.
Place a string along the curve.
Cut the string.
Place the string on a ruler to find its length in inches.

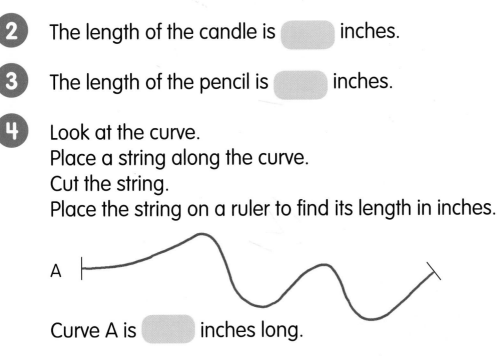

Curve A is ______ inches long.

Learn You can use a ruler to measure height and length of objects to the nearest inch.

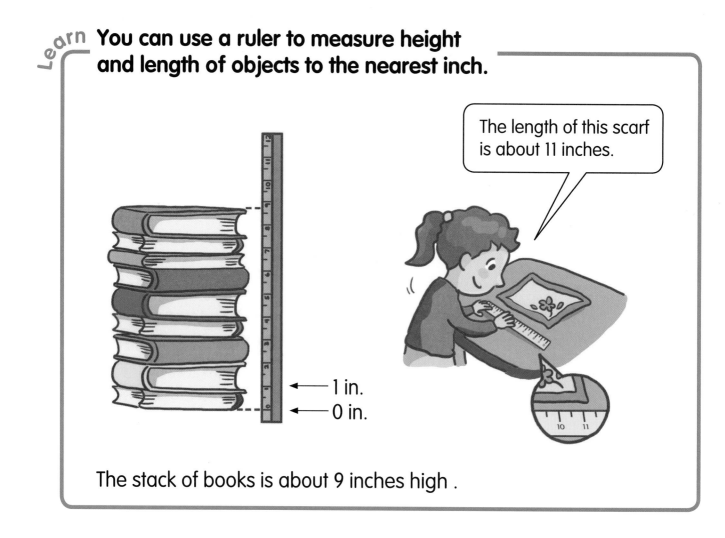

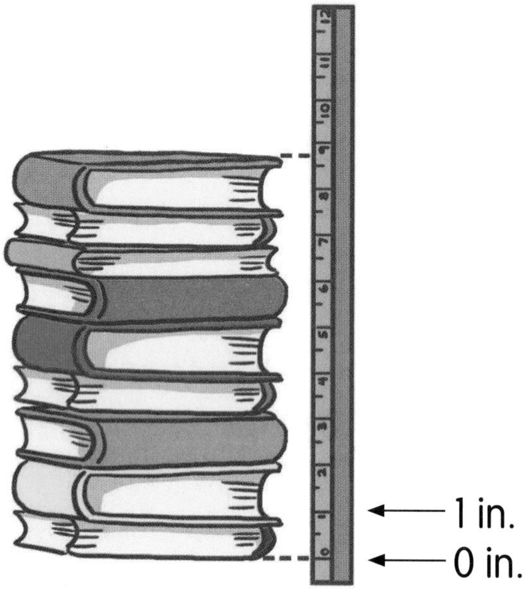

The length of this scarf is about 11 inches.
10
11

The stack of books is about 9 inches high .

Guided Practice

Find the missing numbers.

5

a. The vase is about ____ inches long.

b. The mouth of the vase is about ____ inches wide.

Learn

You can measure objects using a different start point.

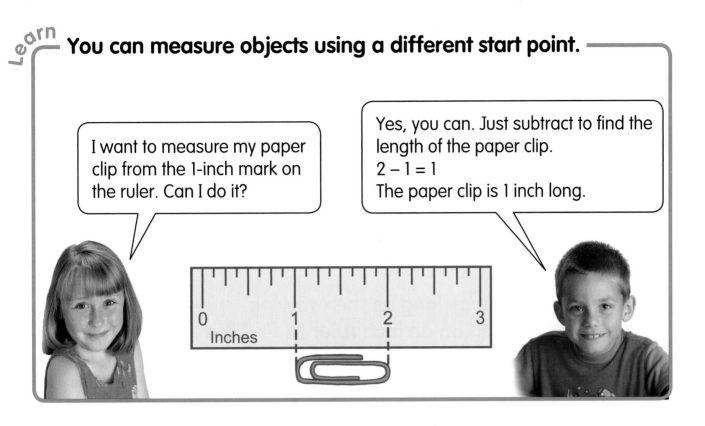

I want to measure my paper clip from the 1-inch mark on the ruler. Can I do it?

Yes, you can. Just subtract to find the length of the paper clip.
$2 - 1 = 1$
The paper clip is 1 inch long.

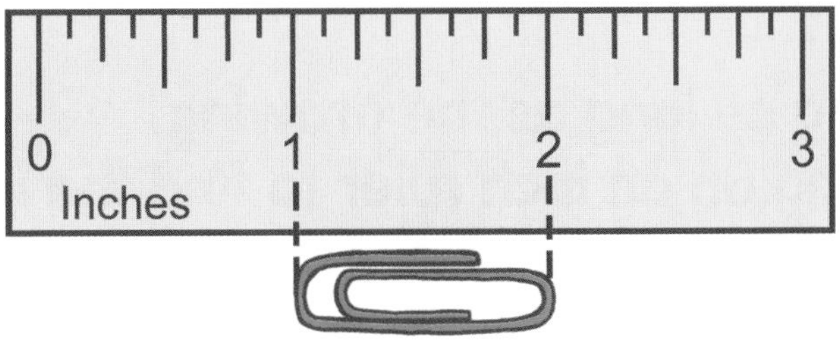

Guided Practice

Use the inch ruler to find the missing numbers.

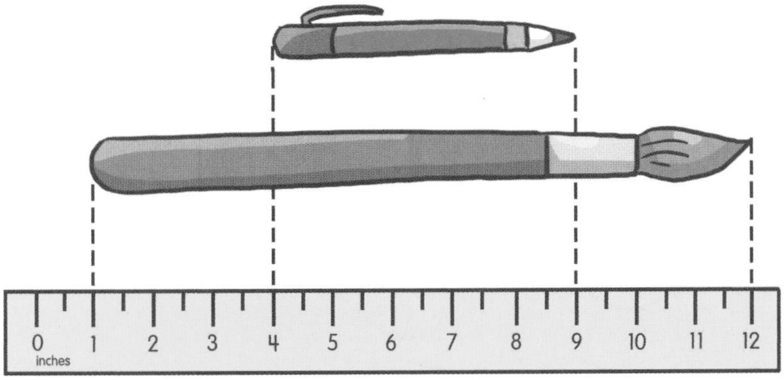

This ruler is smaller than in real life.

6. The paintbrush is ______ inches long.

7. The pen is ______ inches long.

8. Draw parts of lines of different lengths.
Then use a ruler to measure them.

Let's Practice

Measure the length of each part of a line.
Use an inch ruler.

1. part of a line A ____ inches

2. part of a line B ____ inches

Cut a piece of string as long as the drawing.
Then place the string on an inch ruler to find the length.

3. The length of the drawing is about ____ inches.

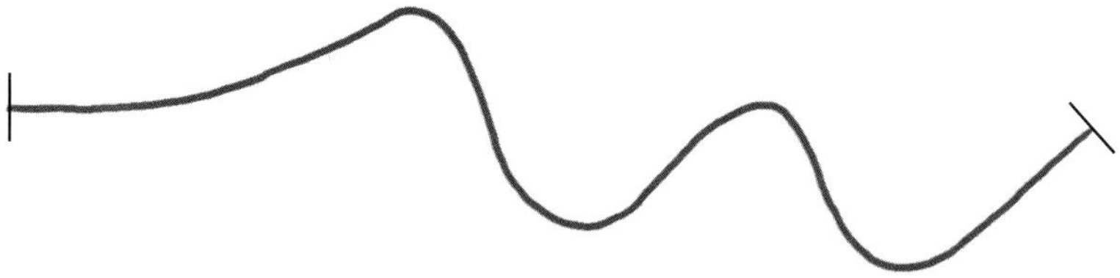

4. The length of the drawing is about ____ inches.

5 Follow these steps.
Then answer the question.

a Draw a part of a line 10 inches long.
Name it Drawing A.

b Draw a part of a line 3 inches longer than Drawing A.
Name it Drawing B.

c Draw a part of a line 5 inches shorter than Drawing B.
Name it Drawing C.

What is the length of Drawing C? ____ inches

Use the inch ruler to find the missing number.

6

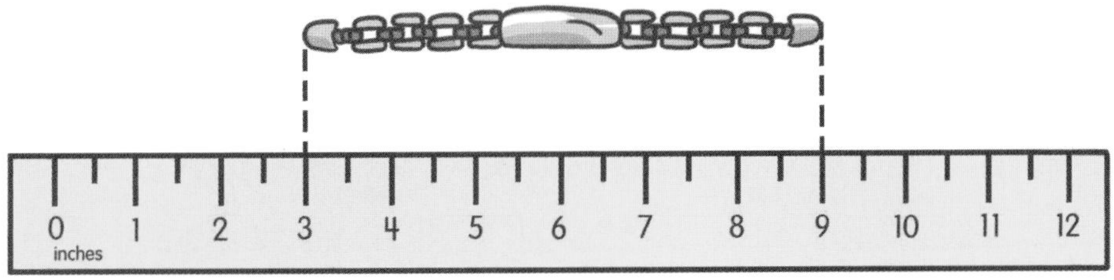

The bracelet is ____ inches long.

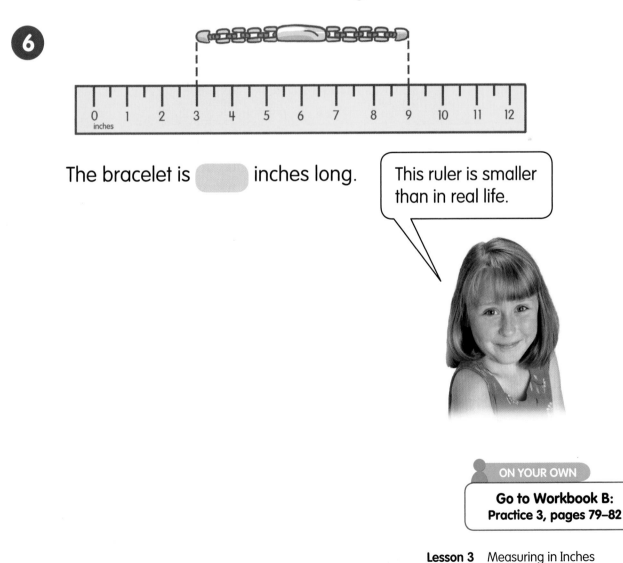

This ruler is smaller than in real life.

ON YOUR OWN

Go to Workbook B:
Practice 3, pages 79–82

LESSON 4

Comparing Lengths in Inches

Lesson Objectives

- Use an inch ruler to measure and compare lengths.
- Find the difference in lengths of objects in inches.

Learn

You can measure in inches to compare the lengths of objects.

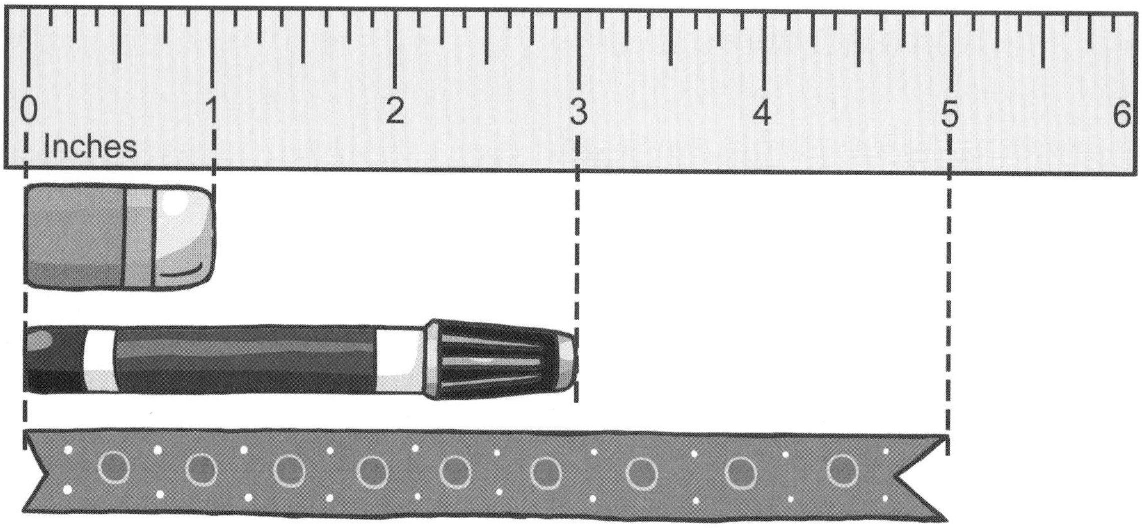

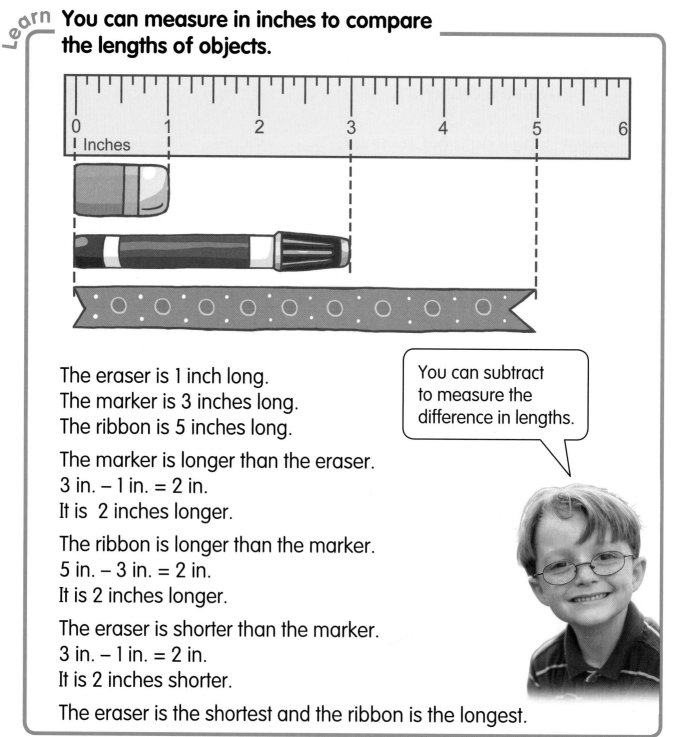

The eraser is 1 inch long.
The marker is 3 inches long.
The ribbon is 5 inches long.

The marker is longer than the eraser.
3 in. – 1 in. = 2 in.
It is 2 inches longer.

The ribbon is longer than the marker.
5 in. – 3 in. = 2 in.
It is 2 inches longer.

The eraser is shorter than the marker.
3 in. – 1 in. = 2 in.
It is 2 inches shorter.

The eraser is the shortest and the ribbon is the longest.

You can subtract to measure the difference in lengths.

Guided Practice

Use the inch rulers to find the missing numbers.

1

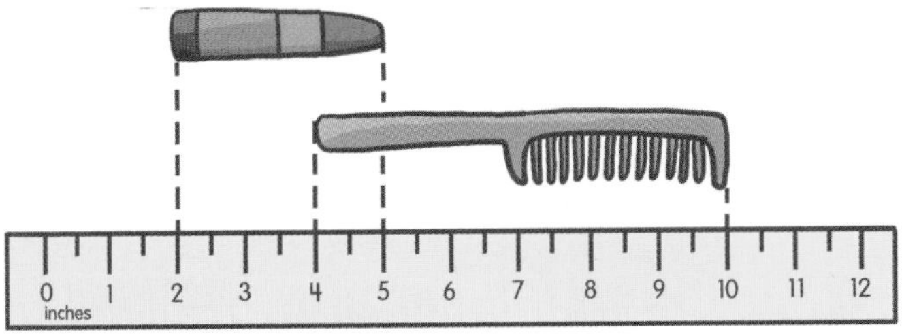

(a) The crayon is ____ inches long.

(b) The comb is ____ inches long.

(c) ____ – ____ = ____

The crayon is ____ inches shorter than the comb.

2

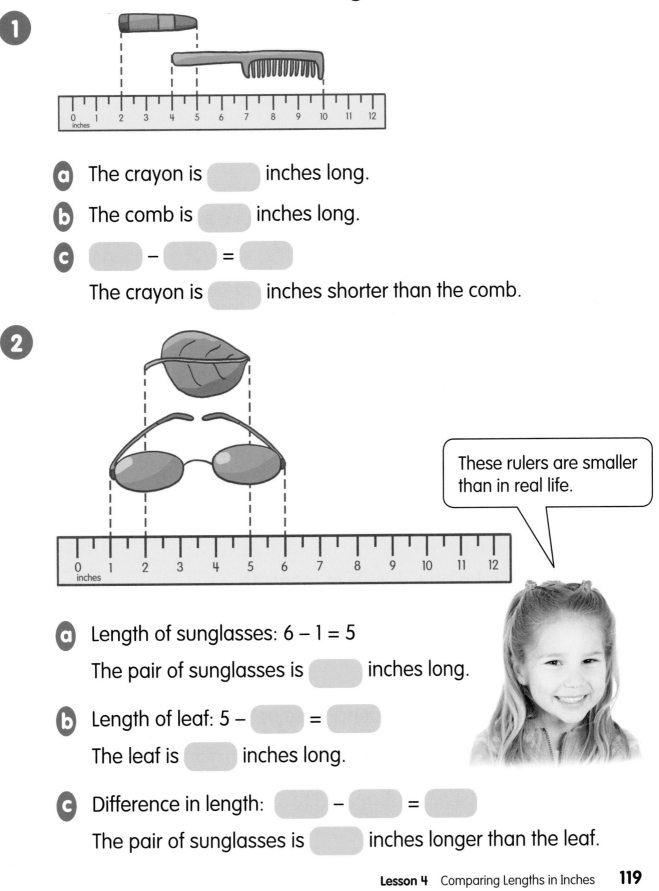

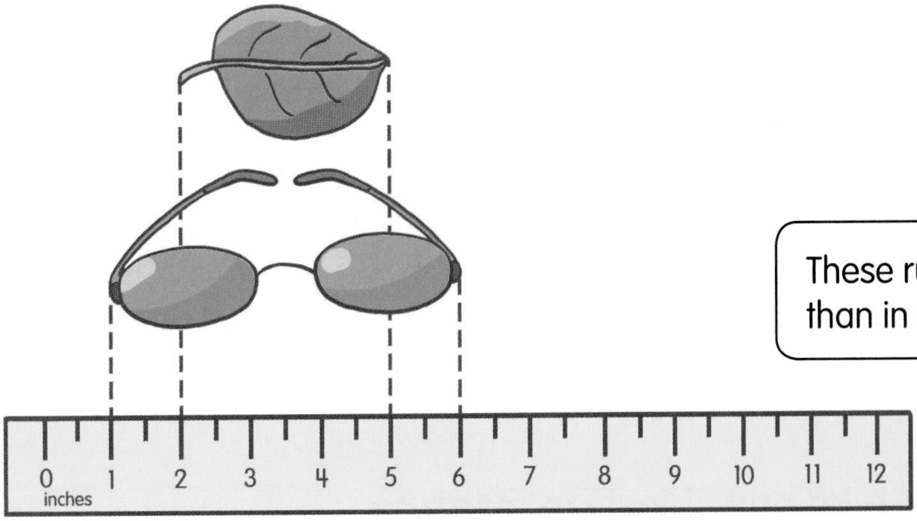

These rulers are smaller than in real life.

(a) Length of sunglasses: 6 – 1 = 5

The pair of sunglasses is ____ inches long.

(b) Length of leaf: 5 – ____ = ____

The leaf is ____ inches long.

(c) Difference in length: ____ – ____ = ____

The pair of sunglasses is ____ inches longer than the leaf.

Guided Practice

Find the missing letters and numbers.

3. Use an inch ruler to measure the lengths of these parts of a line.

Part of a line A

Part of a line B

Part of a line A is ____ inches long.

Part of a line B is ____ inches long.

Part of a line ____ is longer than Line ____.

Part of a line ____ is ____ inches longer than line ____.

Hands-On Activity

Use an inch ruler and objects to measure.

STEP 1 Find the length of your science book.

STEP 2 Then find the length of your pencil case.
Which is shorter, the pencil case or the science book?
How much shorter is it?

STEP 3 Measure the lengths of two other objects.
What is the length of the longer object?
How much longer is it?

Let's Practice

Look at the pictures.
Then answer the questions.

1 Which is longer, Rope A or Rope B?

Rope A 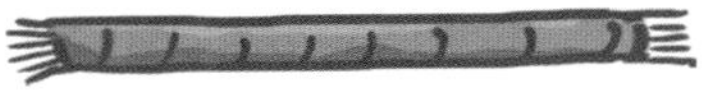

Rope B 

______ is longer.

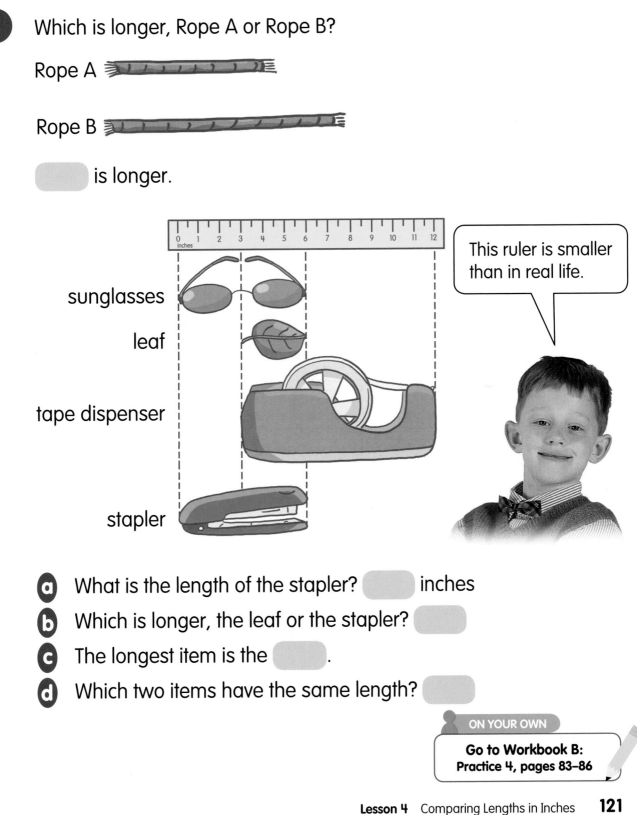

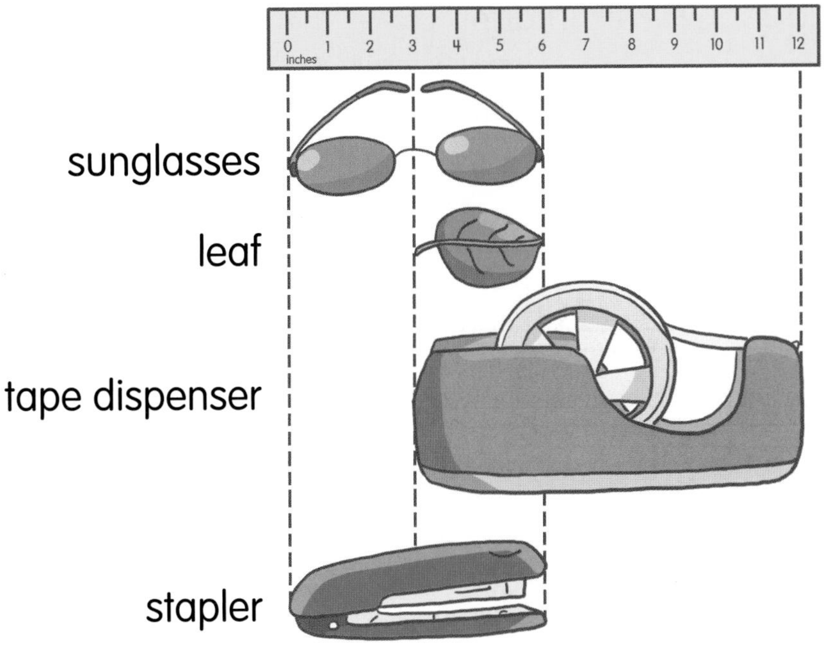

a What is the length of the stapler? ______ inches

b Which is longer, the leaf or the stapler? ______

c The longest item is the ______.

d Which two items have the same length? ______

ON YOUR OWN

Go to Workbook B: Practice 4, pages 83–86

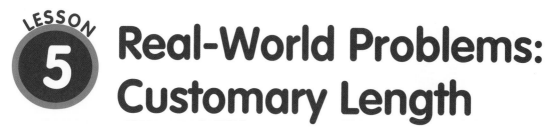

LESSON 5 Real-World Problems: Customary Length

Lesson Objectives

- Solve one- and two-step problems involving length.
- Draw bar models to solve real-world problems.

Learn You can use bar models to solve measurement problems.

Jenny walked 32 feet.
Then she turned right and walked 47 feet.

a How far did Jenny walk in all?

b In which direction did she walk farther, the first direction or the second direction?
How much farther?

a

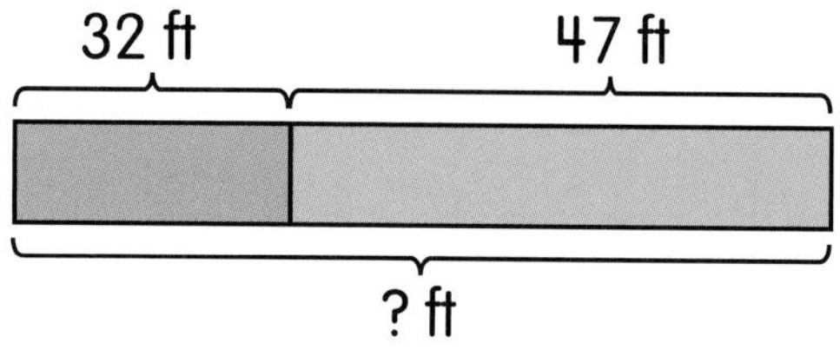

32 + 47 = 79
Jenny walks 79 feet in all.

b

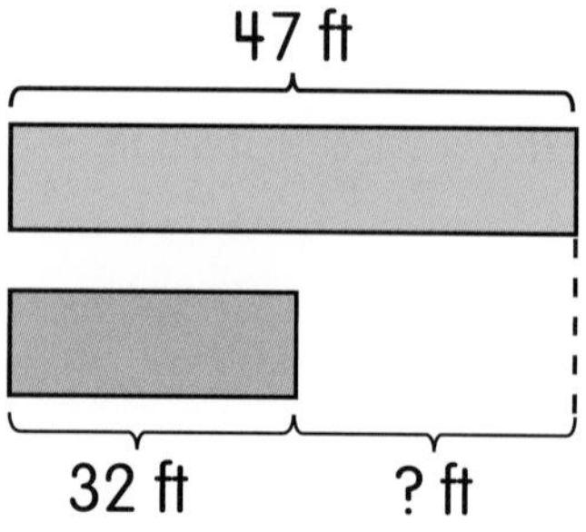

47 – 32 = 15
She walked 15 feet farther in the second direction.

Guided Practice

Solve.
Use bar models to help you.

1

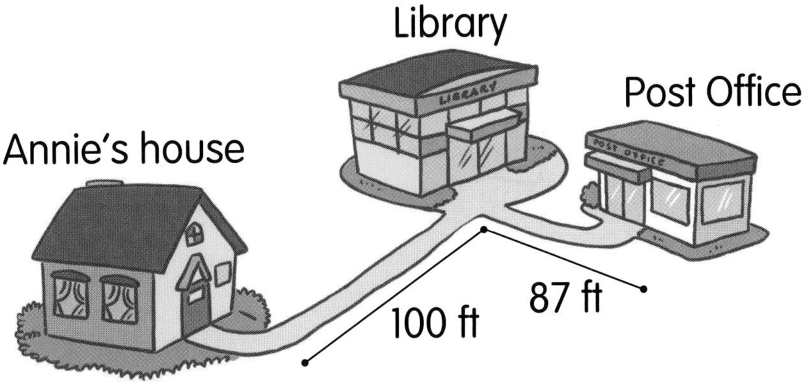

Annie walks from her house to the Post Office to mail a package.
On her way, she passes the Library.
How far does she walk in all?

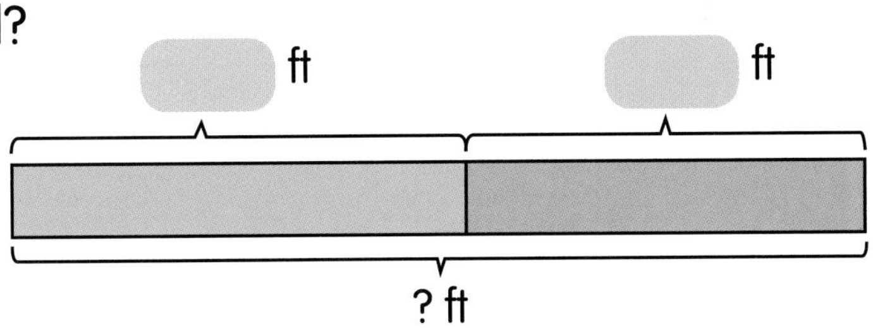

___ + ___ = ___

She walks ___ feet in all.

2

How far is the man from the Boat A?

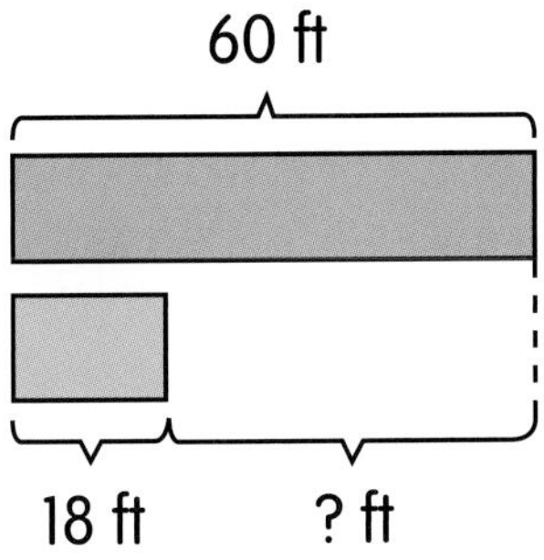

___ − ___ = ___

The man is ___ feet from Boat A.

Learn You can use bar models to solve measurement problems.

Gina wraps gifts for her friends.
She cuts a 47-inch long strip of wrapping paper into 3 pieces.
The first piece is 14 inches long.
The second piece is 18 inches long.

a Find the total length of the first and second pieces.

b What is the length of the third piece?

a

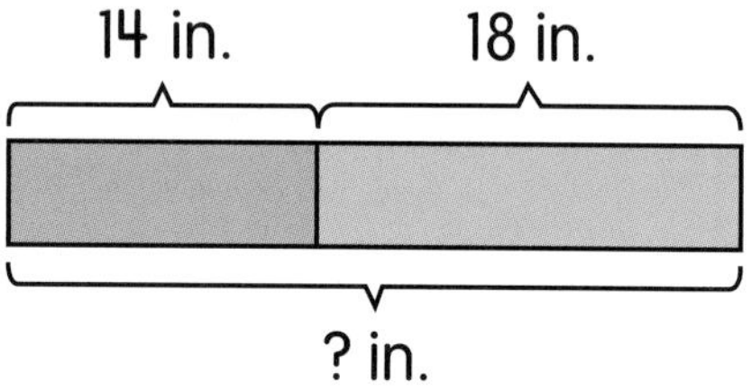

First, find the total length of the first and second pieces.

$14 + 18 = 32$

The total length of the first and second pieces is 32 inches.

b

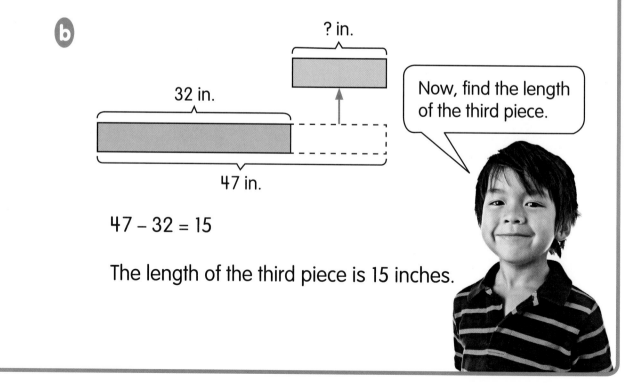

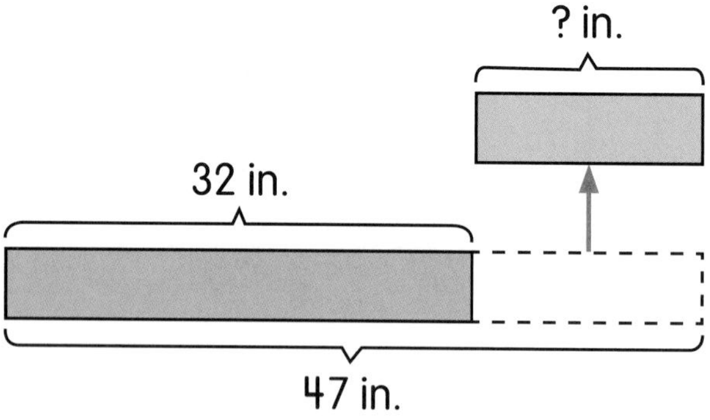

Now, find the length of the third piece.

$47 - 32 = 15$

The length of the third piece is 15 inches.

Guided Practice

Solve.
Use bar models to help you.

3 A dressmaker has a piece of red cloth 50 inches long.
She cuts 28 inches from the red cloth.
Then she sews a piece of yellow cloth that is 43 inches long to the remaining piece of red cloth.
What is the total length of cloth now?

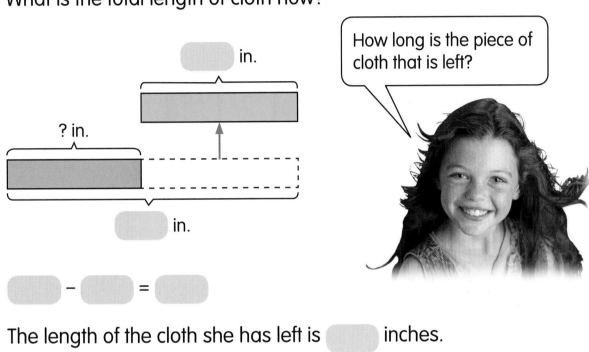

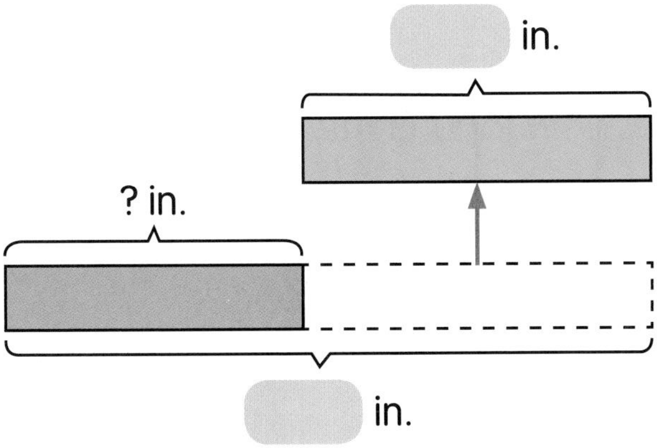

How long is the piece of cloth that is left?

____ – ____ = ____

The length of the cloth she has left is ____ inches.

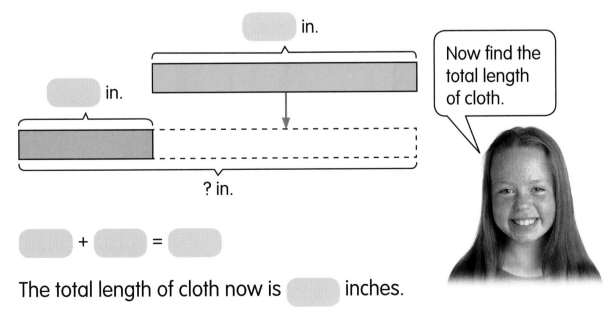

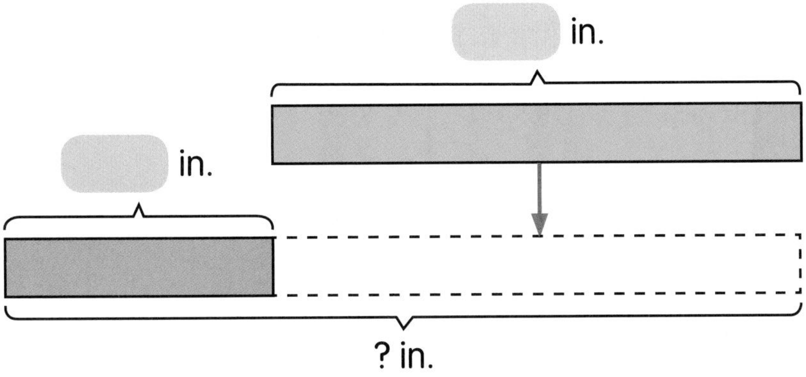

Now find the total length of cloth.

____ + ____ = ____

The total length of cloth now is ____ inches.

Let's Practice

Solve.
Draw bar models to help you.

1. Todd has two gardens.
His vegetable garden is 240 feet long.
His flower garden is 150 feet long.
How long are both gardens?

2. A ribbon, 72 inches long, is cut into 2 pieces.
If one piece is 38 inches long, how long is the other piece?

3. Misha stretches a tape measure to 245 inches.
Naomi stretches her tape measure 28 inches longer.
How far does Naomi stretch her tape measure?

4. Albert is 60 inches tall.
His sister is 17 inches shorter.
How tall is Albert's sister?

5. A wire is cut into two pieces.
The first piece is 34 inches.
It is 18 inches longer than the second piece.
   a. How long is the second piece?
   b. What is the difference in length between the two pieces?

ON YOUR OWN

Go to Workbook B:
Practice 5, pages 87–90

CRITICAL THINKING SKILLS

Put On Your Thinking Cap!

PROBLEM SOLVING

A rectangular field has a length of 50 feet.
A farmer sticks posts along the length of the field from Point A to Point B.
If the distance between the posts is 10 feet, how many posts are there?

ON YOUR OWN

Go to Workbook B: Put on Your Thinking Cap! pages 91–92

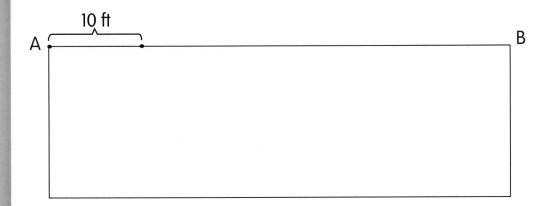

Chapter Wrap Up

You have learned...

Customary Length

Measure

1. 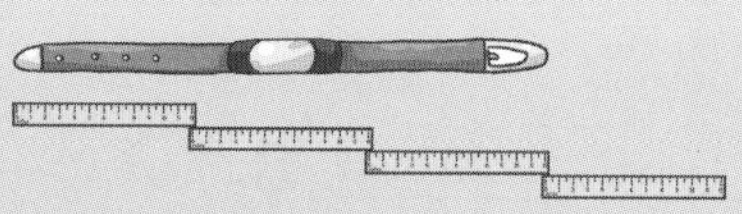

The belt is less than 4 feet long.

2. 

The pencil sharpener is 2 inches long.

3. 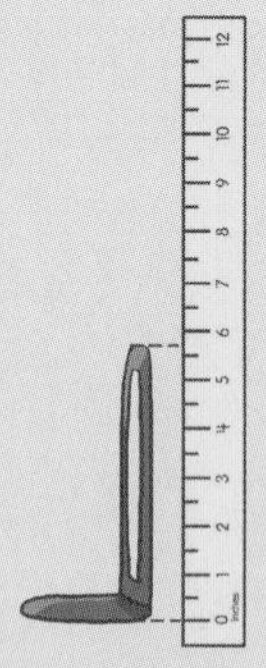

The bookend is about 6 inches tall.

Compare

1. 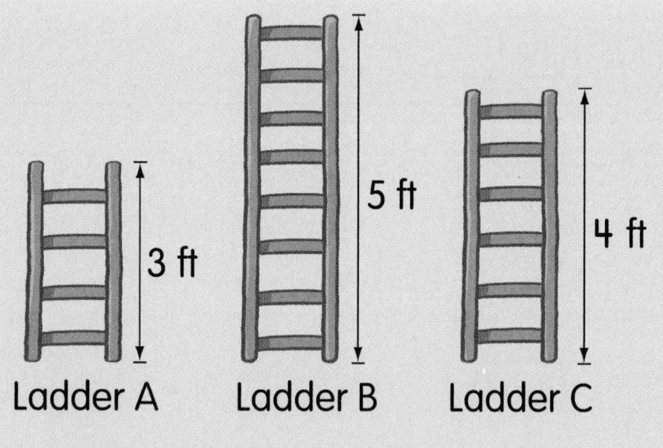

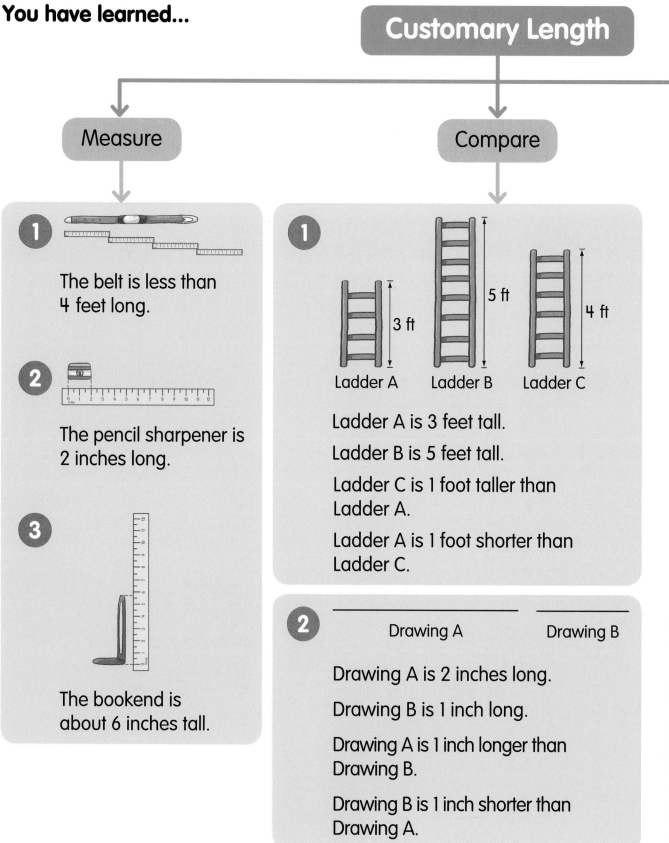

Ladder A is 3 feet tall.

Ladder B is 5 feet tall.

Ladder C is 1 foot taller than Ladder A.

Ladder A is 1 foot shorter than Ladder C.

2. Drawing A Drawing B

Drawing A is 2 inches long.

Drawing B is 1 inch long.

Drawing A is 1 inch longer than Drawing B.

Drawing B is 1 inch shorter than Drawing A.

BIG IDEA

Rulers can be used to measure and compare how long and how tall things are.

Solve Real-World Problems

1 Gabby's mom has 13 feet of tape.
She uses 5 feet of the tape.
How much tape does she have left?
13 – 5 = 8
She has 8 feet of tape left.

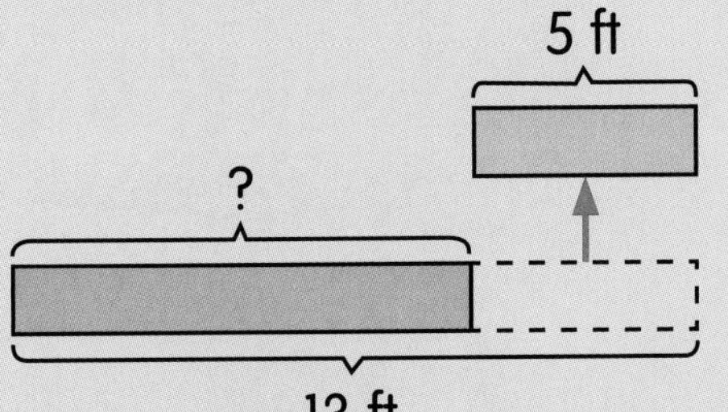

2 Adrian has 7 inches of rope.
He needs 4 inches more of rope to tie a box.
How much rope does he need to tie the box?
4 + 7 = 11
He needs 11 inches of rope.

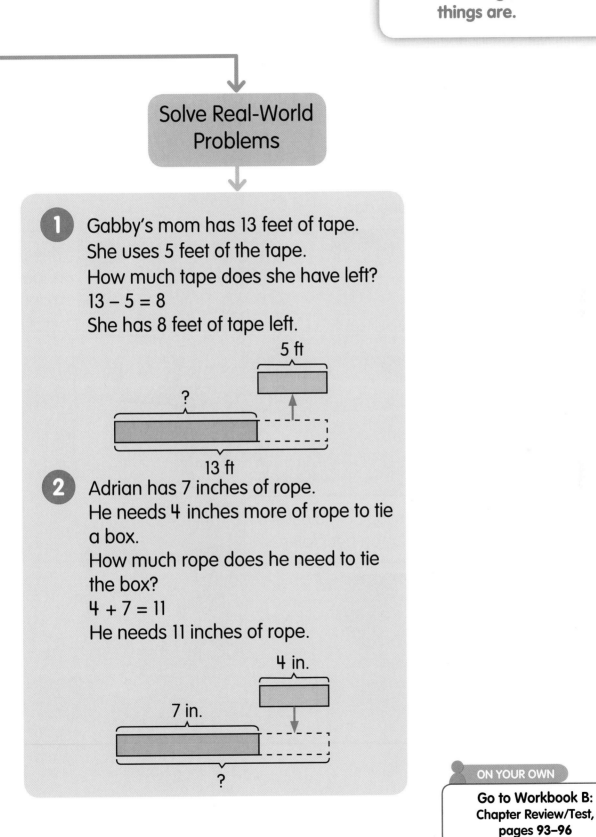

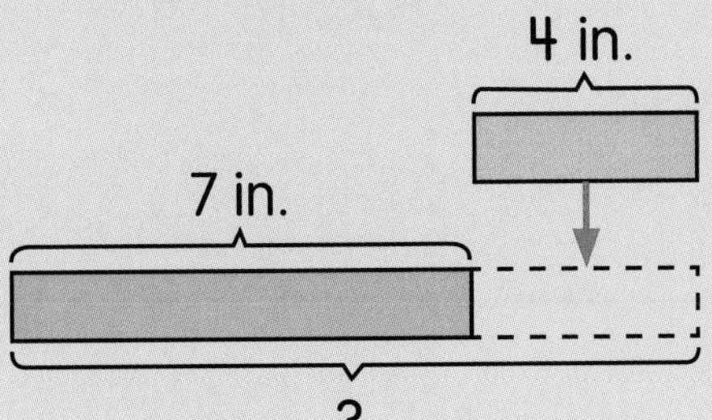

ON YOUR OWN

Go to Workbook B: Chapter Review/Test, pages 93–96

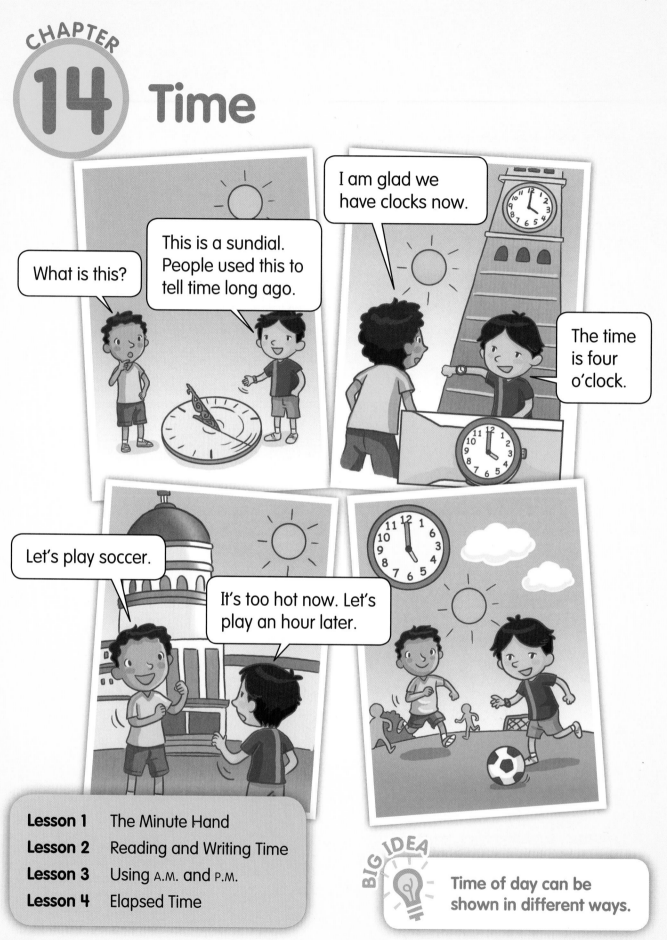

CHAPTER

14 Time

BIG IDEA

Time of day can be shown in different ways.

Recall Prior Knowledge

Skip-counting by 5s

5	10	15	20	25	30
five	ten	fifteen	twenty	twenty-five	thirty

35	40	45	50	55	60
thirty-five	forty	forty-five	fifty	fifty-five	sixty

Finding numbers in a pattern by adding or subtracting

5	10	15	20	25	30	35	40	45	50	55	60

15 is 5 more than 10.
20 is 5 more than 15.

60 is 10 more than 50.
45 is 10 less than 55.

Telling time

It is 9 o'clock.

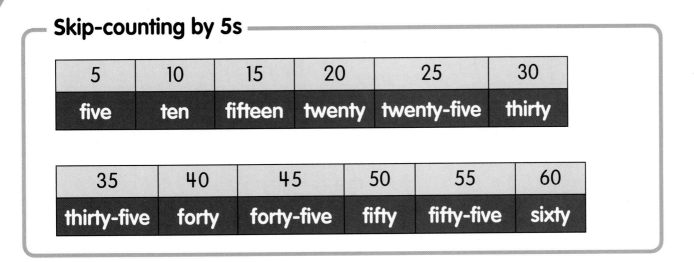

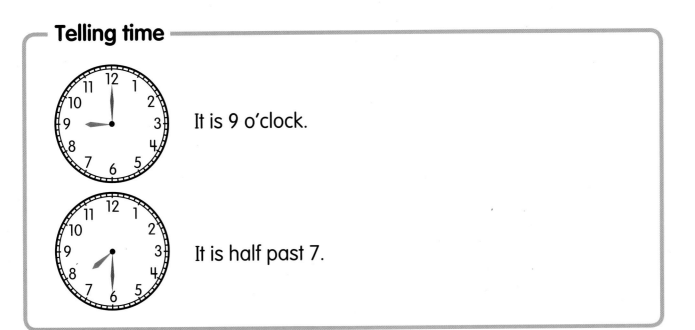

It is half past 7.

✔ Quick Check

Find the missing numbers or words.

1

5		15		25	
	ten		twenty		thirty

2

35	40			55	60
		forty-five	fifty		

Find the missing numbers.

3 10 is 5 more than ___.

4 25 is 10 less than ___.

What is the time?

5

6

7

8

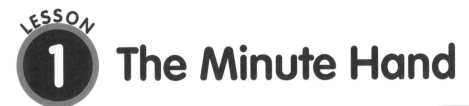

LESSON 1
The Minute Hand

Lesson Objective:

- Use the minute hand to show and tell the number for every five minutes after the hour.

Vocabulary

hour hand
minute hand
minute
hour
o'clock
after
clock face

Learn **You can skip-count by 5s to find how many minutes have passed.**

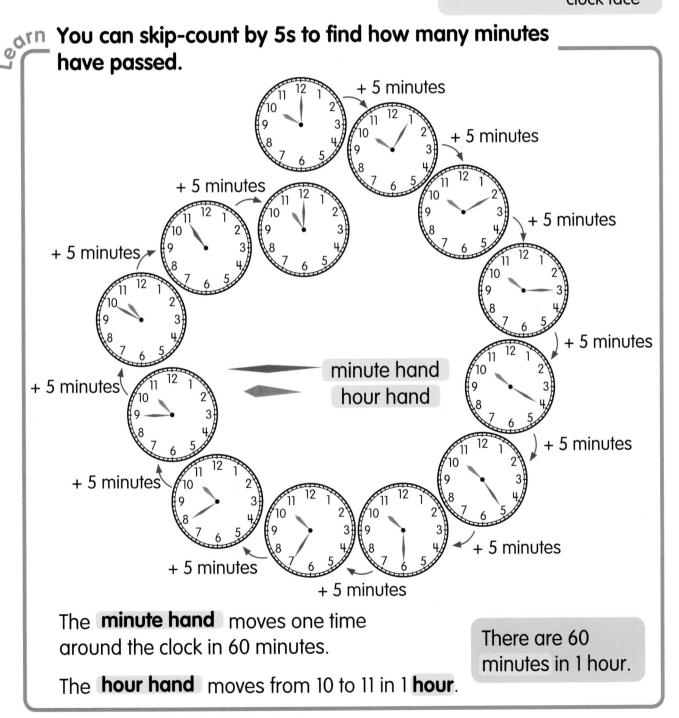

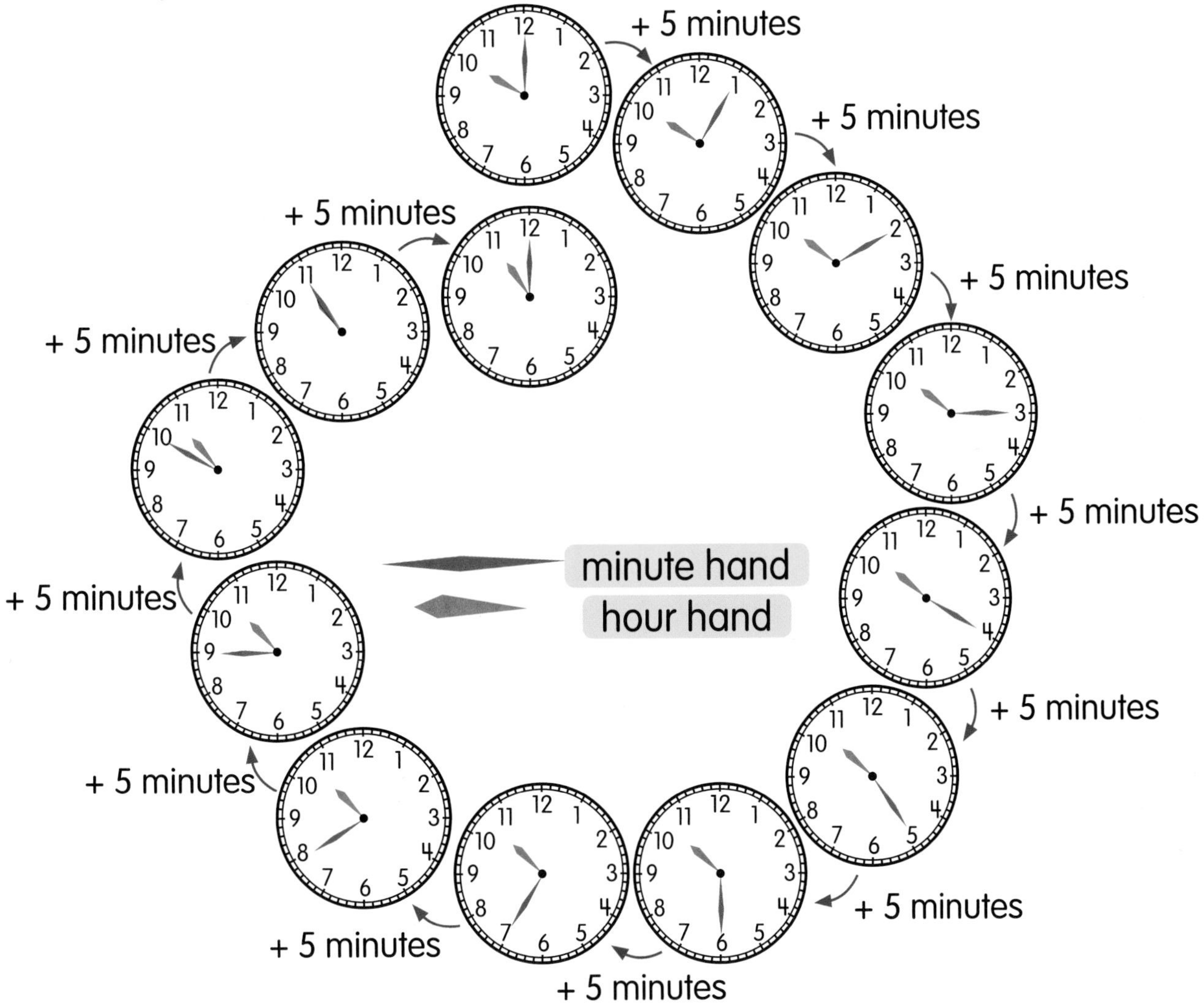

The **minute hand** moves one time around the clock in 60 minutes.

The **hour hand** moves from 10 to 11 in 1 **hour**.

There are 60 minutes in 1 hour.

Learn **You can use the numbers on the clock to skip-count by 5s starting at 12.**

5 minutes later →

5

8 o'clock

5 minutes after 8 o'clock

40 minutes later →

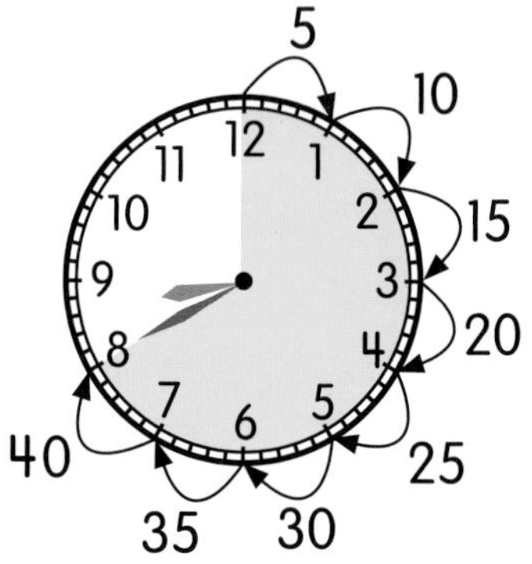
5
10
15
20
25
30
35
40

8 o'clock

40 minutes after 8 o'clock

I count in fives.
5, 10, 15, 20, 25,
30, 35, 40.

Guided Practice

Find the missing number.
Skip-count by 5s to help you.

1

____ minutes later →

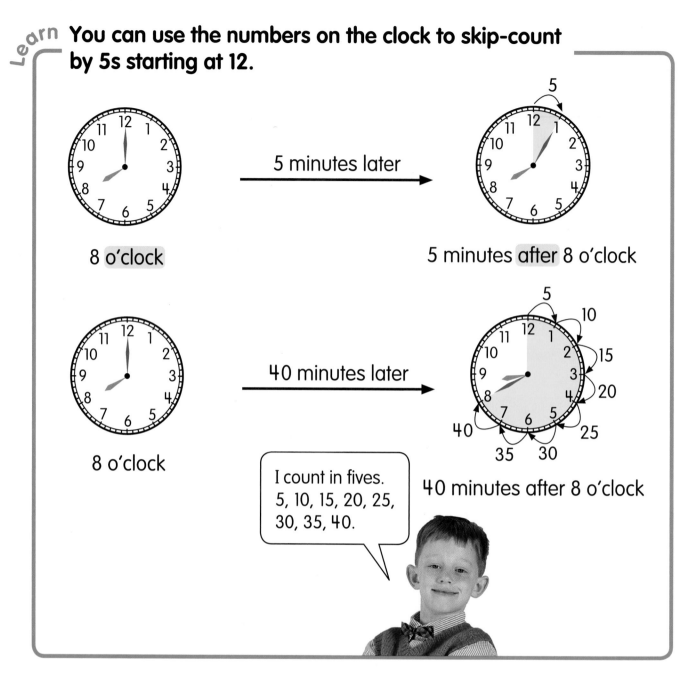

8 o'clock

____ minutes after 8 o'clock

Find the missing number.
Skip-count by 5s to help you.

2 

___ minutes after 10 o'clock

3 

___ minutes after 10 o'clock

Where should the minute hand be to show the time?

4 

20 minutes after 4 o'clock

5 

55 minutes after 8 o'clock

Hands-On Activity

WORK IN PAIRS

Use this clock face.
Your partner says the minutes after the hour.
You point to the correct number on the clock face.
Your partner will check your answer.

1. 15 minutes
2. 30 minutes
3. 45 minutes

Let's Practice

Look at the minute hand.
Then write how many minutes after the hour it shows.

1

____ minutes

2

____ minutes

Find the missing number. Skip-count by 5s to help you.

3

____ minutes after 5 o'clock

4

____ minutes after 8 o'clock

Draw the minute hand to show the time.

5 30 minutes after 1 o'clock

6 45 minutes after 9 o'clock

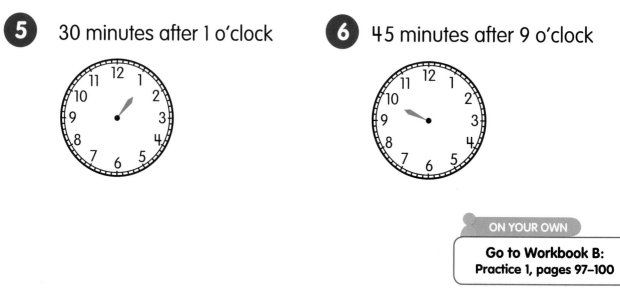

ON YOUR OWN

Go to Workbook B:
Practice 1, pages 97–100

LESSON 2 Reading and Writing Time

Lesson Objective

- Show and tell time in hours and minutes.

Learn You can use a clock to tell time in hours and minutes.

Julia, Nadine, Alvin, and Robert are going on a field trip.
They cannot wait to get to school!

hour → 6:35 ← minute

My school bus will come at **six thirty-five**.

Write six thirty-five as 6:35.

hour → 6:45 ← minute

It's **six forty-five**.
The bus is not here yet!

Write six forty-five as 6:45.

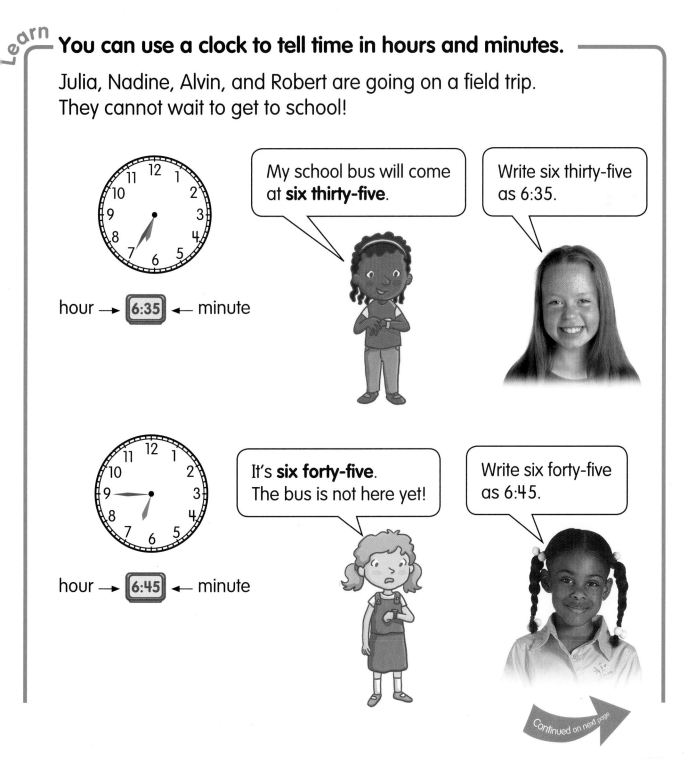

Continued on next page

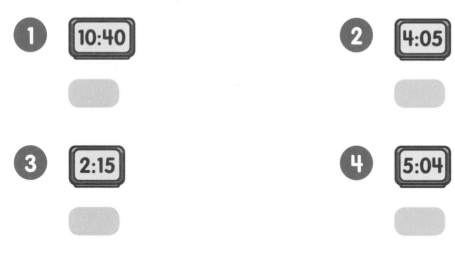

Guided Practice

Give the time in words.

1. 10:40

2. 4:05

3. 2:15

4. 5:04

Learn

You can use a clock to see how time passes.

See how the minute hand and hour hand move as time passes.

Here's how to read the time.

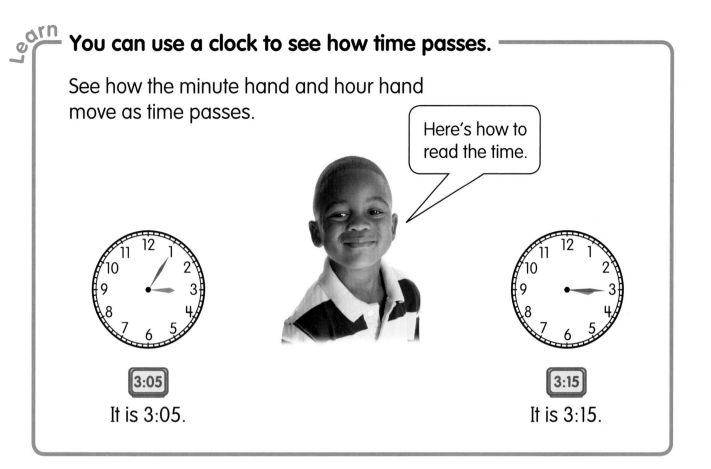

3:05

It is 3:05.

3:15

It is 3:15.

Guided Practice

Tell the time.

5 

6 

7 

8 

Show where the missing hands should be.

Example

9:25

9

12:10

10

4:45

11

3:30

12

8:20

13

5:35

Let's Practice

Tell the time.

1

2

3

Give the time in words.

4

5

6

7

8

9

Show where the missing hands should be.

10

8:00

11

11:05

12

8:45

13

5:15

14

12:30

15

3:20

ON YOUR OWN

Go to Workbook B: Practice 2, pages 101–106

LESSON 3 Using A.M. and P.M.

Lesson Objectives

- Use A.M. and P.M. to show morning, afternoon, or night.
- Order events by time.

Vocabulary

A.M.

P.M.

Learn

You can use the clock and events to tell if it is A.M. or P.M.

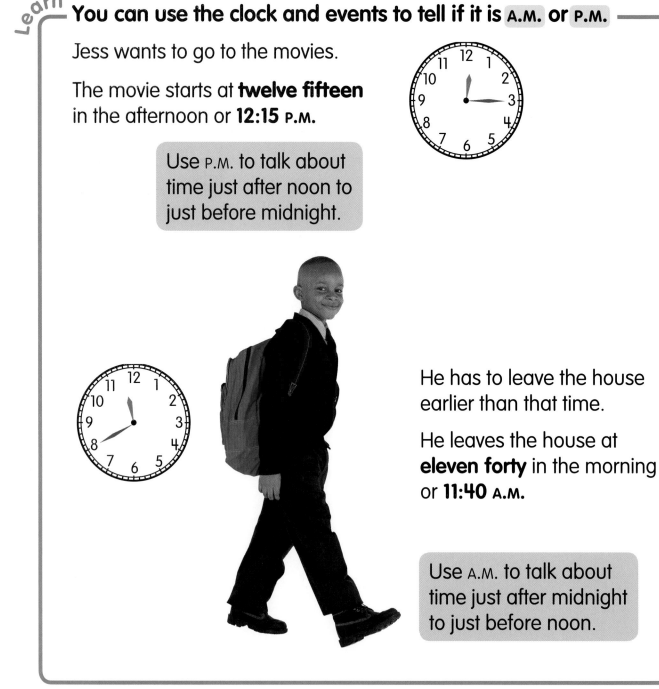

Jess wants to go to the movies.

The movie starts at **twelve fifteen** in the afternoon or **12:15 P.M.**

Use P.M. to talk about time just after noon to just before midnight.

He has to leave the house earlier than that time.

He leaves the house at **eleven forty** in the morning or **11:40 A.M.**

Use A.M. to talk about time just after midnight to just before noon.

Guided Practice

Write A.M. or P.M.

1 It is 4 hours after midnight.
The time is 4:00 ______

2 It is 2 hours after noon.
The time is 2:00 ______

3 Ms. Philips goes to work in the morning.
She leaves home at 8:00 ______

Ms. Philips goes home after work in the evening.
She goes home at 5:00 ______

Read and write the time shown on each clock. Use A.M. or P.M. to show time of the day. Explain your answers.

4

Jason wakes up at ______

5

Alison eats a snack at ______

6

The July Fourth celebration ended at ______

7

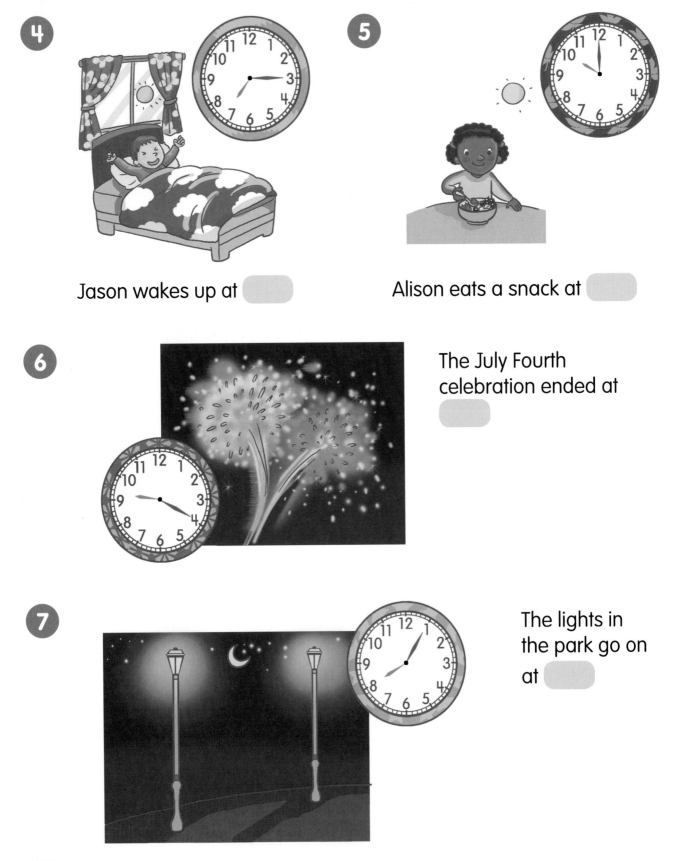

The lights in the park go on at ______

8 In summer, the sun usually comes up at ______

9

This father walks his baby every morning at ______

10 **List the times in Exercises 4–9.**
Arrange them in order from the beginning of the day.

______ ______ ______ ______ ______ ______

Earliest

Write A.M. or P.M.

11. Al plays tennis after school at 4:30 ____
12. Andy does his homework at 8:15 ____ before he goes to bed.
13. Ellie leaves home at 7:30 ____ to go to school.
14. Mr. Davis starts preparing lunch at his restaurant at 10:15 ____

READING AND WRITING MATH

Math Journal

Choose a day of the week.
Describe what you do at these times on this day.

Day: ____

7:00 A.M.: ____

10:00 A.M.: ____

Noon: ____

1:00 P.M.: ____

Read each activity.
Then write the time using A.M. or P.M.

Eat breakfast: ____

Arrive at school: ____

Eat dinner: ____

Go to bed: ____

Let's Practice

Choose the picture that shows noon.

1

Write A.M. or P.M.

2 Mr. and Mrs. Smith went for a midnight movie at 11:50 ____
They returned home at 1:30 ____

3 Kenneth went to the library 3 hours after noon.
The time was 3:00 ____

Look at the pictures.
Fill in the blanks with A.M. or P.M.

4. Hillary plays with Nia until 6:00 ______
Then Hillary returns home.

5. After dinner, Hillary does her homework.
Then she goes to bed at 8:30 ______

6 Hillary wakes up at 7:00 ______

She has breakfast and goes to school.

7 After school, Hillary goes to Nia's house at 2:00 ______

8 **List the times in Exercises 4–7.**
Arrange them in order from the beginning of the day.

______ ______ ______ ______

Earliest

ON YOUR OWN

Go to Workbook B:
Practice 3, pages 107–110

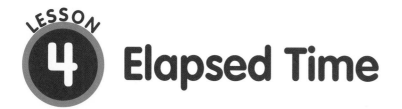

LESSON 4

Elapsed Time

Lesson Objective

- Determine how much time has passed.

Learn

You can use a clock to find how much time has passed.

Math class starts at 9:00 A.M. and ends at 10:00 A.M.

Start
9:00 A.M.

End
10:00 A.M.

Lesson Time
1 hour

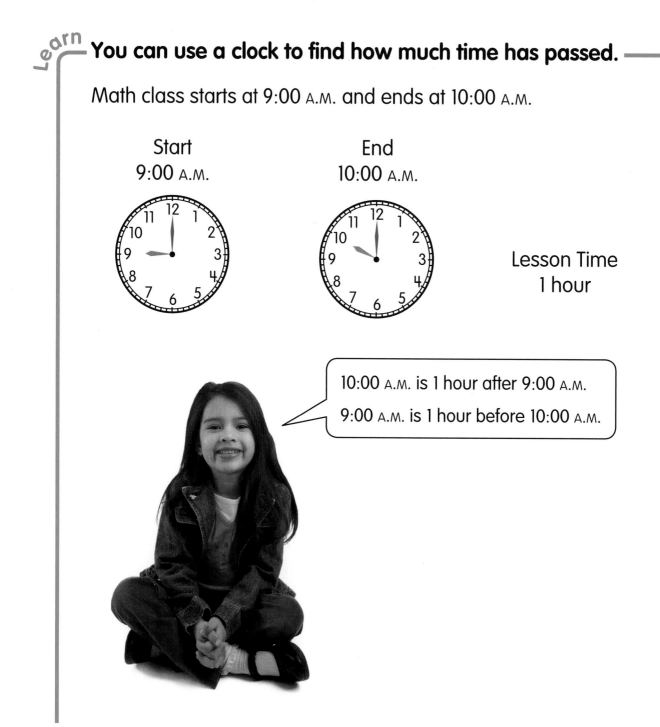

10:00 A.M. is 1 hour after 9:00 A.M.

9:00 A.M. is 1 hour before 10:00 A.M.

Jan got on the school bus at 3:00 P.M. and reached home at 3:30 P.M.

How long was the ride home?

Start
3:00 P.M.

End
3:30 P.M.

Time Taken
30 minutes

3:30 P.M. is 30 minutes after 3:00 P.M.

3:00 P.M. is 30 minutes before 3:30 P.M.

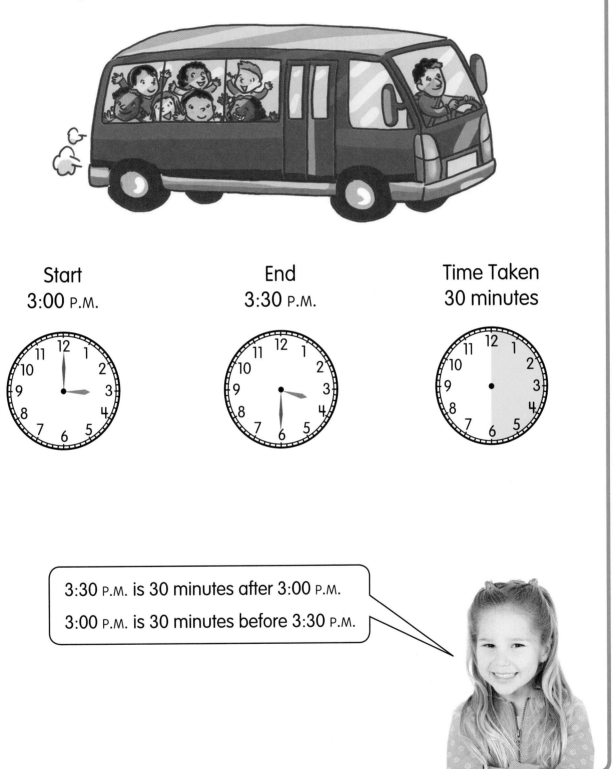

Guided Practice

Complete.

1 Pat and his family arrive at the park at 10:00 A.M.

They leave the park at ______.

They spent ______ at the park.

10:00 A.M. is 1 hour before ______.

______ is 1 hour after ______.

2 Sam fell asleep at 5:00 P.M.

He woke up after 30 minutes or half an hour.

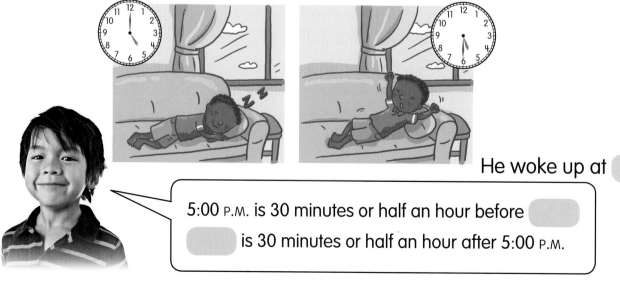

He woke up at ______.

5:00 P.M. is 30 minutes or half an hour before ______.

______ is 30 minutes or half an hour after 5:00 P.M.

Tell the time.

3. 1 hour after 8:00 P.M.

   The time is ______

4. 1 hour before 4:00 P.M.

   The time is ______

5. 30 minutes after 2:00 A.M.

   The time is ______

6. 30 minutes before 7:00 P.M.

   The time is ______

7. half an hour before noon

   The time is ______

8. half an hour after noon

   The time is ______

Hands-On Activity

Use the schedule.
Look at the programs shown from 4:00 P.M. to 10:00 P.M.

WOOO Channel Program Schedule October 4, Saturday	
4:00 to 4:30 P.M.	Planet Z
4:30 to 5:30 P.M.	Road to Victory
5:30 to 6:30 P.M.	Kids Just Want to Have Fun
6:30 to 7:00 P.M.	Playhouse Wooo
7:00 to 8:00 P.M.	The Reporter
8:00 to 8:30 P.M.	Amazing Places
8:30 to 10:00 P.M.	Wooo Movies

1. Find two programs that are each 30 minutes long.
2. Find two programs that are each 1 hour long.
3. Fill in a copy of this chart showing the programs you chose.

Program	Start	End

Let's Practice

Find the start or end time.

		Starts at		Ends at
1	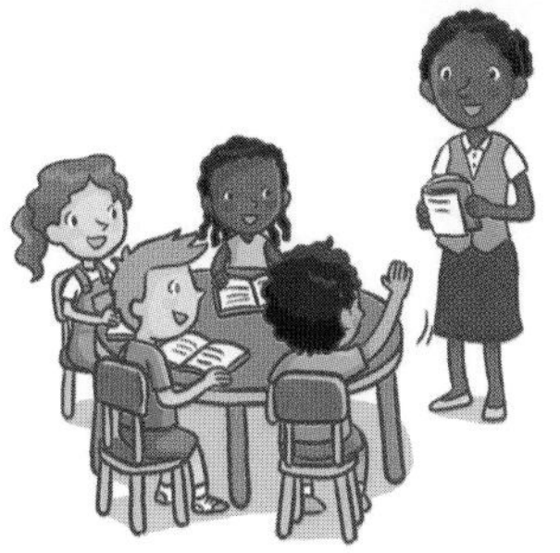		1 hour after is	10:30 A.M.
2		9:30 P.M.	30 minutes after is	

Show where the missing hands point.

3 It is . 30 minutes after is .

4 It is . 1 hour after is .

5 It is . 30 minutes before is .

6 It is . 1 hour before is .

Answer each question.

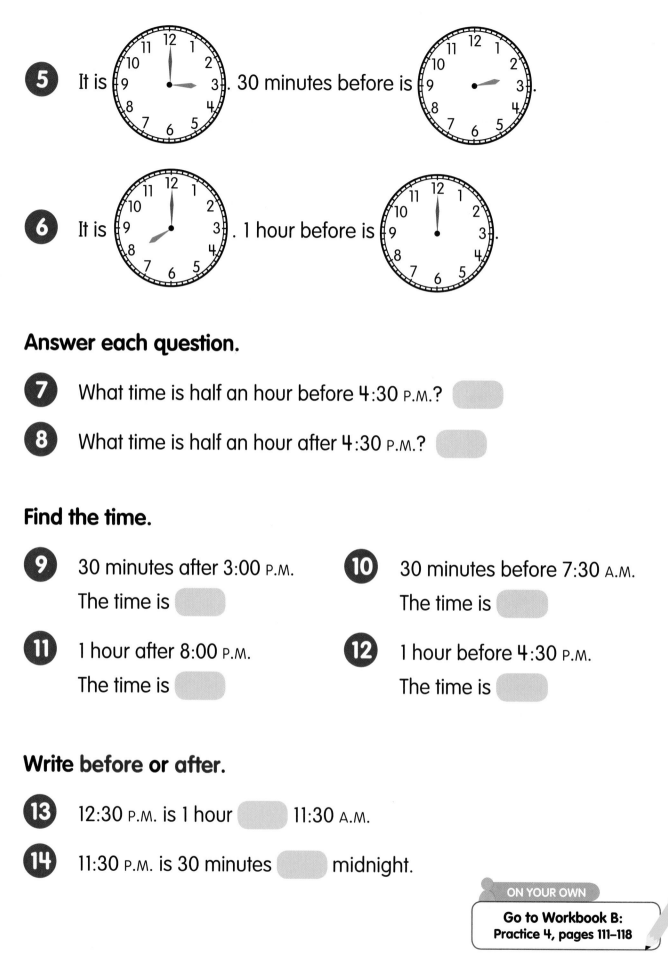

7 What time is half an hour before 4:30 P.M.? ____

8 What time is half an hour after 4:30 P.M.? ____

Find the time.

9 30 minutes after 3:00 P.M.
The time is ____

10 30 minutes before 7:30 A.M.
The time is ____

11 1 hour after 8:00 P.M.
The time is ____

12 1 hour before 4:30 P.M.
The time is ____

Write before or after.

13 12:30 P.M. is 1 hour ____ 11:30 A.M.

14 11:30 P.M. is 30 minutes ____ midnight.

ON YOUR OWN

Go to Workbook B: Practice 4, pages 111–118

Put On Your Thinking Cap!

PROBLEM SOLVING

Look at the clock.
Then look at the pictures.
Which is unlikely to take place at this time?
Explain your answer to your friends.

1

2

ON YOUR OWN

Go to Workbook B:
Put on Your Thinking Cap!
pages 119–120

Chapter Wrap Up

You have learned...

BIG IDEA
Time of day can be shown in different ways.

Time

Read and Write Time to the Minute

Example

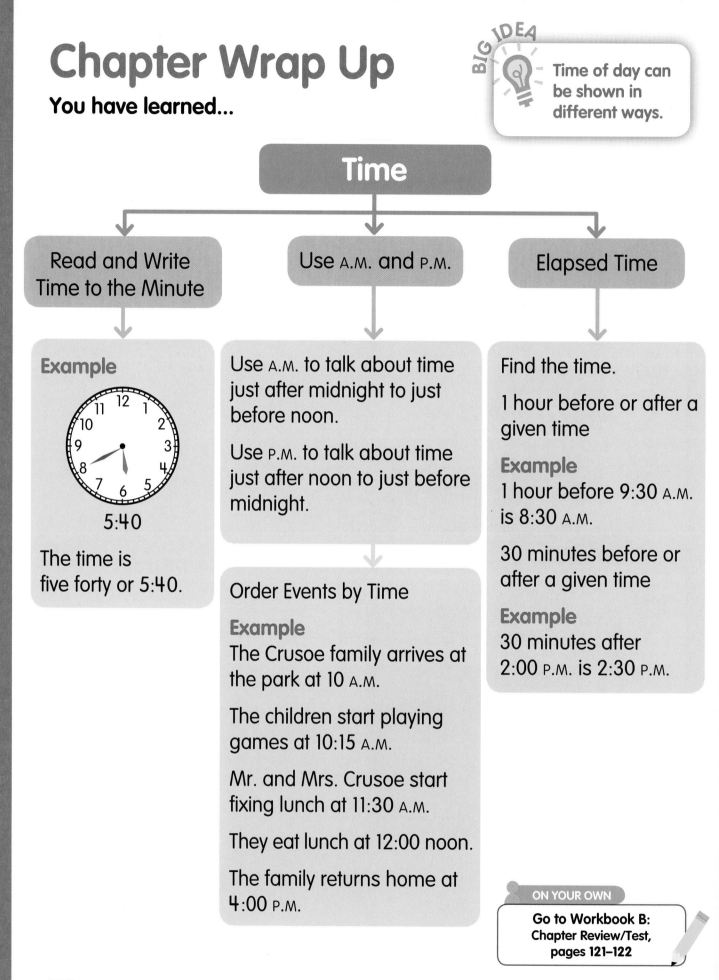

5:40

The time is five forty or 5:40.

Use A.M. and P.M.

Use A.M. to talk about time just after midnight to just before noon.

Use P.M. to talk about time just after noon to just before midnight.

Order Events by Time

Example
The Crusoe family arrives at the park at 10 A.M.

The children start playing games at 10:15 A.M.

Mr. and Mrs. Crusoe start fixing lunch at 11:30 A.M.

They eat lunch at 12:00 noon.

The family returns home at 4:00 P.M.

Elapsed Time

Find the time.

1 hour before or after a given time

Example
1 hour before 9:30 A.M. is 8:30 A.M.

30 minutes before or after a given time

Example
30 minutes after 2:00 P.M. is 2:30 P.M.

ON YOUR OWN

Go to Workbook B: Chapter Review/Test, pages 121–122

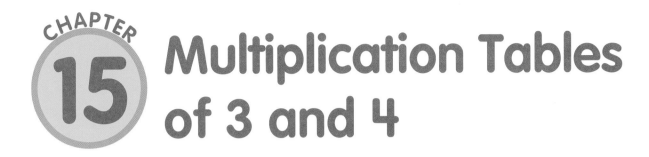

CHAPTER 15

Multiplication Tables of 3 and 4

Multiplication Chart

	1	2	3	4	5	6	7	8	9	10
1	1	2	3	4	5	6	7	8	9	10
2	2	4	6	8	10	12	14	16	18	20
3	3	6	9	12	15	18	21	24	27	30
4	4	8	12	16	20	24	28	32	36	40
5	5	10	15	20	25	30	35	40	45	50
6	6	12	18	24	30	36	42	48	54	60
7	7	14	21	28	35	42	49	56	63	70
8	8	16	24	32	40	48	56	64	72	80
9	9	18	27	36	45	54	63	72	81	90
10	10	20	30	40	50	60	70	80	90	100

Look at the multiplication chart. What patterns can you find?

BIG IDEA

Known multiplication facts can be used to find other multiplication and division facts.

Recall Prior Knowledge

Skip-counting by 2s, 5s, and 10s

2, 4, 6, 8, 10, 12, 14, 16, 18, 20

5, 10, 15, 20, 25, 30, 35, 40, 45, 50

10, 20, 30, 40, 50, 60, 70, 80, 90, 100

Adding equal groups

$$2 + 2 + 2 + 2 + 2 = 5 \times 2$$
$$= 10$$

$$5 + 5 + 5 + 5 = 4 \times 5$$
$$= 20$$

$$10 + 10 + 10 = 3 \times 10$$
$$= 30$$

Rewriting statements

4 twos = 4 groups of 2

3 fives = 3 groups of 5

2 tens = 2 groups of 10

Multiplying using skip-counting

$5 \times 2 = 10$

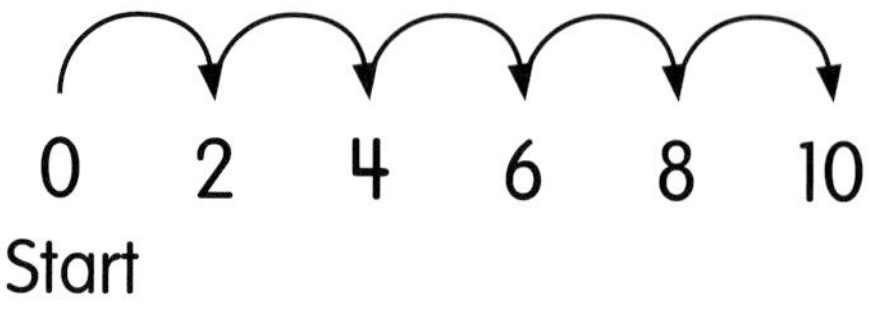

$7 \times 10 = 70$

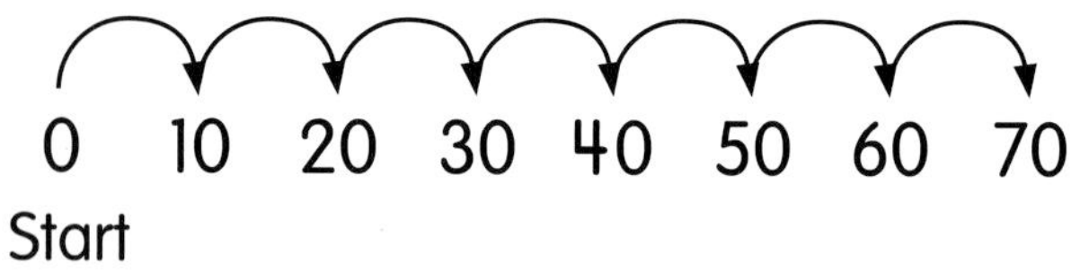

Multiplying using dot paper

$9 \times 5 = 45$

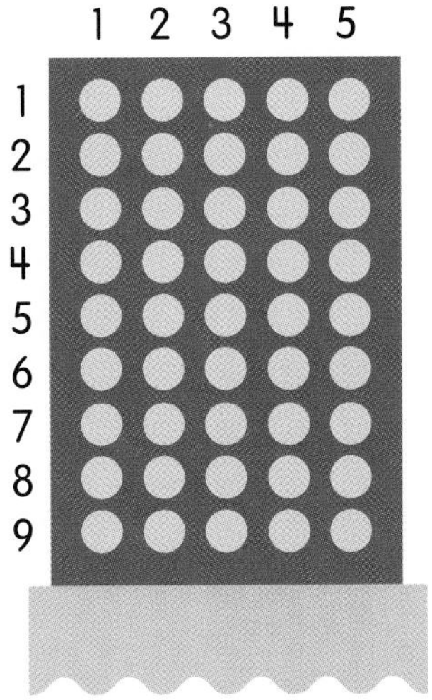

Multiplying in any order

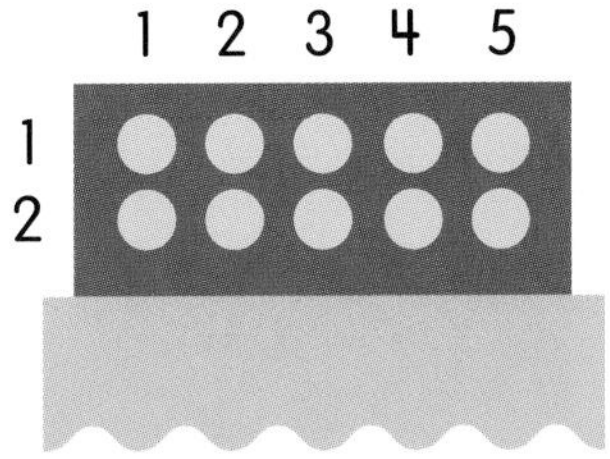

$2 \times 5 = 10$

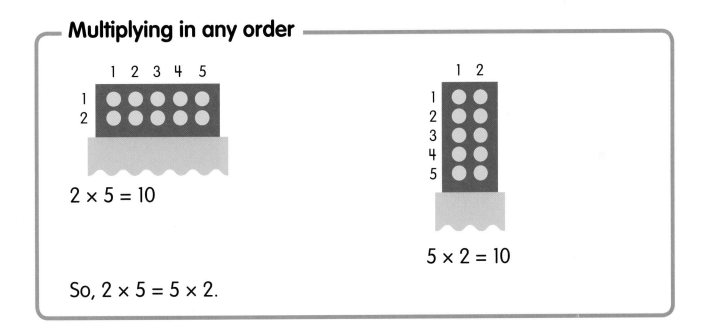

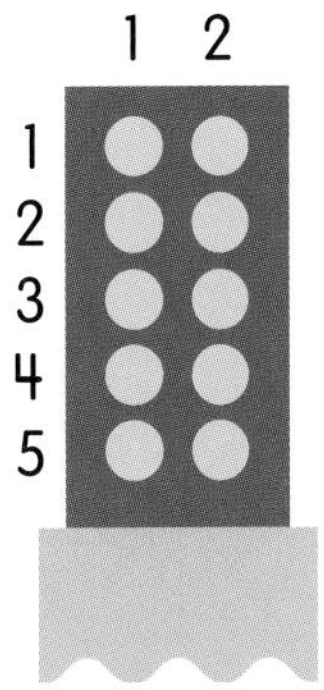

$5 \times 2 = 10$

So, $2 \times 5 = 5 \times 2$.

Using multiplication facts you know to find other multiplication facts

$8 \times 2 = 16$

Start with 10 groups of 2.

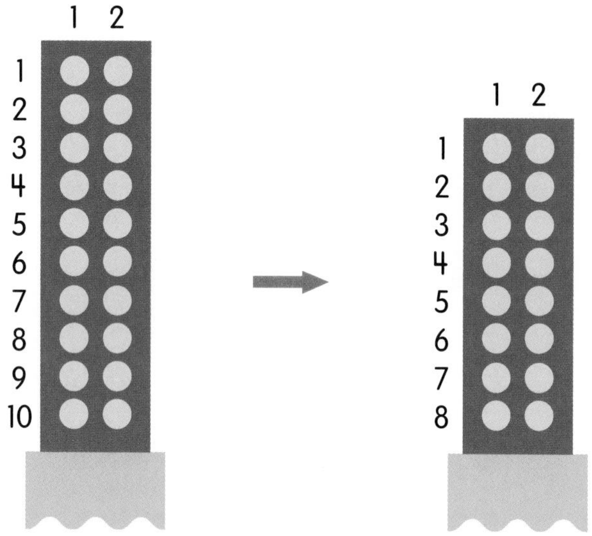

$10 \times 2 = 20$

$$\begin{aligned} 8 \times 2 &= 10 \text{ groups of } 2 - 2 \text{ groups of } 2 \\ &= 20 - 4 \\ &= 16 \end{aligned}$$

Relating multiplication to divison

$20 \div 2 = 10$

$10 \times 2 = 20$
So, $20 \div 2 = 10$.

$30 \div 5 = 6$

$6 \times 5 = 30$
So, $30 \div 5 = 6$.

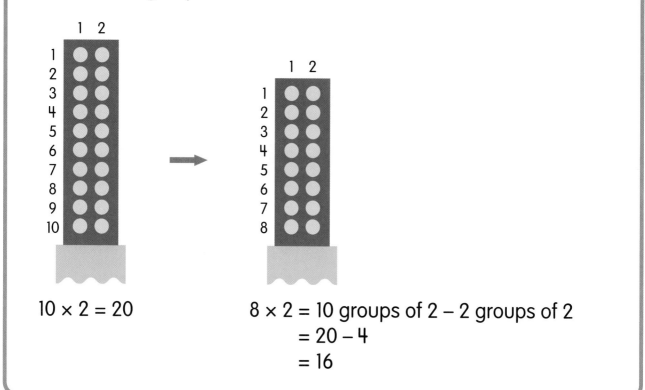

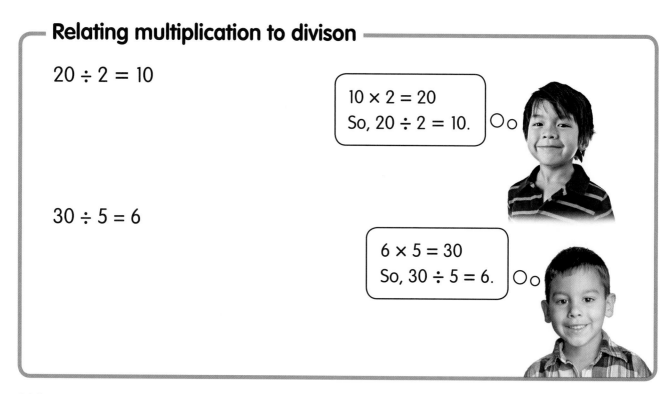

✔ Quick Check

Find the missing numbers.

1. ___, ___, 15, 20, ___, ___, 35, 40, ___, 50

2. 10, 20, 30, 40, ___, ___, ___, ___, ___, 100

Fill in the missing numbers.

3. 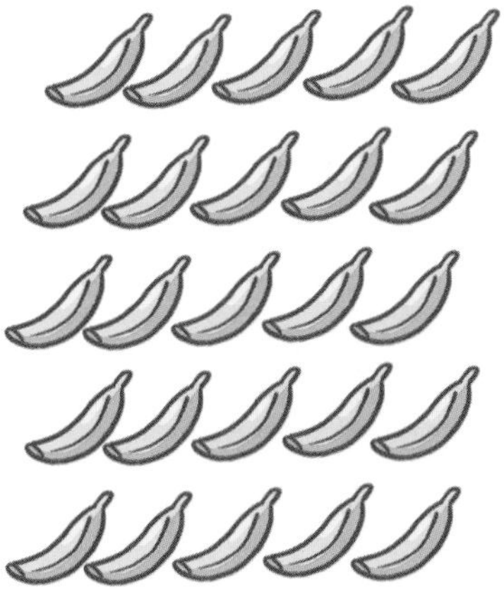

___ fives = ___ groups of ___

4. 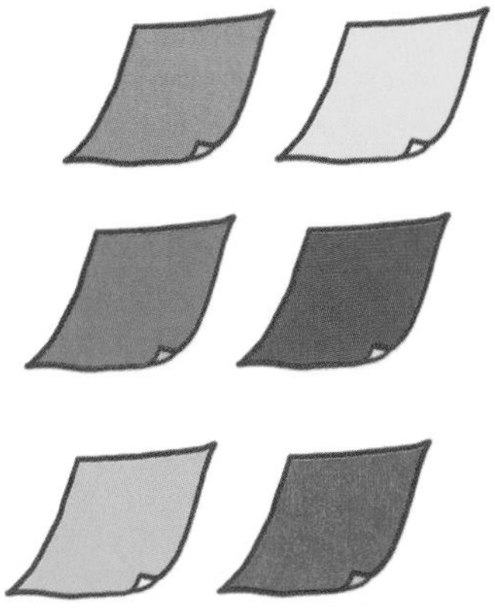

___ twos = ___ groups of ___

Use skip-counting to find the missing numbers.

5. $6 \times 2 =$ ___

6. $7 \times 5 =$ ___

7. $7 \times 10 =$ ___

Use dot paper to find the missing numbers.

8. ___ $\times$ ___ $= 30$ ___ $\times$ ___ $= 35$

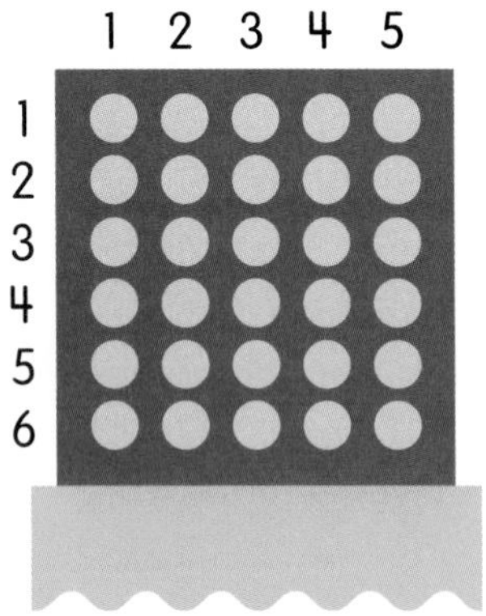

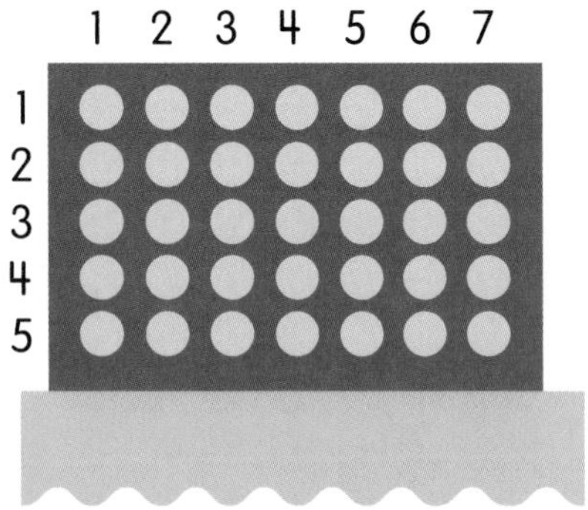

Use dot paper to help you find the missing numbers.

9. $7 \times 2 =$ ___

   $2 \times 7 =$ ___

10. $8 \times 5 =$ ___

    $5 \times 8 =$ ___

Find the missing numbers.

11. $5 \times 2 =$ ___

$7 \times 2 =$ ___ $+ 4 =$ ___

$8 \times 2 =$ ___ $+ 6 =$ ___

12. $10 \times 5 =$ ___

$9 \times 5 =$ ___ $- 5 =$ ___

$8 \times 5 =$ ___ $- 10 =$ ___

Find the missing numbers.

13. $14 \div 2 =$ ___ . . . . . ___ $\times 2 = 14$

14. $50 \div 5 =$ ___ . . . . . ___ $\times 5 = 50$

Solve.

15. A baker has 50 muffins.
He packs them equally in 5 boxes.
How many muffins are in each box? ___

16. Jamal has 18 stickers.
He gives 2 stickers to each of his friends.
How many of his friends get stickers? ___

17. A day camp has 8 groups.
Each group gets 5 paint sets.
How many paint sets are there in all? ___

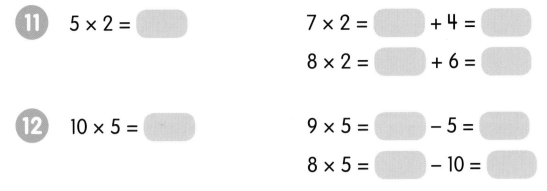

LESSON 1 Multiplying 3: Skip-counting

Lesson Objectives

- Skip-count by 3s.
- Solve multiplication word problems.

Vocabulary
skip-count

Learn

You can skip-count by 3s to find how many there are.

There are 3 marbles in a bag.

1 group of 3 marbles

$1 \times 3 = 3$

How many marbles are in 10 bags?

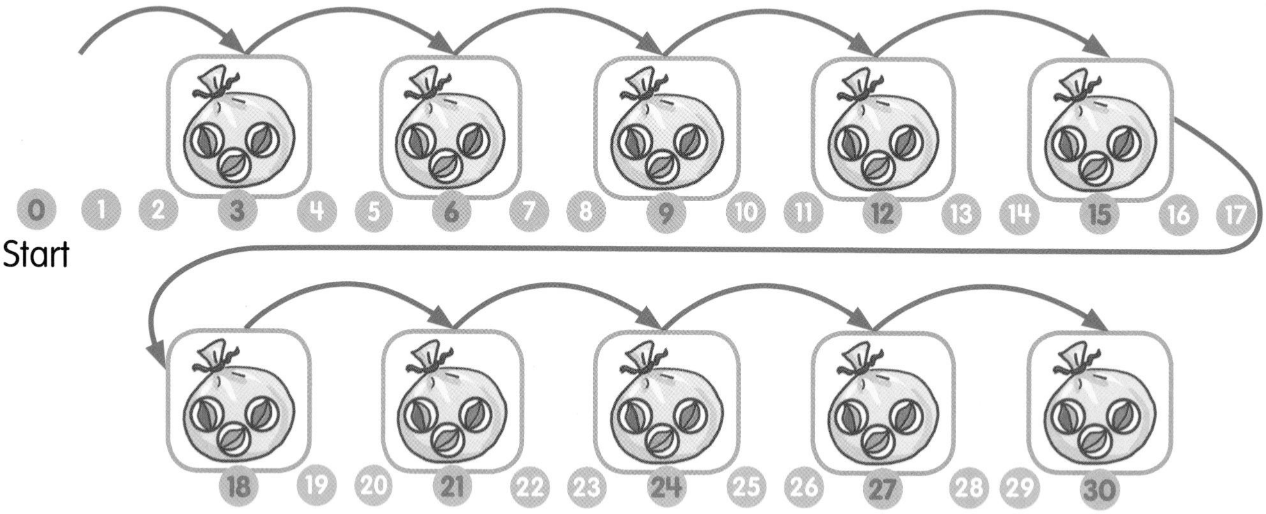

3, 6, 9, 12, 15, 18, 21, 24, 27, 30

$10 \times 3 = 30$

There are 30 marbles in 10 bags.

I count by 3s.

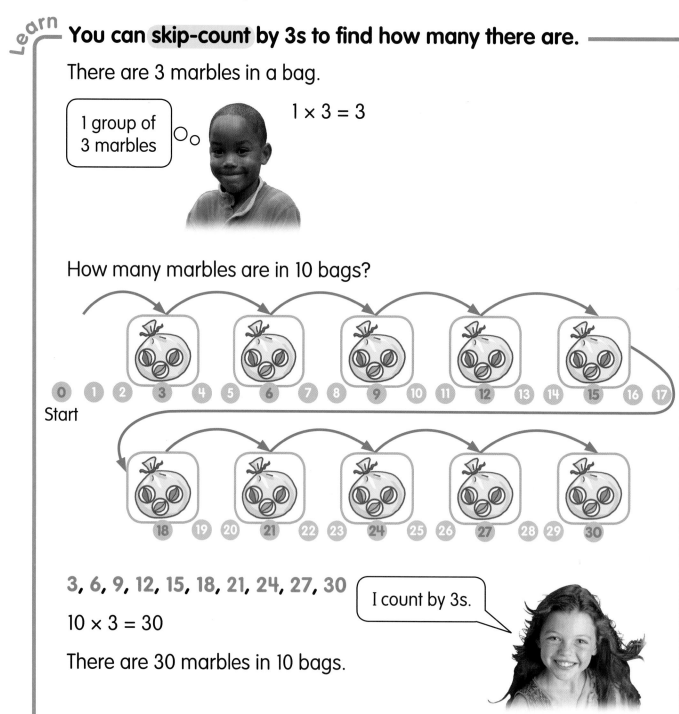

Here are 4 bowls.
3 potatoes are in each bowl.
How many potatoes are there in all?

4 groups of 3 potatoes
4 × 3 = ?

I count by 3s.
3, 6, 9, 12

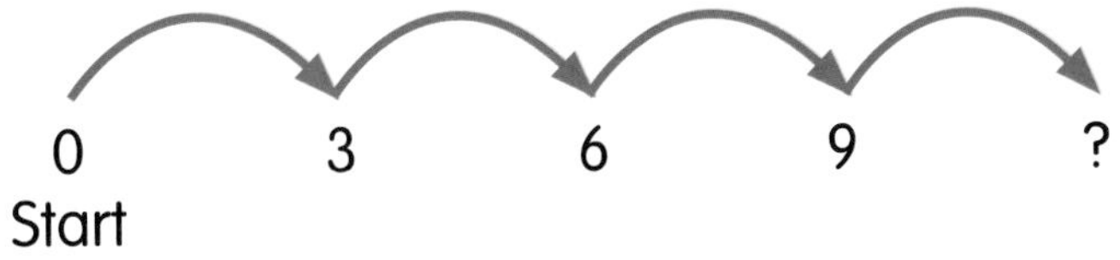

There are 12 potatoes in all.

Guided Practice

Use skip-counting to find the missing numbers.

1 A sticker album has 8 pages.
There are 3 stickers on each page.
How many stickers are there in all?

___ × ___ = ___

There are ___ stickers in all.

I count by 3s.
3, ___, ___, ___, ___, ___, ___, ___

8 groups of 3 stickers

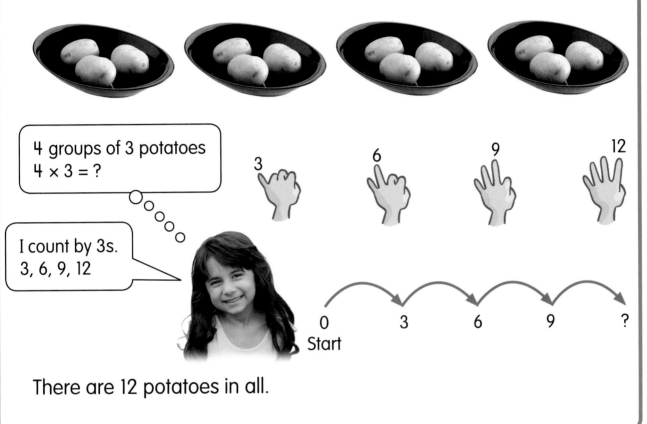

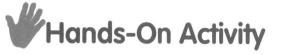

Hands-On Activity

Look at your copy of the Number Wheel.

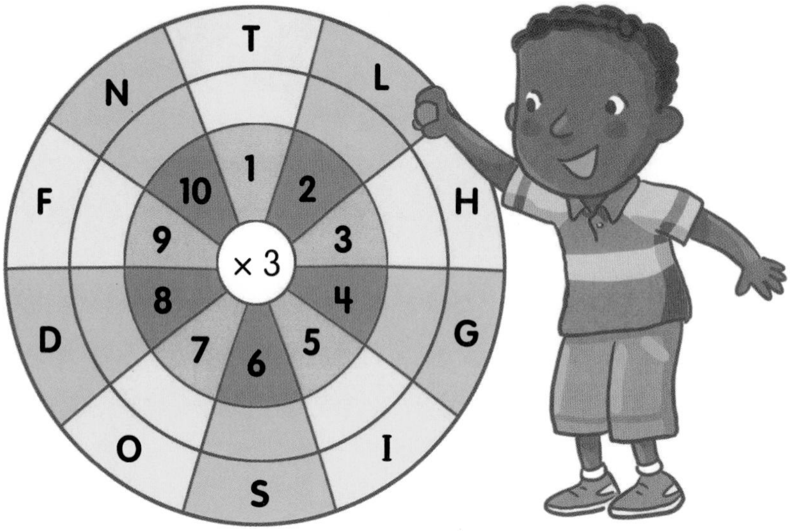

Fill in the empty spaces on the wheel.
First, find each missing number.

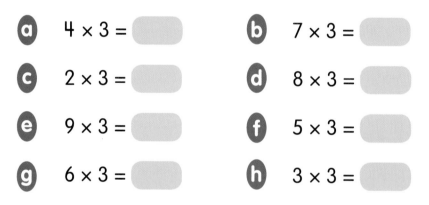

(a) $4 \times 3 =$ ____ (b) $7 \times 3 =$ ____

(c) $2 \times 3 =$ ____ (d) $8 \times 3 =$ ____

(e) $9 \times 3 =$ ____ (f) $5 \times 3 =$ ____

(g) $6 \times 3 =$ ____ (h) $3 \times 3 =$ ____

Then follow the directions to find out Jake's prize!
Match the letters on the wheel to your answers.
Then you will know the prize that Jake gets!

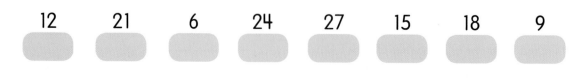

12	21	6	24	27	15	18	9

Let's Practice

Use skip-counting to find the missing numbers.

Example

$5 \times 3 = 15$

$3 \times 5 = 15$

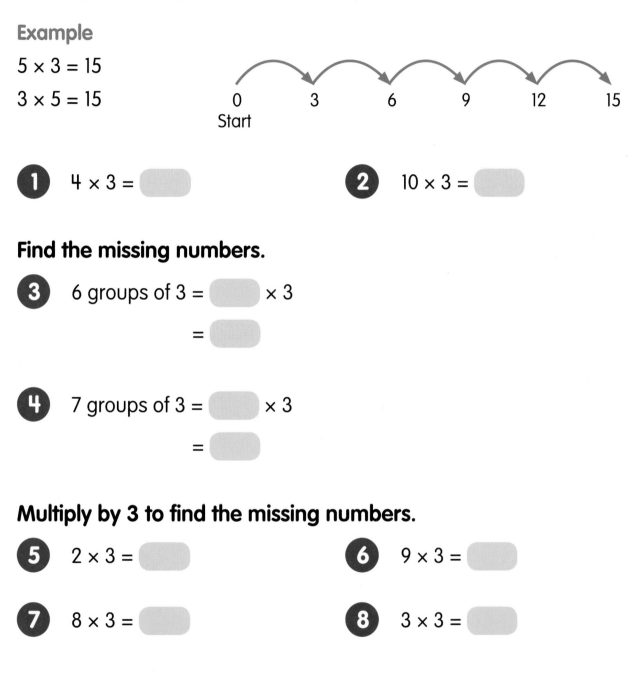

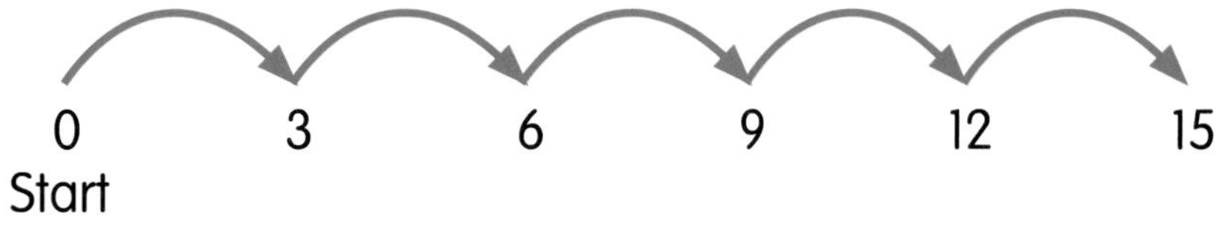

1 $4 \times 3 =$ ___

2 $10 \times 3 =$ ___

Find the missing numbers.

3 6 groups of 3 = ___ $\times$ 3

= ___

4 7 groups of 3 = ___ $\times$ 3

= ___

Multiply by 3 to find the missing numbers.

5 $2 \times 3 =$ ___

6 $9 \times 3 =$ ___

7 $8 \times 3 =$ ___

8 $3 \times 3 =$ ___

Solve.

9 There are 7 children in a painting class.
Each child has 3 paintbrushes.
How many paintbrushes are there in all?

ON YOUR OWN

**Go to Workbook B:
Practice 1, pages 133–134**

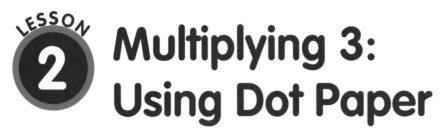

LESSON 2

Multiplying 3: Using Dot Paper

Lesson Objectives

- Use dot paper to multiply by 3.
- Use known multiplication facts to find new multiplication facts.
- Identify related multiplication facts.
- Solve multiplication word problems.

Vocabulary
dot paper
related multiplication facts

Learn

You can use dot paper to multiply by 3.

There are 4 hens.
Each hen lays 3 eggs.
How many eggs do they lay in all?

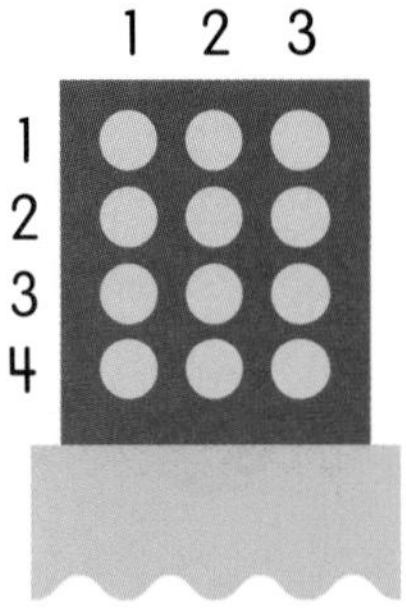

$4 \times 3 = 12$

They lay 12 eggs in all.

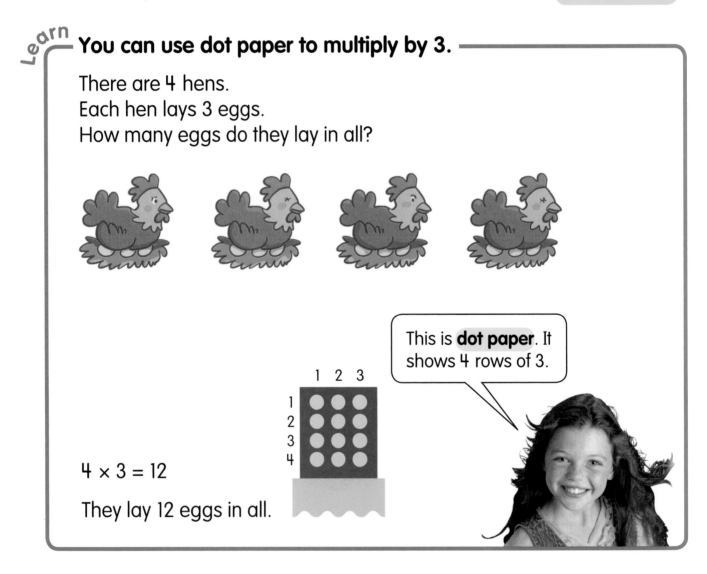

This is **dot paper**. It shows 4 rows of 3.

Guided Practice

1 A baker puts 3 loaves of bread into 1 bag.
How many loaves are in 5 bags?

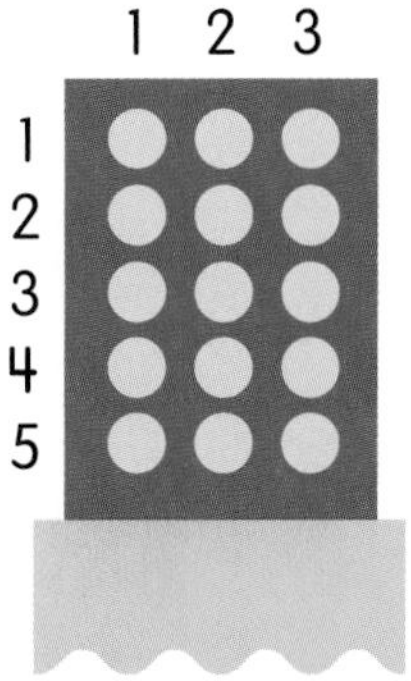

$5 \times 3 =$ ____

There are ____ loaves in 5 bags.

Learn **You can use multiplication facts you know to find other multiplication facts.**

$6 \times 3 = ?$
Start with 5 groups of 3.

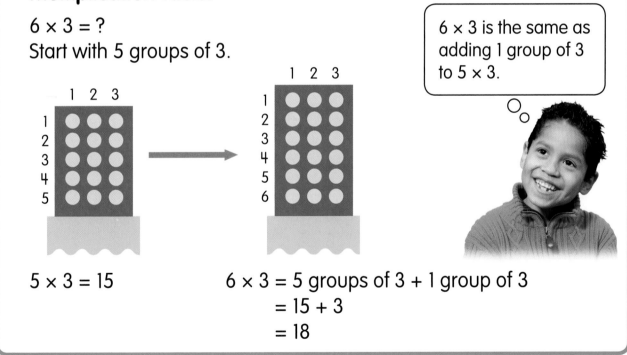

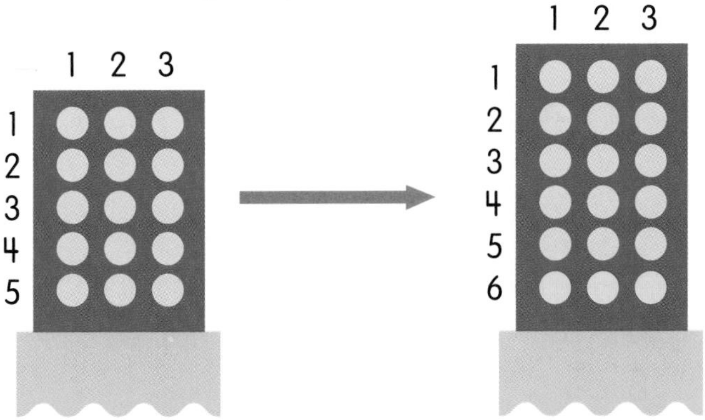

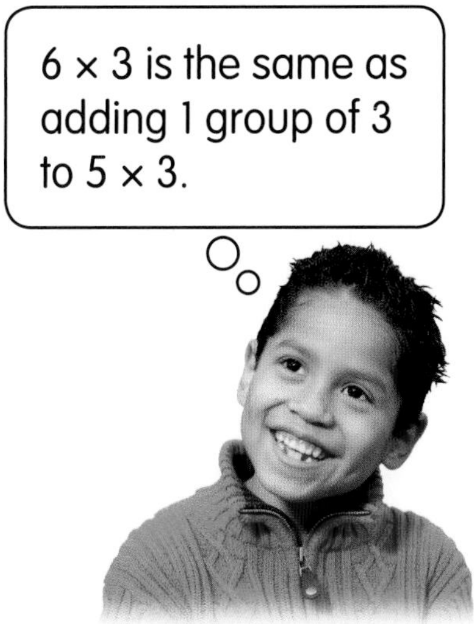

6 × 3 is the same as adding 1 group of 3 to 5 × 3.

$5 \times 3 = 15$

$6 \times 3 = 5 \text{ groups of } 3 + 1 \text{ group of } 3$
$= 15 + 3$
$= 18$

Guided Practice

Use facts you know to find the missing numbers.

2 $8 \times 3 = ?$

Start with 10 groups of 3.

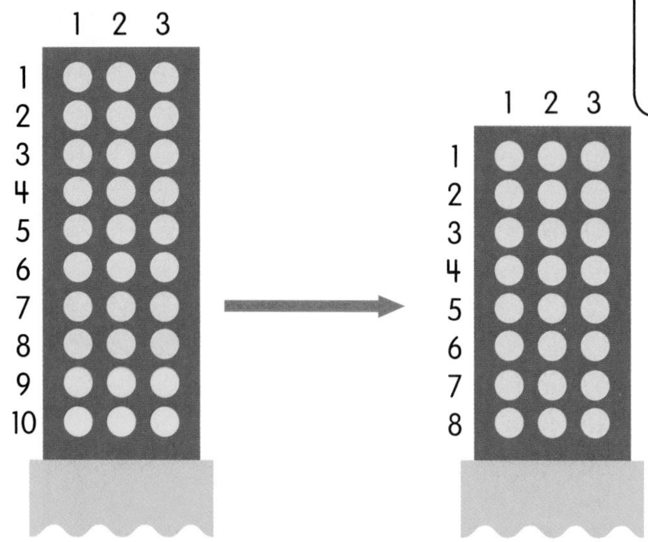

8 × 3 is the same as subtracting ____ groups of 3 from 10 × 3.

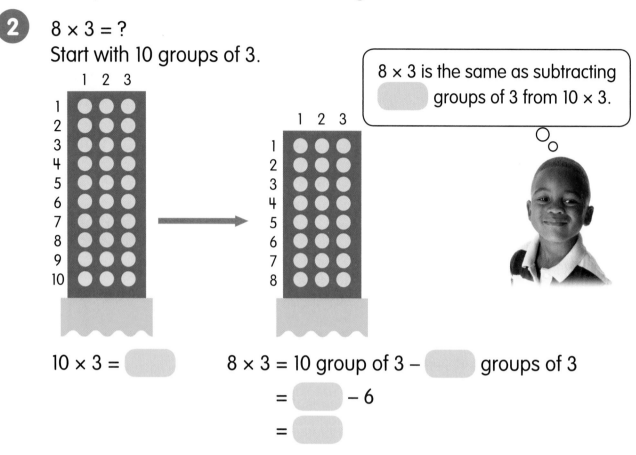

$10 \times 3 =$ ____

$8 \times 3 =$ 10 group of 3 – ____ groups of 3

$=$ ____ $- 6$

$=$ ____

Multiplication Table of 3

1	×	3	=	3
2	×	3	=	6
3	×	3	=	9
4	×	3	=	12
5	×	3	=	15
6	×	3	=	18
7	×	3	=	21
8	×	3	=	24
9	×	3	=	27
10	×	3	=	30

Learn

You can multiply numbers in any order.

4 × 3 = 12

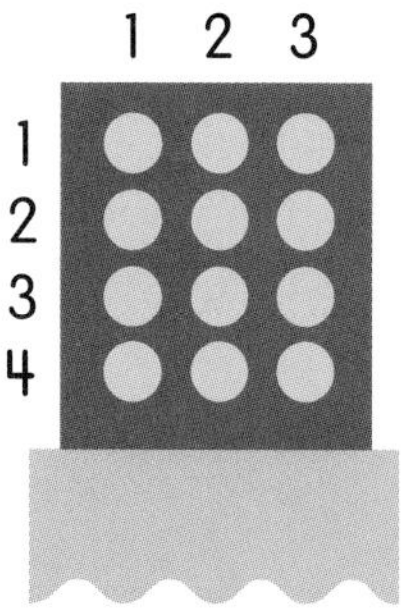

3 × 4 = 12

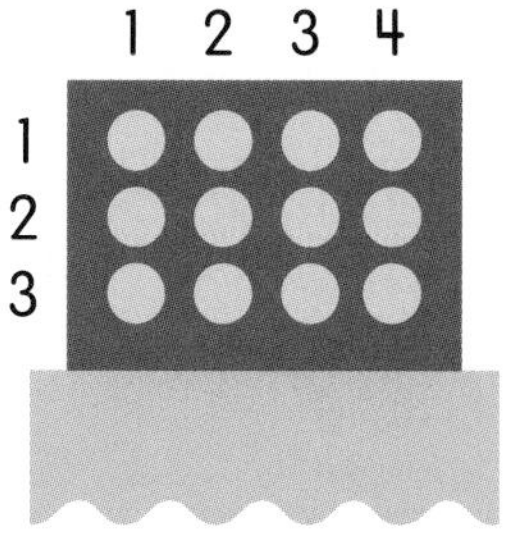

4 × 3 = 3 × 4
These are **related multiplication facts**.

Guided Practice

Use dot paper to find the missing numbers.

3 ___ × ___ = 21

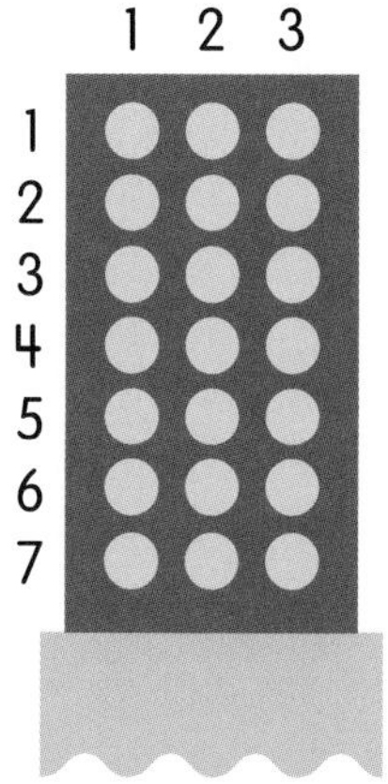

___ × ___ = 21

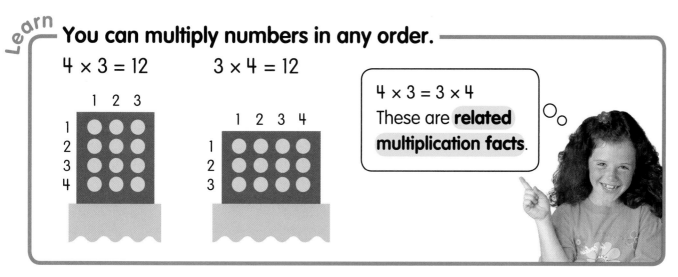

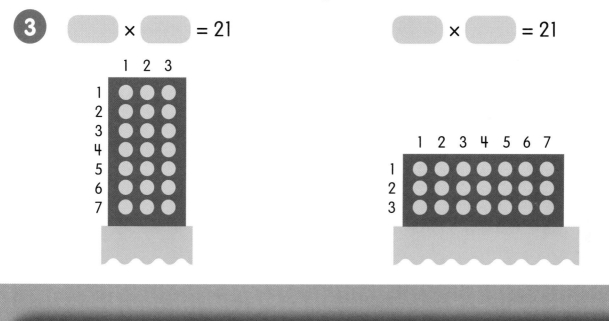

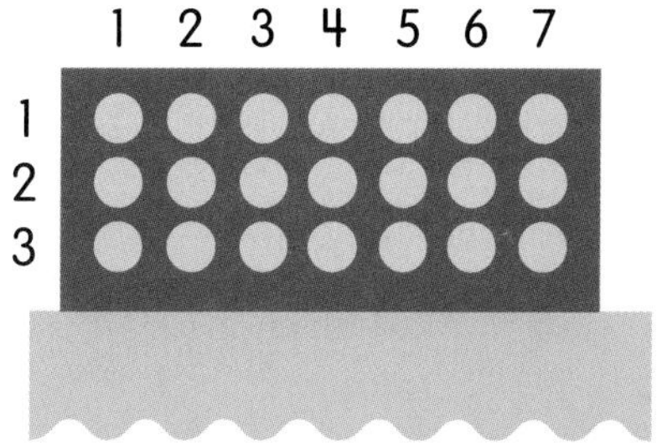

Let's Explore!

WORKING TOGETHER

Multiply.
Then find other ways to find the same answer.

1 3 × 6

2 9 × 3

Let's Practice

Find the missing numbers.

1 $5 \times 3 = \_\_\_$

$6 \times 3 = 5$ groups of 3 + ___ group of 3

$= \_\_\_ + 3$

$= \_\_\_$

$7 \times 3 = 5$ groups of 3 + ___ groups of 3

$= \_\_\_ + \_\_\_$

$= \_\_\_$

2 $10 \times 3 = \_\_\_$

$9 \times 3 = 10$ groups of 3 – ___ group of 3

$= \_\_\_ - 3$

$= \_\_\_$

$8 \times 3 = 10$ groups of 3 – ___ groups of 3

$= \_\_\_ - \_\_\_$

$= \_\_\_$

Use dot paper to find the missing numbers.

3 $5 \times 3 = \_\_\_$

$3 \times 5 = \_\_\_$

4 $7 \times 3 = \_\_\_$

$3 \times 7 = \_\_\_$

5 $9 \times 3 = \_\_\_$

$3 \times 9 = \_\_\_$

6 $8 \times 3 = \_\_\_$

$3 \times 8 = \_\_\_$

ON YOUR OWN

Go to Workbook B: Practice 2, pages 135–140

LESSON 3 Multiplying 4: Skip-counting

Lesson Objectives

- Skip-count by 4s.
- Solve multiplication word problems.

Learn

You can skip-count by 4s to find how many there are.

4 clothes pins are in 1 group.

$2 \times 4 = 8$

How many clothes pins are in 10 groups?

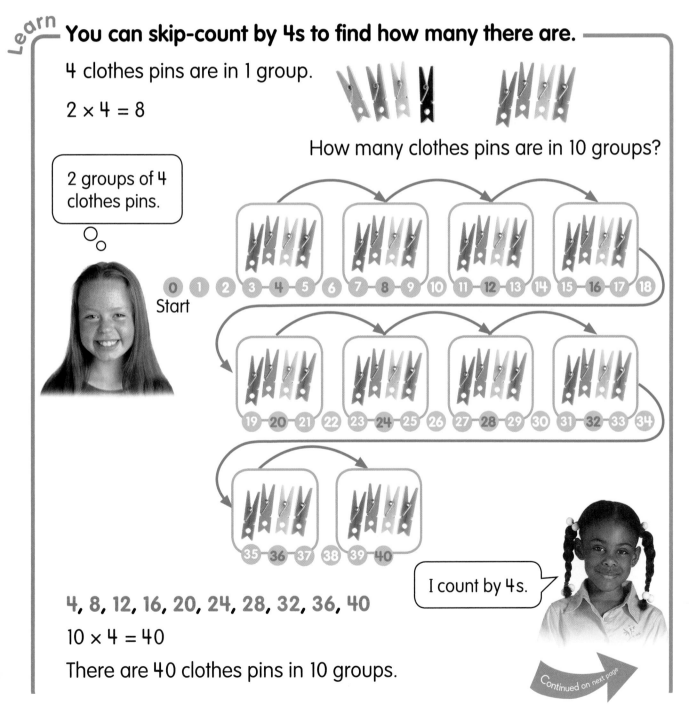

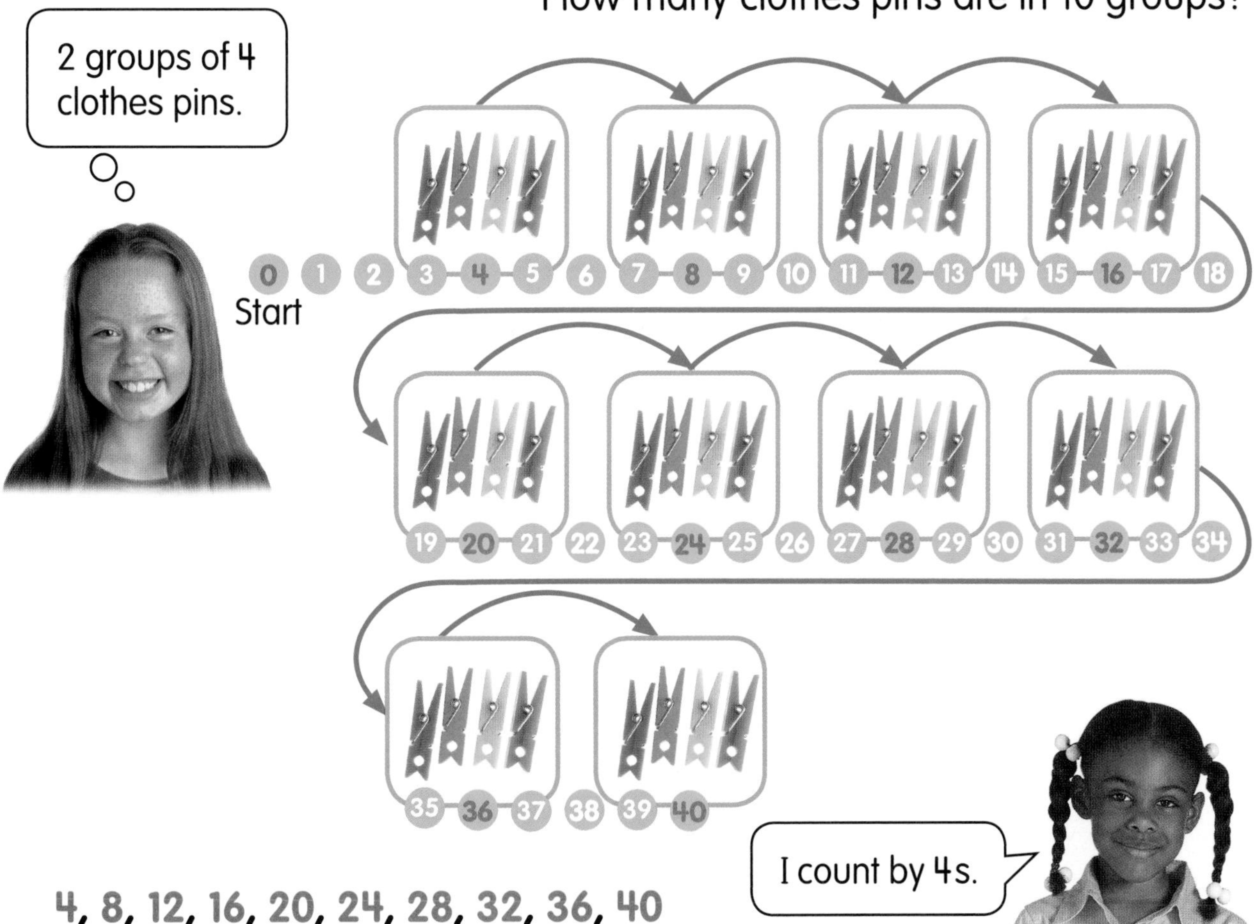

4, 8, 12, 16, 20, 24, 28, 32, 36, 40

$10 \times 4 = 40$

There are 40 clothes pins in 10 groups.

Continued on next page

There are 7 bags.
4 marbles are in each bag.
How many marbles are there in all?

7 groups of 4 marbles
$7 \times 4 = ?$

I count by 4s.
4, 8, 12, 16,
20, 24, 28

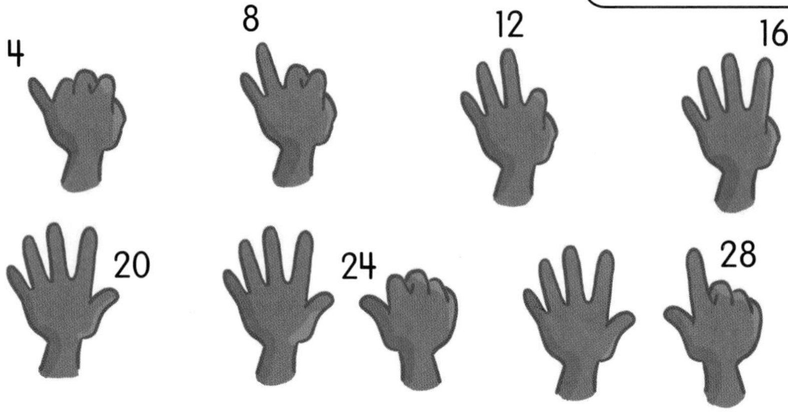

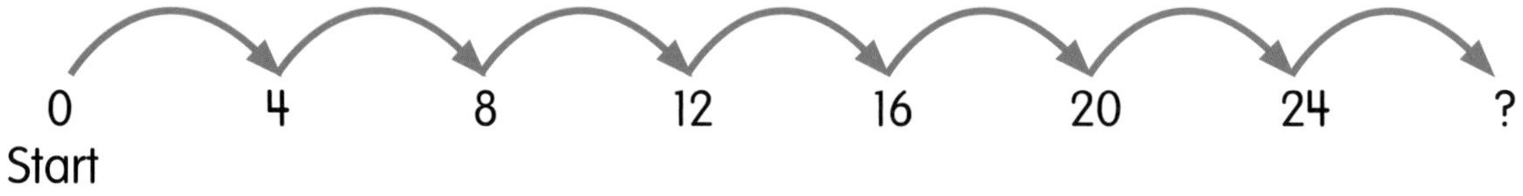

There are 28 marbles in all.

Guided Practice

Use skip-counting to find the missing numbers.

1 3 frogs are playing in a pond.
Each frog has 4 legs.
How many legs do the frogs have in all?

3 groups of 4 legs

I count in 4s.
4, ____, ____

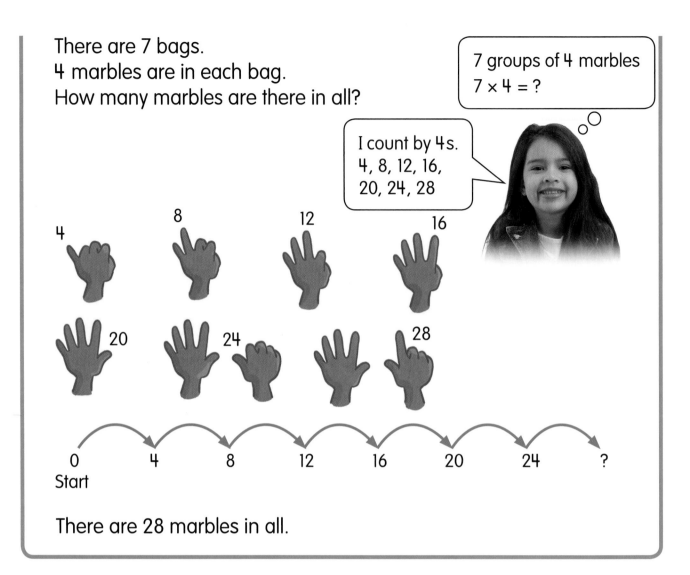

____ × ____ = ____

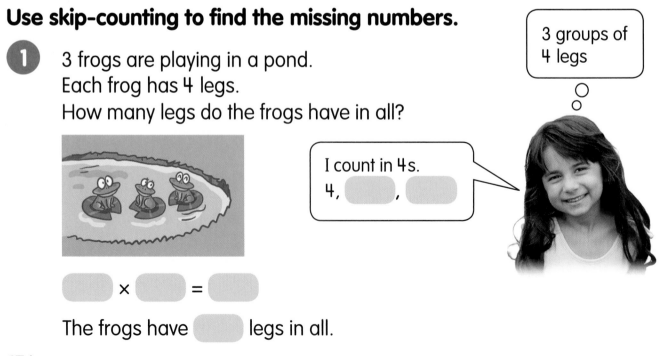

The frogs have ____ legs in all.

WORKING TOGETHER **Game**

Number Cube Game!

Players: 4–6
You need:
- Rocket Ship recording sheet
- number cards from 2–9
- blank number cubes
- number stickers

STEP 1 Write these numbers on the stickers. Paste them on the number cube.

2	3	4	2	3	4

STEP 2 Put the number cards in a stack. Each player uses a Rocket Ship recording sheet.

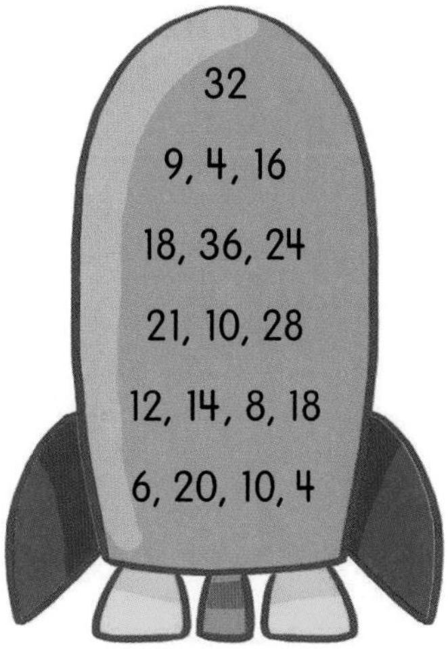

STEP 3 Player 1 rolls the number cube and draws a number card.

STEP 4 Player 1 multiplies the two numbers. The other players check the answer.

STEP 5 If Player 1 gives the correct answer, he or she circles the number on the rocket. If not, Player 1 loses his or her turn.

Players take turns.

The first player to circle 5 numbers on the rocket wins!

Let's Practice

Find the missing numbers.

1. 3 groups of 4 = ___ × 4
   = ___

2. 5 groups of 4 = ___ × ___
   = ___

3. 6 groups of 4 = ___ × ___
   = ___

4. 9 groups of 4 = ___ × ___
   = ___

Multiply by 4 to find the missing numbers.

5. 2 × 4 = ___

6. 4 × 4 = ___

7. 7 × 4 = ___

8. 8 × 4 = ___

Solve.

9. Tom has 8 packs of trading cards.
   There are 4 cards in each pack.
   How many cards does Tom have?

10. The Jones family has 5 rabbits.
    Each rabbit has 4 carrots.
    How many carrots do the rabbits have in all?

ON YOUR OWN

Go to Workbook B:
Practice 3, pages 141–142

LESSON 4 Multiplying 4: Using Dot Paper

Lesson Objectives

- Use dot paper to multiply by 4.
- Use known multiplication facts to find new multiplication facts.
- Identify related multiplication facts.
- Solve multiplication word problems.

Learn — You can use dot paper to multiply by 4.

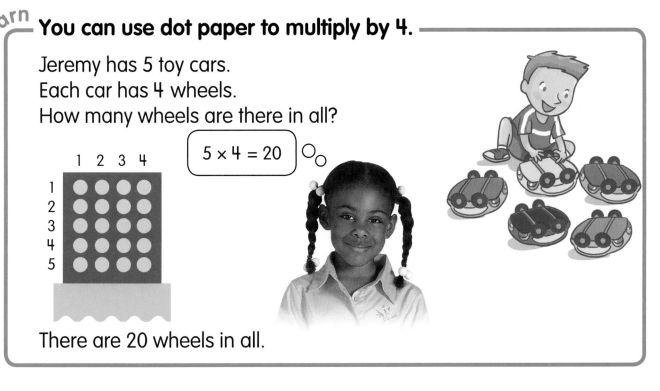

Jeremy has 5 toy cars.
Each car has 4 wheels.
How many wheels are there in all?

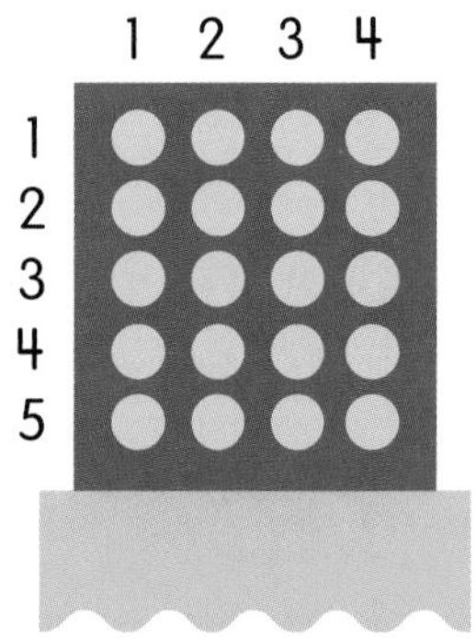

$5 \times 4 = 20$

There are 20 wheels in all.

Guided Practice

Use dot paper to find the missing numbers.

1. Miguel has 9 photos.
He puts a piece of tape at the 4 corners of each photo.
How many pieces of tape does Miguel use?

$9 \times 4 = $ ____

Miguel uses ____ pieces of tape.

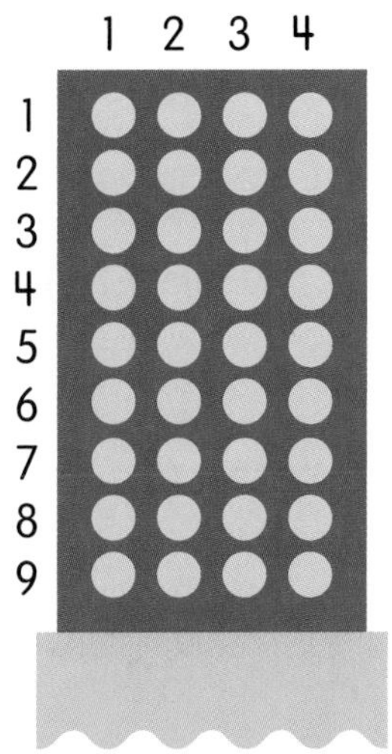

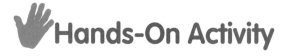

Hands-On Activity

Wheel of Numbers

Amy uses this number wheel to solve riddles.

Complete each multiplication sentence.
Then help Amy find the answer for each letter on the wheel.

a. 6 × 4 = ____

b. 5 × 4 = ____

c. 3 × 4 = ____

d. 8 × 4 = ____

e. 9 × 4 = ____

f. 10 × 4 = ____

g. 4 × 4 = ____

h. 1 × 4 = ____

i. 2 × 4 = ____

j. 7 × 4 = ____

What are two words that tell about computers?
Find out by matching the letters on the wheel to the answers.

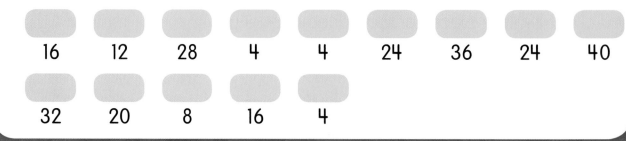

____	____	____	____	____	____	____	____	____
16	12	28	4	4	24	36	24	40
____	____	____	____	____				
32	20	8	16	4				

Learn

You can use multiplication facts you know to find other multiplication facts.

$6 \times 4 = ?$
Start with 5 groups of 4.

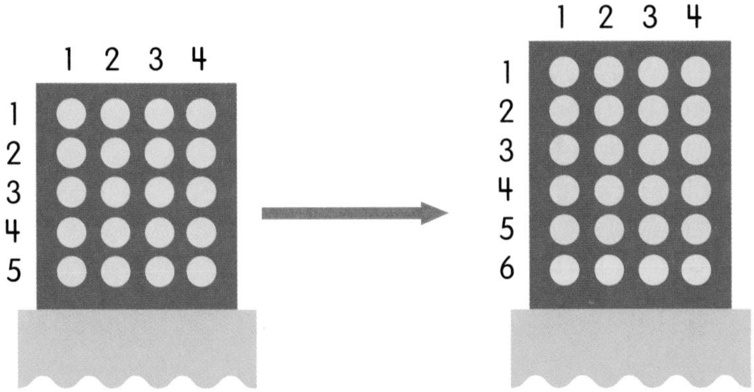

6 × 4 is the same as adding 1 group of 4 to 5 × 4.

$5 \times 4 = 20$

$6 \times 4 = 5$ groups of $4 + 1$ group of 4
$= 20 + 4$
$= 24$

Guided Practice

Use facts you know to find the missing numbers.

2 $8 \times 4 = ?$
Start with 10 groups of 4.

8 × 4 is the same as subtracting ____ groups of 4 from 10 × 4.

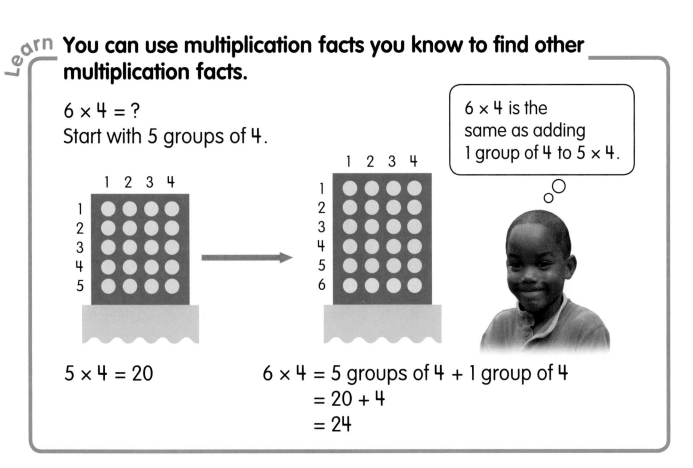

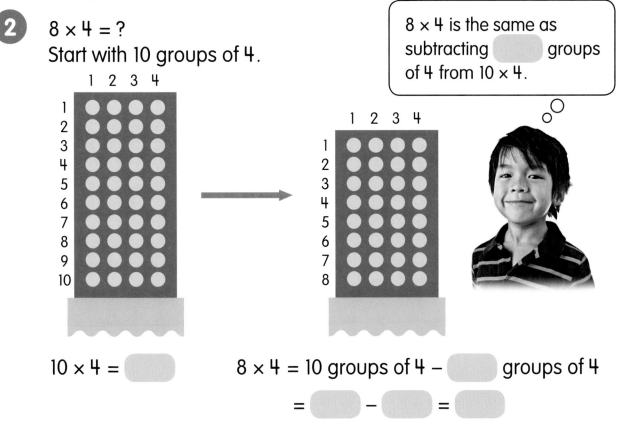

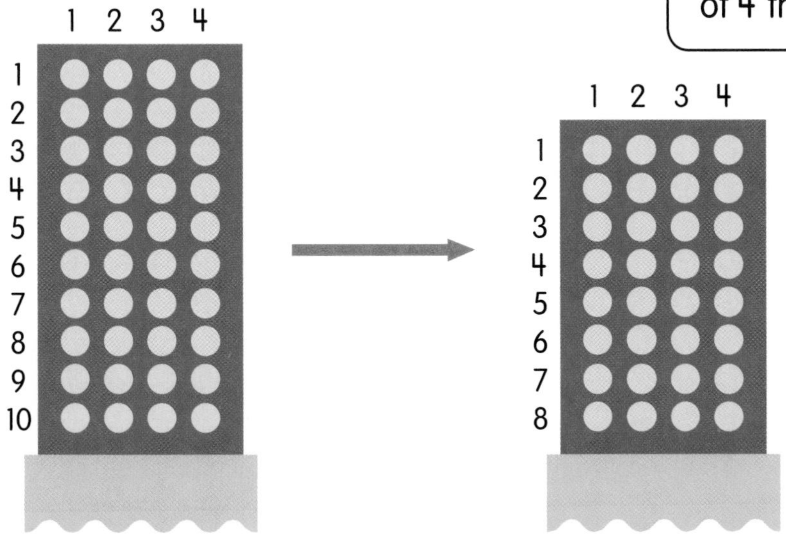

$10 \times 4 =$ ____

$8 \times 4 = 10$ groups of 4 − ____ groups of 4
= ____ − ____ = ____

Multiplication Table of 4

1	×	4	=	4
2	×	4	=	8
3	×	4	=	12
4	×	4	=	16
5	×	4	=	20
6	×	4	=	24
7	×	4	=	28
8	×	4	=	32
9	×	4	=	36
10	×	4	=	40

Learn

You can multiply numbers in any order.

2 × 4 = 8

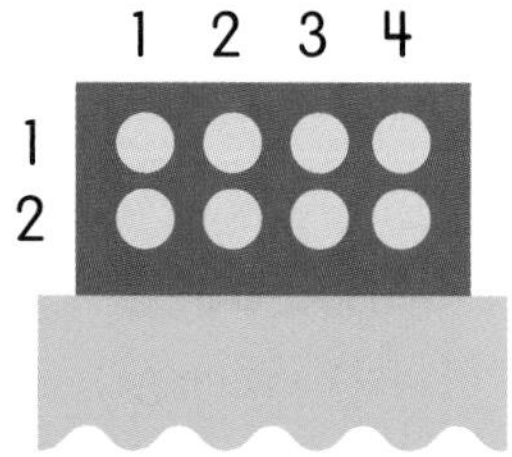

4 × 2 = 8

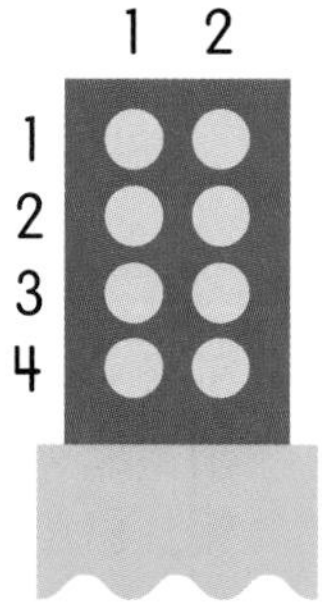

2 × 4 = 4 × 2
These are related multiplication facts.

Guided Practice

Use the dot paper to find the missing numbers.

3 ___ × ___ = 28

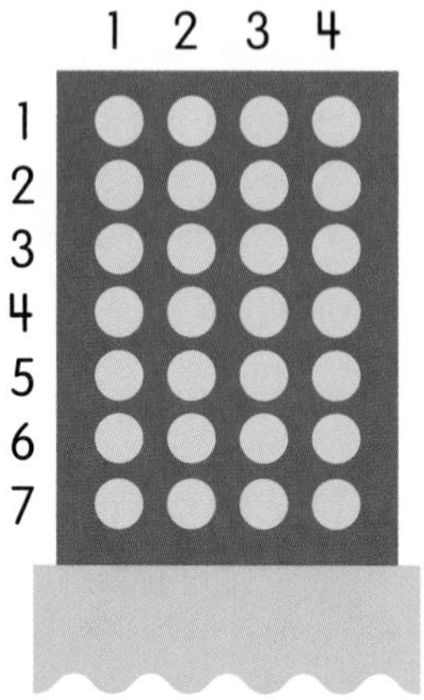

___ × ___ = 28

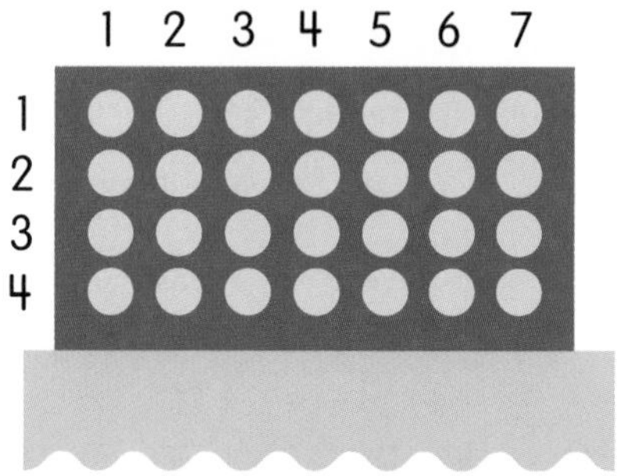

Let's Practice

Find the missing numbers.

1 $5 \times 4 =$ ____

$6 \times 4 =$ 5 groups of 4 + ____ group of 4

$=$ ____ $+ 4$

$=$ ____

$7 \times 4 =$ 5 groups of 4 + ____ groups of 4

$=$ ____ $+$ ____

$=$ ____

2 $10 \times 4 =$ ____

$9 \times 4 =$ 10 groups of 4 − ____ group of 4

$=$ ____ $- 4$

$=$ ____

$8 \times 4 =$ 10 groups of 4 − ____ groups of 4

$=$ ____ $-$ ____

$=$ ____

Use dot paper to find the missing numbers.

3 $3 \times 4 =$ ____

$4 \times 3 =$ ____

4 $6 \times 4 =$ ____

$4 \times 6 =$ ____

5 $5 \times 4 =$ ____

$4 \times 5 =$ ____

6 $8 \times 4 =$ ____

$4 \times 8 =$ ____

ON YOUR OWN

Go to Workbook B: Practice 4, pages 143–146

LESSON 5

Divide Using Related Multiplication Facts

Lesson Objectives:

- Find division facts using related multiplication facts.
- Write a multiplication sentence and a related division sentence.
- Solve division word problems.

Learn You can use related multiplication facts to divide when sharing equally.

Divide 12 spoons into 3 equal groups.
How many spoons are in each group?

$12 \div 3 = ?$

There are 4 spoons in each group.

$3 \times 4 = 12$
So, $12 \div 3 =$ ____.

Guided Practice

Find the missing numbers.
Use related multiplication facts to help you divide.

1. Divide 24 buttons into 4 equal groups.
How many buttons are in each group?

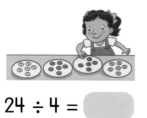

$24 \div 4 =$ ____

There are ____ buttons in each group.

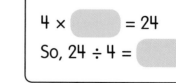

$4 \times$ ____ $= 24$
So, $24 \div 4 =$ ____.

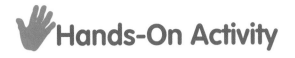

Hands-On Activity

Tell a division story.
Ask a classmate to use counters to **act out** the division story.
Then use counters to solve the division story.
Take turns telling division stories!

Learn

You can use related multiplication facts to divide when putting things in equal groups.

Divide 15 peanuts into equal groups.
There are 3 peanuts in each group.
How many groups are there?

$15 \div 3 = ?$

$5 \times 3 = 15$

So, $15 \div 3 = 5$.

There are 5 groups.

Guided Practice

Use related multiplication facts to find the missing numbers.

2 Divide 36 beads into equal groups.
There are 4 beads in each group.
How many groups are there?

$36 \div 4 = ?$

There are ____ groups.

Let's Explore!

Josh has fewer than 8 coloring books.
He puts them into groups.
This is what he finds.

First he puts 2 coloring books in each group.
No coloring books are left.

Then he puts 3 coloring books in each group.
No coloring books are left.

How many coloring books does Josh have?

WORKING TOGETHER **Game**

Number Game!

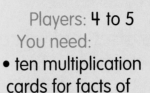

Players: 4 to 5
You need:
- ten multiplication cards for facts of 2, 3, 4, 5, and 10

STEP **1** Mix up the multiplication cards.
Player 1 draws a card.

STEP **2** The other players write one division sentence for the multiplication card drawn.

Example

Card $2 \times 4 = 8$ is drawn.

Players write

$8 \div 2 = 4$ or $8 \div 4 = 2$

STEP **3** Player 1 checks their answers.

STEP **4** Players take turns drawing a card.
Play until all the cards have been used.

The player with the greatest number of correct answers wins!

Let's Practice

Use related multiplication facts to find the missing numbers.

1. 18 ÷ 3 = ___

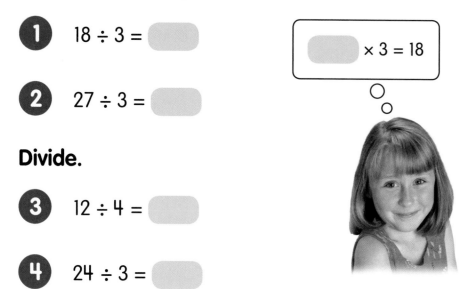

2. 27 ÷ 3 = ___

Divide.

3. 12 ÷ 4 = ___

4. 24 ÷ 3 = ___

Use related multiplication facts to find the missing numbers.

5. 3 x 4 = 12 4 x 3 = ___ 12 ÷ 3 = ___ 12 ÷ 4 = ___

6. 4 x 5 = 20 5 x 4 = ___ 20 ÷ 4 = ___ 20 ÷ 5 = ___

Find the missing numbers.
Then write three related number sentences.
Make one multiplication sentence and two division sentences.

7. 5 x 3 = 15
   ___ x ___ = 15
   15 ÷ ___ = ___
   15 ÷ ___ = 3

8. 2 x 4 = 8
   ___ x ___ = 8
   8 ÷ ___ = ___
   8 ÷ ___ = ___

Use related multiplication facts to solve.

9. Divide 15 children into 3 equal groups.
How many children are in each group?

10. Tonia puts 14 cards equally into 2 bags.
How many cards are in each bag?

11. Maureen and Yumi have 24 colored pencils.
They tie the colored pencils into bundles of 3.
How many bundles are there?

12. Diego has 30 marbles.
He puts 3 marbles into each jar.
How many jars are there?

13. Fran divides 24 stickers equally among 4 friends.
How many stickers does each friend get?

14. The art teacher shares 24 crayons equally
among her students.
Each student gets 4 crayons.
How many students are there?

ON YOUR OWN

Go to Workbook B:
Practice 5, pages 147–150

CRITICAL THINKING SKILLS
Put On Your Thinking Cap!

PROBLEM SOLVING

Linda starts reading a book from page 1.
She reads the same number of pages each day.
She stops at page 12 after 3 days.
How many pages does she read each day?

Use the diagram to help you.

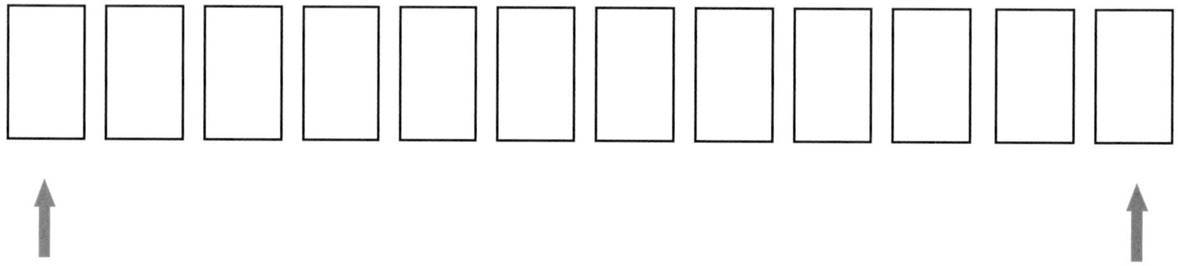

Page 1 Page 12

Use the diagram to help you.

ON YOUR OWN

Go to Workbook B: Put on Your Thinking Cap! pages 151–152

Chapter Wrap Up

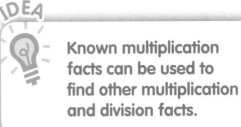

You have learned...

BIG IDEA

Known multiplication facts can be used to find other multiplication and division facts.

Multiplying 3 and 4 using:

Skip-counting

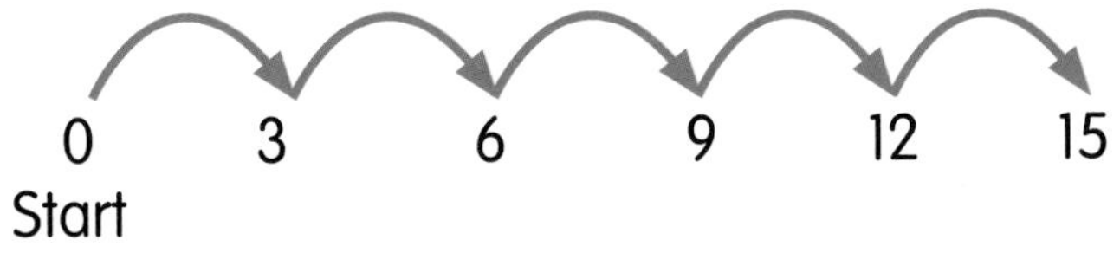

5 × 3 = 15

Dot paper

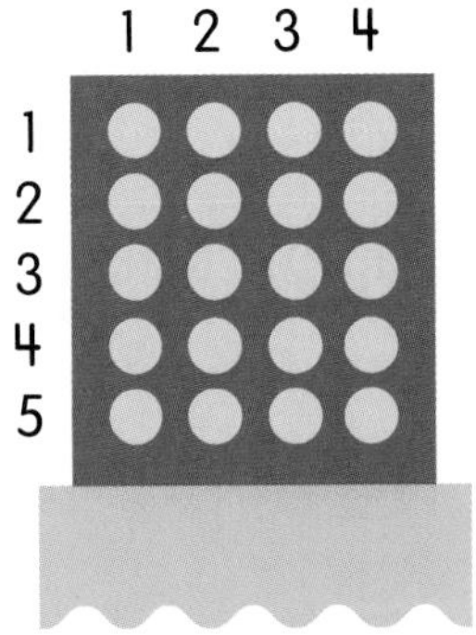

5 × 4 = 20

Multiplication tables of 3 and 4.

1	×	3	=	3
2	×	3	=	6
3	×	3	=	9
4	×	3	=	12
5	×	3	=	15
6	×	3	=	18
7	×	3	=	21
8	×	3	=	24
9	×	3	=	27
10	×	3	=	30

1	×	4	=	4
2	×	4	=	8
3	×	4	=	12
4	×	4	=	16
5	×	4	=	20
6	×	4	=	24
7	×	4	=	28
8	×	4	=	32
9	×	4	=	36
10	×	4	=	40

to multiply numbers in any order.

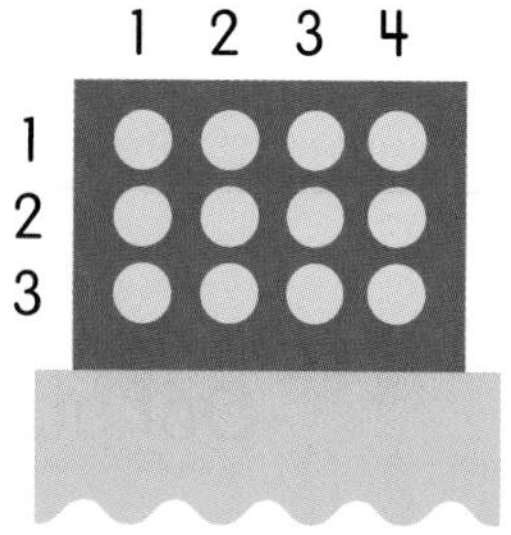

$3 \times 4 = 12$

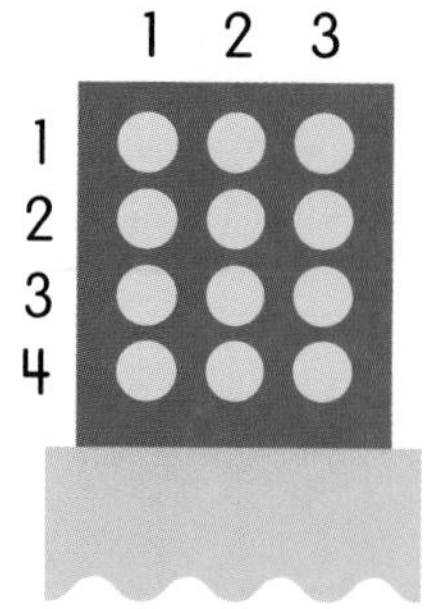

$4 \times 3 = 12$

to use multiplication facts you know to find new multiplication facts.

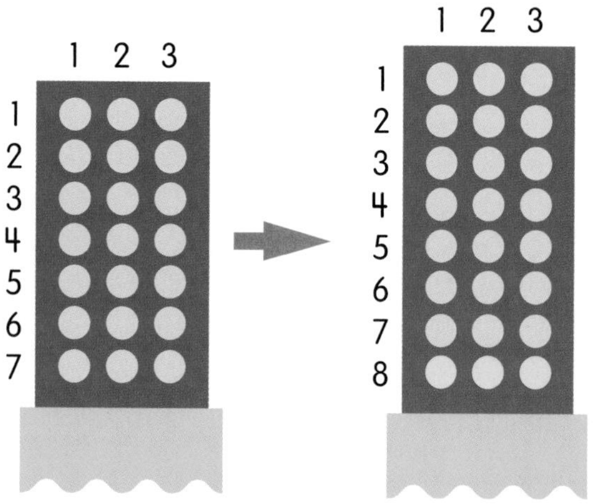

$7 \times 3 = 21$

$8 \times 3 = 7$ groups of 3
+ 1 group of 3
$= 21 + 3$
$= 24$

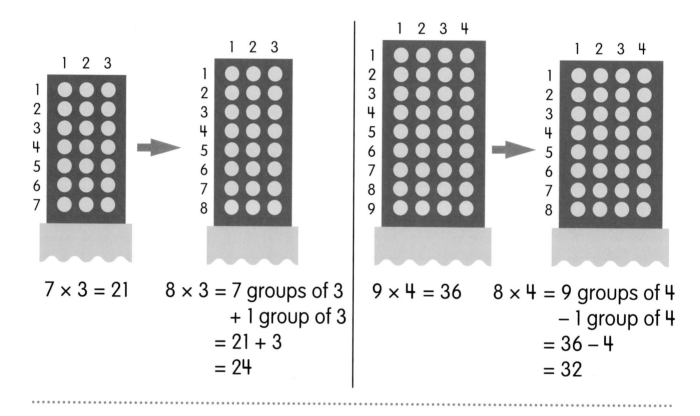

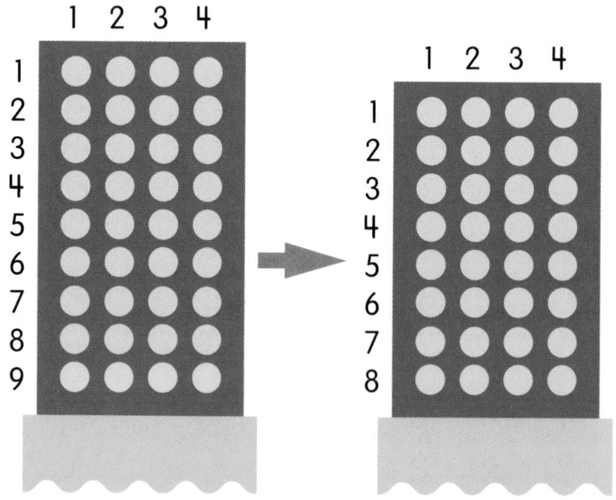

$9 \times 4 = 36$

$8 \times 4 = 9$ groups of 4
− 1 group of 4
$= 36 - 4$
$= 32$

to divide using a related multiplication fact.

$32 \div 4 = 8$

$8 \times 4 = 32$
So, $32 \div 4 = 8$

to write multiplication sentences and related division sentences.

$8 \times 3 = 24$	$7 \times 4 = 28$
$3 \times 8 = 24$	$4 \times 7 = 28$
So, $24 \div 3 = 8$	So, $28 \div 4 = 7$
$24 \div 8 = 3$	$28 \div 7 = 4$

to solve multiplication and division word problems.

There are 8 tables in the classroom.
Each table has 4 chairs.
How many chairs are there in all?

$8 \times 4 = 32$

There are 32 chairs in all.

Mrs. Dempsey divides 40 pieces of craft paper equally among her students.
She has 20 students.
How many pieces of craft paper does each student get?

$40 \div 20 = 2$

Each students gets 2 pieces of craft paper.

ON YOUR OWN

Go to Workbook B: Chapter Review/Test, pages 153–154

CHAPTER 16 Using Bar Models: Multiplication and Division

How much does each child's ticket cost?
The children's tickets cost $ 24.
TICKETS
?
$24

BIG IDEA

Bar models can be used to solve multiplication and division word problems.

Recall Prior Knowledge

Using equal groups and repeated addition to multiply

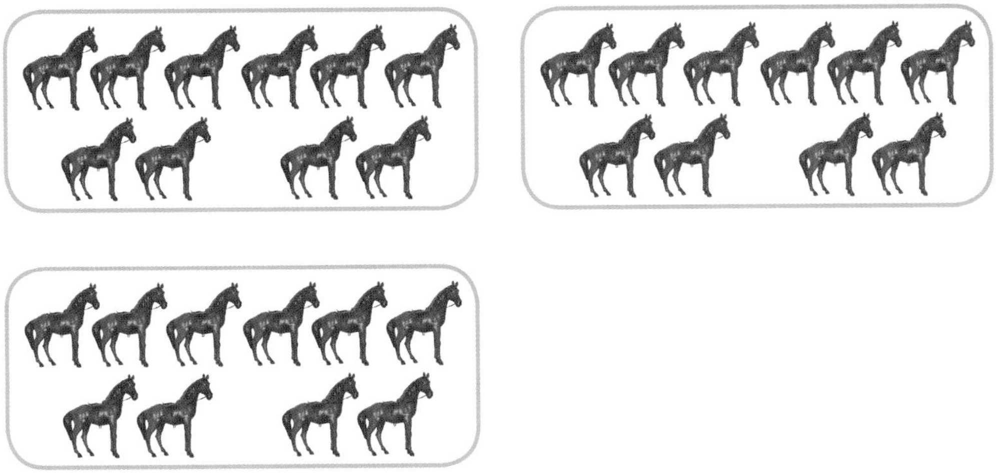

10 + 10 + 10 = 30
3 × 10 = 30

There are 30 horses in all.
3 × 10 = 30 is a **multiplication sentence**.

× is read as **times**.
It means to **multiply,** or to put all the equal groups together.

Sharing equally to divide

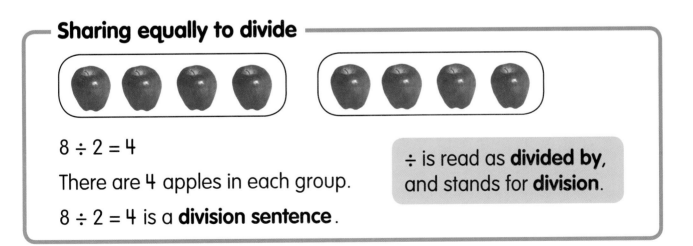

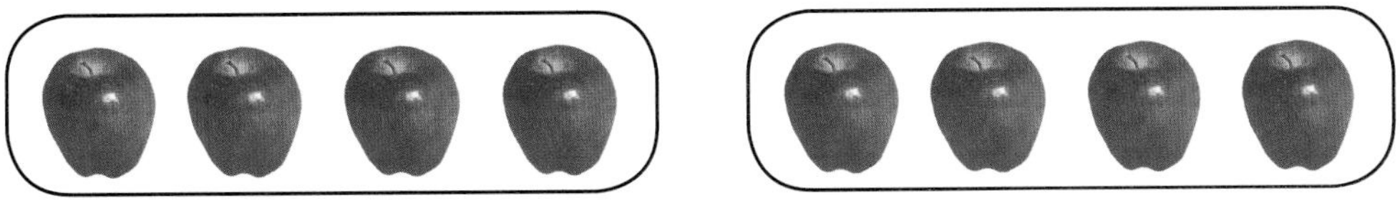

8 ÷ 2 = 4

There are 4 apples in each group.

8 ÷ 2 = 4 is a **division sentence**.

÷ is read as **divided by,** and stands for **division**.

Multiplying by 2, 3, 4, 5, and 10

$5 \times 2 = 10$ $6 \times 3 = 18$
$7 \times 4 = 28$ $8 \times 5 = 40$
$9 \times 10 = 90$

Multiplying in any order

$5 \times 2 = 10$ $7 \times 4 = 28$
$2 \times 5 = 10$ $4 \times 7 = 28$

Using related multiplication facts to divide

$18 \div 3 =$ ▭

$6 \times 3 = 18$
So, $18 \div 3 = 6$

$40 \div 5 =$ ▭

$8 \times 5 = 40$
So, $40 \div 5 = 8$

$90 \div 10 =$ ▭

$9 \times 10 = 90$
So, $90 \div 10 = 9$

✓Quick Check

Multiply.

1. $3 \times 4 =$ ___
2. $7 \times 5 =$ ___
3. $8 \times 10 =$ ___
4. $8 \times 3 =$ ___

Divide.
Use related multiplication facts to help you.

5. $15 \div 5 =$ ___
6. $21 \div 3 =$ ___
7. $16 \div 4 =$ ___
8. $18 \div 2 =$ ___

Solve.

9. Catherine has 7 vases.
She puts 2 flowers in each vase.
How many flowers does Catherine have in all?

10. Celeste has 24 cherries.
She gives 4 cherries to each of her friends.
How many friends does she have in all?

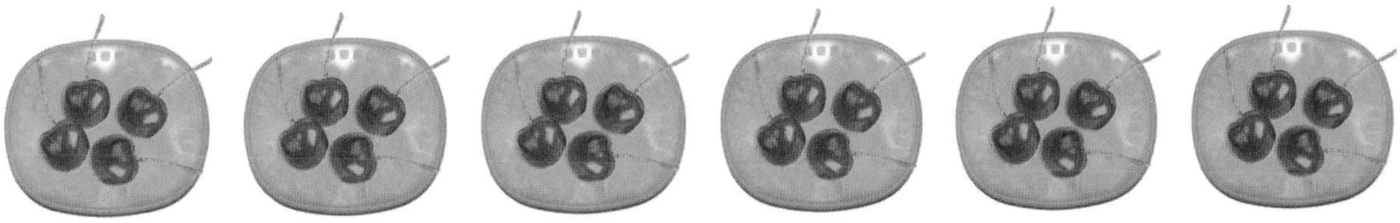

LESSON 1 Real-World Problems: Multiplication

Lesson Objectives

- Use bar models to solve real-world multiplication problems.
- Write multiplication sentences to solve real-world problems.

Learn **You can use bar models to solve multiplication word problems.**

5 crackers are in each bag.
There are 4 bags.
How many crackers are there in all?

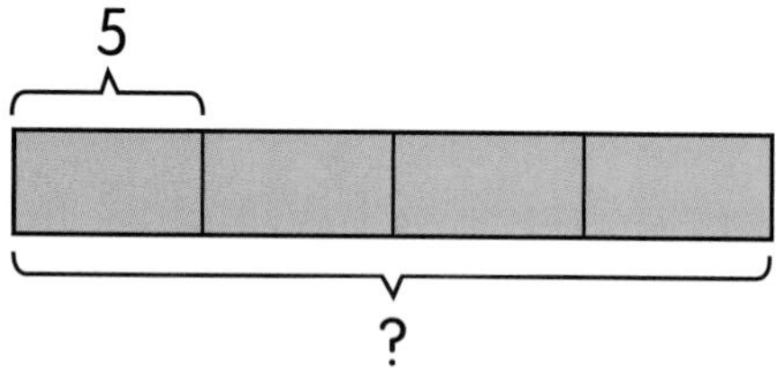

4 × 5 = 20

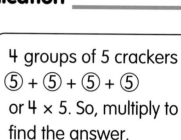

There are 20 crackers in all.

4 groups of 5 crackers
⑤ + ⑤ + ⑤ + ⑤
or 4 × 5. So, multiply to find the answer.

Guided Practice

Solve.
Use bar models to help you.

3 groups of 5 birds

1 There are 3 nests in a tree.
5 birds are in each nest.
How many birds are there in all?

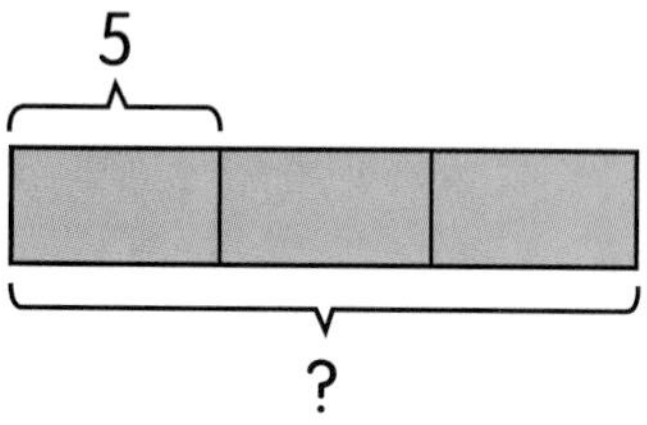

____ ○ ____ = ____

There are ____ birds in all.

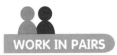

Hands-On Activity

WORK IN PAIRS

Use colored strips of paper.
Use the strips to make bar models.
Then solve the multiplication word problems.

Example

Trish has 4 plates of strawberries.
There are 3 strawberries on each plate.
How many strawberries are there in all?

STEP 1 Choose 4 colored strips of the same length to show 4 plates.
Glue them on a sheet of paper to make a bar model.

STEP 2 Label the bar model with the data in the word problem.
Write 3 above one strip to show 3 strawberries Show what has to be solved with a question mark (?).

STEP 3 Write the multiplication sentence to find the answer.
Then write the answer statement.
$4 \times 3 = 12$
There are 12 strawberries in all.

1. Jack and Megan each have 5 CDs.
How many CDs do they have in all?

2. The art teacher uses 10 shapes to make a poster.
She makes 4 posters.
How many shapes does the teacher use in all?

READING AND WRITING MATH

Math Journal

Use the bar model and the words to write a word problem. Then solve it.

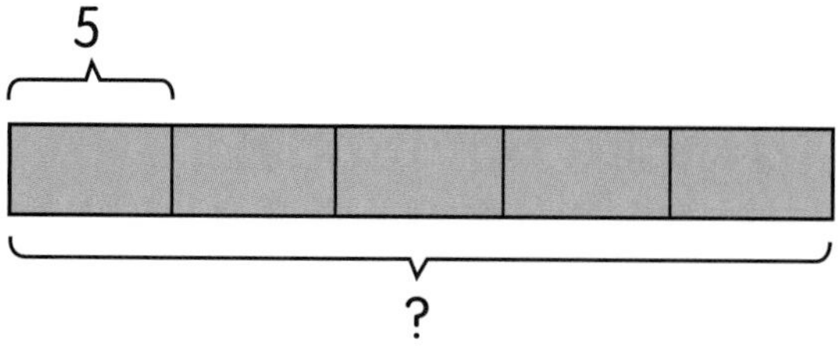

Sam | chicken | eggs | lay | many

Let's Practice

Show a bar model for each.

1. 2 groups of 4 puppies
2. 4 groups of 10 kittens

Draw 2 boxes and put the number 4 in each box.

Solve.
Draw bar models to help you.

3. Katy uses 10 beads to make a bracelet.
   She makes 5 bracelets.
   How many beads does she use?
4. Shannon reads 3 pages of her book each day.
   How many pages does she read in 5 days?
5. 5 glasses are on each tray.
   There are 5 trays.
   How many glasses are there in all?

ON YOUR OWN

Go to Workbook B: Practice 1, pages 155–160

LESSON 2 Real-World Problems: Division

Lesson Objectives

- Use bar models to solve division word problems.
- Write division sentences to solve word problems.

Learn You can use bar models to solve division word problems.

Barry buys 12 muffins.
He puts an equal number of muffins into 3 boxes.
How many muffins are in each box?

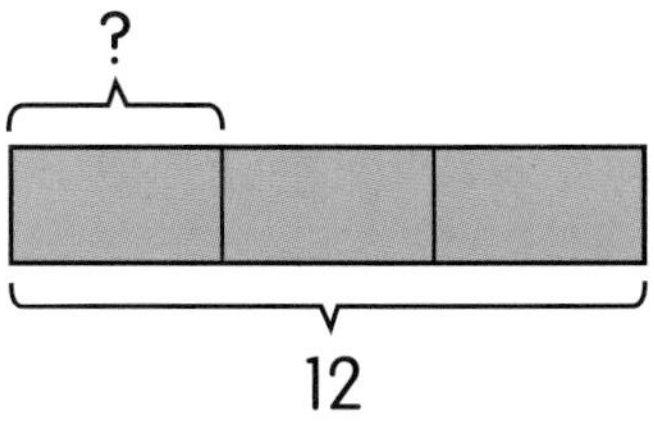

Use a related multiplication fact to divide.
$3 \times ? = 12$
$3 \times 4 = 12$

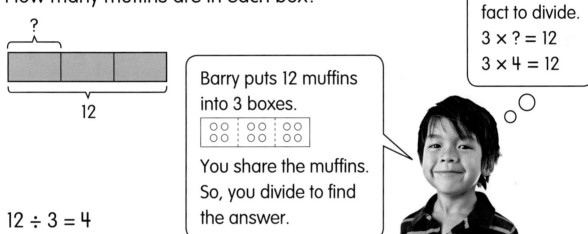

Barry puts 12 muffins into 3 boxes.

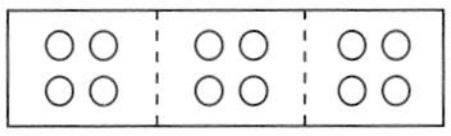

You share the muffins. So, you divide to find the answer.

$12 \div 3 = 4$

There are 4 muffins in each box.

Jason packs 15 shirts into boxes.
He puts 3 shirts in each box.
How many boxes does Jason use?

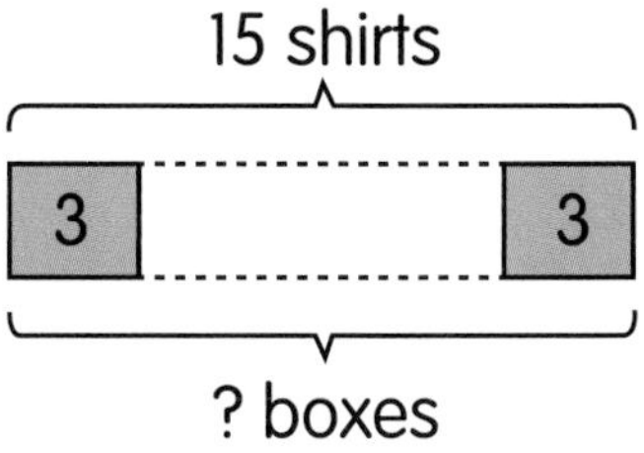

$15 \div 3 = 5$

Jason uses 5 boxes.

Each box has 3 shirts.
$3 \times ? = 15$
$3 \times 5 = 15$

Guided Practice

Solve.
Use bar models to help you.

1 The art teacher puts 50 crayons into 5 groups.
Each group has the same number of crayons.
How many crayons are in one group?

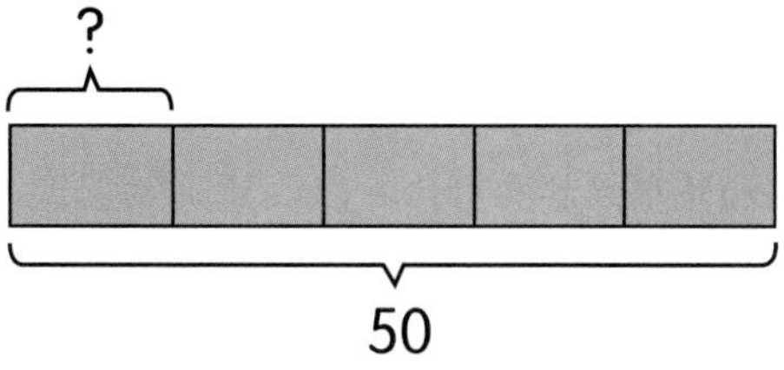

I divide 50 crayons into 5 groups.

Use a related multiplication fact to divide
5 × ? = 50
5 × 10 = 50

50 ÷ 5 = ______

There are ______ crayons in each group.

2 Brad has 20 table legs.
Each table needs 4 legs.
How many tables can Brad make?

Each table needs 4 legs.
4 × ? = 20
4 × 5 = 20

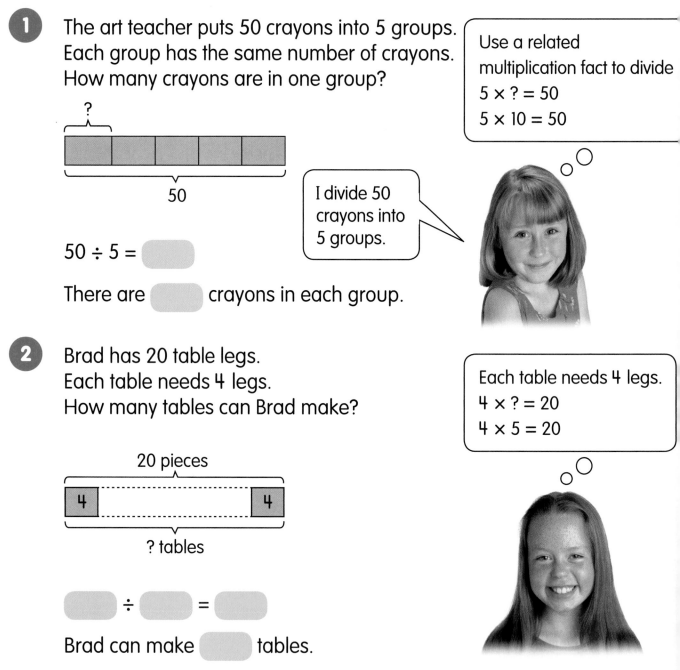

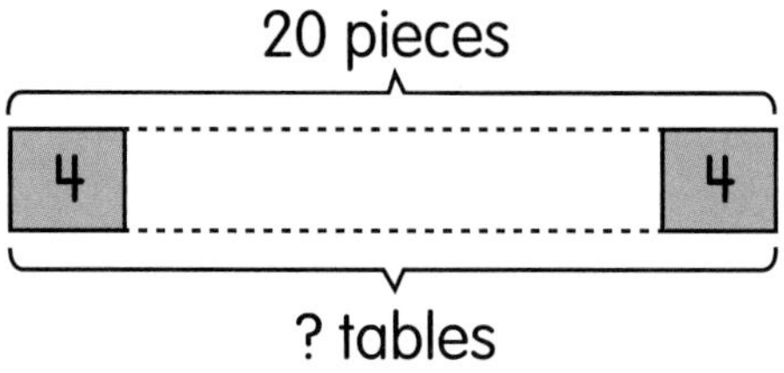

______ ÷ ______ = ______

Brad can make ______ tables.

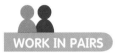

Hands-On Activity

WORK IN PAIRS

Use colored strips of paper.
Use the strips to make bar models.
Then solve the division word problems.

Example

Miss Lee has 15 folders.
She gives these folders equally to 5 students.
How many folders does each student get?

STEP 1 Choose 5 strips of the same length to show 5 students.
Paste them on paper to make a bar model.

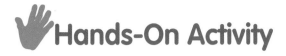

STEP 2 Label the bar model with the data in the word problem.

STEP 3 Write the division sentence to find the answer.
$15 \div 5 = 3$

1. Julie has 10 stamps and 5 envelopes.
   She puts the same number of stamps on each envelope.
   How many stamps does she put on each envelope?

2. Mr. Singh buys 6 cartons of milk.
   The clerk packs them equally into 3 bags.
   How many cartons of milk are in each bag?

READING AND WRITING MATH

Math Journal

Use each bar model and the words to write a word problem. Then solve it.

1. 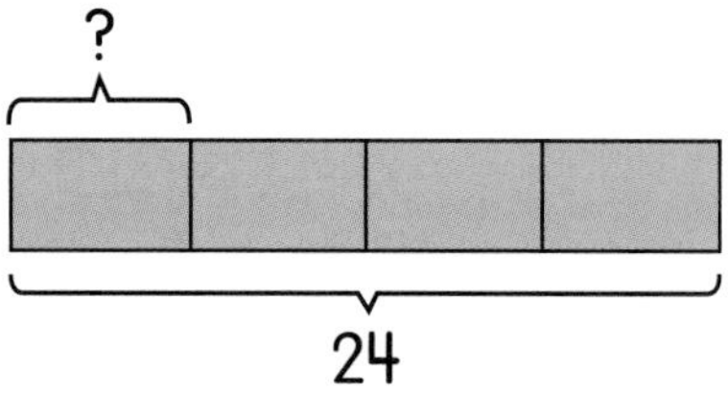

   buys apples bags many packs Rita

2. 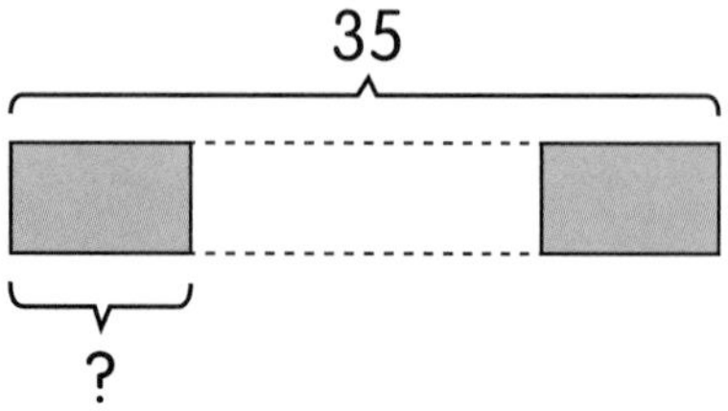

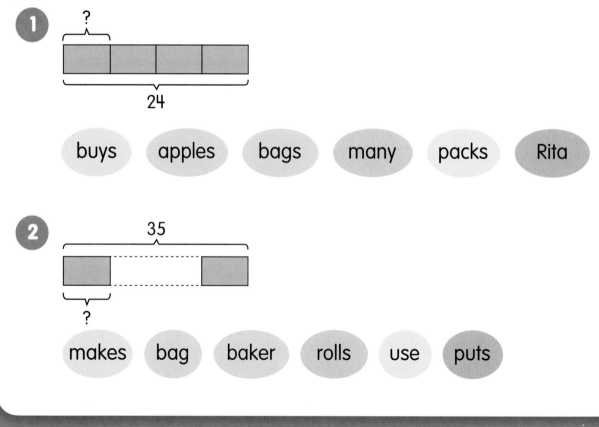

   makes bag baker rolls use puts

Let's Practice

Solve.
Use bar models to help you.

Draw 2 boxes to show 2 children.

1. Divide 10 cherries equally between 2 children.
   Each child gets ___ cherries.

2. Put 24 muffins equally on 4 plates.
   Each plate has ___ muffins.

Solve.
Draw bar models to help you.

3. Frank puts 18 stamps equally on 3 pages of an album.
   How many stamps are on each page?

4. Jim has 30 pieces of wood.
   He uses an equal number of pieces to make 5 picture frames.
   How many pieces does he need to make each frame?

5. Kara feeds 18 treats to some cats.
   Each cat eats 3 treats.
   How many cats are there?

6. Anton draws 24 pictures in his journal.
   He draws 4 pictures on each page.
   How many pages does he use?

7. Mr. Ruiz has 12 apples.
   He puts 4 apples in each bowl.
   How many bowls of apples does he have?

8. Liza has 20 craft sticks.
   She uses 4 craft sticks to make a square.
   How many squares does Liza make?

ON YOUR OWN

Go to Workbook B: Practice 2, pages 161–164

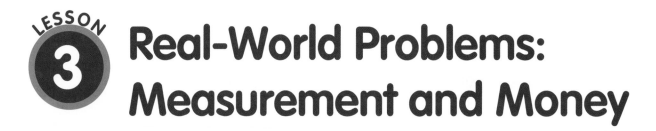

LESSON 3

Real-World Problems: Measurement and Money

Lesson Objective

- Use bar models to solve real-world problems on measurement and money.

Learn — Read, understand, and solve this word problem.

4 colored strips are 3 centimeters long each.
They are placed side by side to make a long strip.
How long is the strip?

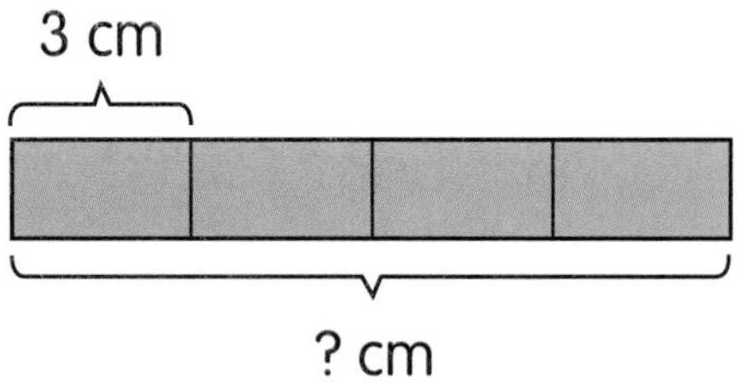

$4 \times 3 = 12$

The strip is 12 centimeters long.

4 groups of 3 centimeters

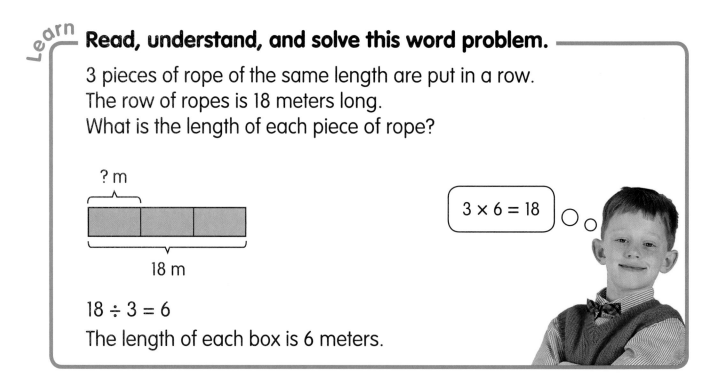

Learn — Read, understand, and solve this word problem.

3 pieces of rope of the same length are put in a row.
The row of ropes is 18 meters long.
What is the length of each piece of rope?

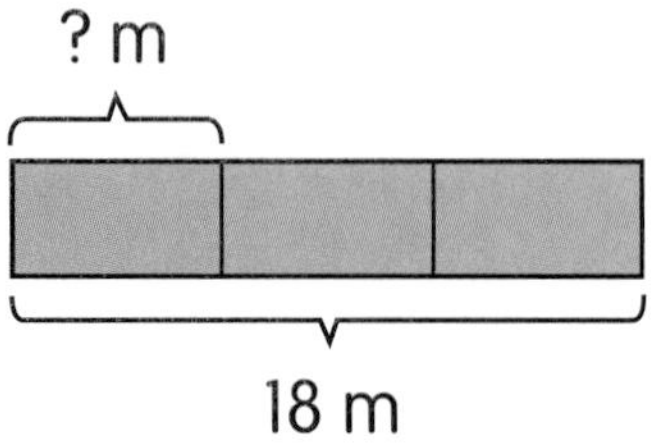

$18 \div 3 = 6$

The length of each box is 6 meters.

$3 \times 6 = 18$

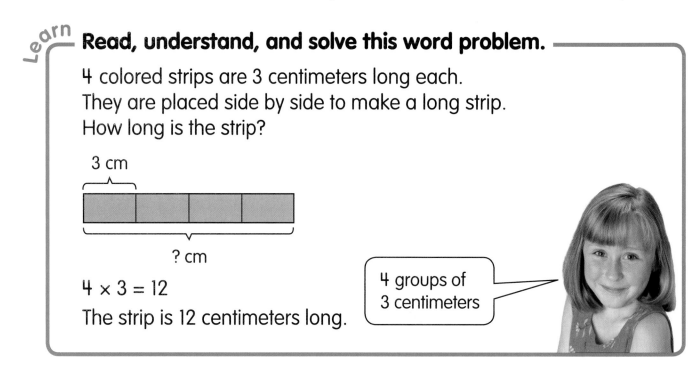

Guided Practice

**Tell whether you need to multiply or divide.
Explain how you know.
Then solve.
Use bar models to help you.**

1 Mike lines up bricks along a wall.
The length of each brick is 10 inches.
What is the length of the 5 bricks?

5 groups of 10 inches.

___ in.

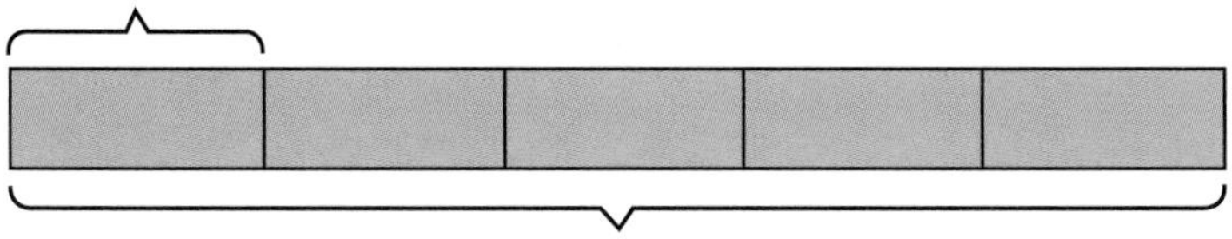

? in.

___ ◯ ___ = ___

The length of the 5 bricks is ___ inches.

2 Tara has a 20-foot long ribbon.
She cuts it into 4 equal pieces.
What is the length of each piece of ribbon?

? ft

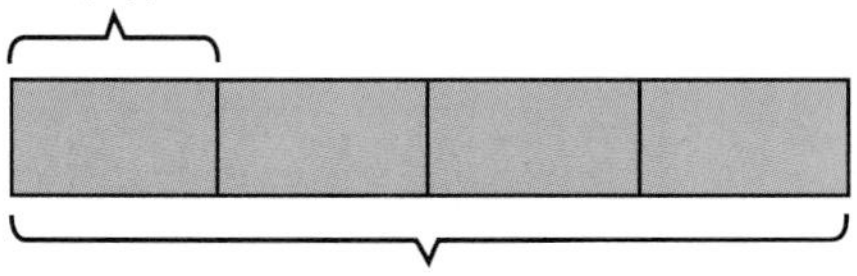

20 ft

4 × ___ = 20

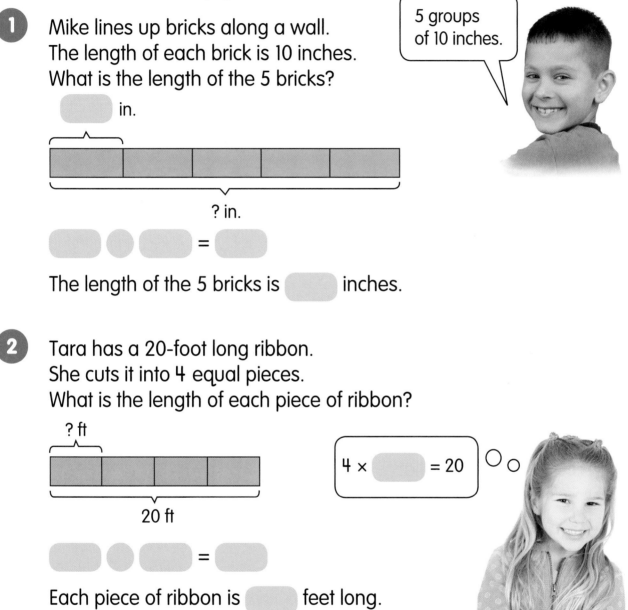

___ ◯ ___ = ___

Each piece of ribbon is ___ feet long.

3 Sam arranges 8 square tiles in a row.
Each square tile is 4 centimeters long.
What is the length of the row of tiles?

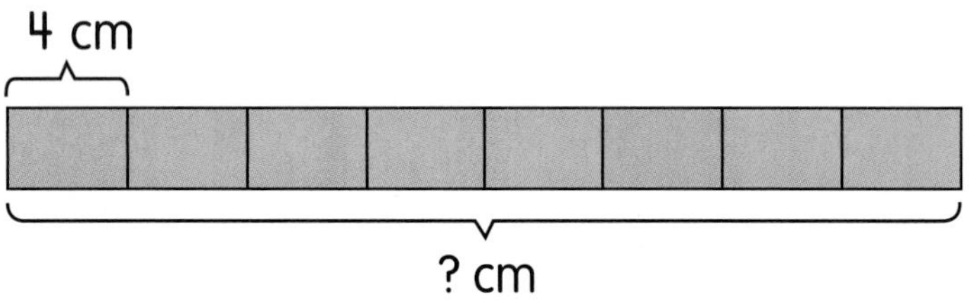

[ ] ( ) [ ] = [ ]

The length of the row of tiles is [ ] centimeters.

4 The total length of a tube is 45 feet.
The tube is cut into equal pieces 5 feet long.
How many pieces of tube are there?

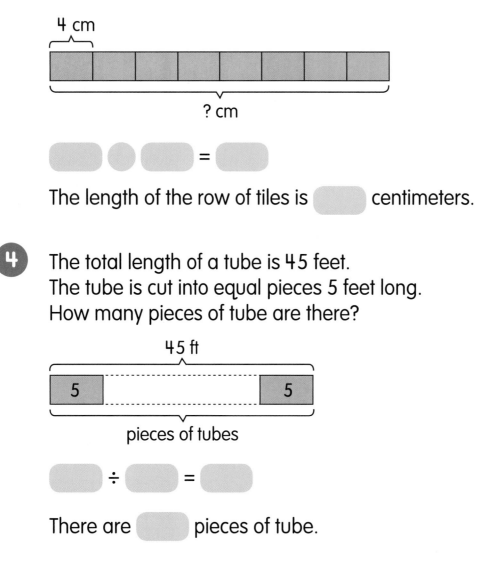

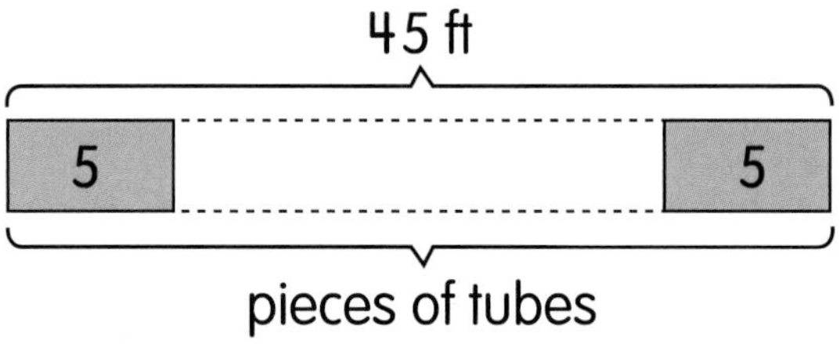

[ ] ÷ [ ] = [ ]

There are [ ] pieces of tube.

Learn

Read, understand, and solve these word problems.

There are 5 bags of rice.
The mass of each bag of rice is 10 kilograms.
What is the mass of the 5 bags of rice?

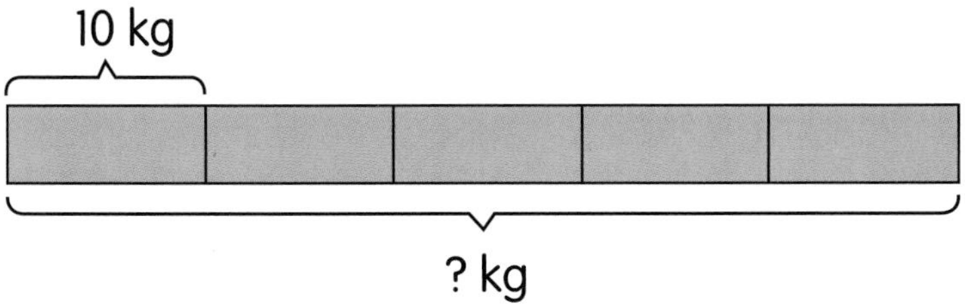

$5 \times 10 = 50$

The mass of the 5 bags of rice is 50 kilograms.

15 liters of fruit juice is prepared for a party.
All of it is poured equally into 3 pitchers.
How many liters of fruit juice can each pitcher hold?

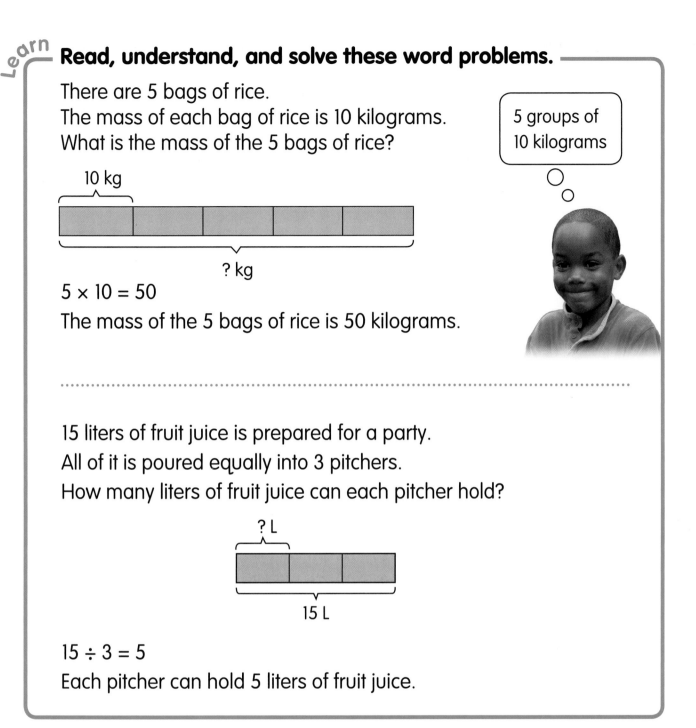

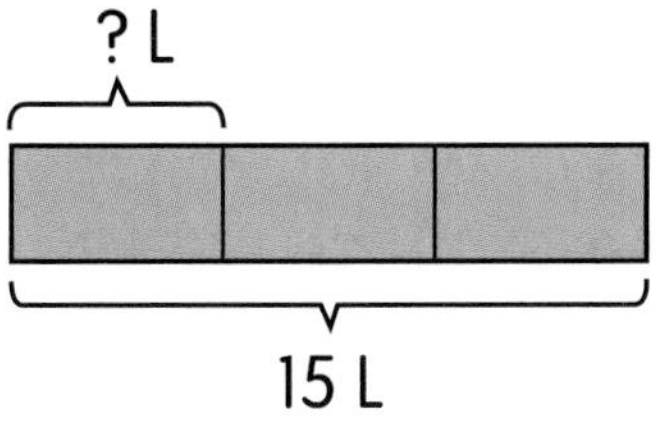

$15 \div 3 = 5$

Each pitcher can hold 5 liters of fruit juice.

Guided Practice

Tell whether need to multiply or divide.
Explain how you know.
Then solve.
Use bar models to help you.

5 The mass of 5 melons is 30 kilograms.
Each melon has the same mass.
What is the mass of each melon?

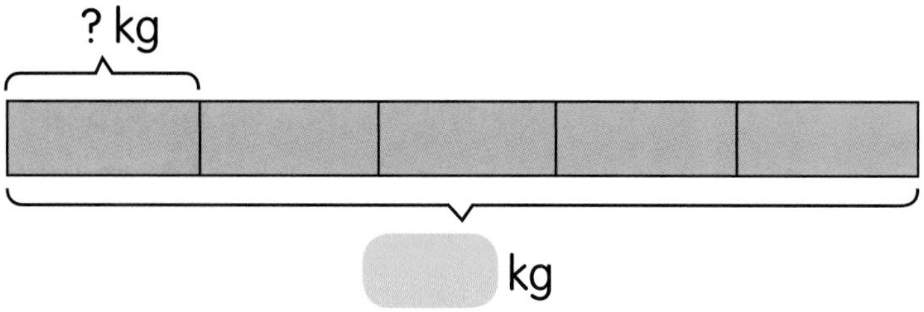

___ ÷ ___ = ___

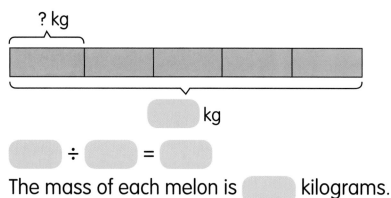

The mass of each melon is ___ kilograms.

6 Sam collected 9 pails of rainwater.
Each pail contained 3 liters of water.
How many liters of rainwater did Sam collect?

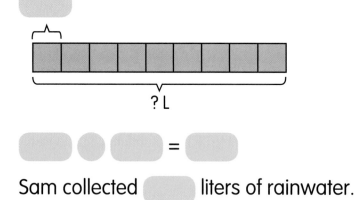

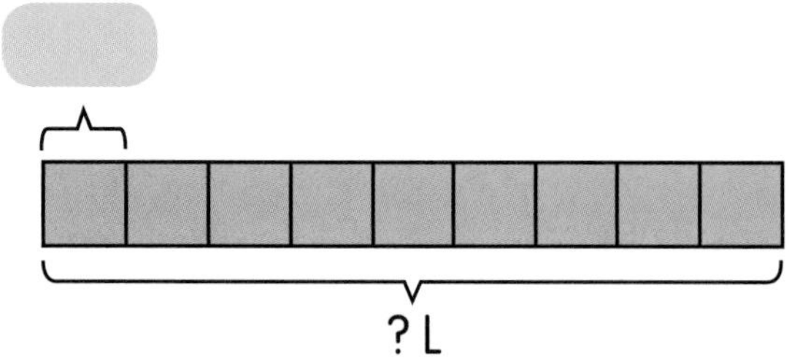

___ ___ ___ = ___

Sam collected ___ liters of rainwater.

7 Agnes has 16 liters of water to fill some vases.
Each vase can hold 4 liters of water.
How many vases does Agnes need?

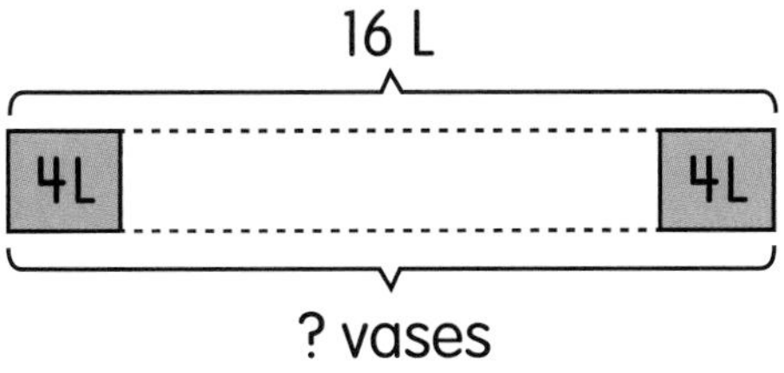

____ ○ ____ = ____

Agnes needs ____ vases.

8 Amber has 6 rings.
The mass of each ring is 3 grams.
What is the mass of the 6 rings?

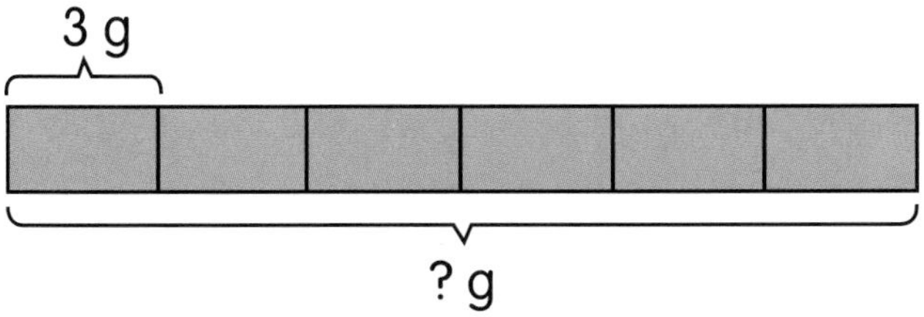

____ ○ ____ = ____

The mass of the 6 rings is ____ grams.

9 Alex used 14 liters of paint to paint his bedroom.
He used 7 cans of paint.
How many liters of paint did each can contain?

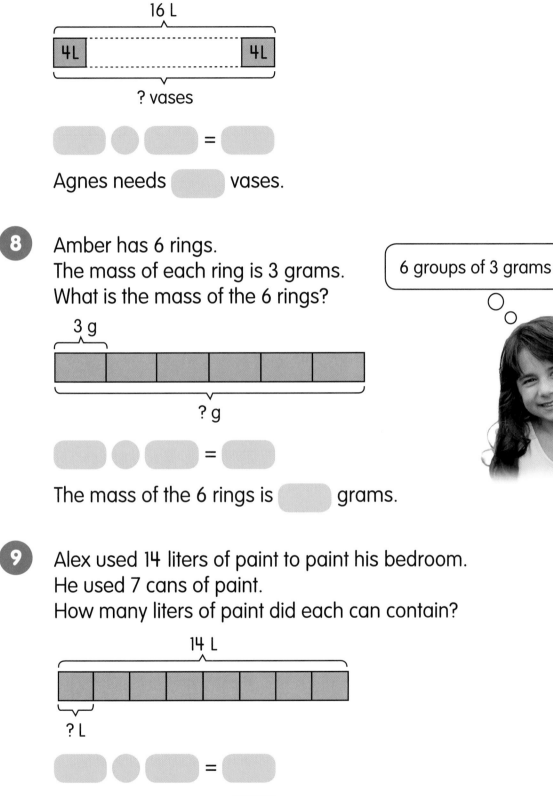

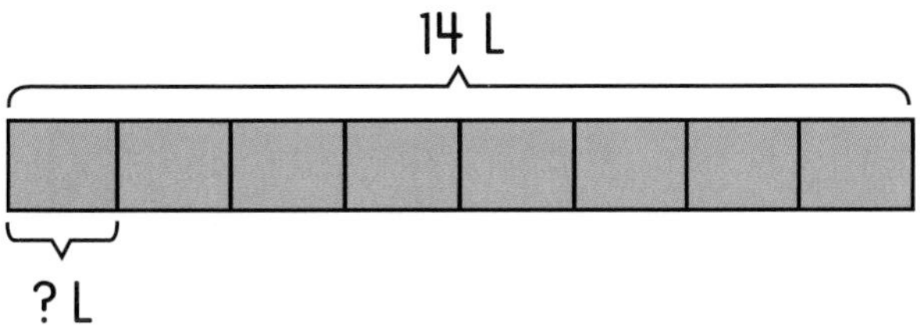

____ ○ ____ = ____

Each can contained ____ liters of paint.

10 Some bags of seeds are in a bin.
The total mass of the seeds is 36 grams.
Each bag of seeds has a mass of 4 grams.
How many bags of seeds are in the bin?

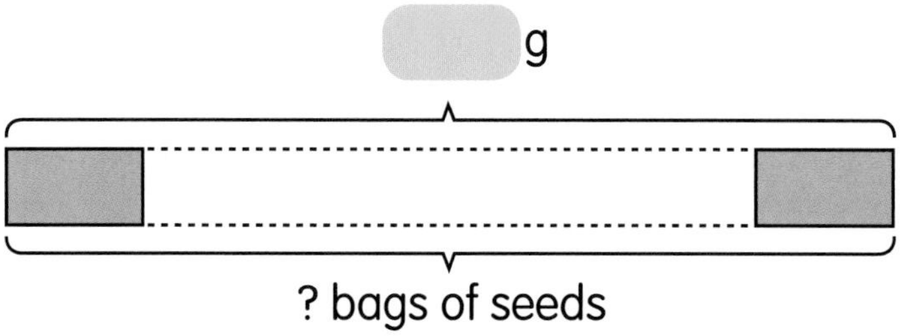

___ ◯ ___ = ___

There are ___ bags of seeds in the bin.

11 Rita pours 30 liters of oil into some bottles.
Each bottle contains 3 liters of oil.
How many bottles are there in all?

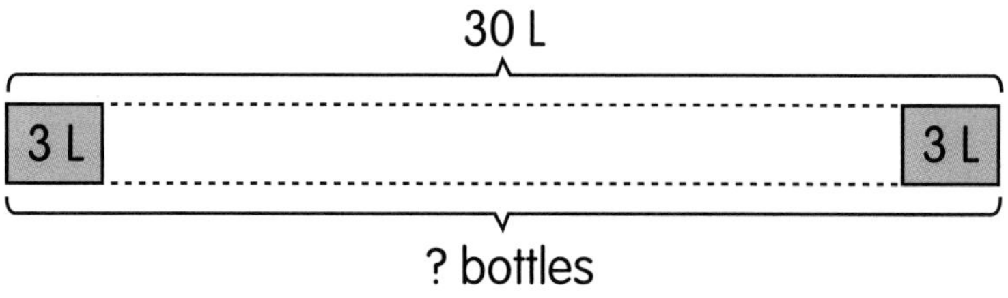

___ ◯ ___ = ___

There are ___ bottles in all.

Learn

Read and understand these word problems.

Lucy gives $3 each to her 5 children.
How much money does Lucy give her children in all?

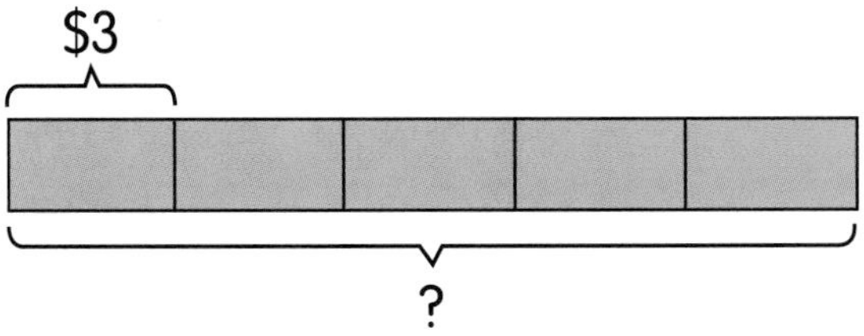

5 × $3 = $15
Lucy gives her children $15 in all.

Tim saves $20 in 4 days.
He saves an equal amount each day.
How much does Tim save each day?

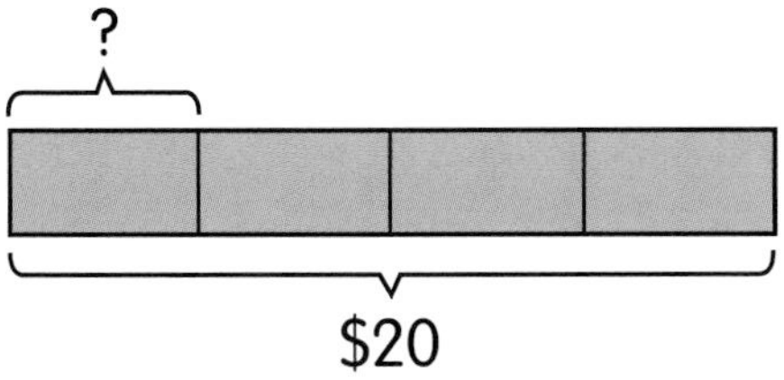

20 ÷ 4 = 5
Tim saves $5 each day.

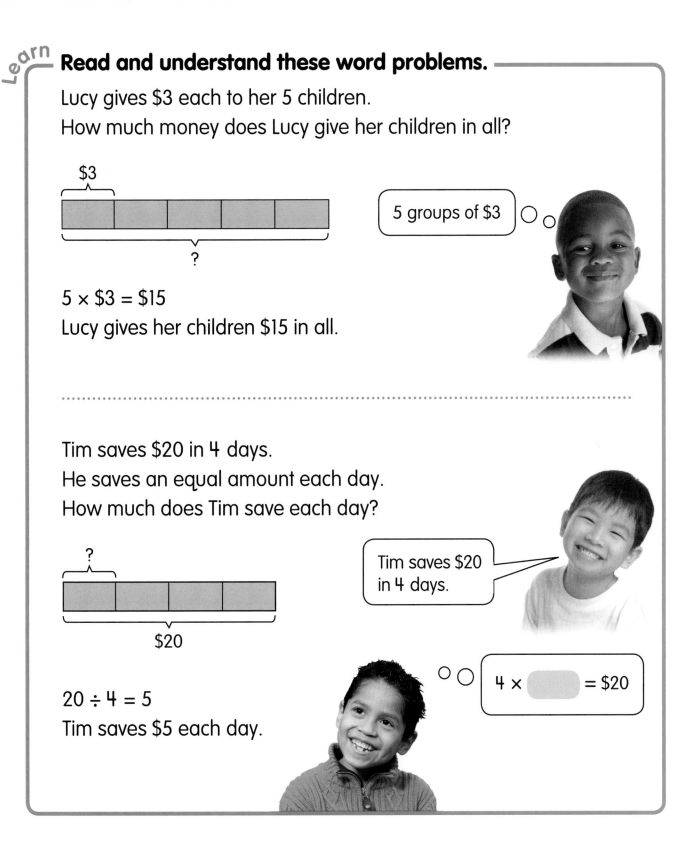

Guided Practice

Tell whether need to multiply or divide.
Explain how you know.
Then solve.
Use bar models to help you.

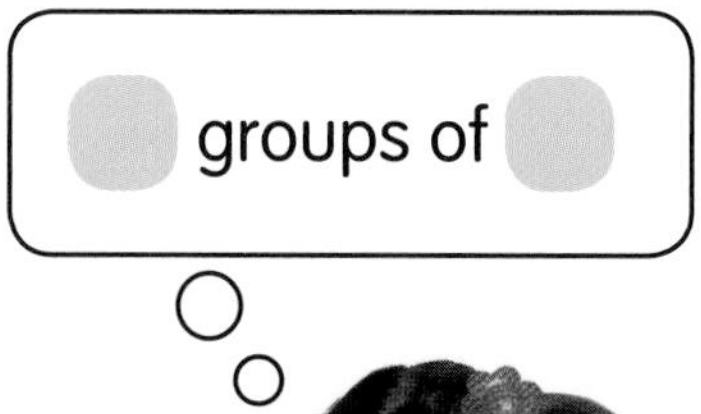

12 Elena spends \$5 each day.
How much does she spend in 8 days?

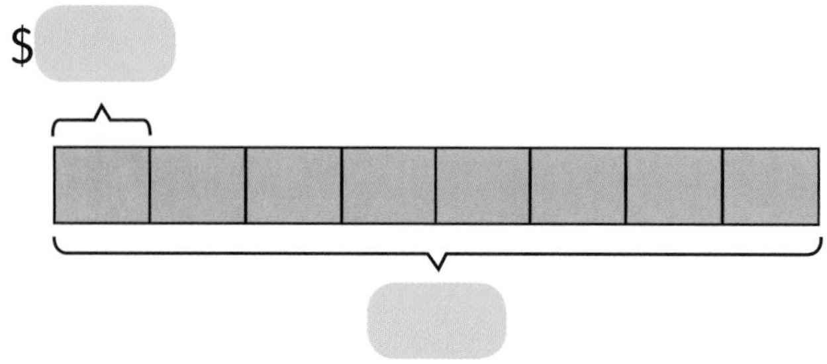

____ ____ \$____ = \$____

Elena spends \$____ in 8 days.

13 5 movie tickets cost \$35.
How much does each movie ticket cost?

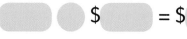

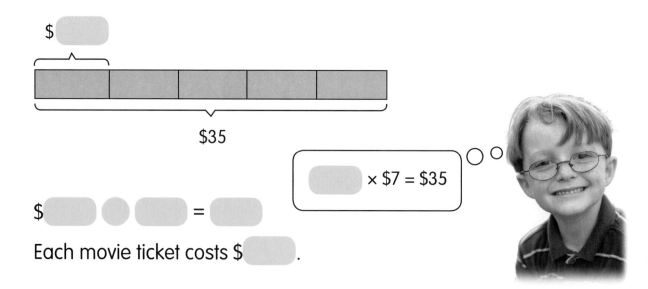

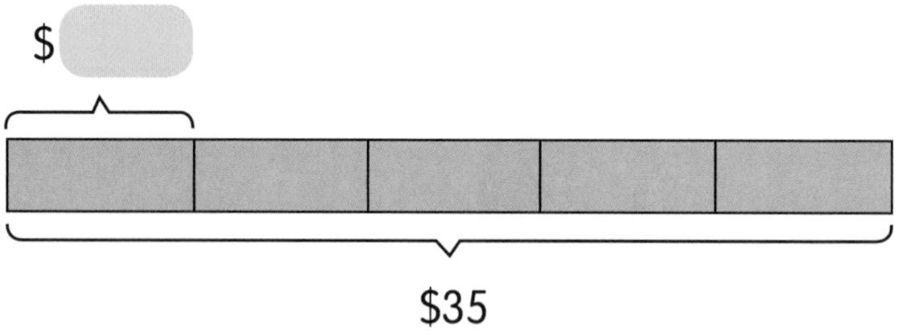

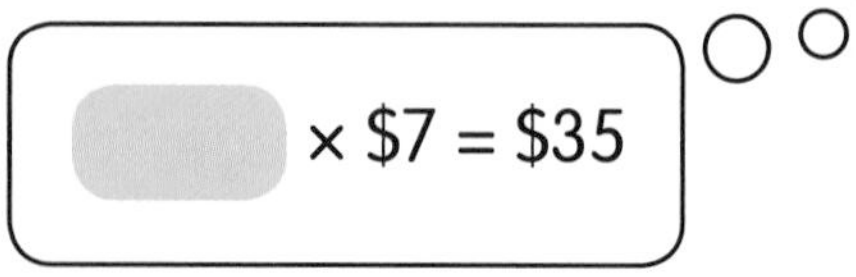

\$____ ____ ____ = ____

Each movie ticket costs \$____.

14 Mrs. Benedict spends $28 on her sons' baseball caps.
Each baseball cap costs $7.
How many sons does Mrs. Benedict have?

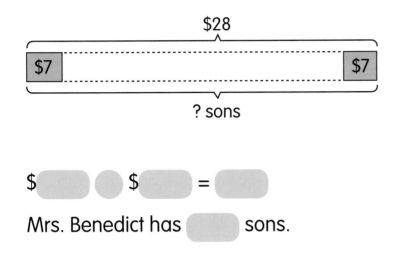

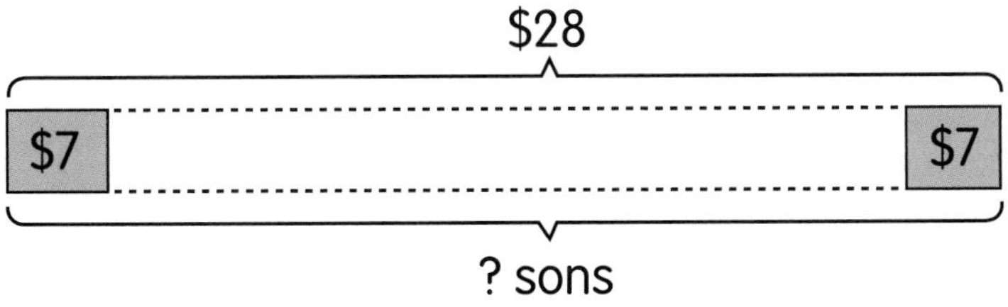

$ ___ ___ $ ___ = ___

Mrs. Benedict has ___ sons.

Let's Practice

Tell whether you need to multiply or divide.
Solve.
Draw bar models to help you.

1. Krish cuts a piece of wire 21 feet long into 3 equal pieces.
What is the length of each piece?

2. Joe made a wooden frame for a square window.
The piece of wood he used was 12 meters long.
How long is each side of the window?

3. The total mass of 2 bags of flour is 18 kilograms.
Each bag has the same mass.
What is the mass of each bag?

4. The mass of each pack of paper clips is 10 grams.
What is the total mass of 7 packs of paper clips?

5. There are some bundles of newspapers.
The total mass of the bundles of newspapers is 24 kilograms.
Each bundle has a mass of 3 kilograms.
How many bundles of newspapers are there?

6. Mrs. William's children drink 8 liters of milk in a week.
How many liters of milk do the children drink in 4 weeks?

7. Dave needs 27 liters of water to fill 3 tanks of the same size.
How many liters of water does Dave need to fill each tank?

8. Anthony helps his father pour 20 liters of water into a number of tanks.
Each tank contains 5 liters of water.
How many tanks are there in all?

9. A book costs $9.
Hal buys 2 books.
How much does he pay in all?

10. Kathy brings her 3 children to a toy store.
She spends $15 on them.
How much does she spend for 1 child?

11. Mrs. Tanner buys shirts for her children at $5 each.
She pays $20 for the shirts.
How many children does Mrs. Tanner have?

ON YOUR OWN

Go to Workbook 2B: Practice 3, pages 165–172

CRITICAL THINKING SKILLS

Put On Your Thinking Cap!

PROBLEM SOLVING

Solve.

Meena has 28 counters.
She puts some in a bag.
She puts the rest of the counters into 5 boxes.
If each box contains 5 counters, how many counters are in the bag?

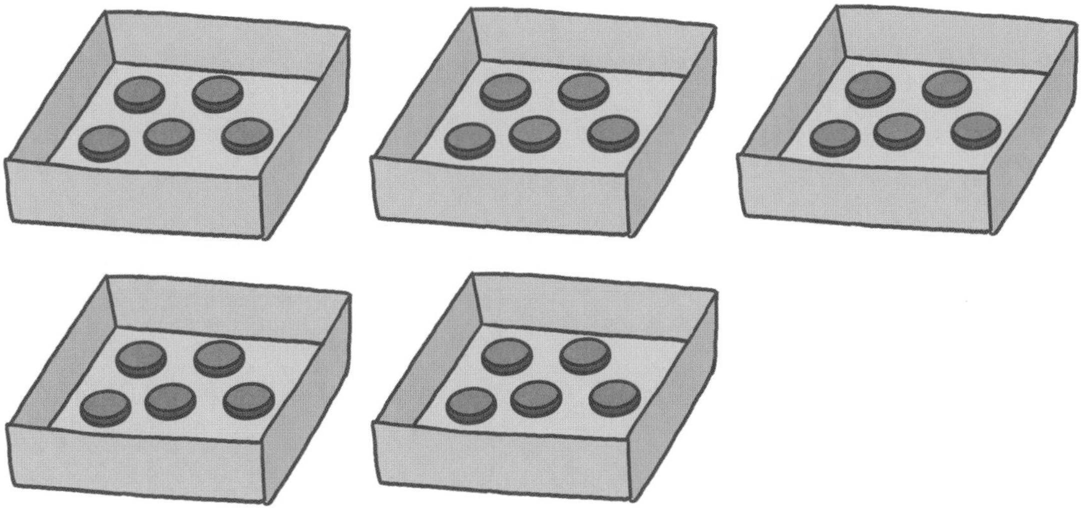

There are ______ counters in the bag.

ON YOUR OWN

Go to Workbook B:
Put On Your Thinking Cap!
pages 173–174

Chapter Wrap Up

You have learned...

Using Bar Models: Multiplication and Division

Multiplication

- to find the number in several equal groups

There are 6 markers in each box.
There are 5 boxes in all.
How many markers are there in all?

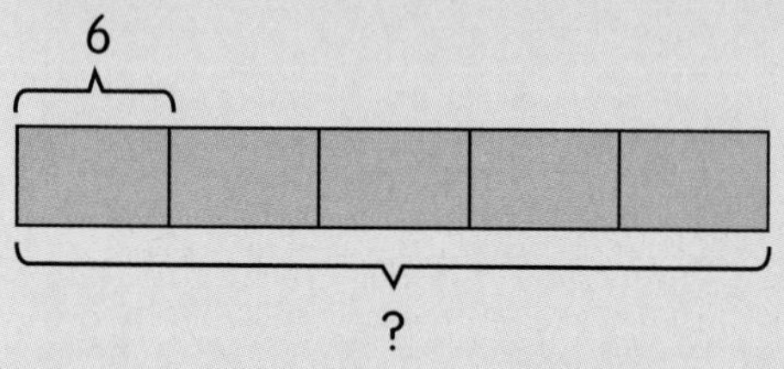

$5 \times 6 = 30$
There are 30 markers in all.

Measurement and Money

- Length

Grace joins 7 strings of beads.
The length of each string is 10 inches.
What is the total length of the 7 strings?

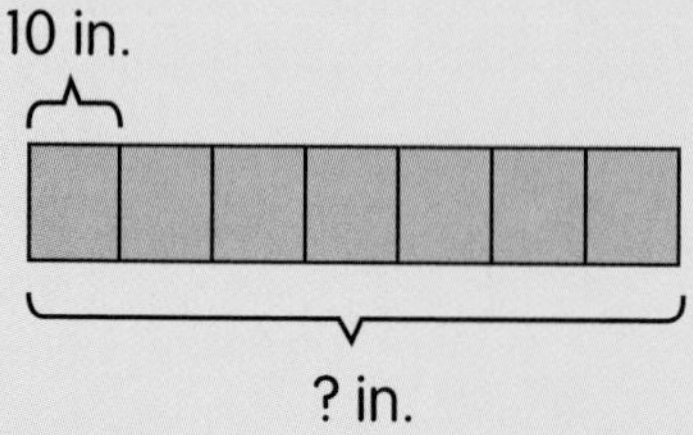

$7 \times 10 = 70$
The total length of the 7 strings of beads is 70 inches.

- Mass

There are 8 bunches of flowers.
Their total mass is 32 kilograms.
Each bunch has the same mass.
What is the mass of each bunch?

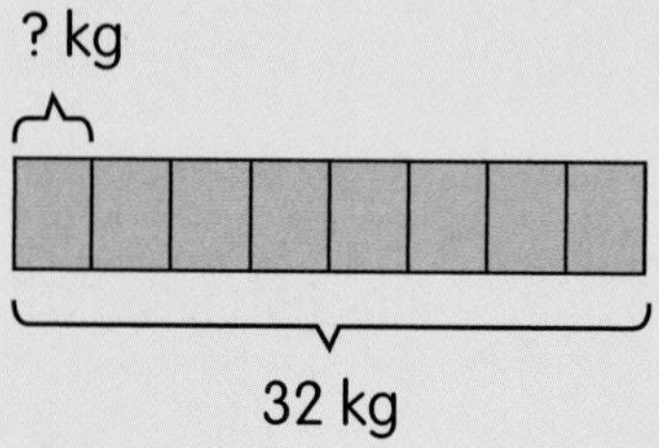

$32 \div 8 = 4$
The mass of each bunch of flowers is 4 kilograms.

BIG IDEA

Bar models can be used to solve multiplication and division word problems.

Division

- to find the number in each group

There are 30 markers.
An equal number of markers is put in 5 boxes.
How many markers are there in each box?

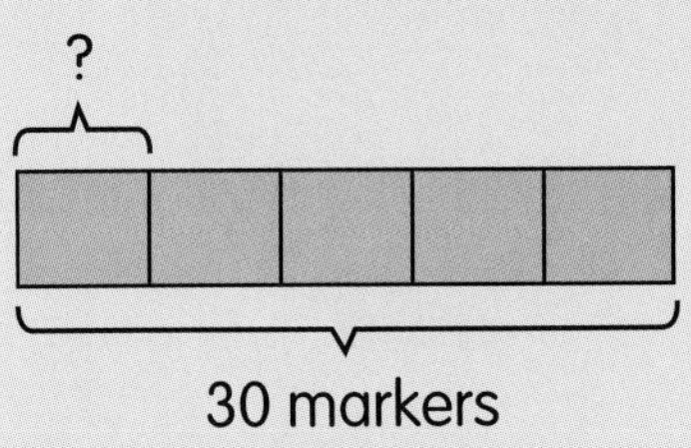

30 ÷ 5 = 6
There are 6 markers in each box.

- to find the number of groups

There are 30 crayons.
6 crayons are put in each box.
How many boxes are there?

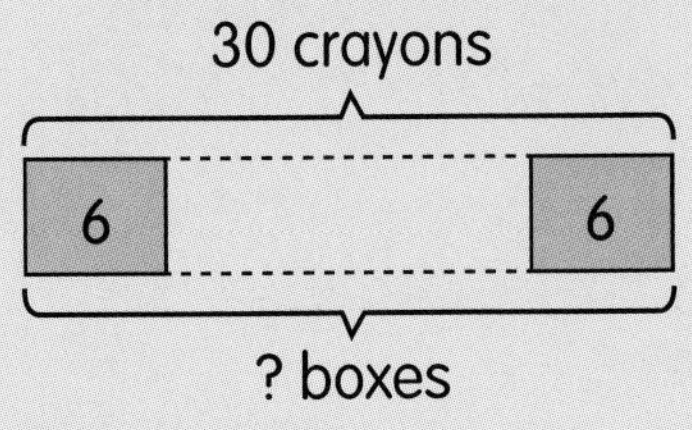

30 ÷ 6 = 5
There are 5 boxes.

- Volume

4 liters of paint is needed to paint a bookshelf.
There are 3 bookshelves.
How many liters of paint are needed in all?

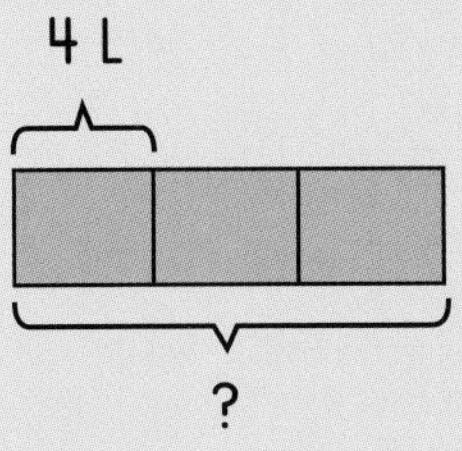

3 × 4 = 12
12 liters of paint are needed.

- Money

Mrs. Estrada has $36.
She divides the money equally among her 4 children.
How much money does each child get?

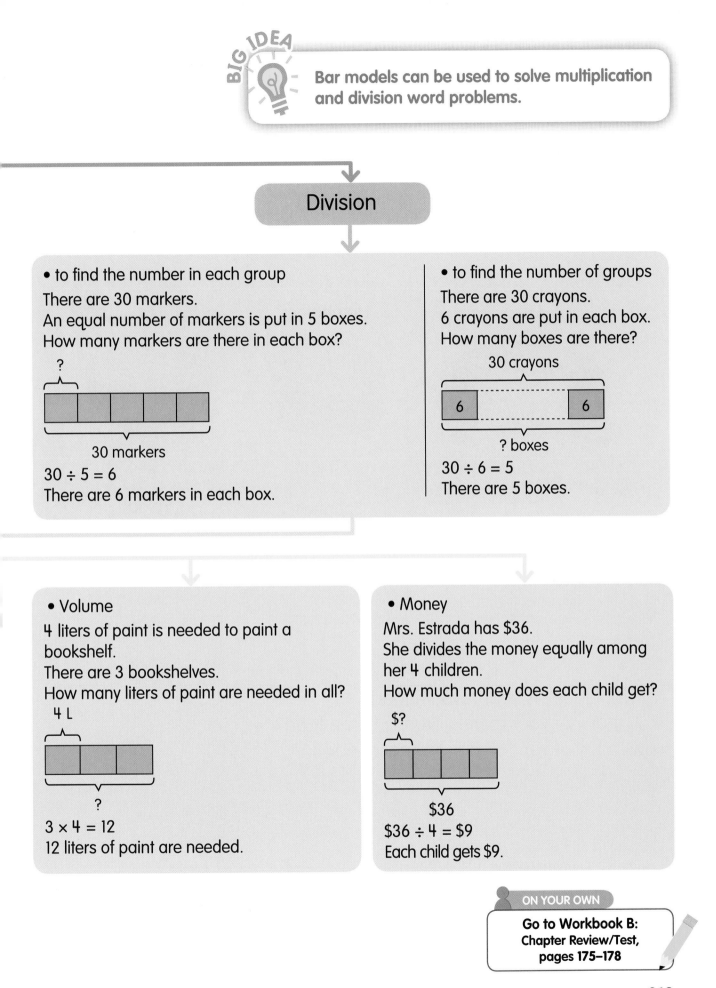

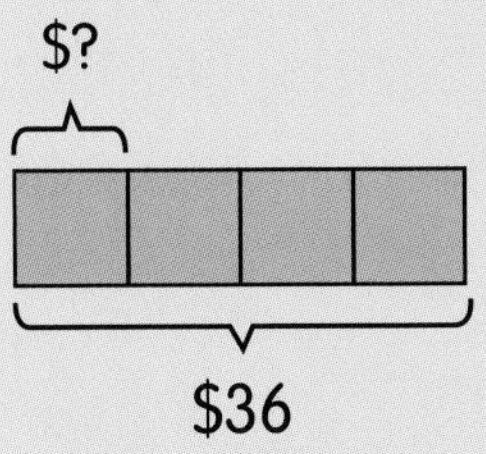

$36 ÷ 4 = $9
Each child gets $9.

ON YOUR OWN

Go to Workbook B: Chapter Review/Test, pages 175–178

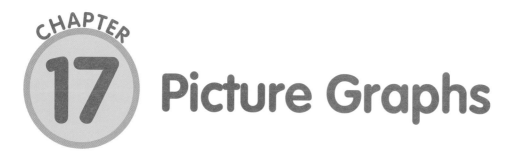

CHAPTER 17

Picture Graphs

Here are the favorite foods of some second graders.

Pizza

Hamburger

Chicken soup

Tacos

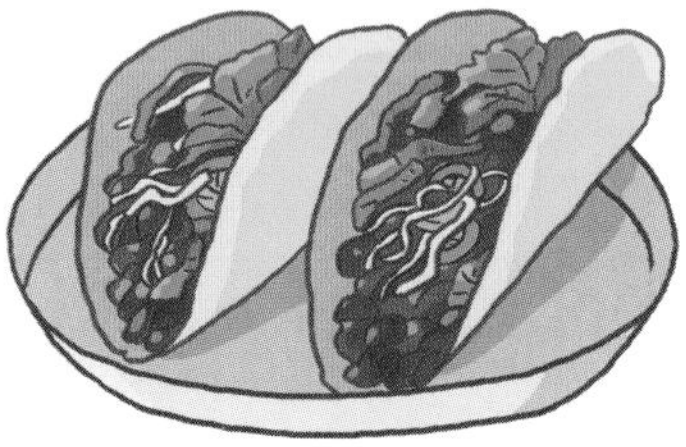

Spaghetti

Salad

Which of these is your favorite food?
How many of your friends like the same food?
How many of your friends like each food?

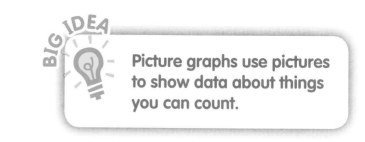

BIG IDEA

Picture graphs use pictures to show data about things you can count.

Recall Prior Knowledge

Showing data with pictures

Count the number of each kind of animal.

Animals at the Zoo

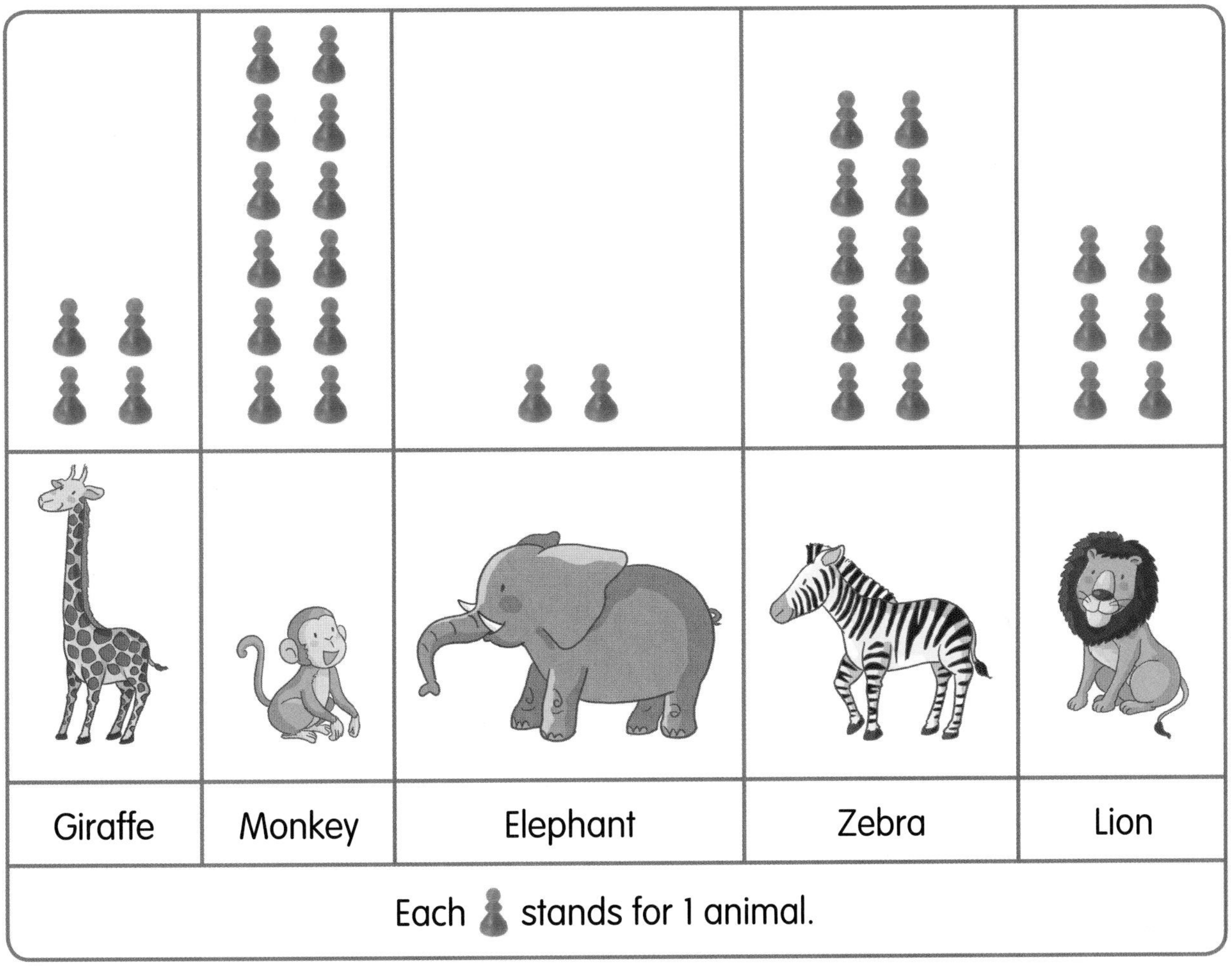

There are 5 kinds of animals.

There are 4 giraffes.

There are 12 monkeys and 2 elephants.

There are 10 zebras and 6 lions.

There are 34 animals altogether.

Making a tally chart

Kelly made this tally chart to show the solid shapes she has.

Solid Shape	Tally	Number of Solid Shapes
	~~////~~	5
	///	3
	~~////~~ ~~////~~	10
	//	2
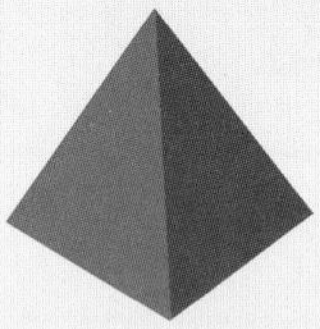	////	4

You can find the total number of shapes.

Count the ~~////~~ first.

Then count the remaining tallies.

5, 10, 15, 16, 17, 18, 19, 20, 21, 22, 23, 24

✔Quick Check

Look at the stickers that James collects.
Complete a copy of the tally chart and the sentences below it.

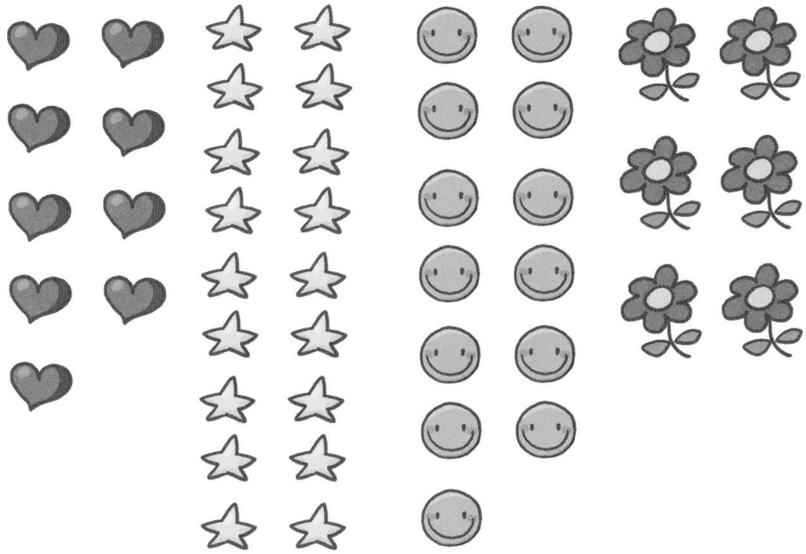

Sticker	Tally	Number of Stickers

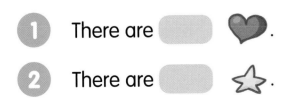

1. There are ___ .
2. There are ___ .

LESSON 1

Reading Picture Graphs with Scales

Lesson Objectives

- Read, analyze, and interpret picture graphs.
- Complete picture graphs.

Vocabulary
picture graph
key
symbol

Learn

You use the key on a picture graph when you read it.

There are four kinds of balls.
The **picture graph** shows the number of each kind of ball.

Kinds of Balls

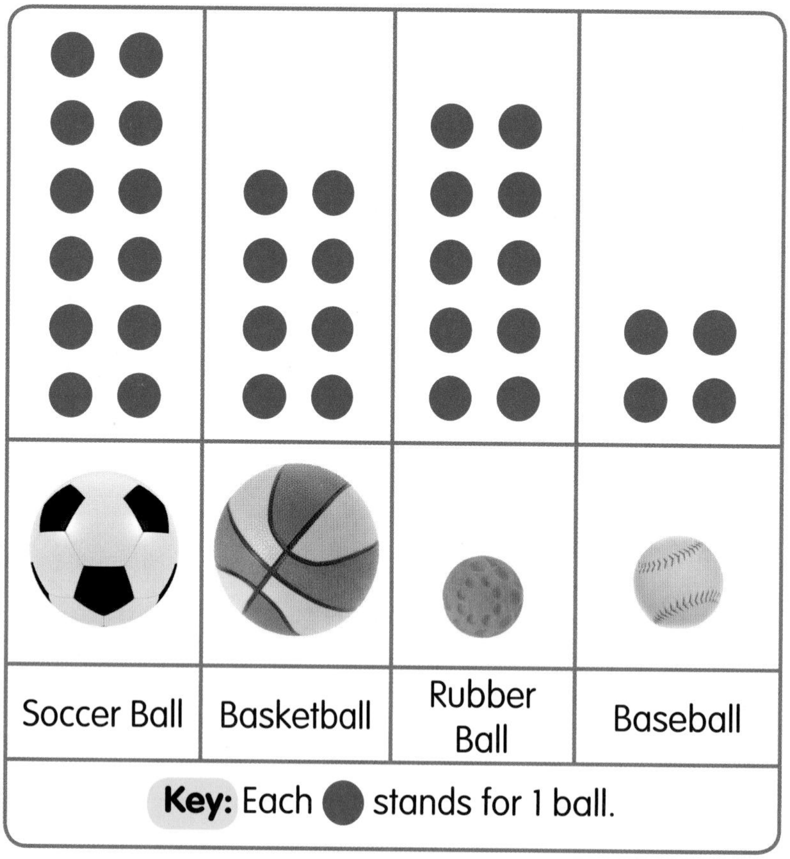

1 ● stands for 1 ball. So, you can read this picture graph by counting the pictures.

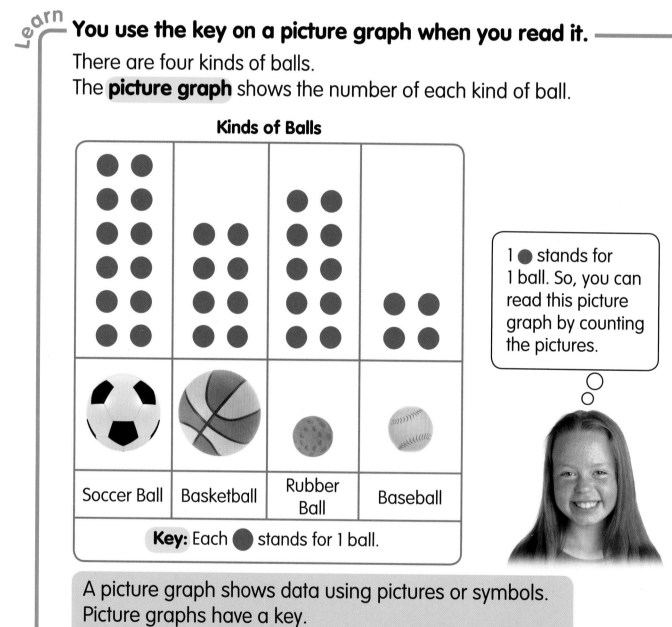

A picture graph shows data using pictures or symbols.
Picture graphs have a key.
The key shows what each picture or **symbol** stands for.

You can change the key on a picture graph.

Now use one ● to stand for 2 balls.

Kinds of Balls

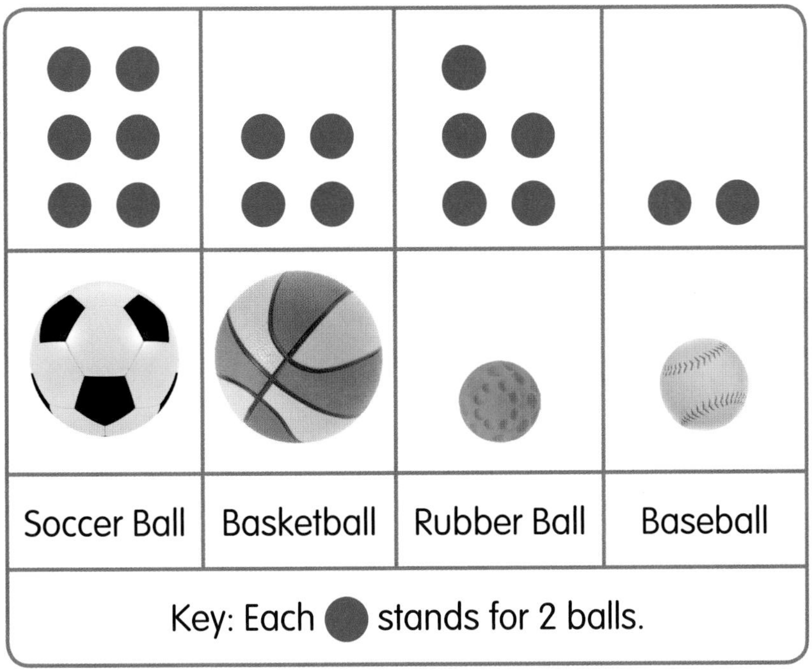

1 How many soccer balls are there?

The graph shows 6 ● for soccer balls.
1 ● stands for 2 soccer balls.
So, this picture graph has a scale of 2.

You read this picture graph by counting and multiplying. Since the scale is 2, you multiply by 2.

$6 \times 2 = 12$

There are 12 soccer balls.

Continued on next page

2 How many more soccer balls than basketballs are there?
There are 2 more ● for soccer balls than basketballs.

$2 \times 2 = 4$

There are 4 more soccer balls than basketballs.

It is easy to compare data using a picture graph.

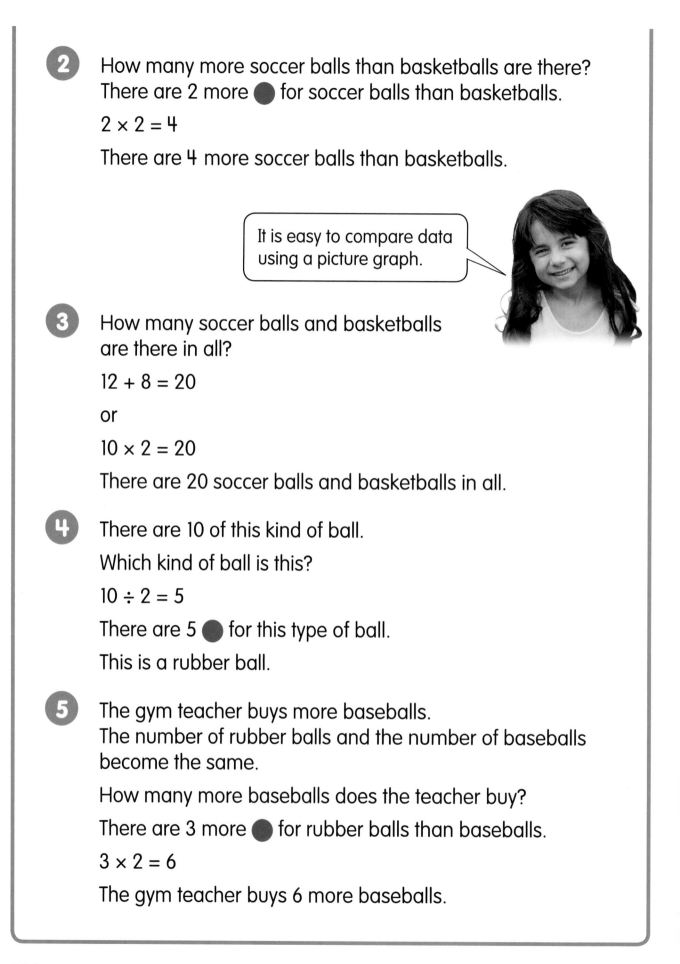

3 How many soccer balls and basketballs are there in all?

$12 + 8 = 20$

or

$10 \times 2 = 20$

There are 20 soccer balls and basketballs in all.

4 There are 10 of this kind of ball.

Which kind of ball is this?

$10 \div 2 = 5$

There are 5 ● for this type of ball.

This is a rubber ball.

5 The gym teacher buys more baseballs.
The number of rubber balls and the number of baseballs become the same.

How many more baseballs does the teacher buy?

There are 3 more ● for rubber balls than baseballs.

$3 \times 2 = 6$

The gym teacher buys 6 more baseballs.

Guided Practice

Use the picture graphs to find the missing numbers.

Sam's friends have lost some of their teeth.
He draws a picture graph to show the number of friends who have lost teeth.

Number of Teeth Lost

one tooth	♥
two teeth	♥ ♥ ♥
three teeth	♥ ♥
four teeth	♥ ♥ ♥
Key: Each ♥ stands for 3 friends.	

3 children have each lost only one tooth.

6 children have each lost three teeth.

1. The number of children who have lost ____ teeth is the same as those who have lost ____ teeth.

2. Sam has ____ friends in all.

Ms. Bishop owns a pet shop.
She starts to draw a picture graph of her pets.
It shows the number of each kind of pet in her shop.

Kinds of Pets

🐢	Turtle	▲ ▲ ▲
🐟	Fish	▲ ▲ ▲ ▲ ▲
🐹	Hamster	▲
🐰	Rabbit	
🐱	Cat	▲ ▲ ▲
🐦	Bird	▲ ▲ ▲ ▲ ▲ ▲

Key: Each ▲ stands for ____ animals.

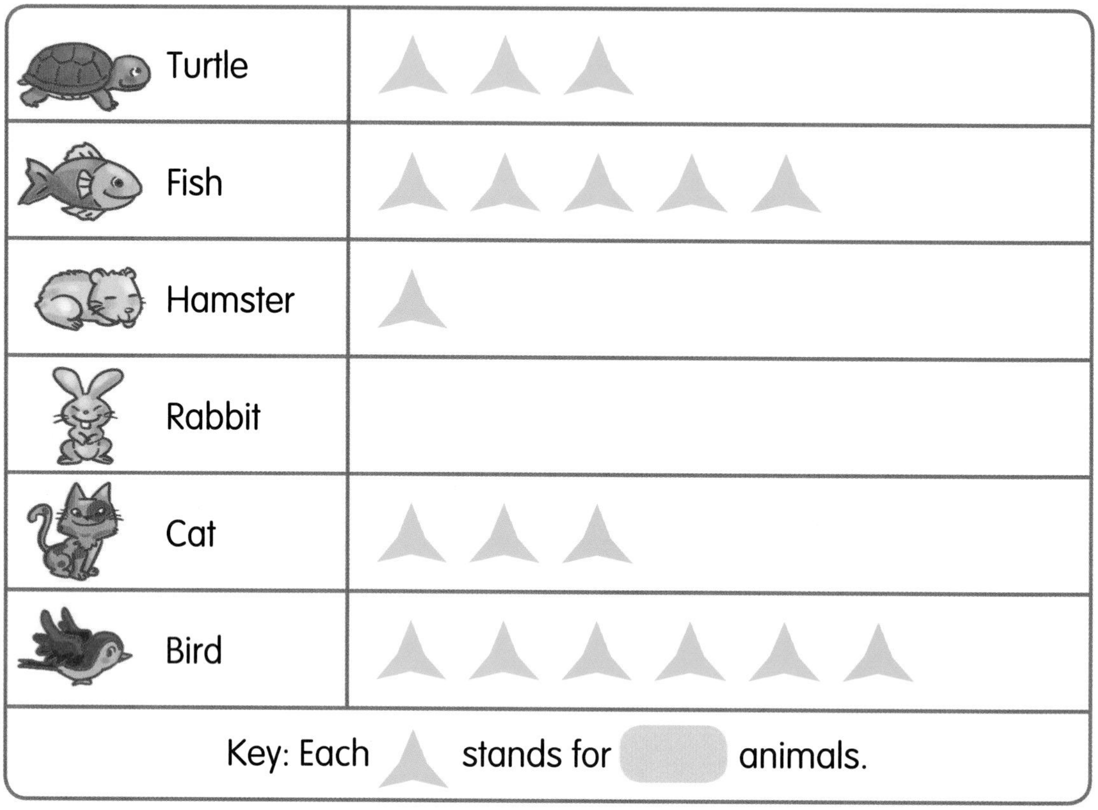

3 She has 20 fish.
Each ▲ stands for ____ animals.

4 She has ____ more birds than hamsters.

5 There are ____ cats and birds in all.

6 She has 16 rabbits.
She draws ____ ▲ on the graph.

7 She buys 8 more turtles.
She will draw ____ more ▲ on the graph.

The second graders visit the zoo.
They start to draw a picture graph of what they see on the way.
It shows the number of cars and trucks they see.

Kinds of Cars and Trucks

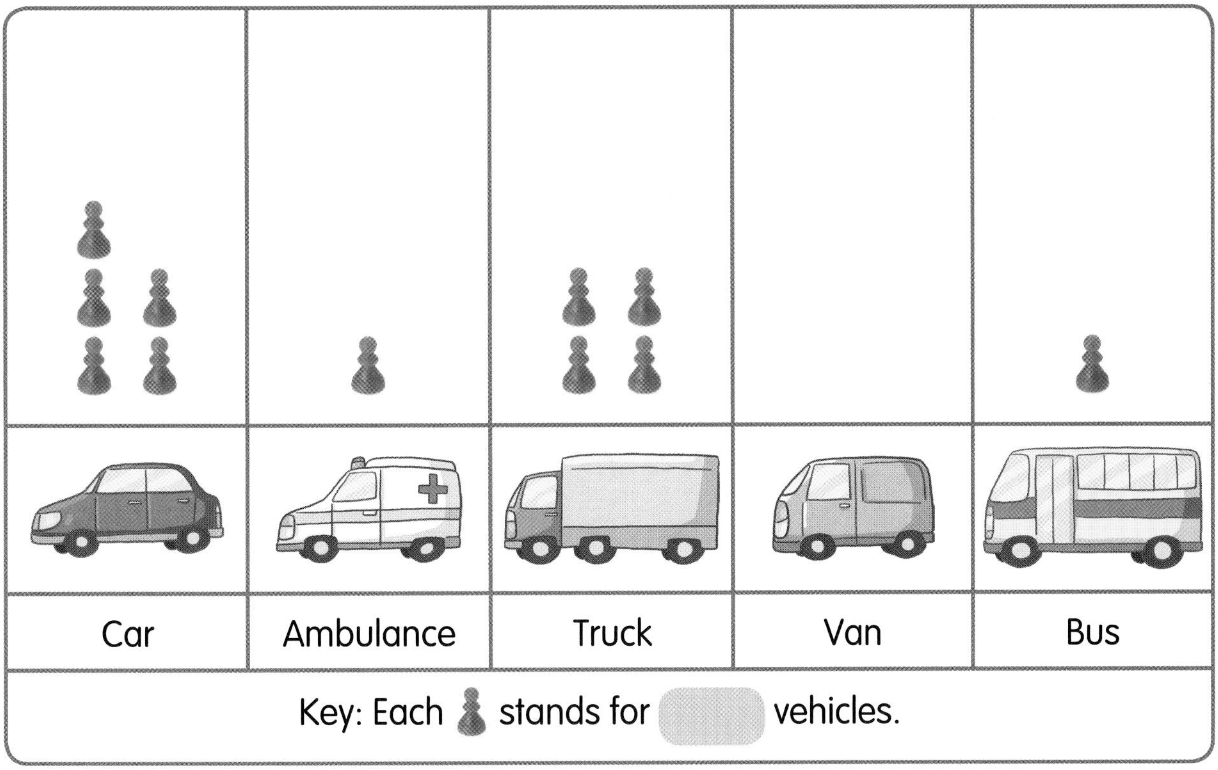

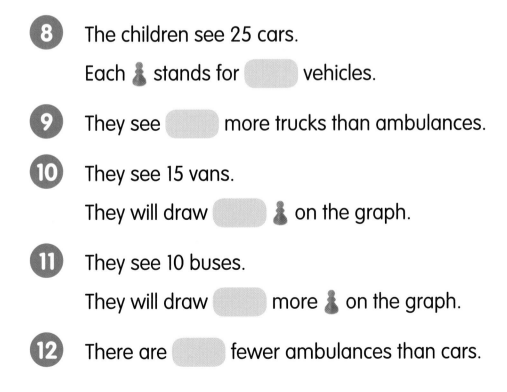

8 The children see 25 cars.

Each ♟ stands for ____ vehicles.

9 They see ____ more trucks than ambulances.

10 They see 15 vans.

They will draw ____ ♟ on the graph.

11 They see 10 buses.

They will draw ____ more ♟ on the graph.

12 There are ____ fewer ambulances than cars.

Mr. Brown sells fruit at the market.
He draws a picture graph of his sales for Monday.
The graph shows the number of each kind of fruit he sold.

Fruit Sold on Monday

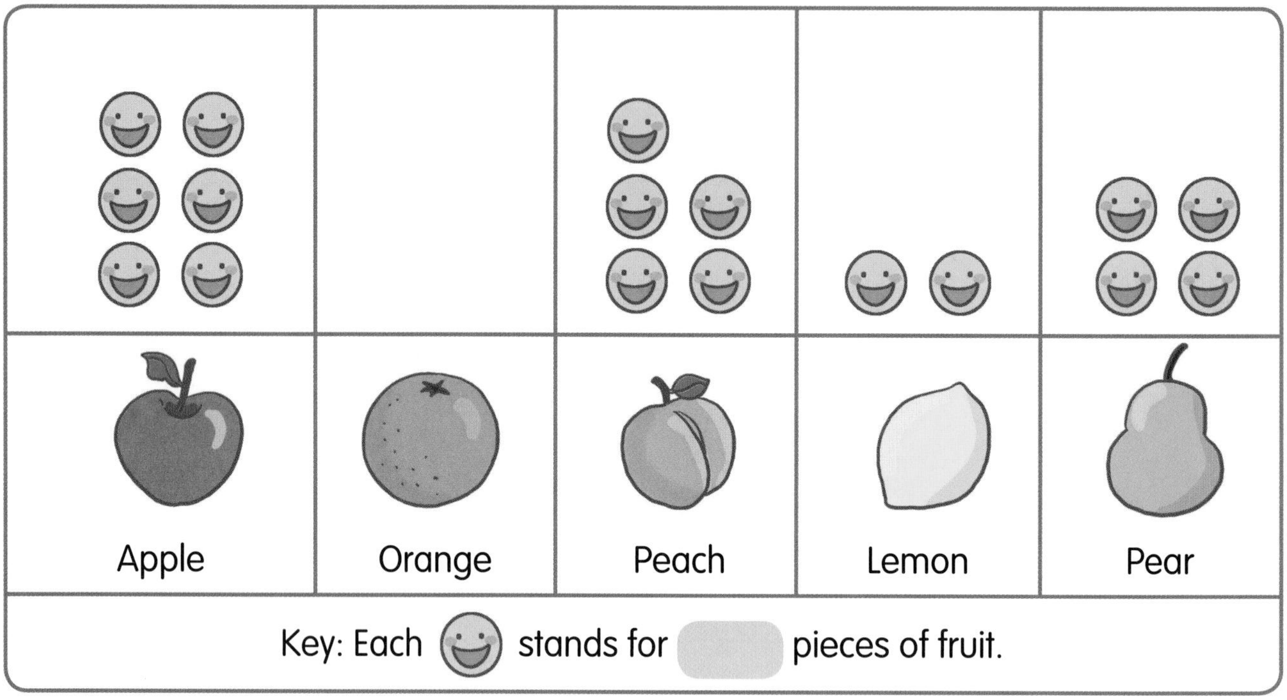

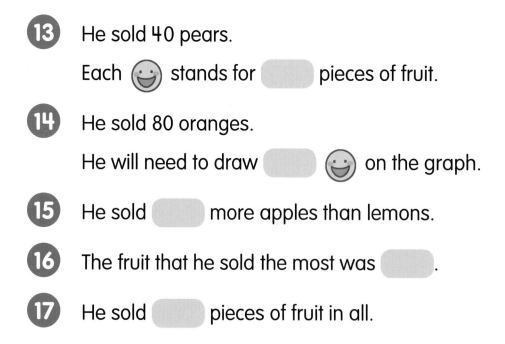

13 He sold 40 pears.

Each stands for ____ pieces of fruit.

14 He sold 80 oranges.

He will need to draw ____ on the graph.

15 He sold ____ more apples than lemons.

16 The fruit that he sold the most was ____.

17 He sold ____ pieces of fruit in all.

Let's Practice

The graph shows the number of different colored bows in a box.

Bows in a Box

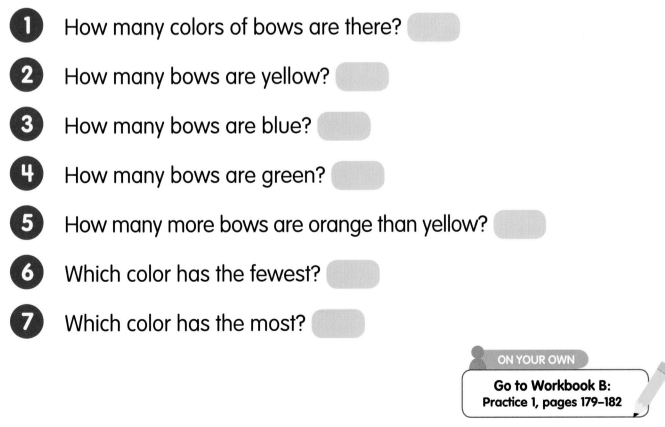

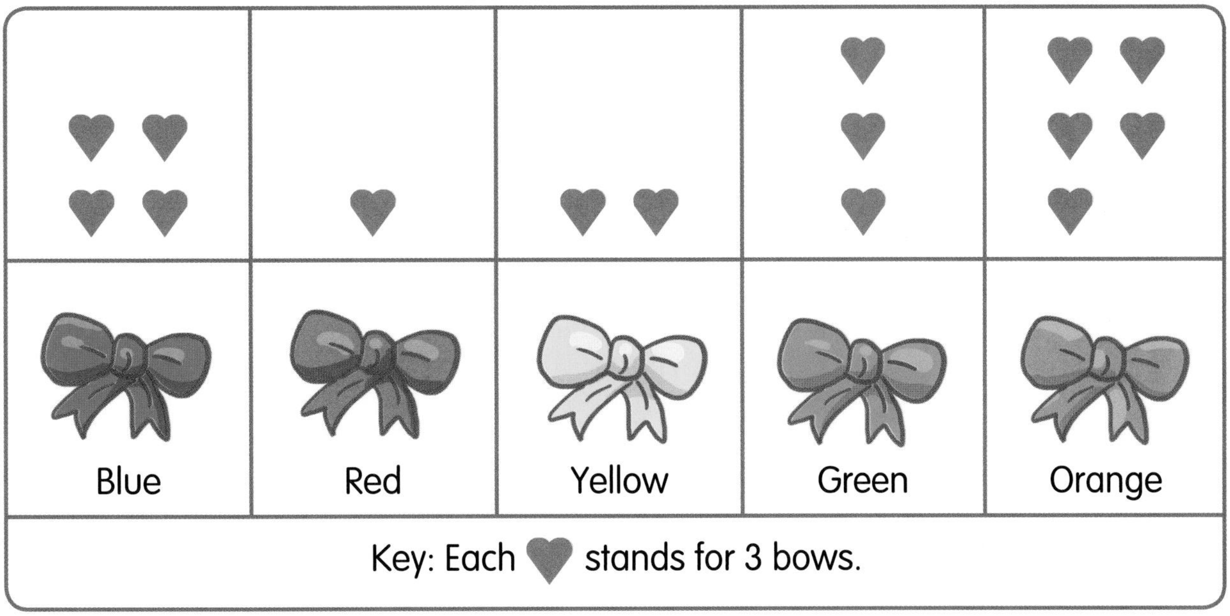

Use the graph to answer these questions.

1. How many colors of bows are there? ____
2. How many bows are yellow? ____
3. How many bows are blue? ____
4. How many bows are green? ____
5. How many more bows are orange than yellow? ____
6. Which color has the fewest? ____
7. Which color has the most? ____

ON YOUR OWN

Go to Workbook B: Practice 1, pages 179–182

LESSON 2 Making Picture Graphs

Lesson Objectives

- Make picture graphs.
- Read and interpret picture graphs.

Vocabulary
record
tally chart

Learn You can make picture graphs to show the number of different items.

Ben's uncle has a farm.
Ben counts each kind of animal on the farm.

He **records** the kinds of animals and their numbers in a **tally chart**.

Animals on the Farm				
Chicken	Cow	Duck	Sheep	Horse
𝍸 𝍸	//	𝍸 𝍸 //	𝍸 /	////

Ben draws a picture graph of his data.
He uses a ♥ to show the numbers of animals.
He puts a key under the graph.
It shows that each ♥ stands for 1 animal.
Then he gives his graph a title.

Kinds of Farm Animals

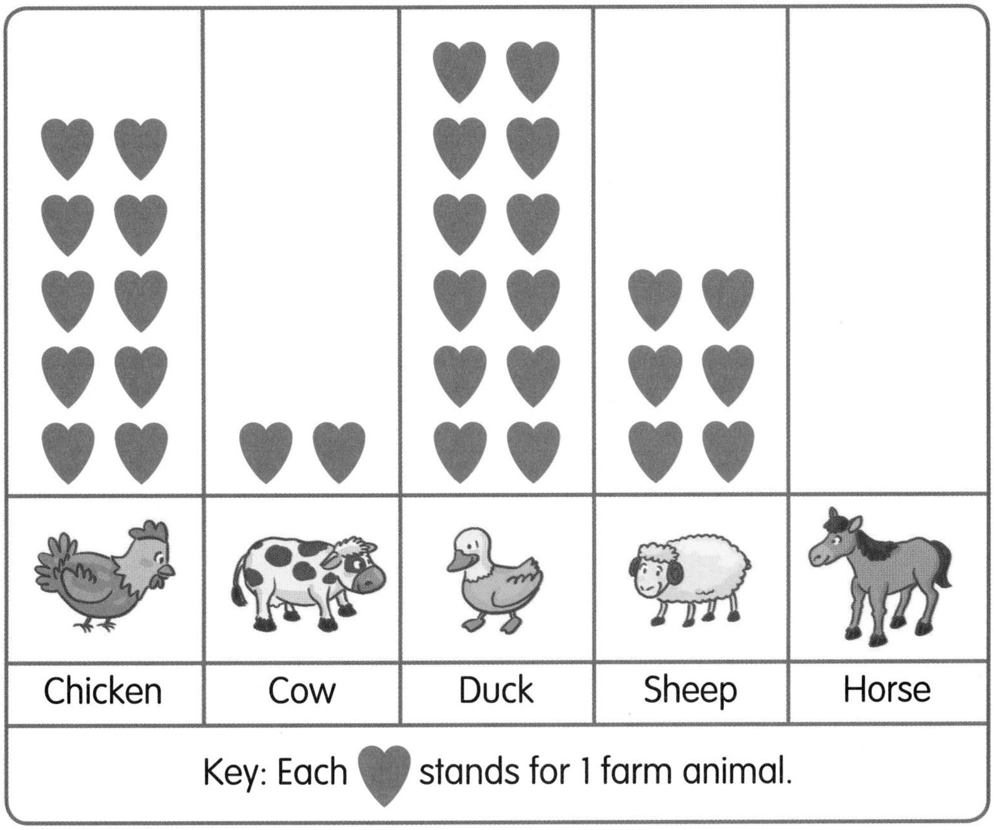

(a) Ben's uncle has 5 kinds of animals.

(b) He has 10 chickens.

(c) He has 12 ducks.

(d) He has 6 sheep and 2 cows.

(e) Ben will draw 4 ♥ to show the number of horses.

(f) Ben's uncle has 34 farm animals in all.

Guided Practice

Complete.

1 Count each color of flower in the picture.
Record your data in a tally chart.

Copy and complete the picture graph.
Give your graph a title.

★ ★			
★ ★			
★ ★			
★ ★			
Red	Yellow	Blue	Pink
Key: Each ★ stands for 2 flowers.			

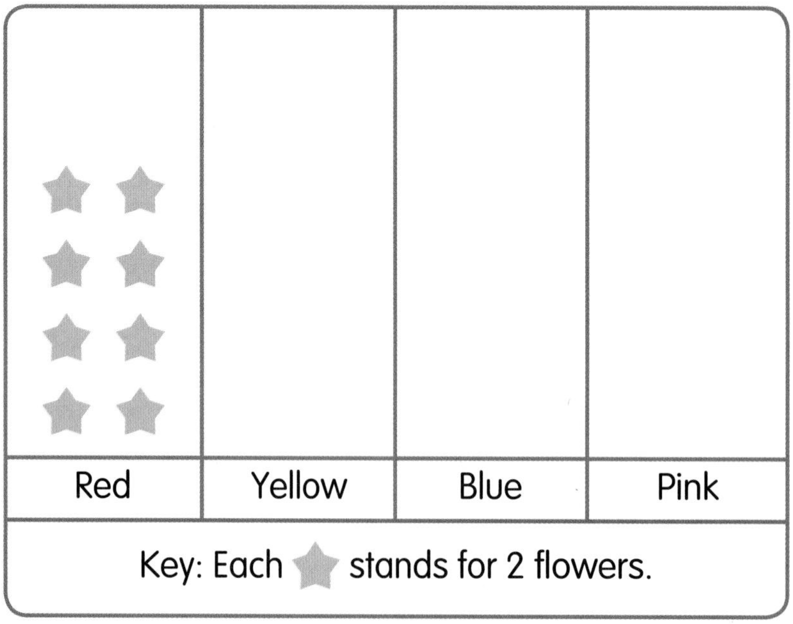

2 Write two problems about your picture graph.
Ask a classmate to solve them.

Hands-On Activity

WORKING TOGETHER

Use 12 colored pencils.

STEP 1 Bundle each pair of the same color.
Put the bundles in a bag.

STEP 2 Take one pair of pencils from the bag.
Record the color on a copy of the picture graph.
Use a ○ of the right color to stand for 2 colored pencils.

Red	
Yellow	
Blue	
Green	
Purple	
Orange	○
Each ○ stands for 2 colored pencils.	

Continued on next page

STEP 3 Put the bundle back in the bag.

STEP 4 Let your partner repeat Step 2 and Step 3.
Take turns taking bundles and drawing ○.
Stop when you have 12 ○ in your graph.

Give your graph a title. Show and explain your graph to the class.

The graph shows the ______ of each kind of ______.

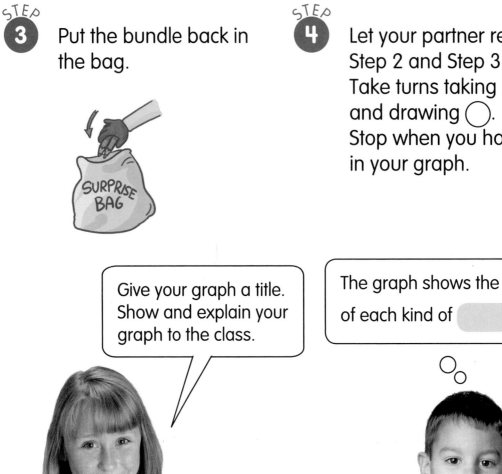

Did you take out the same number of each color?
How can you tell from your graph?
How many red bundles did you take out?
What color did you pull out most often?
How can you tell from your graph?

Let's Practice

The pictures show the farm animals that 24 children like best.

List the animals on a tally chart. Record all the choices.
Then complete a copy of the picture graph below.
Use  to stand for 3 children.

Chicken	
Cow	
Duck	
Sheep	
Horse	

Give your picture graph a title and a key.
Write four problems about your picture graph.
Ask a classmate to solve them.

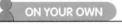

ON YOUR OWN

Go to Workbook B: Practice 2, pages 183–190

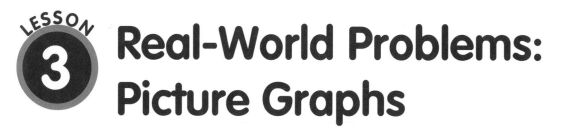

LESSON 3

Real-World Problems: Picture Graphs

Lesson Objective

- Solve real-world problems using picture graphs.

Learn

You can solve word problems using picture graphs.

The picture graph shows the number of stamps 5 children have.

Andy has the most stamps.
There are 8 for Andy.
$3 \times 8 = 24$
Andy has 24 in all.

Susan has 18 stamps in all.

There are 6 for Susan.
$3 \times 6 = 18$
Susan has 6 stamps from Brazil.
The rest are from the United States.

How many stamps does she have from the United States?
$18 - 6 = 12$
She has 12 stamps from the United States.

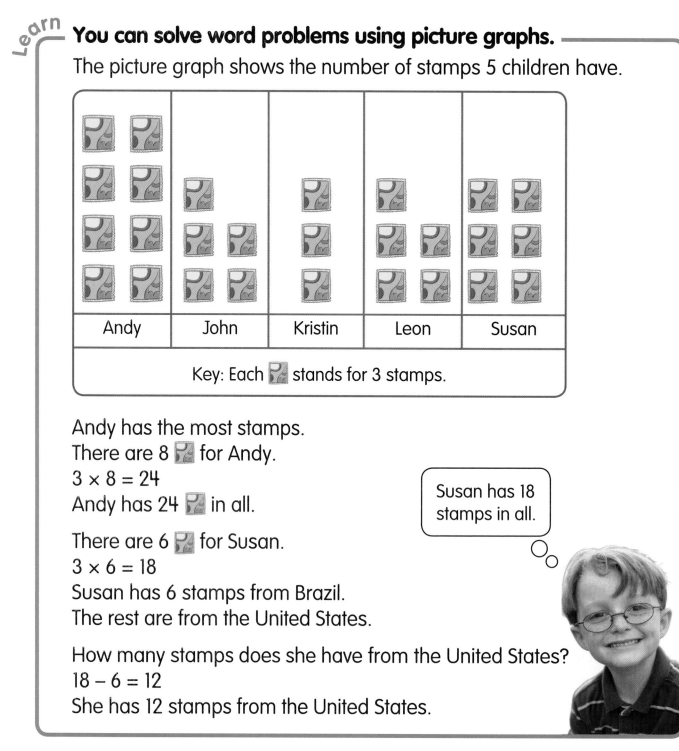

Guided Practice

The graph shows the number of children playing five kinds of games.

Games Children Play

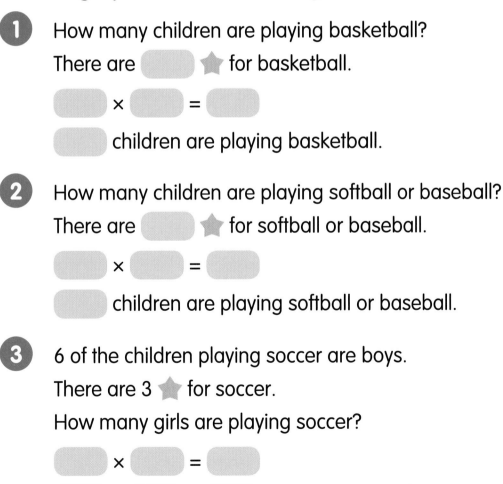

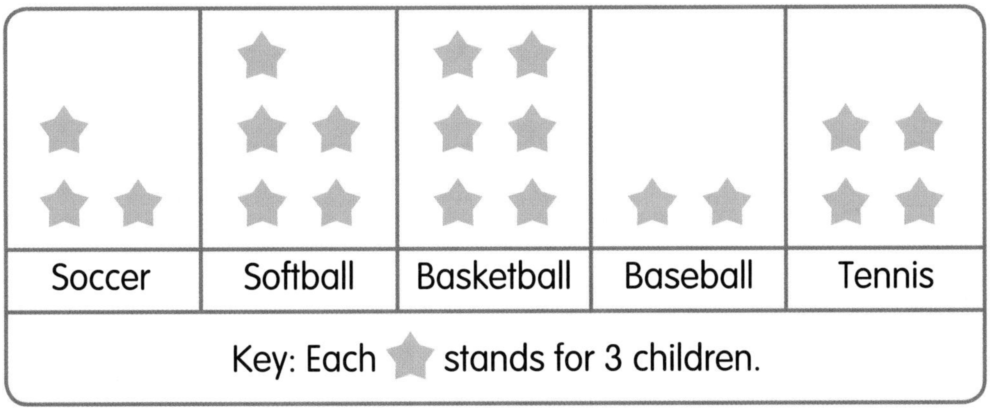

Use the graph to find the missing numbers.

1 How many children are playing basketball?

There are ___ ★ for basketball.

___ × ___ = ___

___ children are playing basketball.

2 How many children are playing softball or baseball?

There are ___ ★ for softball or baseball.

___ × ___ = ___

___ children are playing softball or baseball.

3 6 of the children playing soccer are boys.

There are 3 ★ for soccer.

How many girls are playing soccer?

___ × ___ = ___

___ − ___ = ___

___ girls are playing soccer.

The graph shows the favorite fruit of some students.

Favorite Fruit

Apple	◆ ◆ ◆ ◆
Banana	◆ ◆
Pear	◆
Peach	◆ ◆ ◆ ◆ ◆ ◆
Orange	◆ ◆ ◆ ◆ ◆
Key: Each ◆ stands for 4 students.	

Use the graph to answer these questions.

4 4 of the students who chose Apple are boys.
How many girls chose Apple? ____

5 15 girls chose Peach.
How many boys chose Peach? ____

6 4 girls chose Banana and 9 girls chose Orange.
How many boys chose Banana or Orange? ____

7 3 girls chose Pear.
How many more girls than boys chose Pear? ____

Let's Practice

The graph shows the number of bottles of drinks sold on a Monday.

Bottles of Drinks Sold

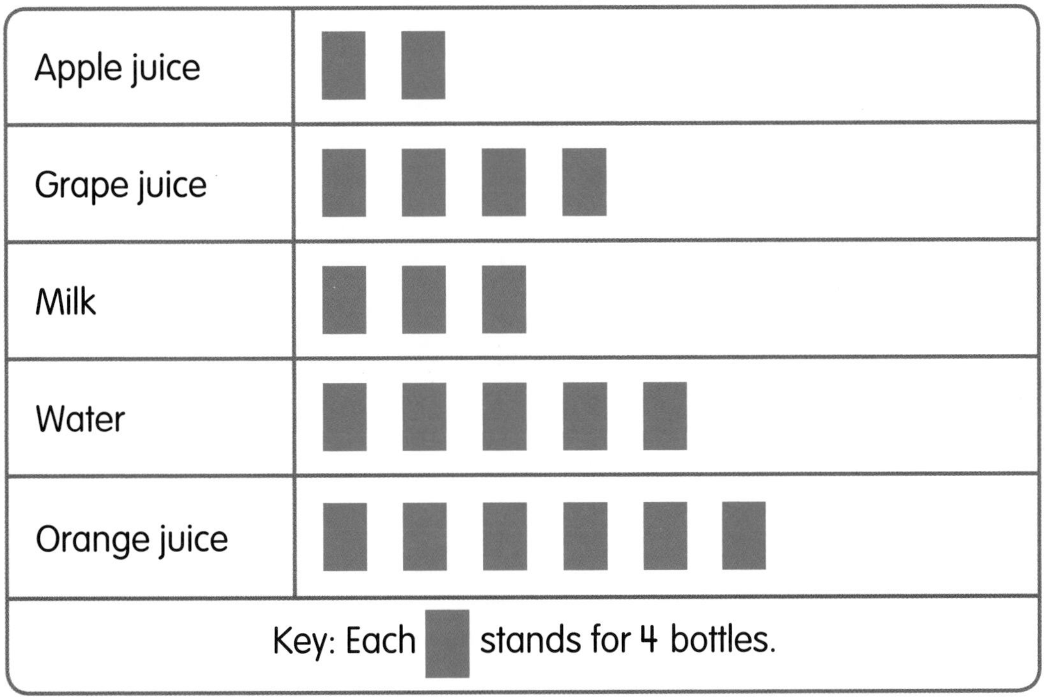

Use the graph to answer these questions.

1. How many bottles of grape juice were sold?
2. Which was the most popular drink?
3. 11 girls bought orange juice.
   How many boys bought orange juice?
4. 16 girls bought grape juice.
   How many boys bought grape juice?
5. One bottle of water cost $2.
   How much did the store owner make by selling water?
6. Write two more questions about this graph.

The graph shows the number of teenagers who went to a movie on a Sunday.

Movies Teenagers Watched

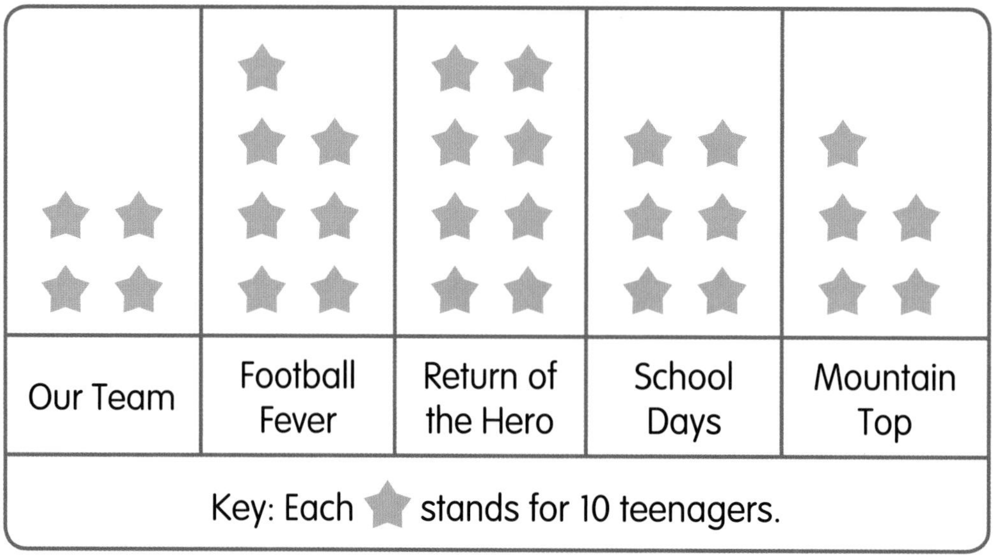

Use the graph to answer the questions.

7 60 boys watched Football Fever.
How many girls watched Football Fever? ______

8 60 girls watched School Days.
How many boys watched School Days? ______

9 20 girls watched Return of the Hero, and 35 girls watched Mountain Top.

How many boys watched Return of the Hero or The Mountain Top? ______

10 10 more girls than boys watched Our Team.
How many girls watched Our Team? ______

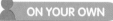

ON YOUR OWN

Go to Workbook B: Practice 3, pages 191–194

CRITICAL THINKING SKILLS

Put On Your Thinking Cap!

PROBLEM SOLVING

Pearl watched her friends at a playground. She made a picture graph of what each friend was doing.

Friends at the Playground

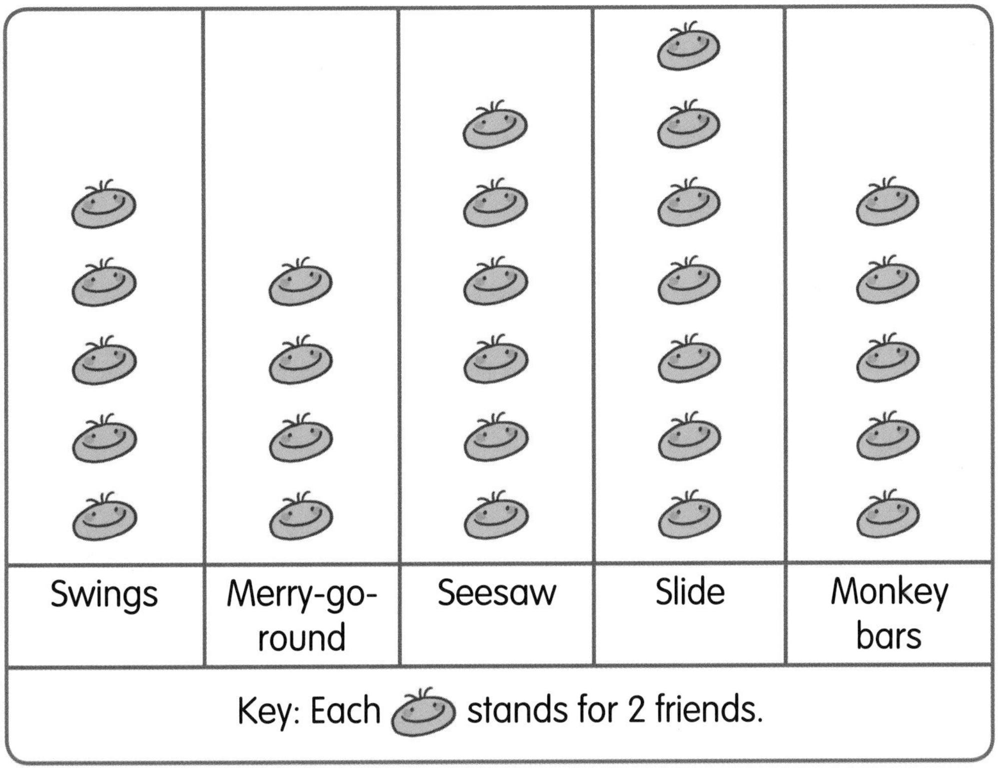

How many friends are doing each activity?

Use the graph on page 243 to answer each question.

1. The merry-go-round can hold two more friends than the monkey bars can. How many more children can get on the merry-go-round?

2. An equal number of friends can be on the slide and the merry-go-round.
How many children need to get off the slide to make an equal number?

3. There should be an equal number of friends on the slide and swings.
How many children need to move to the swings from the slide?

4. Four more friends can be on the seesaw than on the swings.
How many friends need to get off the swings to make this happen?

ON YOUR OWN

Go to Workbook B:
Put on Your Thinking Cap!
pages 195–196

Chapter Wrap Up

BIG IDEA Picture graphs use pictures to show data about things you can count.

You have learned...

to read, analyze, and interpret picture graphs

Prizes Won at the Fair

to find number of things

How many people won a teddy bear?
$5 \times 4 = 20$
20 people won a teddy bear.

to find difference or sum

How many people won a teddy bear or a stuffed animal?
$20 + 12 = 32$
32 people won a teddy bear or a stuffed animal each.

How many more people won a teddy bear than a stuffed animal?
$20 - 12 = 8$
8 more people won a teddy bear than a stuffed animal.

to make picture graphs

Collect and record data in a tally chart.

Snowy Days in December	Tally
First Week	𝍸 /
Second Week	//
Third Week	////
Fourth Week	𝍸 /

Draw a picture graph.

Use to show the number of snowy days.

Make a key.

Show that each stands for 2 days.

Give the graph a title.

Snowy Days in December

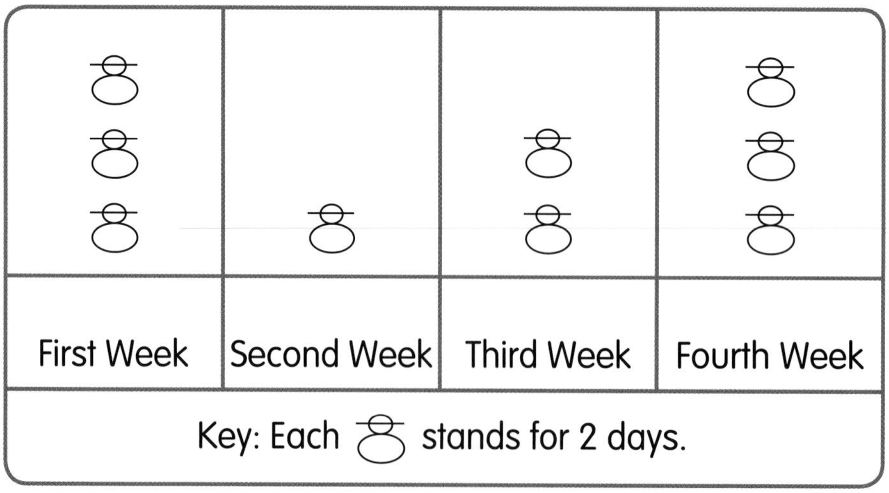

to solve real-world problems using picture graphs

The graph shows the kind of flowers sold on Monday.

Flowers Sold on Monday

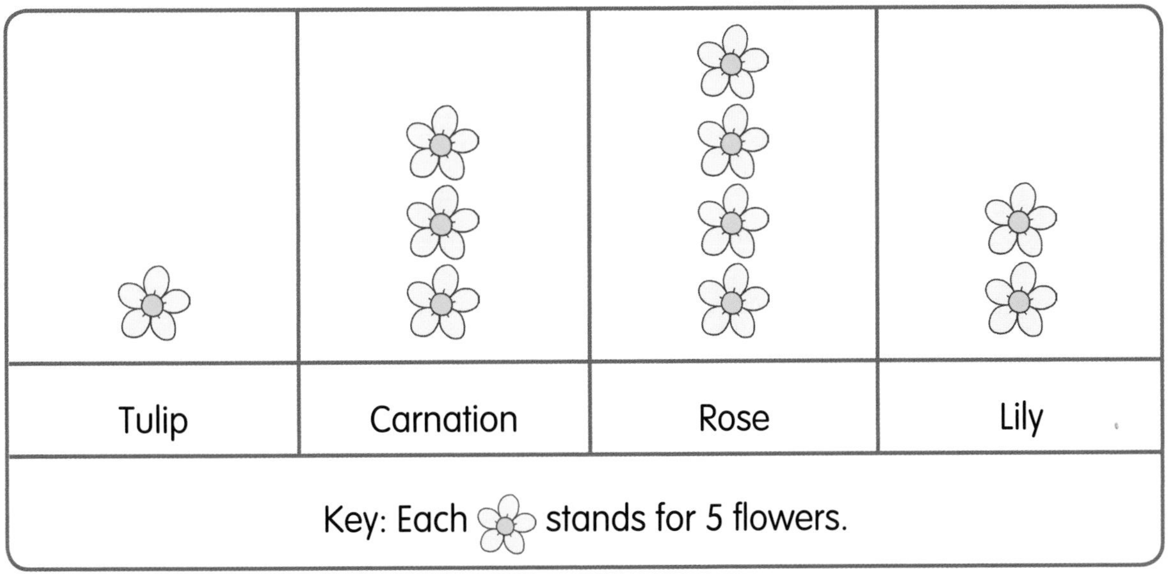

How many carnations were sold?
There are 3  for carnation.
3 × 5 = 15
15 carnations were sold.

How many tulips and lilies were sold in all?
There is 1  for tulips.
1 × 5 = 5
There are 2  for lilies.
2 × 5 = 10
5 + 10 = 15
15 tulips and lilies were sold in all.

5 roses are white and the rest are red.
How many red roses were sold?
There are 4  of roses.
4 × 5 = 20
20 – 5 = 15
15 red roses were sold.

ON YOUR OWN

Go to Workbook B: Chapter Review/Test, pages 197–200

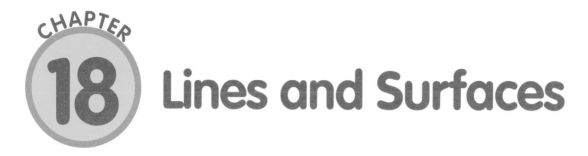

CHAPTER

18 Lines and Surfaces

Look at these drawings.

These drawings are parts of lines.

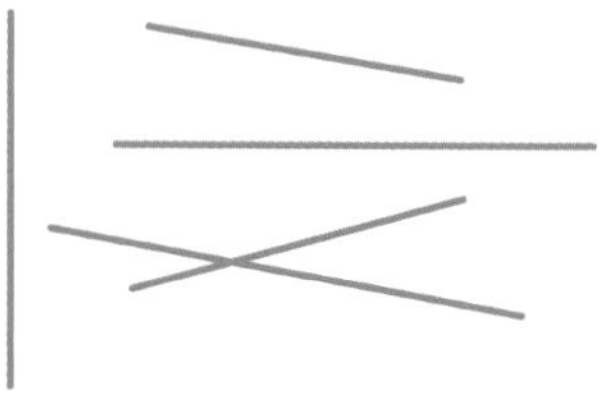

These shapes are made of parts of lines.

These are curves.

Each of these pictures is made of both parts of lines and curves.

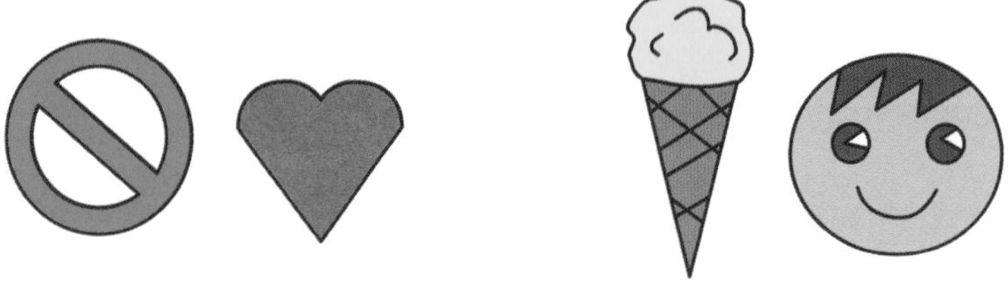

None of these pictures is made of *both* parts of lines and curves.

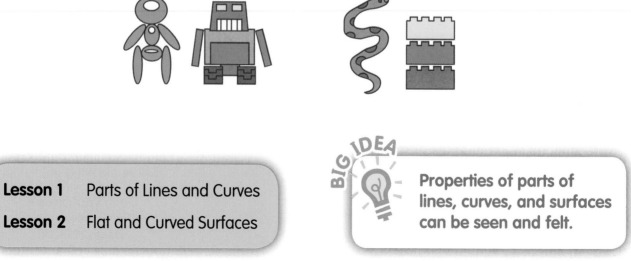

BIG IDEA

Properties of parts of lines, curves, and surfaces can be seen and felt.

Recall Prior Knowledge

Identifying plane shapes

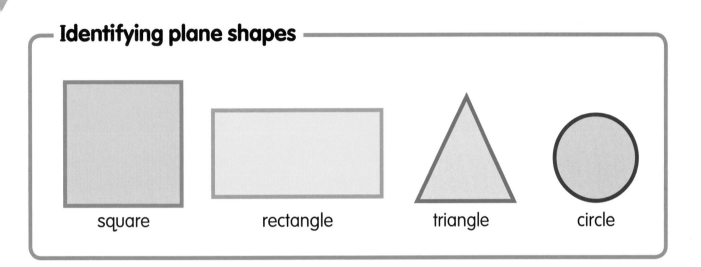

square rectangle triangle circle

Recognizing plane shapes in objects

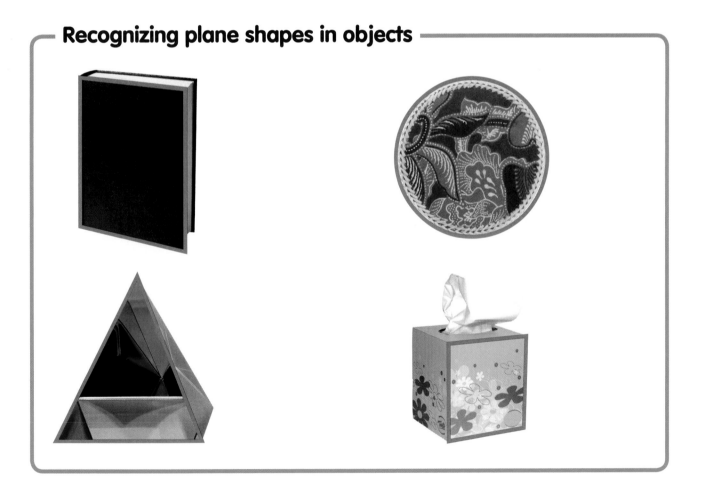

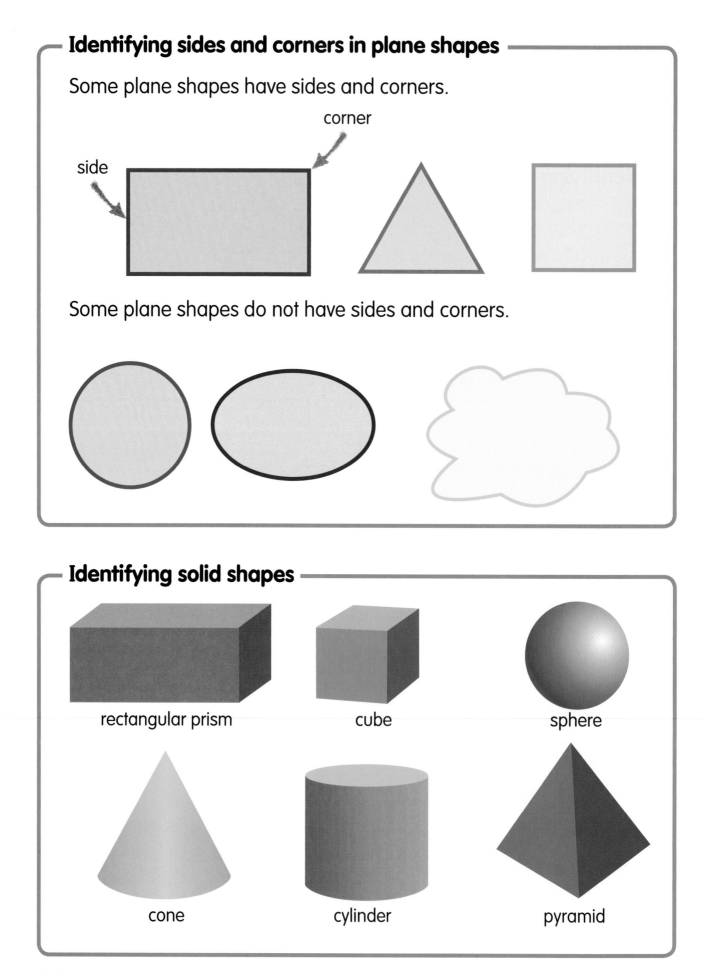

Identifying sides and corners in plane shapes

Some plane shapes have sides and corners.

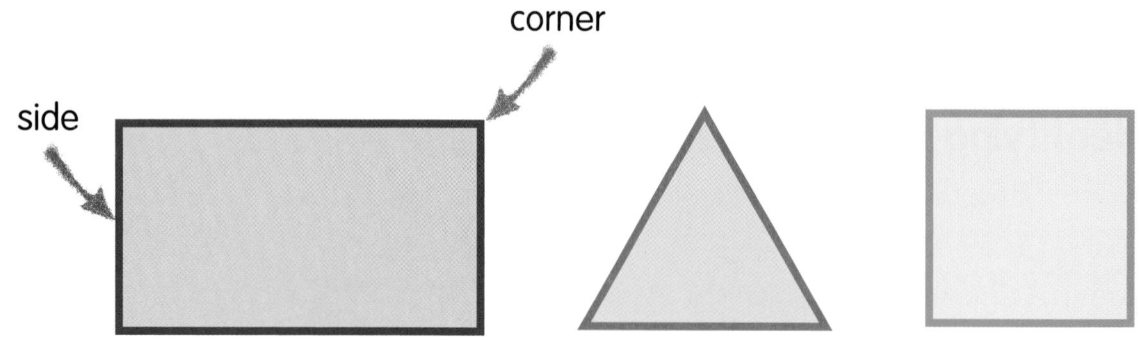

Some plane shapes do not have sides and corners.

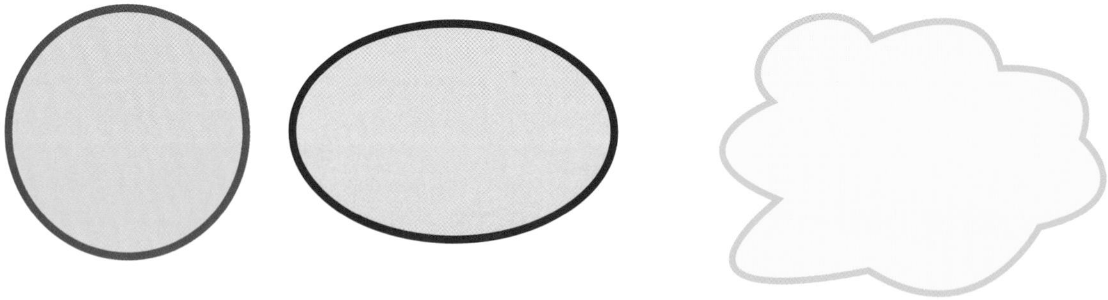

Identifying solid shapes

rectangular prism

cube

sphere

cone

cylinder

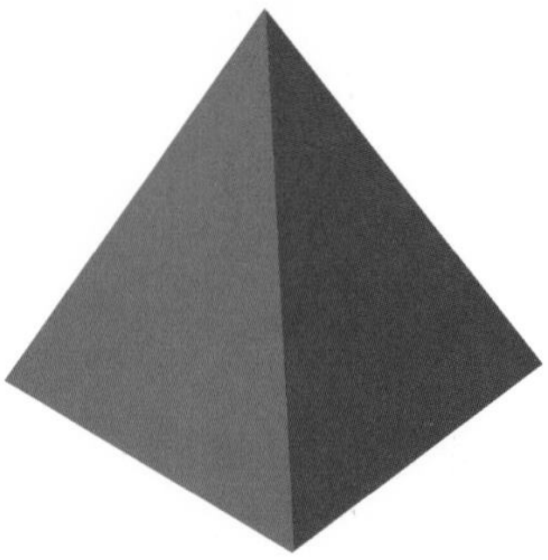
pyramid

Recognizing solid shapes in objects

✔Quick Check

Name the shapes.

1. 

2. 

3. 

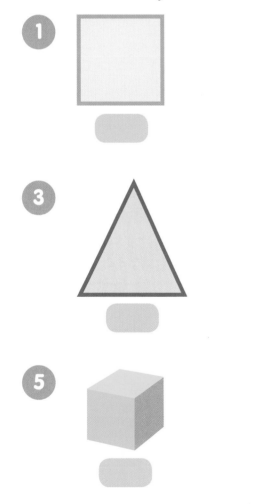

4. 

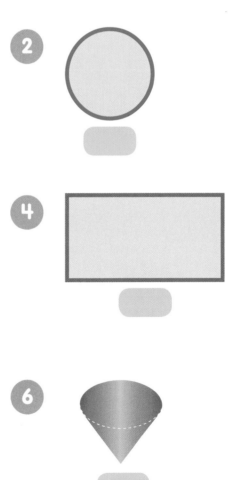

5. 

6. 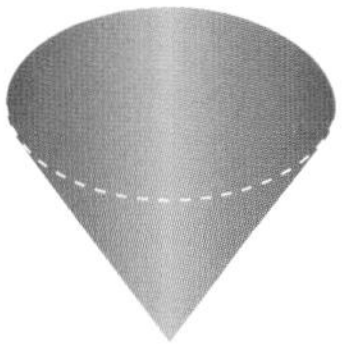

Name the plane shapes you see in these objects.

7 

8 

9 

Count the number of sides.
Then count the number of corners.

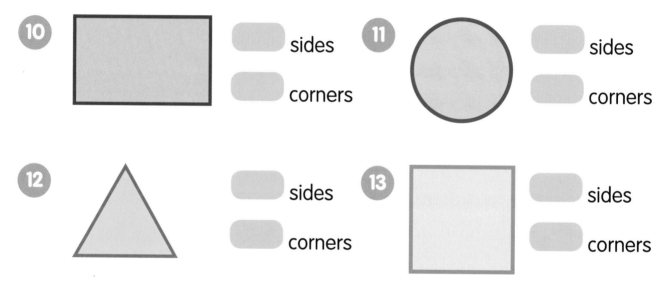

10 

sides

corners

11 

sides

corners

12 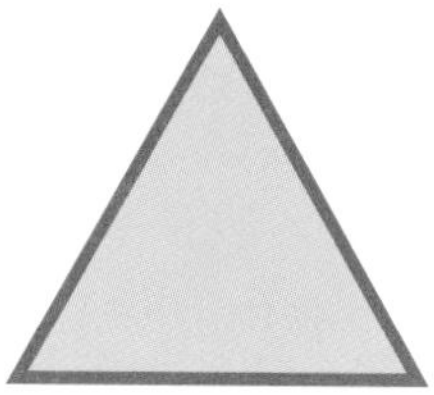

sides

corners

13 

sides

corners

Name the solid shapes you see in these objects.

14 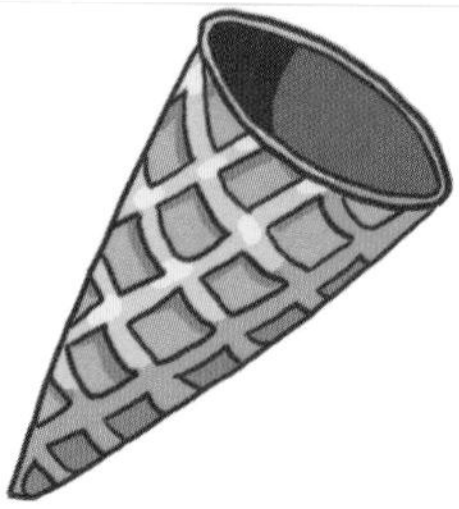

15 

16 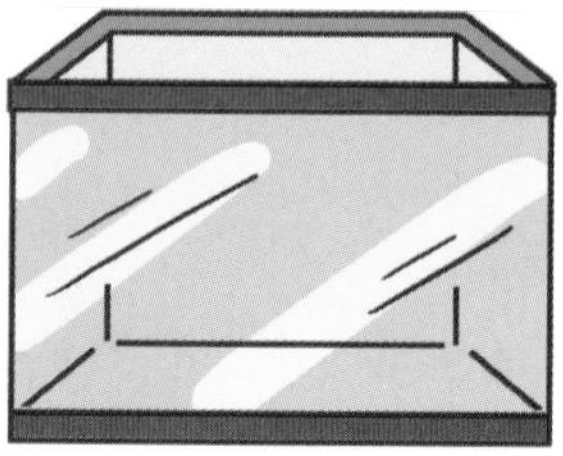

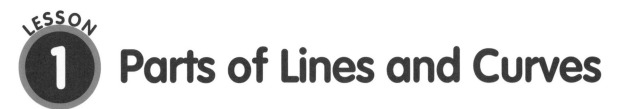

LESSON 1 Parts of Lines and Curves

Lesson Objective

- Recognize, identify, and describe parts of lines and curves.
- Draw parts of lines and curves.

Vocabulary
part of a line
curve

Learn Recognize and identify parts of lines and curves.

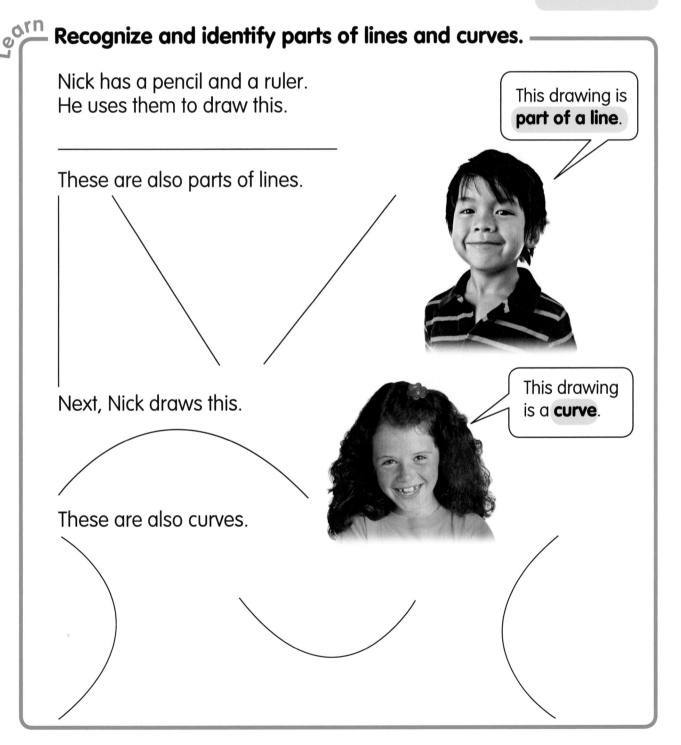

Nick has a pencil and a ruler.
He uses them to draw this.

This drawing is **part of a line**.

These are also parts of lines.

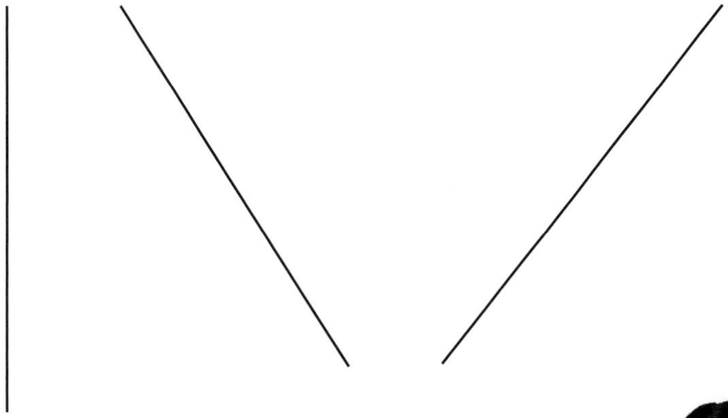

Next, Nick draws this.

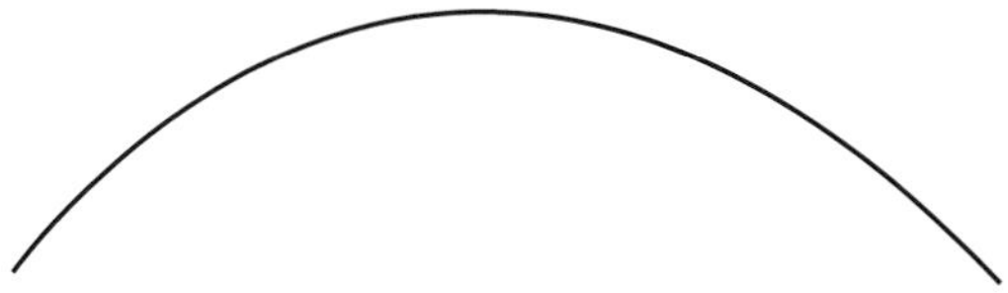

This drawing is a **curve**.

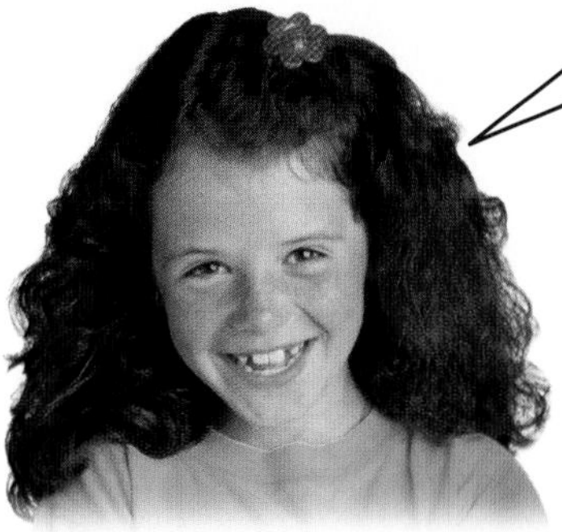

These are also curves.

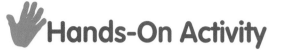

Hands-On Activity

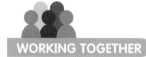

WORKING TOGETHER

Which is a part of a line and which is a curve?
Trace each with your finger.
Then make drawings like:

What do you notice?
Which of these are curves?
Trace each with your finger.

Guided Practice

Look at these drawings.
Then answer each question.

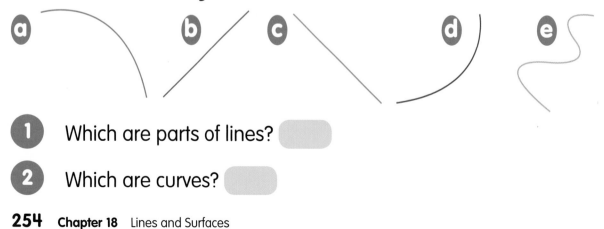

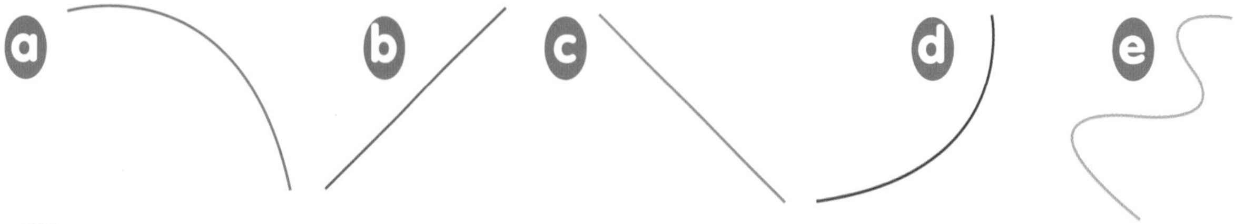

1. Which are parts of lines?
2. Which are curves?

Learn

You can combine parts of lines and curves.

How many parts of lines and curves are there in the drawing?
There are 10 parts of lines and 9 curves.

Guided Practice

Find the missing numbers.
The picture is made with parts of lines and curves.

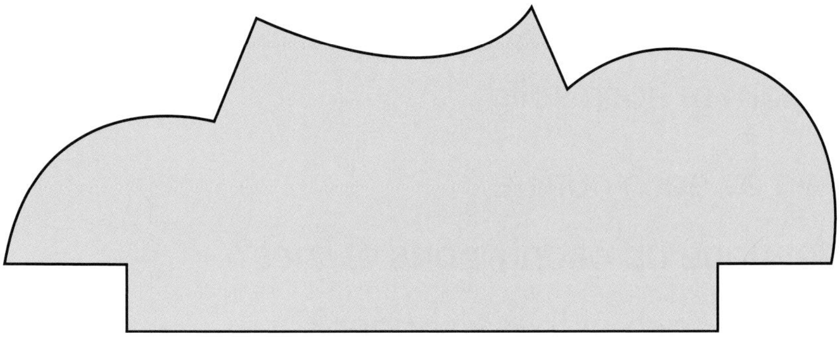

3 There are ____ parts of lines and ____ curves.

The figure has two parts of lines and a curve.

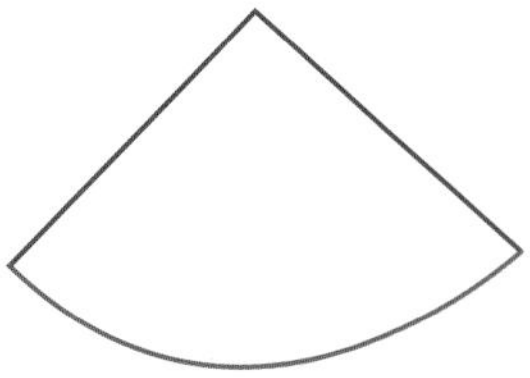

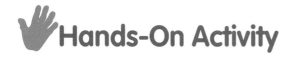

4 Draw two figures that each have 2 parts of lines and 1 curve.

5 Draw two figures that each have 2 curves and 1 part of a line.

6 Draw two figures that each have more than 2 parts of lines and 2 curves. Tell the number of parts of lines and curves in each figure.

Hands-On Activity

Use these solids.

Trace the outline of the bottom of each solid.

Name the flat shape shown by each outline.

Which of these shapes are made up of only parts of lines?

How many parts of lines make each of these shapes?

Are any of these shapes made of curves only?

How many curves make each of these shapes?

Let's Practice

Answer the questions.

1. Look at the picture.
How many parts of lines are there?
How many curves are there?

2. Collect some objects in your classroom.
Draw around the bottom of each object, like this.

Do you know the name of the shape you drew?
If your answer is 'Yes,' name the shape.
Are the shapes made of parts of lines or curves?

ON YOUR OWN

Go to Workbook B: Practice 1, pages 209–214

LESSON 2 Flat and Curved Surfaces

Lesson Objectives

- Identify, classify, and count flat and curved surfaces.
- Identify solids that can stack, slide, and/or roll.

Vocabulary
flat surface
curved surface
slide
stack
roll

Learn You can see and feel flat surfaces.

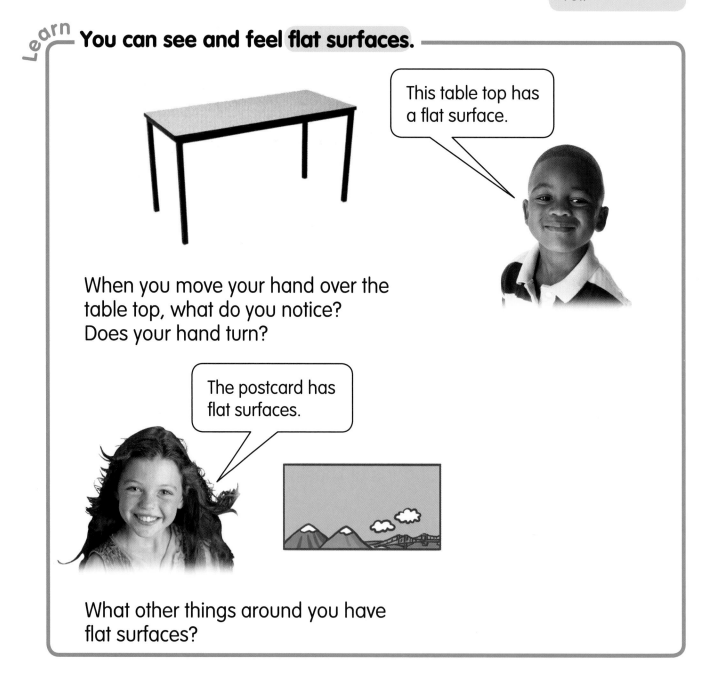

This table top has a flat surface.

When you move your hand over the table top, what do you notice? Does your hand turn?

The postcard has flat surfaces.

What other things around you have flat surfaces?

Learn

You can see and feel surfaces that are not flat.

This ball does not have a flat surface. It has a **curved surface**.

Move your hand over the surface of a ball. Does your hand turn?

Does this watermelon have a curved surface?

What other things around you have curved surfaces?

Guided Practice

Look at the pictures. Then answer the questions.

CD

road sign

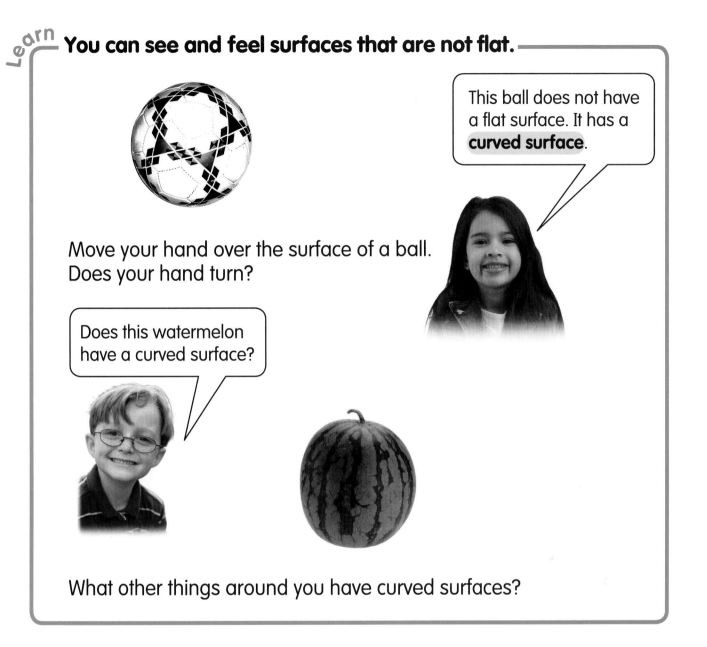

balloon

apple

frame

pencil

scarf

marble

tissue box

glass

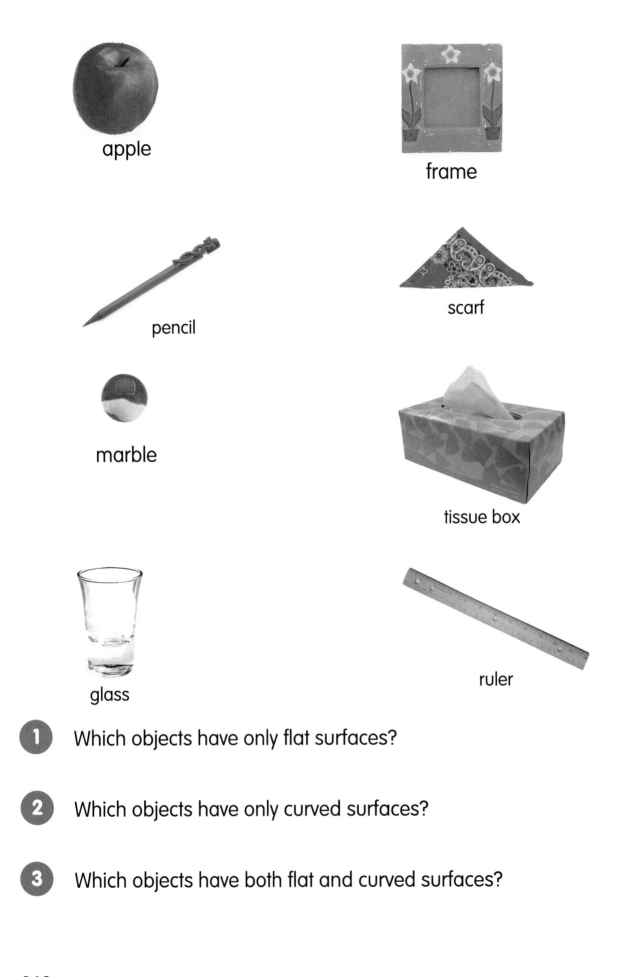

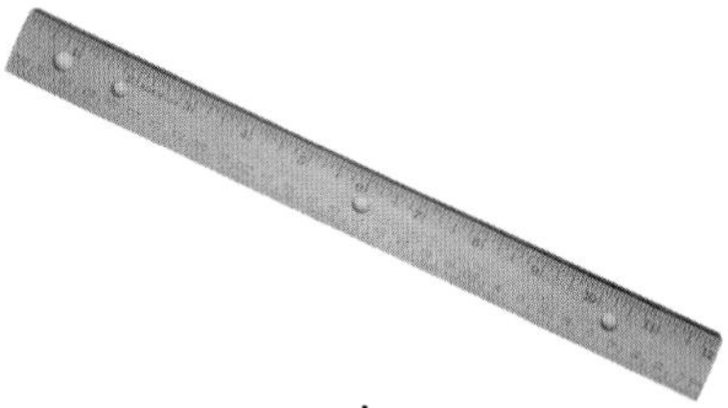

ruler

1. Which objects have only flat surfaces?

2. Which objects have only curved surfaces?

3. Which objects have both flat and curved surfaces?

Learn

You can move objects with flat or curved surfaces.

Some objects have flat surfaces.

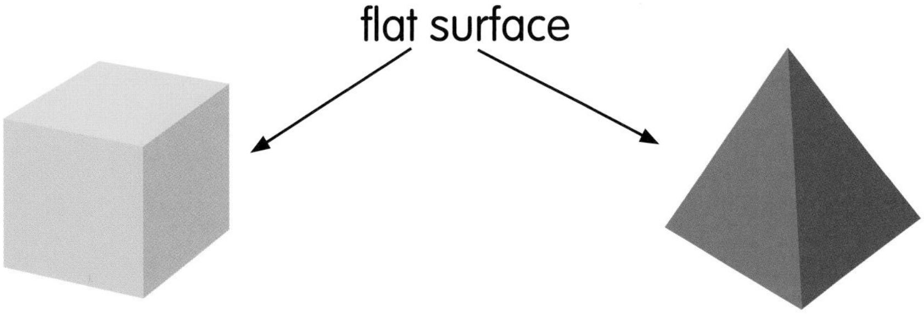

You can **slide** objects that have a flat surface.

You can **stack** some objects that have more than one flat surface.

Some objects have curved surfaces.

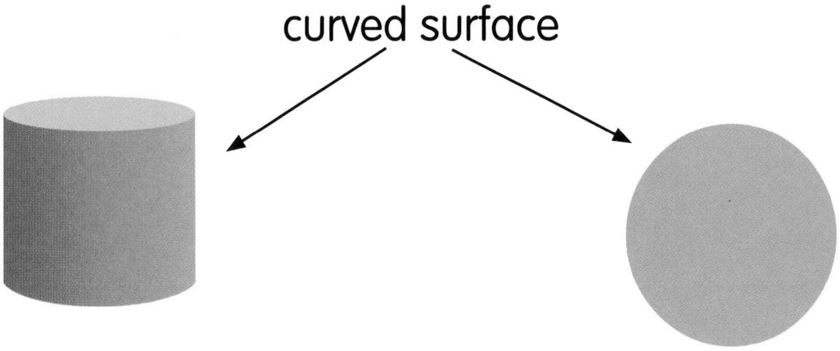

You can **roll** objects that have curved surfaces.

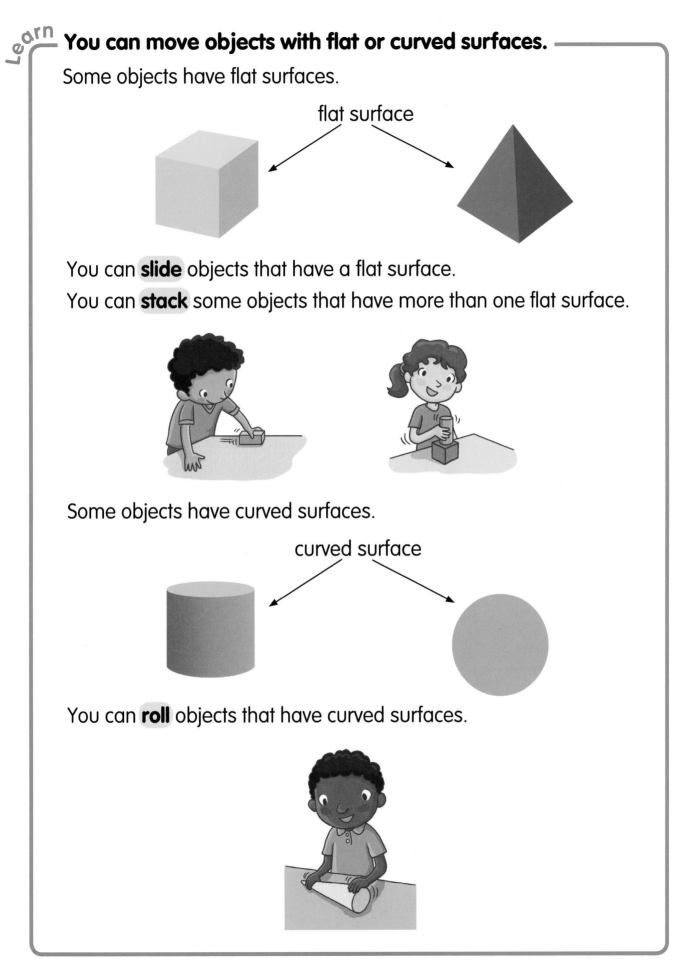

Hands-On Activity

1 **Name the solids shown.**

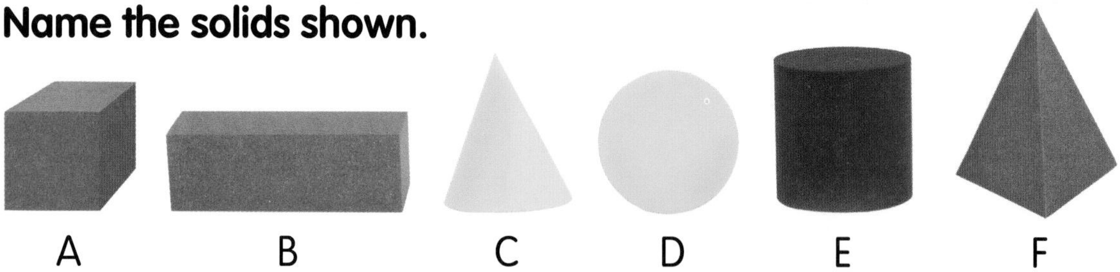

2 **Name and count the flat and curved surfaces on each solid. Then mark (*X*) to show whether you can stack, slide, or roll the solid.**

	Number of flat surfaces	Number of curved surfaces	Stack	Slide	Roll
A					
B					
C					
D					
E					
F					

Now talk about the solids.

3 Which solids have only flat surfaces?

4 Which solids have only curved surfaces?

5 Which solid has both flat and curved surfaces?

6 Which solids can you stack?

7 Which solids can you roll?

8 Which solids can you slide?

9 Which solids can you not slide?

10 Which two solids can you move in the same ways?

11 Is there a solid that you can stack, roll, and slide?

12 If the answer is 'Yes,' name the solid.

13 Then explain why it can move in all these ways.

Guided Practice

Look at the pictures.
Then answer the questions.

4 

This is a box. It can slide.
Why?

5 

This is a ball. It can roll.
Why?

6 

You can stack, slide, or roll this container.
Why?

Let's Practice

Look at the pictures.
Then answer the questions.

cube

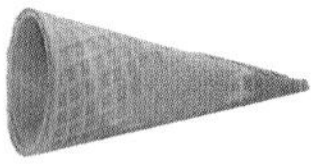
ice cream cone

orange

book

1. Which objects have flat surfaces?
2. Which objects have curved surfaces?
3. Which objects can you slide?
4. Which objects can you stack?
5. Which objects can you roll?
6. Which objects can you slide, stack, and roll?

party hat

soup can

box

marble

7. How many flat surfaces are in each object?
8. How many curved surfaces are in each object?

ON YOUR OWN

Go to Workbook B:
Practice 2, pages 215–220

Put On Your Thinking Cap!

PROBLEM SOLVING

1 Look at the figure.
How many straight lines and curves are needed to make it?

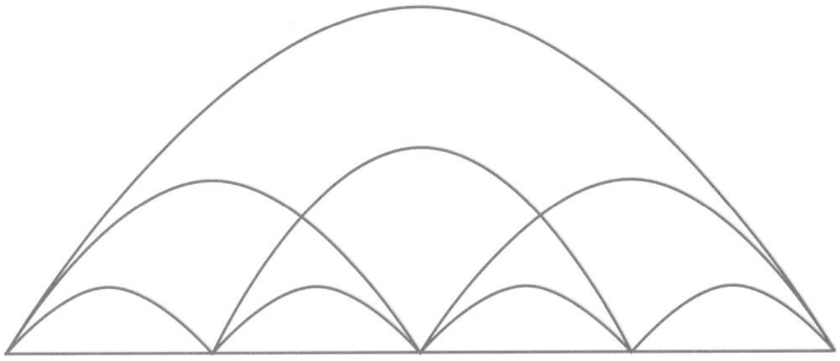

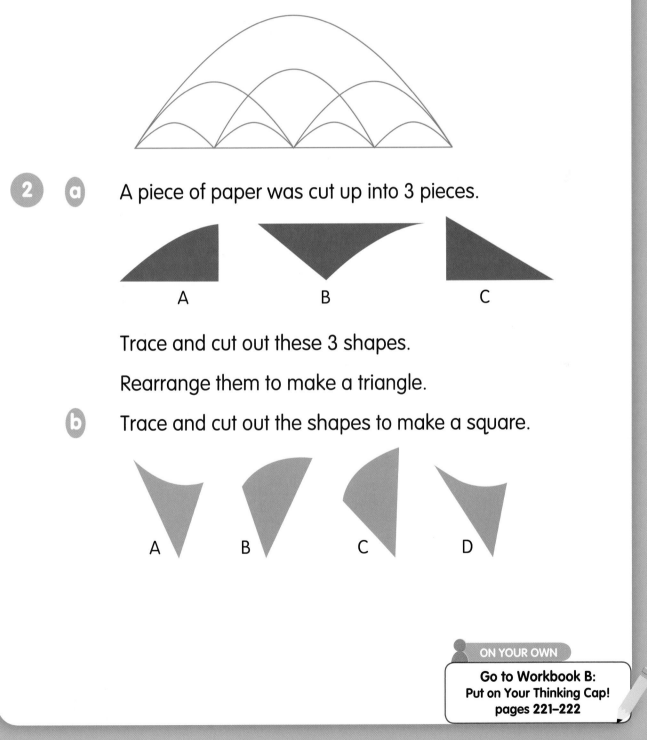

2 a A piece of paper was cut up into 3 pieces.

A B C

Trace and cut out these 3 shapes.

Rearrange them to make a triangle.

b Trace and cut out the shapes to make a square.

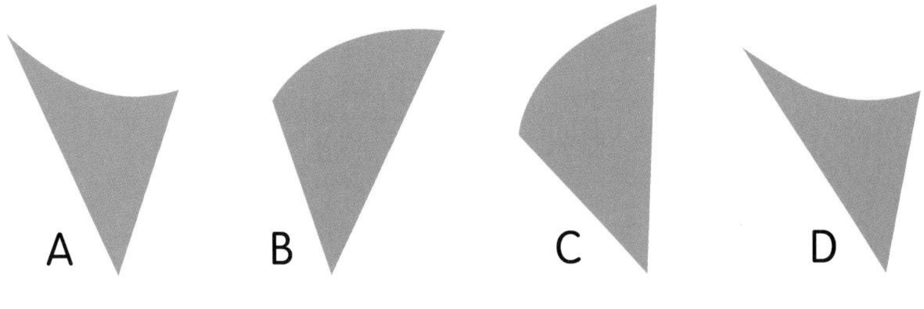

ON YOUR OWN

Go to Workbook B:
Put on Your Thinking Cap!
pages 221–222

Chapter Wrap Up

BIG IDEA
Properties of parts of lines, curves, and surfaces can be seen and felt.

You have learned...

Lines and Surfaces

Lines

Parts of Lines

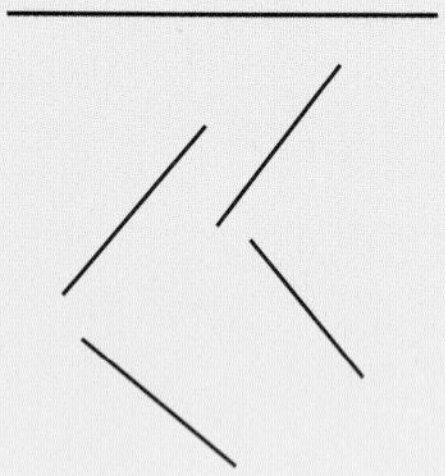

Curves

Parts of lines and curves can be combined to form objects.

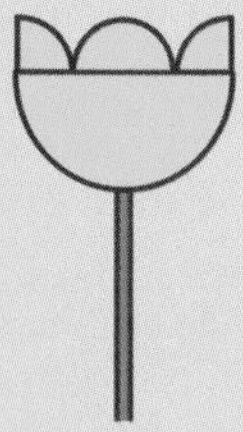

5 parts of lines,
4 curves

Surfaces

Flat surfaces

This book has a flat surface.

Curved surfaces

This globe does not have a flat surface.

can be moved by...

stacking

sliding

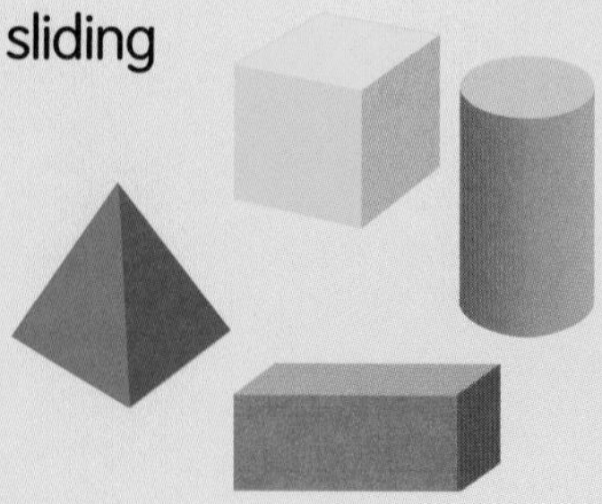

rolling

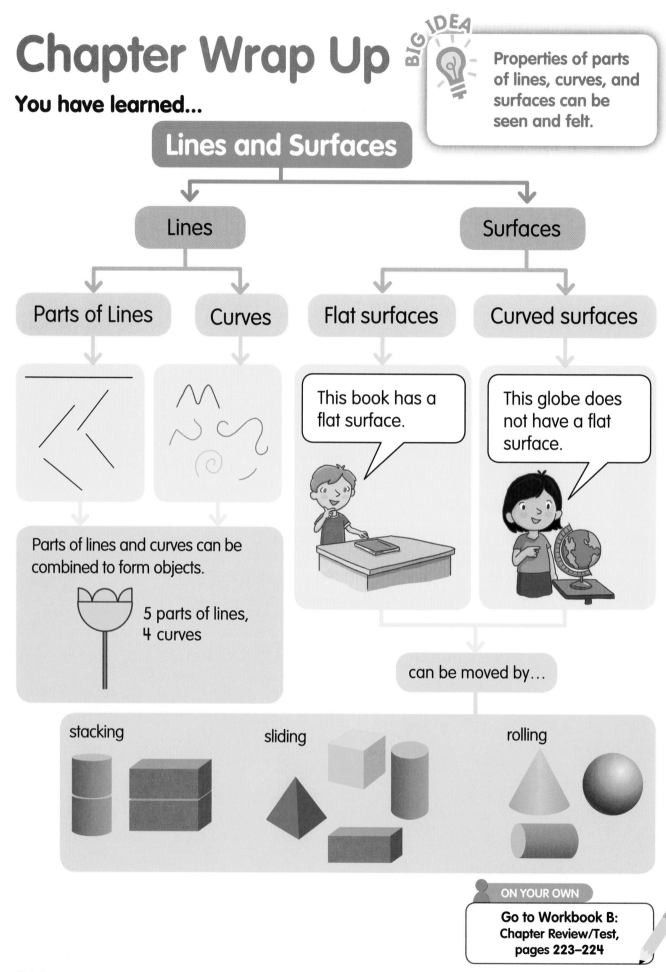

ON YOUR OWN

Go to Workbook B: Chapter Review/Test, pages 223–224

CHAPTER
19 Shapes and Patterns

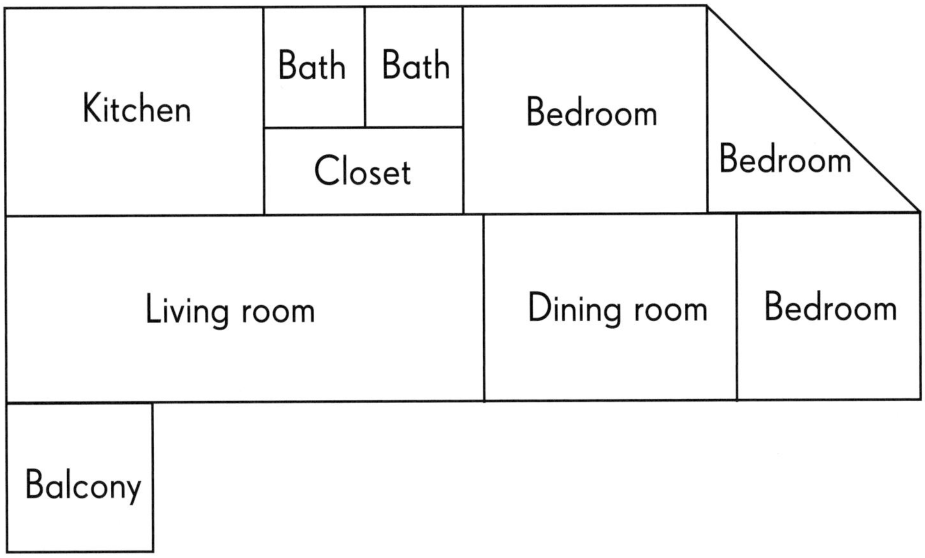

I can draw the rooms in my house like this. Can you identify the plane shapes?

Here are some items found in the living room.

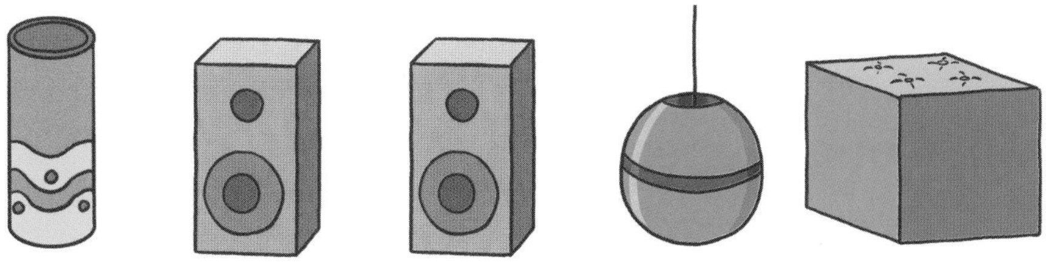

Can you identify the solid shapes?

BIG IDEA

Plane and solid shapes can be identified and classified. They can be separated and combined to make other shapes.

Recall Prior Knowledge

Making pictures with plane shapes

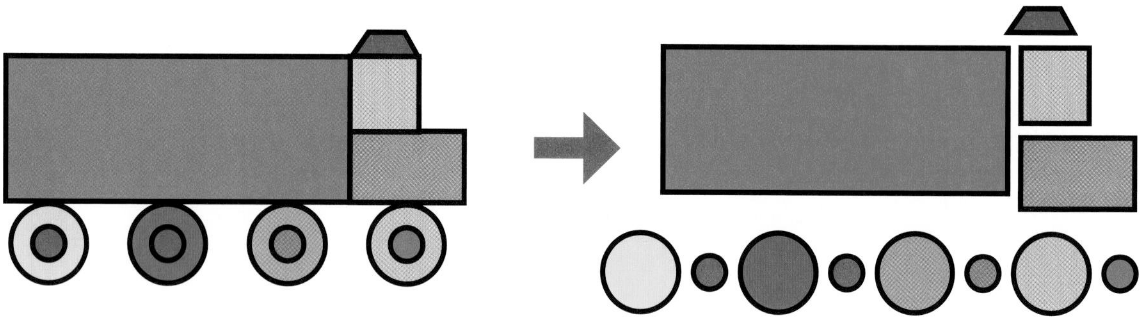

Making models with solid shapes

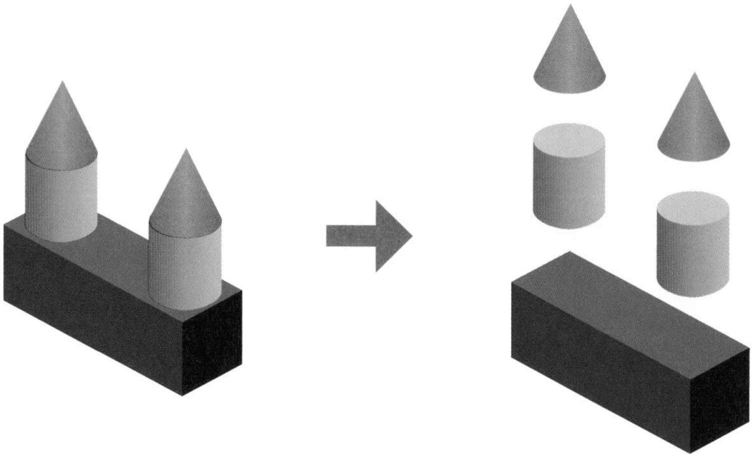

Making patterns with plane shapes

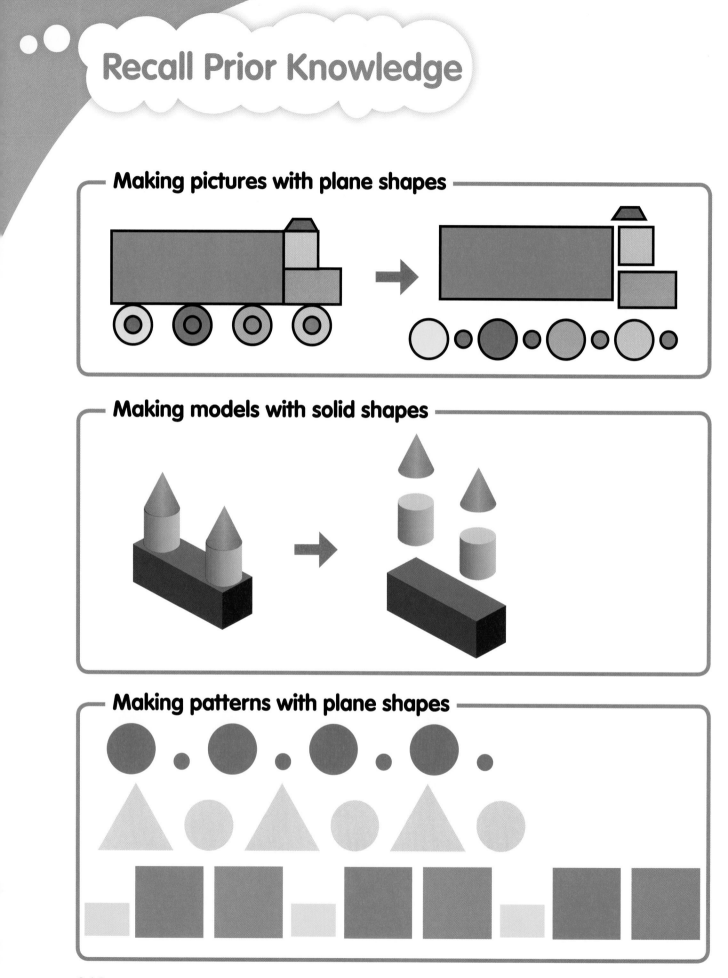

Making patterns with solid shapes

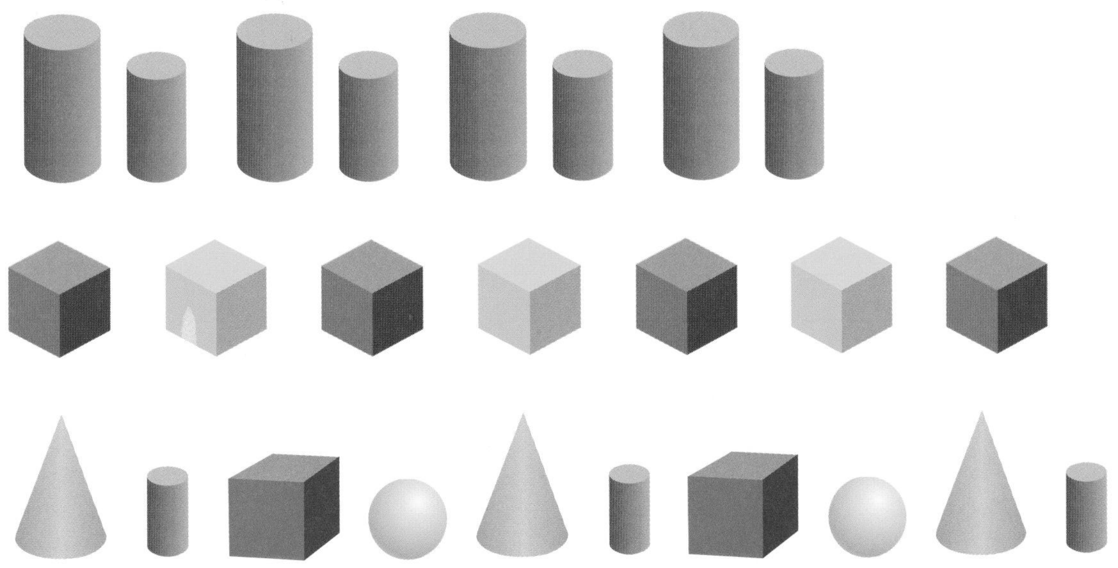

✔Quick Check

1. Name the shapes that make up this picture.
How many of each shape are there?

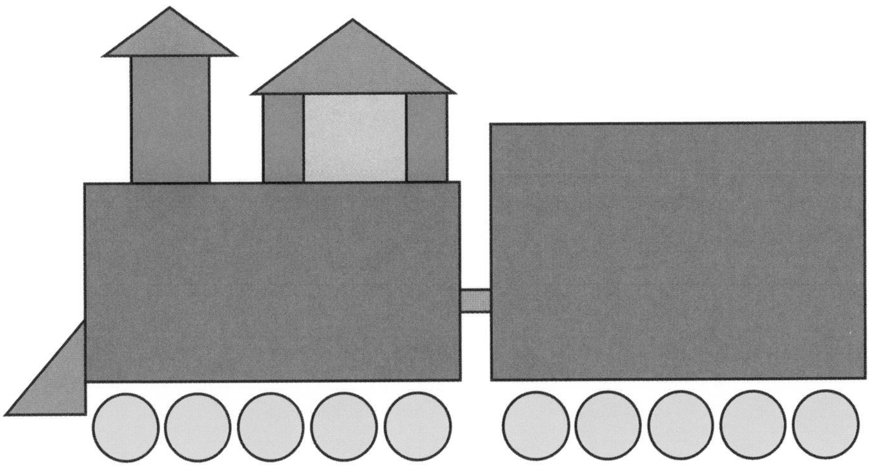

2 Name the solid shapes that make up this model.
How many of each shape are there?

Choose the shape that comes next.

3 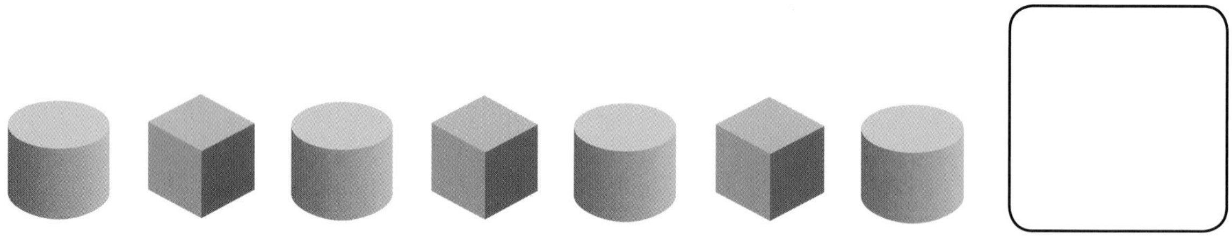

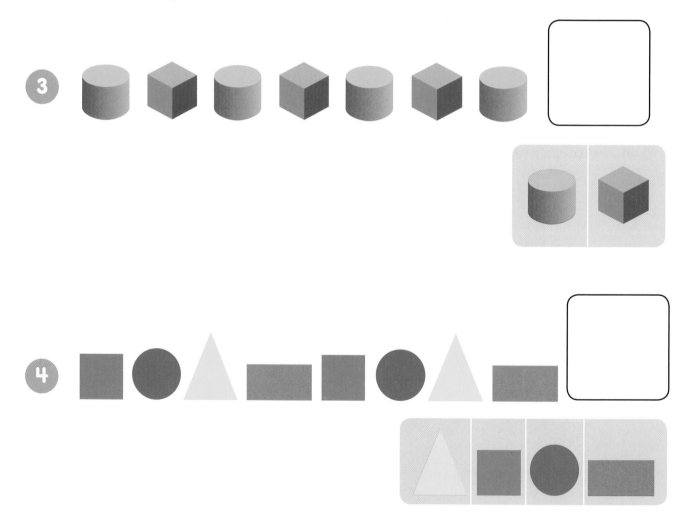

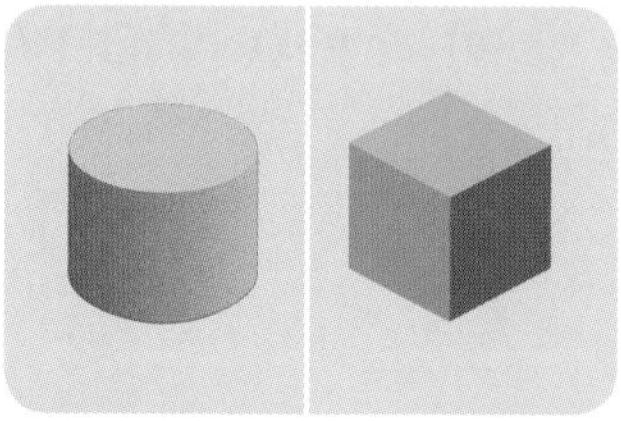

4 

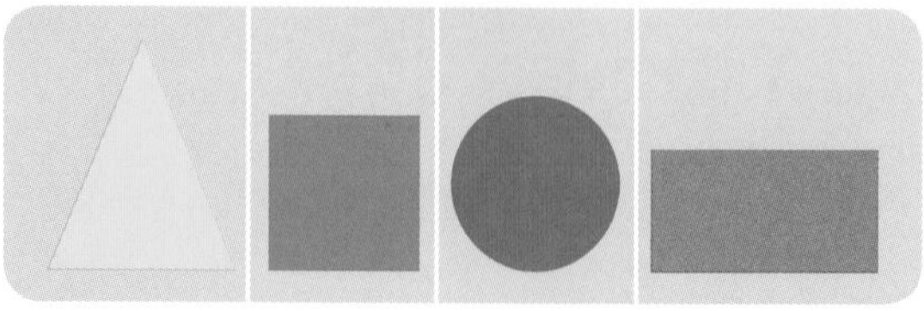

LESSON

1 Plane Shapes

Lesson Objectives

- Recognize and identify plane shapes.
- Combine smaller plane shapes to make larger plane shapes.
- Separate larger plane shapes into smaller plane shapes.
- Combine and separate plane shapes in figures.
- Draw plane shapes and figures on dot paper and square grid paper.

Vocabulary
plane shape
hexagon
trapezoid
figure

Learn

Get to know more plane shapes.

A plane is a flat surface that has length and width but no thickness. A plane shape is a two dimensional shape that lies in a plane. These are plane shapes you know.

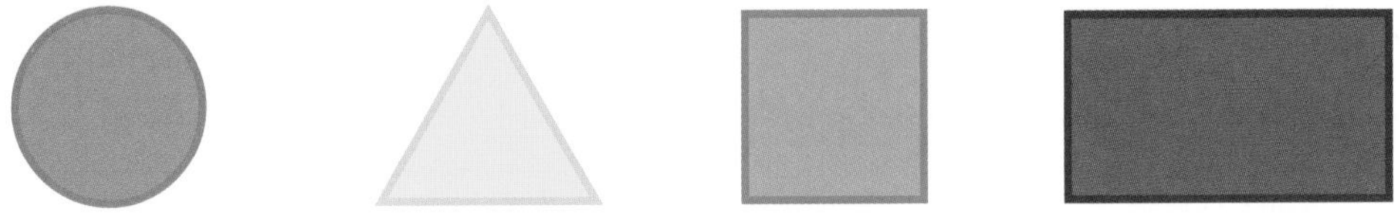

Circle Triangle Square Rectangle

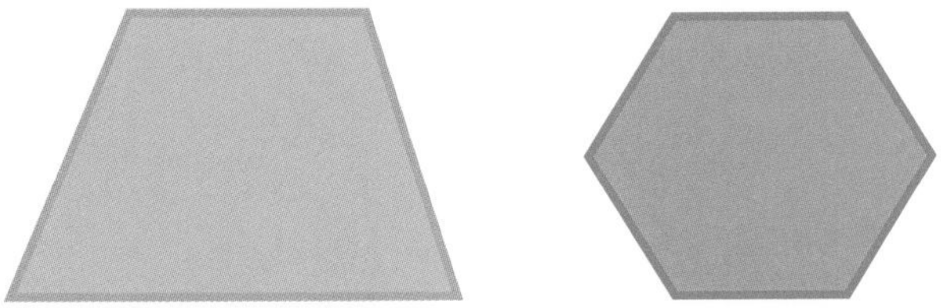

Trapezoid **Hexagon**

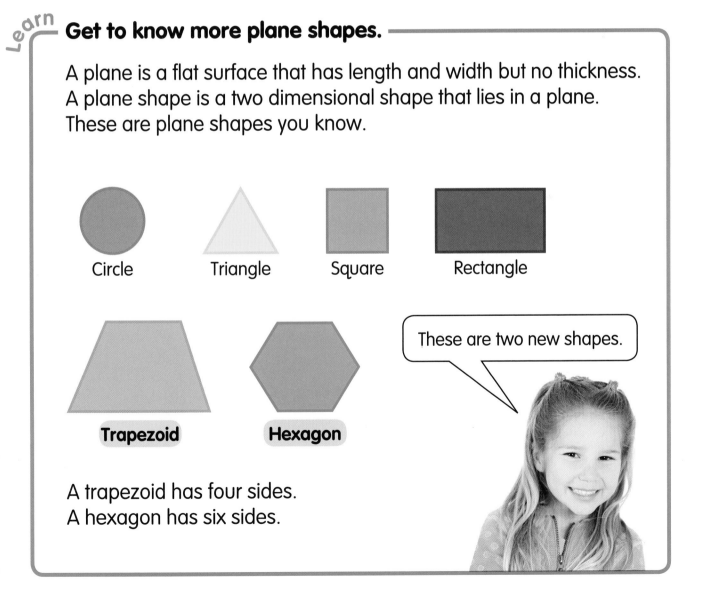

These are two new shapes.

A trapezoid has four sides.
A hexagon has six sides.

Guided Practice

Look at the picture.

1 It is made of many shapes.

How many of these shapes can you find?

Plane Shapes	How many?
triangle	
rectangle	
square	
circle	

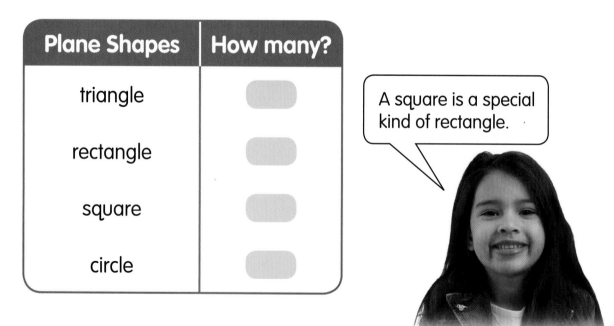

A square is a special kind of rectangle.

Hands-On Activity

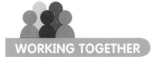

WORKING TOGETHER

Look at the things around you.
Make a list of the things that have plane shapes.

Plane Shapes	Things Around You

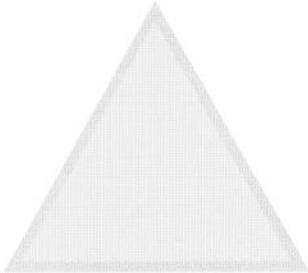	

Learn

You can combine and separate plane shapes.

Combine smaller shapes to make larger shapes.

This is a square.

This is a triangle.

You can combine 4 squares to form a larger square.

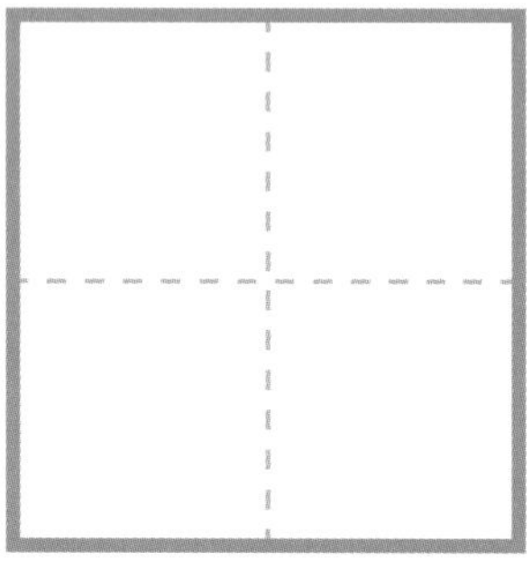

You can combine 6 triangles to form a hexagon.

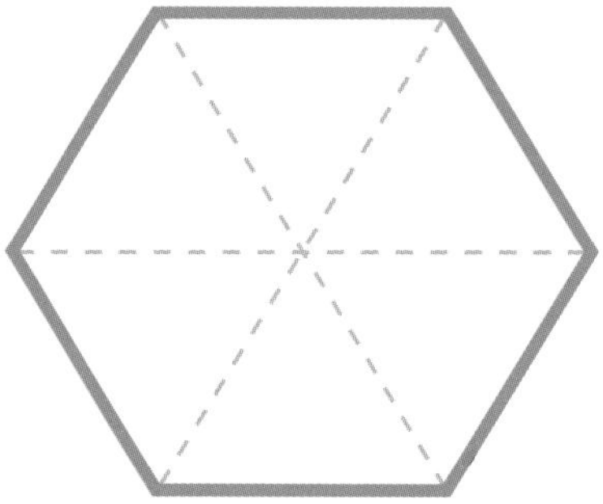

Separate larger shapes to make smaller shapes.

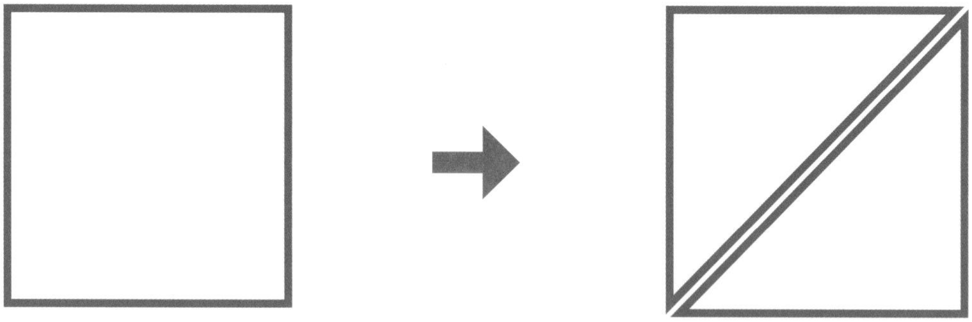

square

two smaller triangles

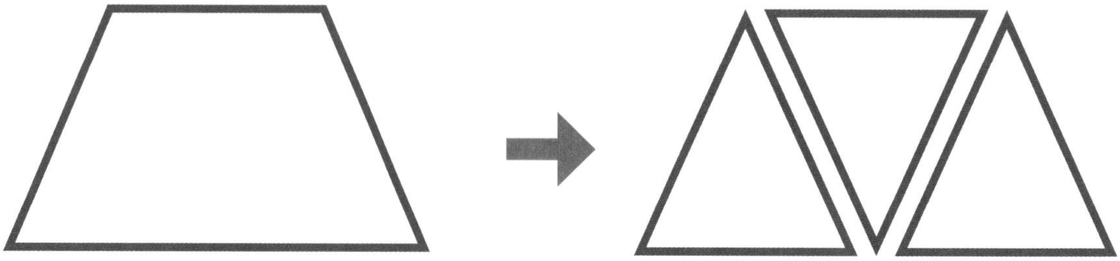

trapezoid

three smaller triangles

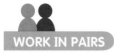

Hands-On Activity

WORK IN PAIRS

1 Each pair of students uses 10 triangles.

Combine some of them to make these shapes.
How many triangles did you use?

a

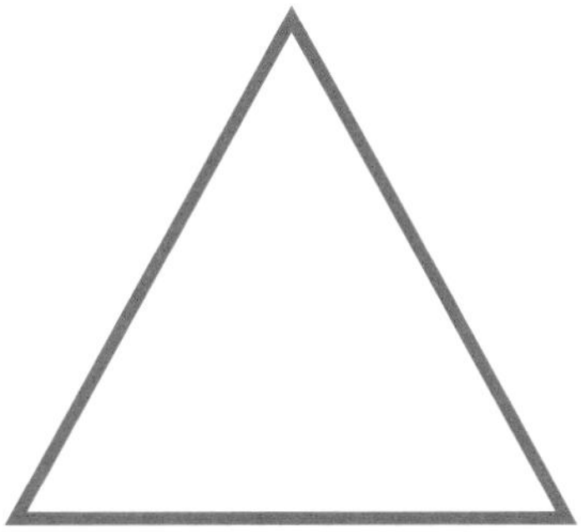

b

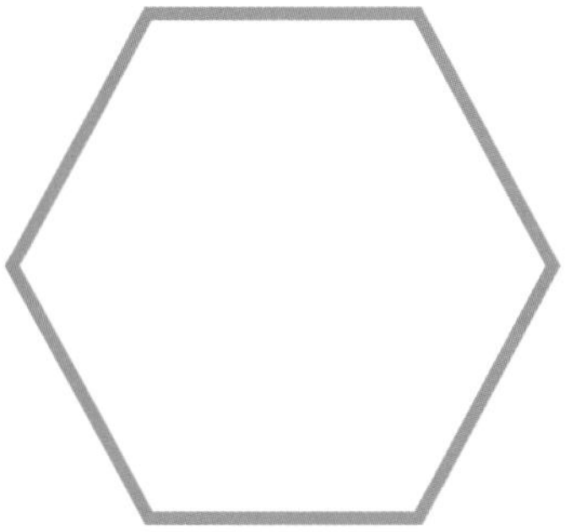

2 Separate each shape to form smaller identical shapes in 3 different ways.

a

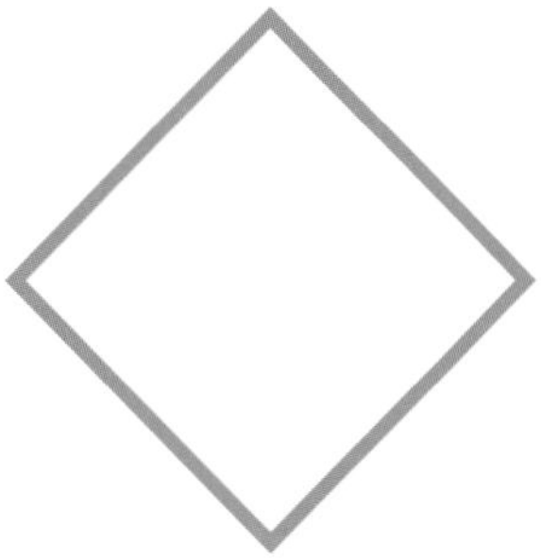

b

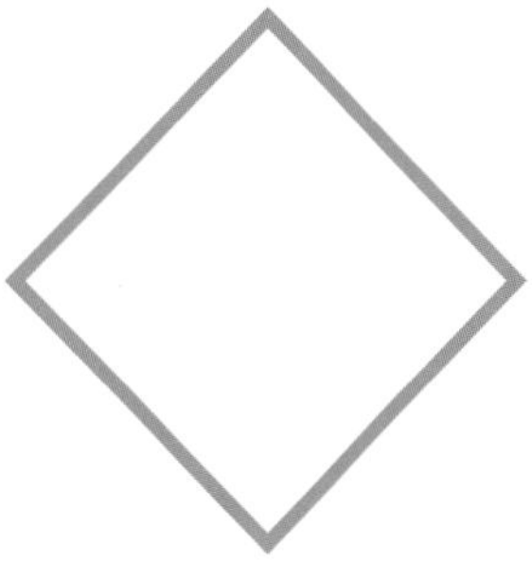

c

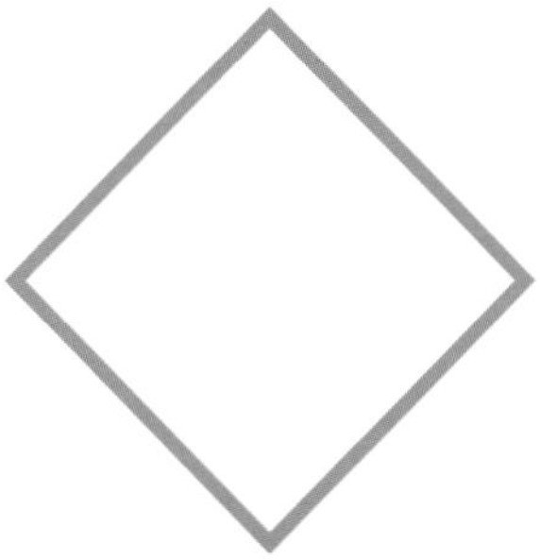

Guided Practice

 2 Cut out 6 copies of the small rectangle.
Combine them to make Shape A.
Then combine them to make Shape B.

Use this shape	Shape A	Shape B
6 ▭	▭	◇

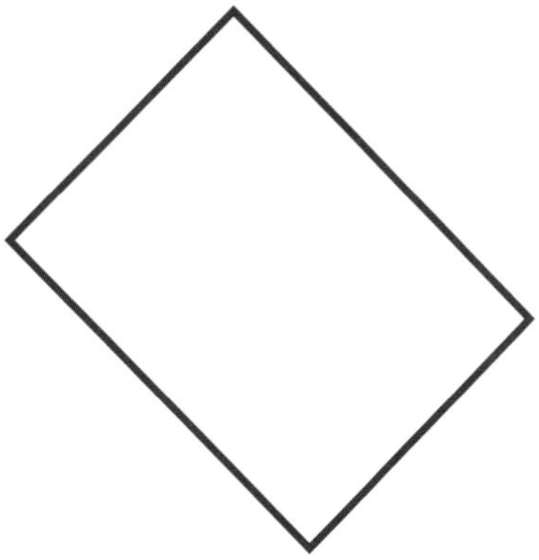

3 Trace this square onto a sheet of paper.
Separate it into smaller identical shapes.

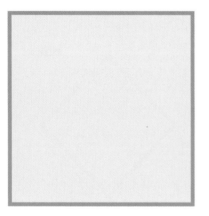

Learn

You can make **figures** by combining different shapes.

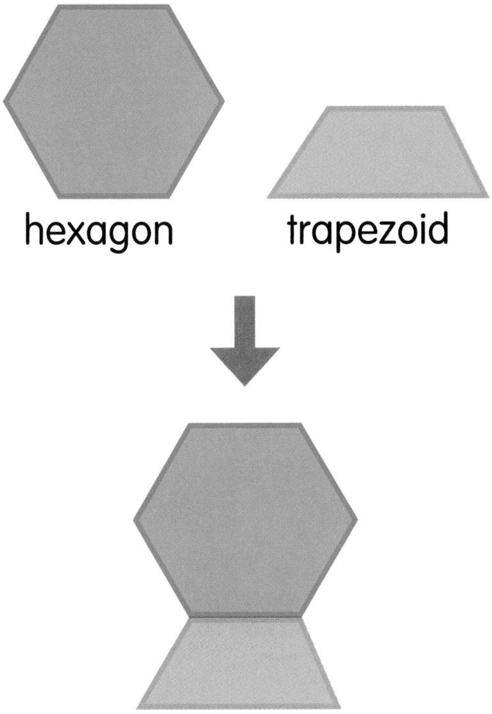

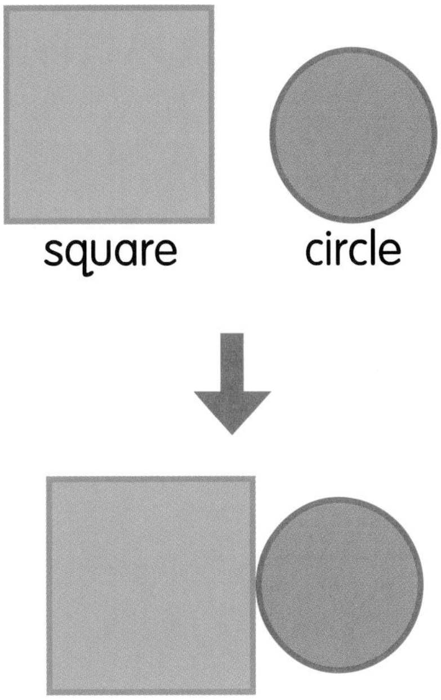

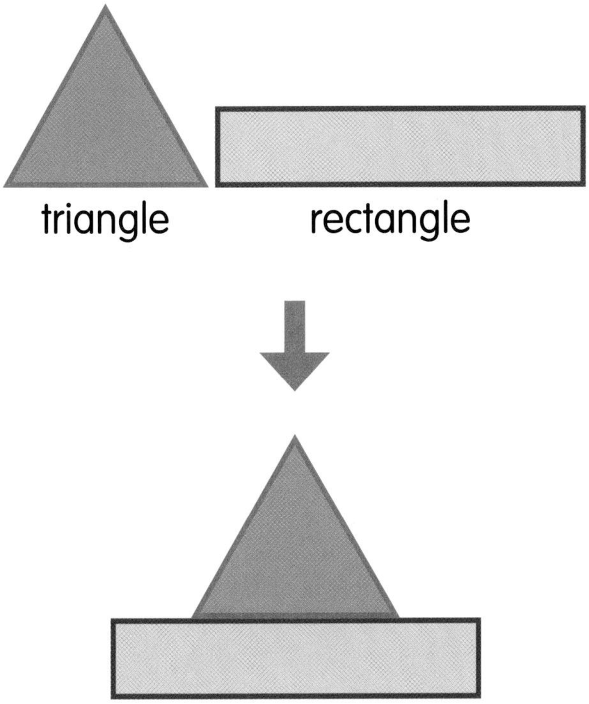

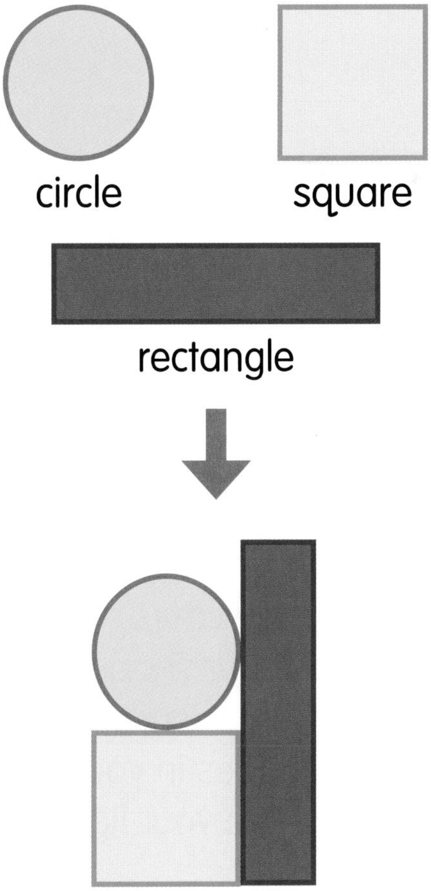

Hands-On Activity

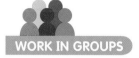

WORK IN GROUPS

Trace four sets of these shapes. Then cut them out.

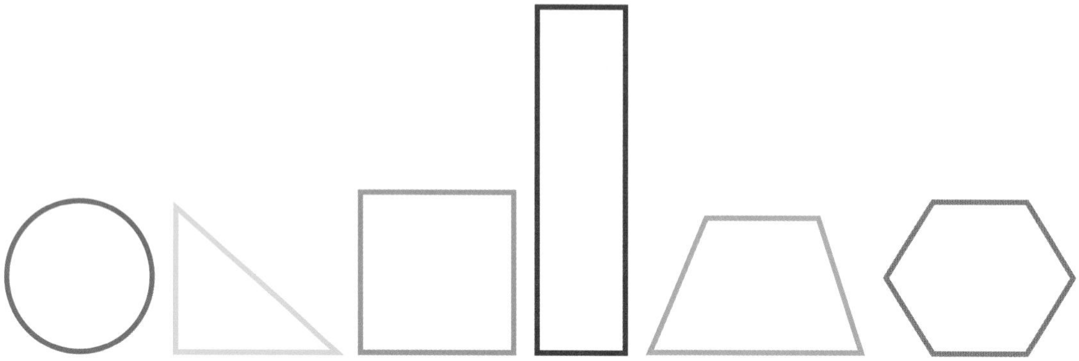

Use the cut-outs to make each figure.

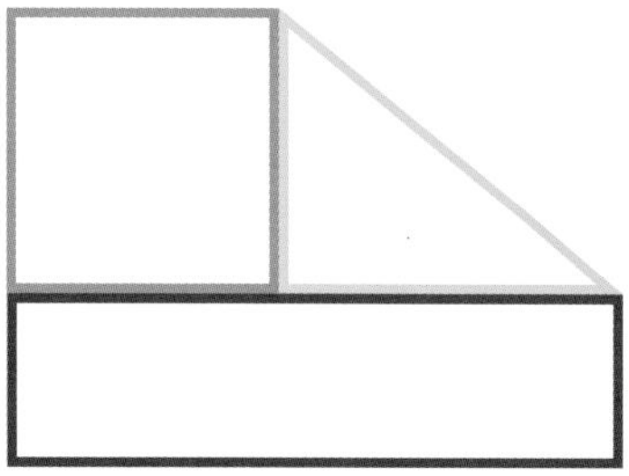

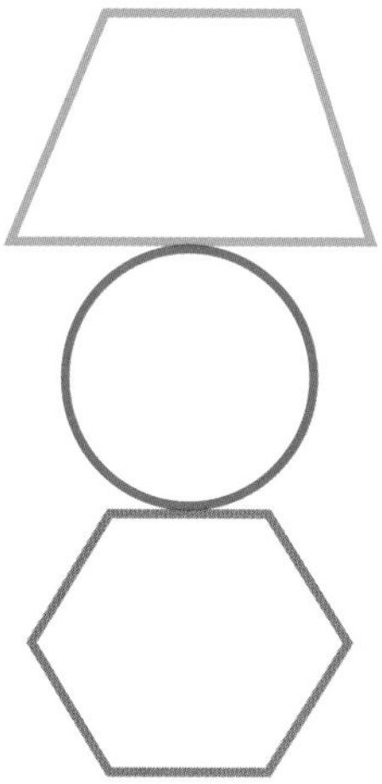

Use the remaining cut-outs to make other figures.
How many different shapes did you use for each figure?
How many of each type of shape did you use for each figure?

Use the shape tools on your computer
to draw a new figure.
Use at least four shapes.

Color the shapes in your figure.
Print and share your figure with
your classmates.

Guided Practice

4 Look at the figure.
It is made of different plane shapes.

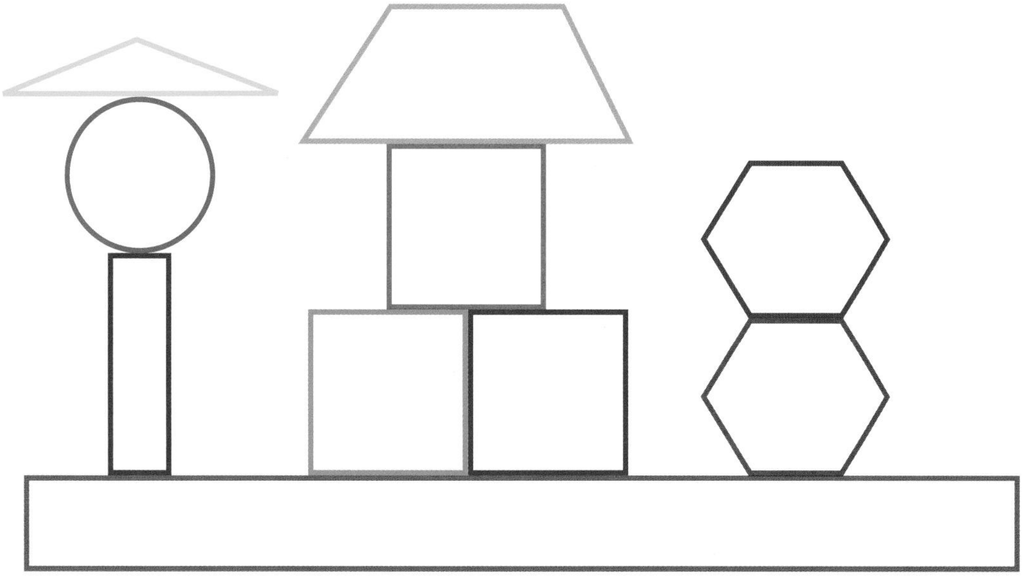

a How many different plane shapes can you find? ____

b How many of each plane shape can you find?

Plane Shapes	How many?
____	____
____	____
____	____
____	____
____	____
____	____

Learn

You can separate the plane shapes that make up a figure.

This figure is made up of three shapes.

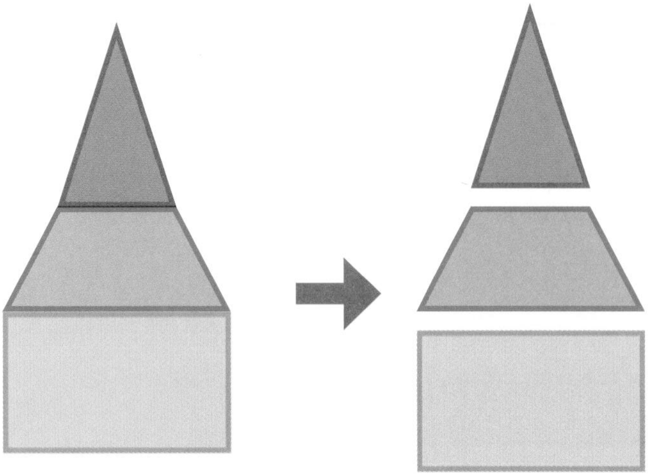

Take apart the figure to see the shapes that make it up.

The three shapes are a rectangle, a trapezoid, and a triangle.

Hands-On Activity

WORK IN GROUP

Which shapes make up these figures?
Draw lines to show the different shapes.
Copy each figure first.

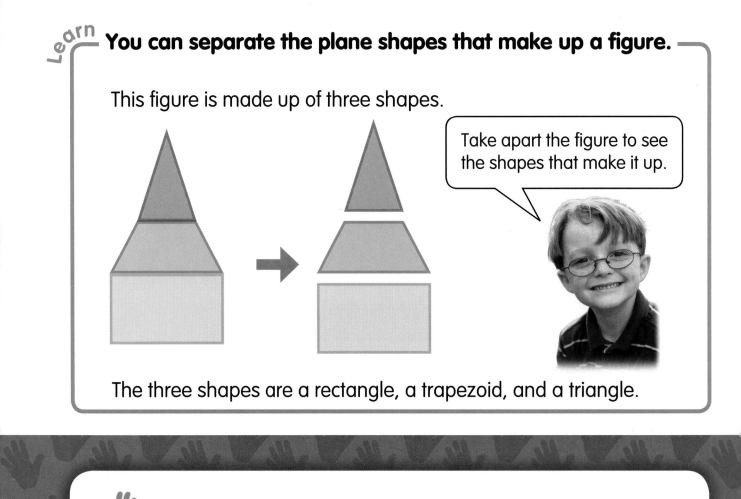

Figure A   Figure B   Figure C

Guided Practice

5 Look at the picture.
It is made of many shapes.

How many of these shapes can you find?

Plane Shapes	How many?
circles	
triangles	
squares	
rectangles	
trapezoids	
hexagons	

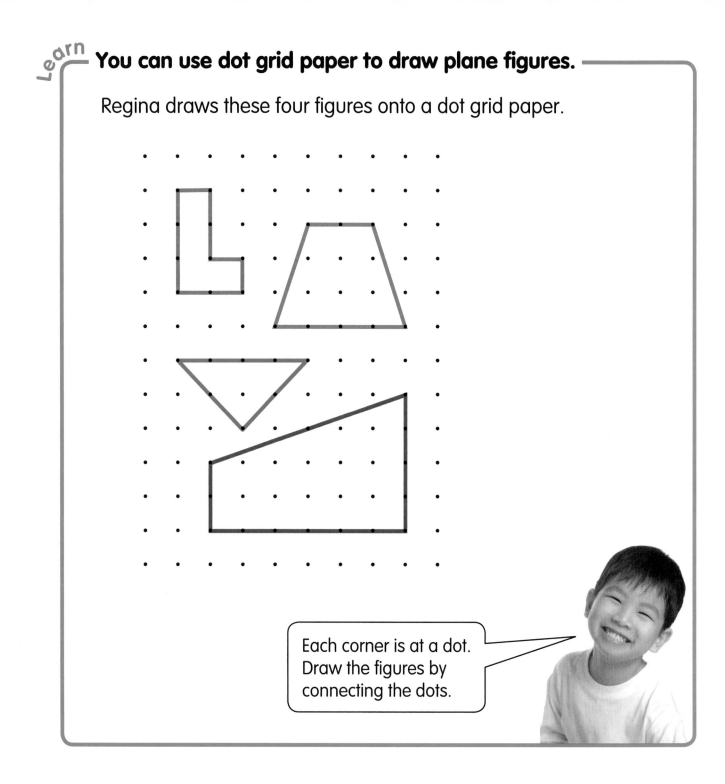

Learn

You can use dot grid paper to draw plane figures.

Regina draws these four figures onto a dot grid paper.

Each corner is at a dot. Draw the figures by connecting the dots.

Guided Practice

6 Copy these figures onto dot grid paper.

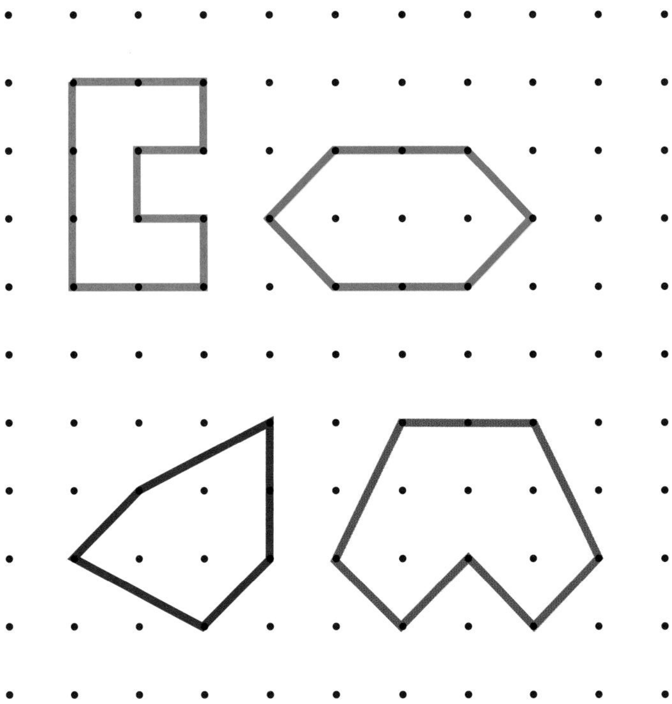

Learn

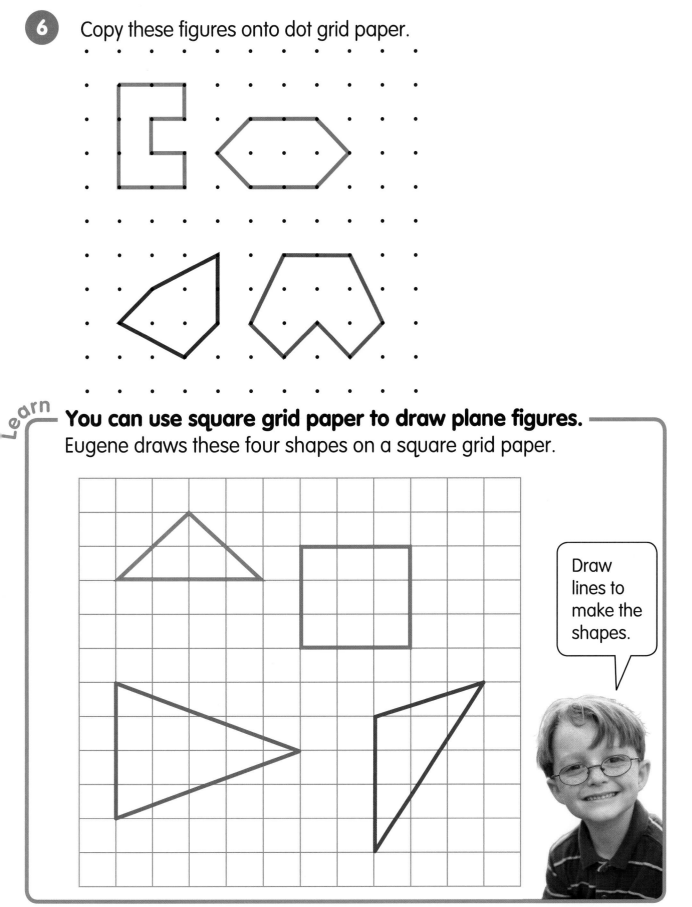

You can use square grid paper to draw plane figures.

Eugene draws these four shapes on a square grid paper.

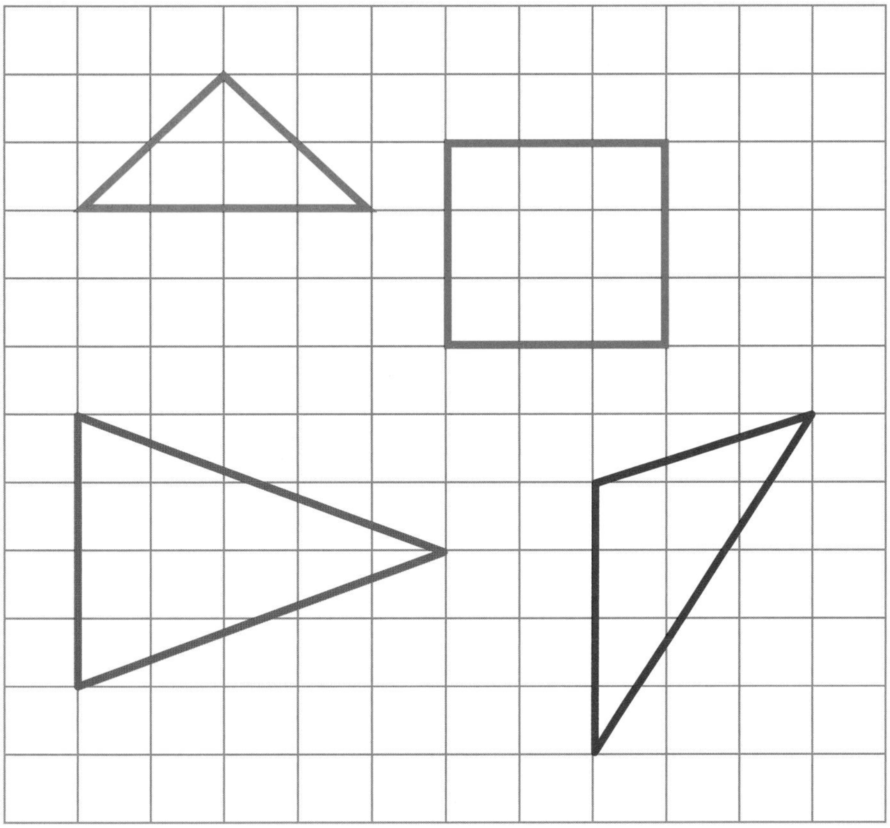

Draw lines to make the shapes.

Guided Practice

7. Copy these figures on square grid paper.

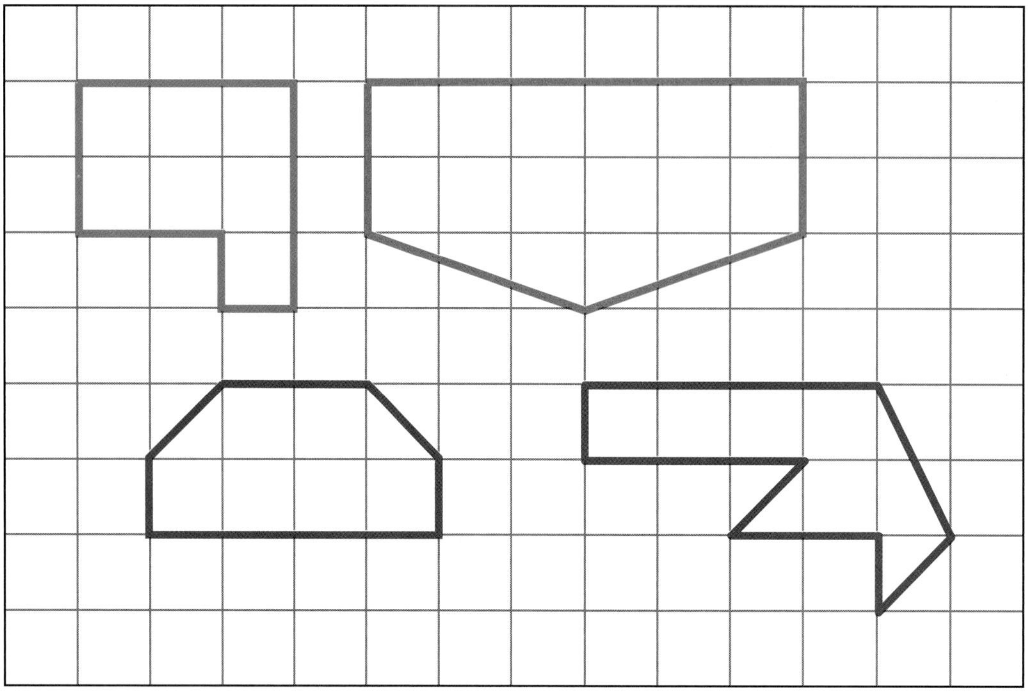

Let's Practice

1. Look at the picture. Identify the shapes.
Then copy the shapes onto a paper and write the names next to each shape.

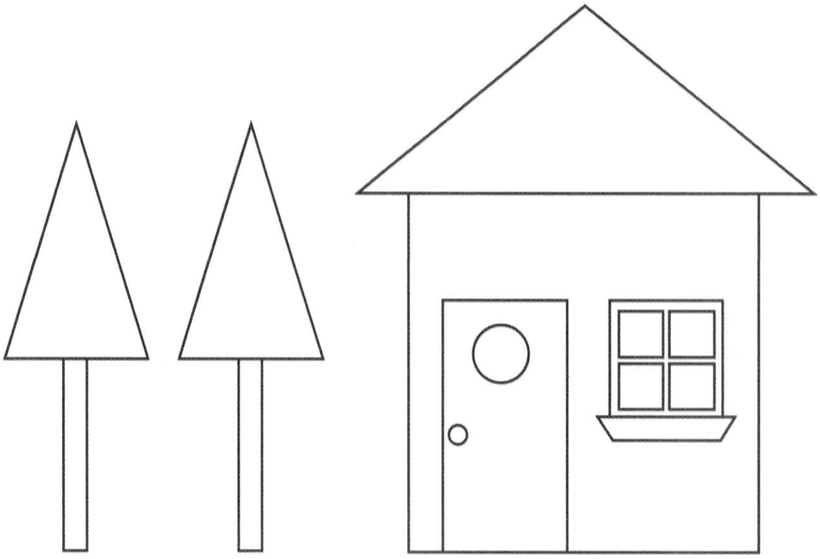

2. Make the big shape on the right by combining a few copies of the smaller shape on the left.
Trace the larger shape.
Then count the number of smaller shapes needed for the large shape.

a 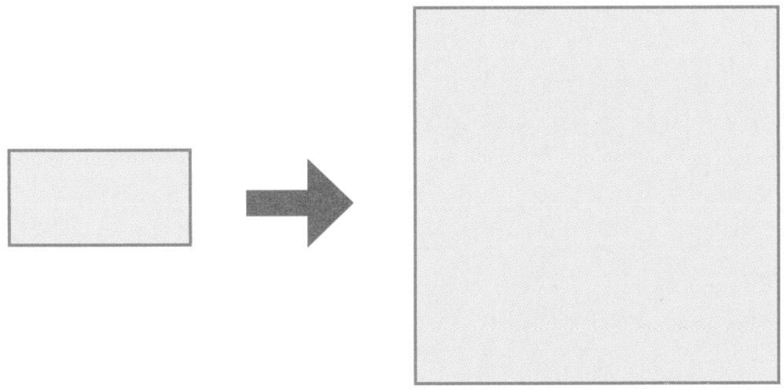

b 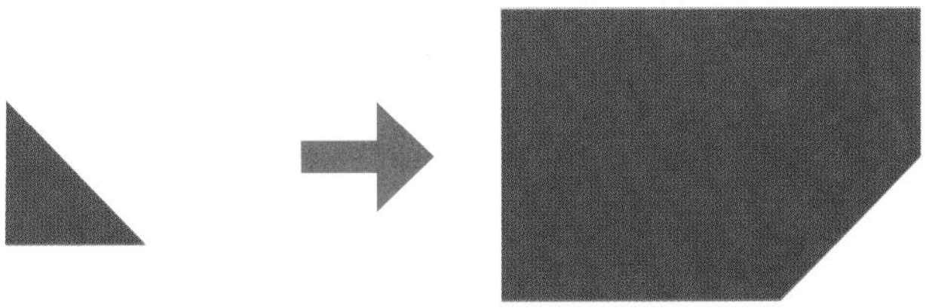

3. Trace the rectangle.
Show how to divide it into two triangles.

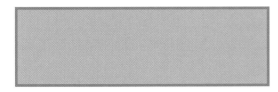

4. Trace the trapezoid.
Show how to divide it into three triangles.

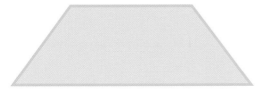

5 Make a figure with a copy of these shapes. Paste it on another sheet of paper.

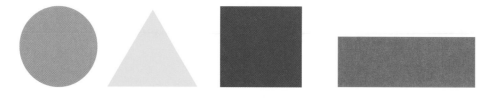

6 Trace the shape. Draw lines to show the different shapes that make up the figure.

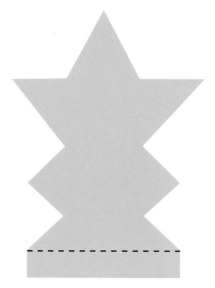

7 Copy this shape on dot grid paper.

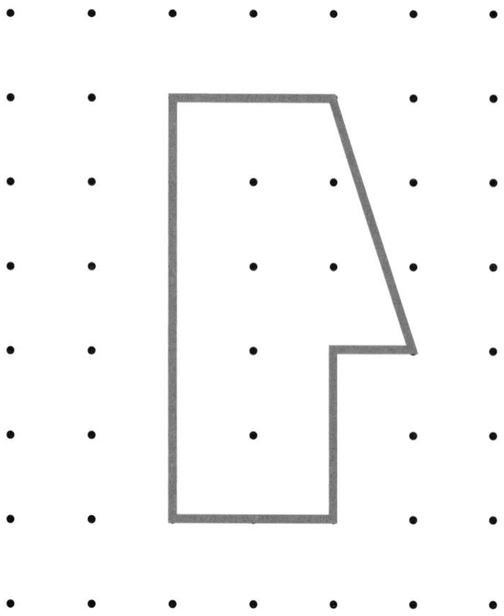

8 Copy this shape on square grid paper.

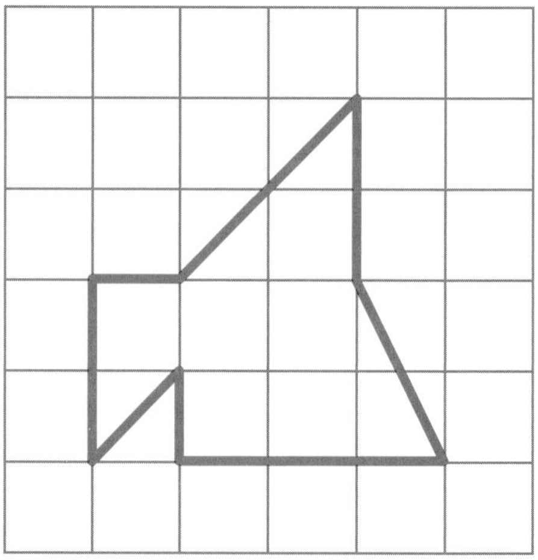

ON YOUR OWN

Go to Workbook B: Practice 1, pages 225–236

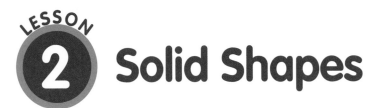

LESSON 2

Solid Shapes

Lesson Objectives

- Recognize and identify solid shapes.
- Build models using solid shapes.
- Combine and separate solid shapes.

Learn

You can build models with solid shapes.

Look at these solid shapes.

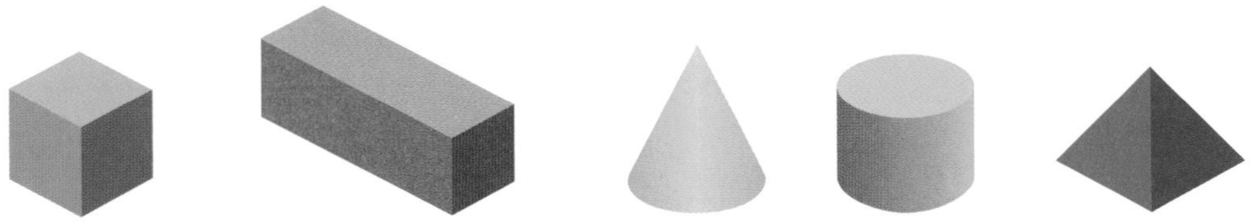

Cube Rectangular prism Cone Cylinder Pyramid

I can make a model using a cube and a rectangular prism.

I can also make a model using a cylinder and a cone.

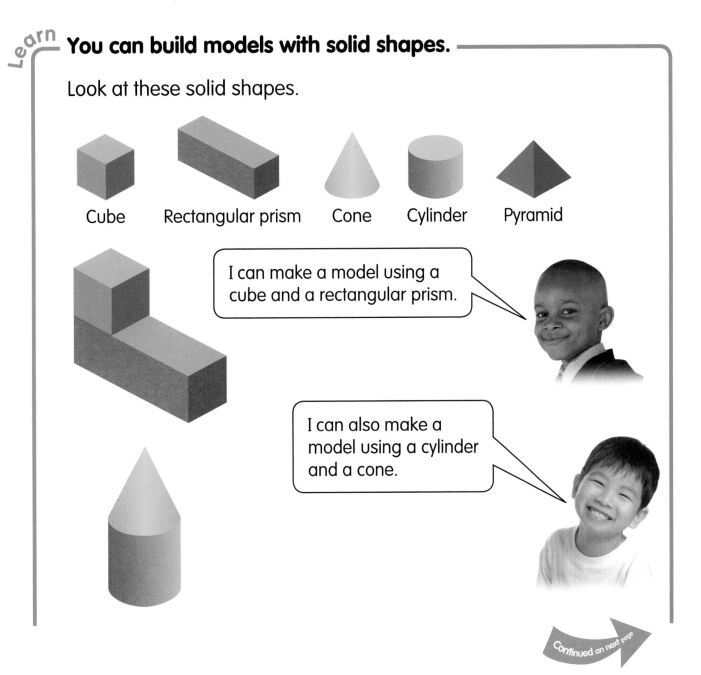

Continued on next page

I can make a model using a pyramid and a rectangular prism.

This model is made of 3 different solid shapes.

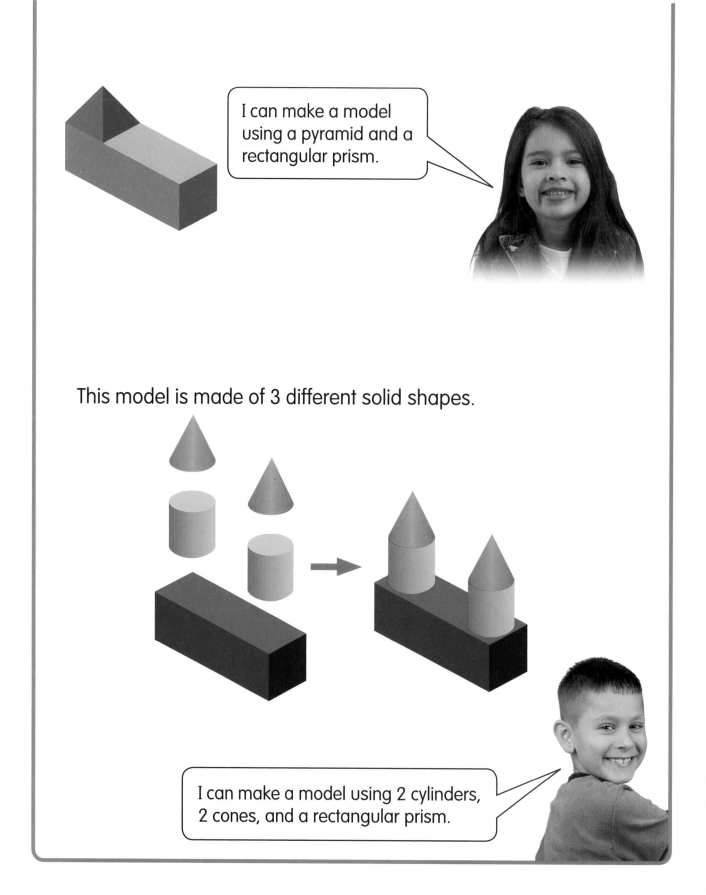

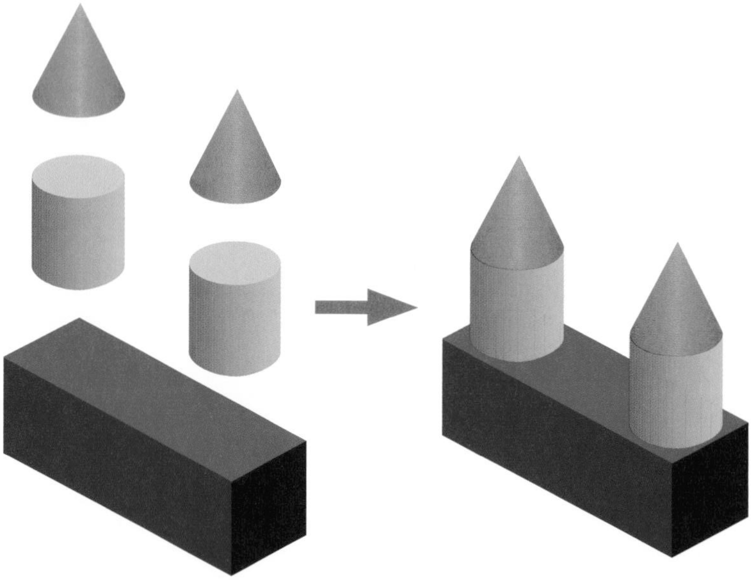

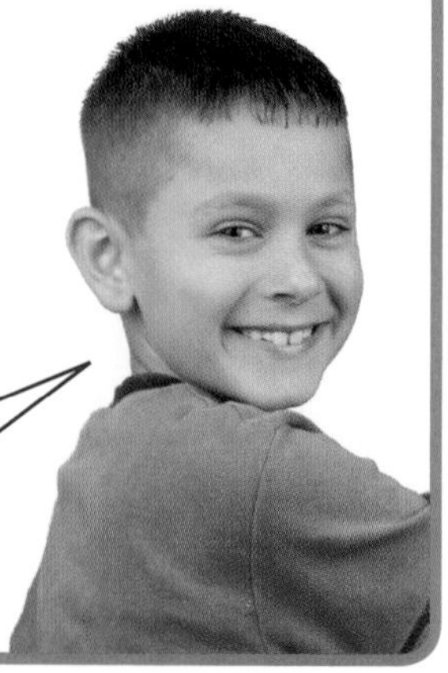

I can make a model using 2 cylinders, 2 cones, and a rectangular prism.

Guided Practice

Look at these models.

1

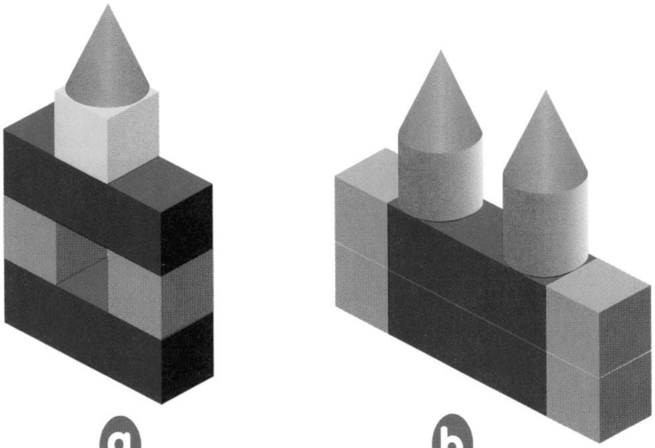

a b

Which solids make up the models?

a

b

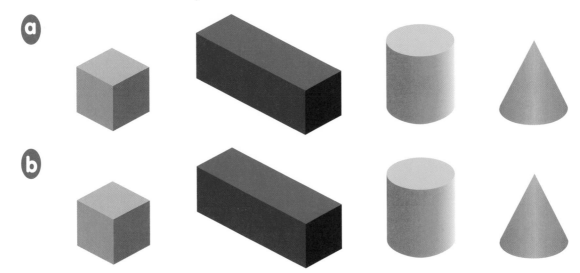

Look at the model.
Find the number of each solid shape that makes up this model.

2

___ cubes

___ rectangular prisms

___ cylinders

___ cones

Hands-On Activity

WORK IN GROUPS

1 Use these solid shapes.

Make a model using

a any four solid shapes.

b at least two solid shapes of each type.

2 Use 2 sets of these.

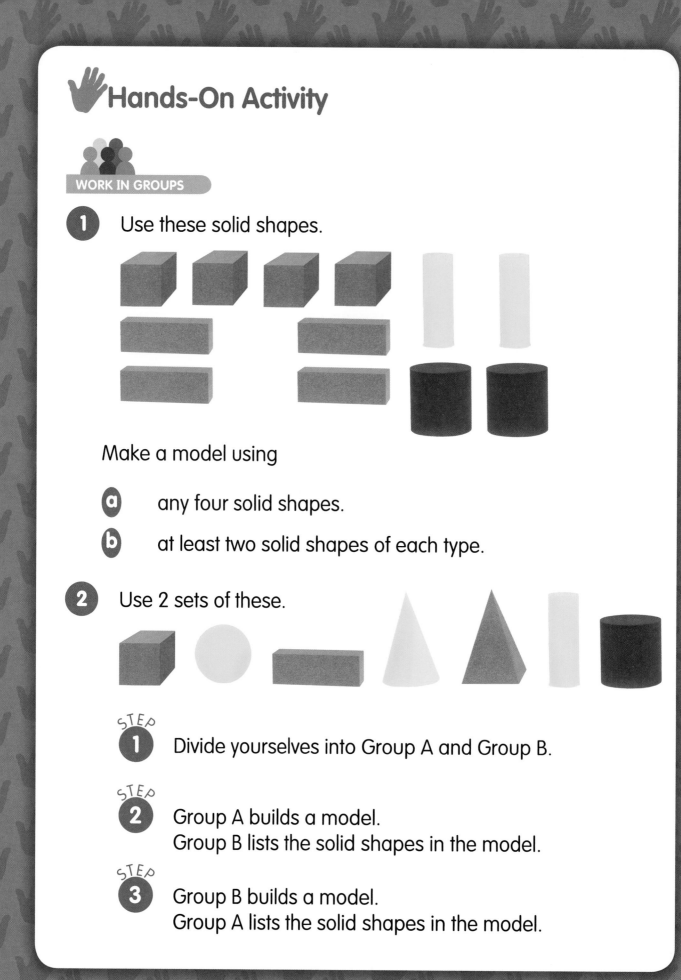

STEP **1** Divide yourselves into Group A and Group B.

STEP **2** Group A builds a model.
Group B lists the solid shapes in the model.

STEP **3** Group B builds a model.
Group A lists the solid shapes in the model.

Let's Practice

This model is made of solid shapes.
Find the number of each solid shape used.

1

Solid Shape	How many?
cube	
rectangular prism	
cylinder	

This model is made of solid shapes.

2 How many of each solid shape are used to make the model?

3 Use solid shapes to make the same model.

ON YOUR OWN

Go to Workbook B:
Practice 2, pages 237–238

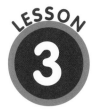

LESSON 3 Making Patterns

Lesson Objective

- Identify, describe, extend, and create patterns using different sizes, shapes, colors, and positions (turning).

Vocabulary

pattern	repeating pattern
pattern unit	size
shape	turning

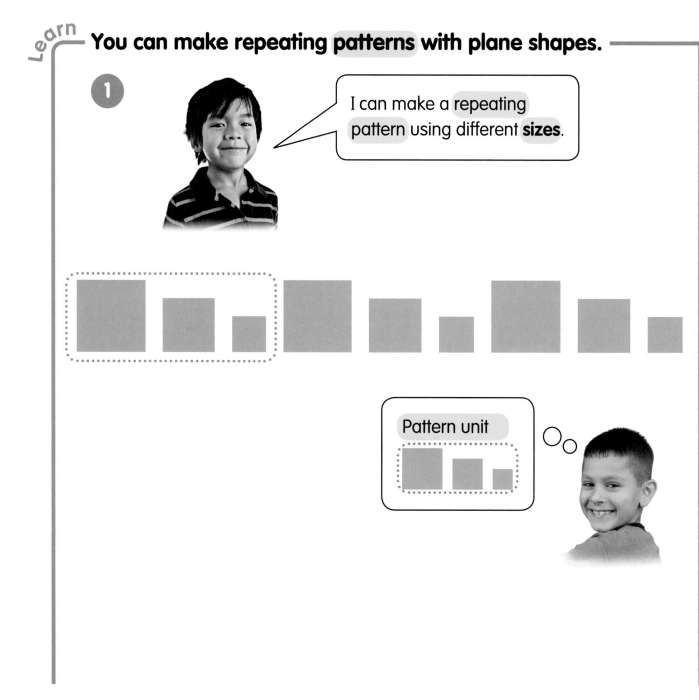

Learn You can make repeating patterns with plane shapes.

1

I can make a repeating pattern using different **sizes**.

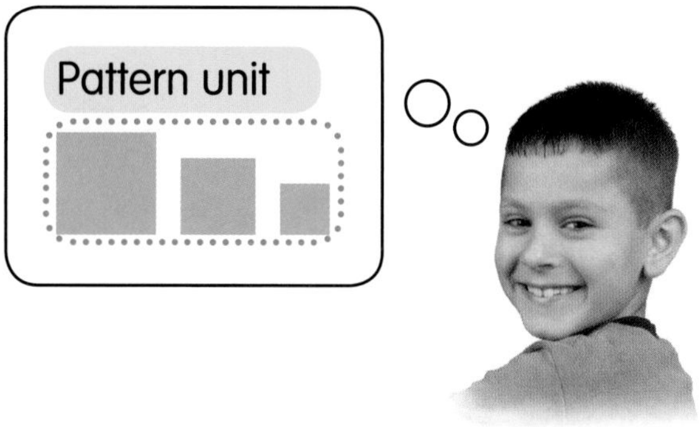

2

I can make a repeating pattern using different **shapes**.

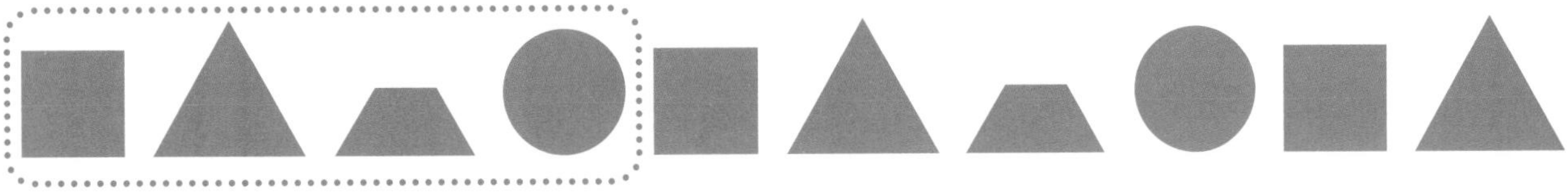

3

I can make a repeating pattern using different **colors**.

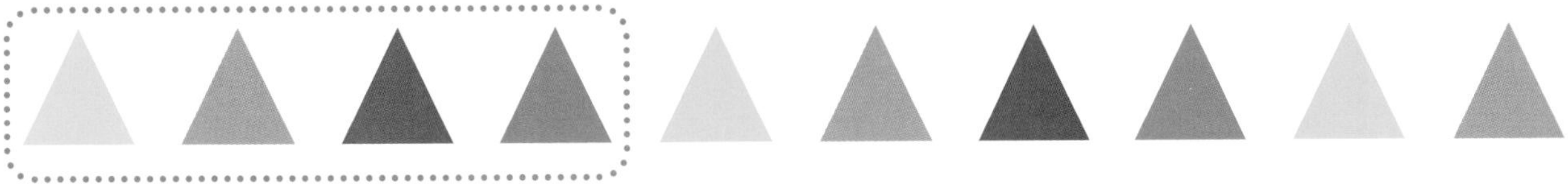

4

I can make a repeating pattern by **turning** the shapes like this.

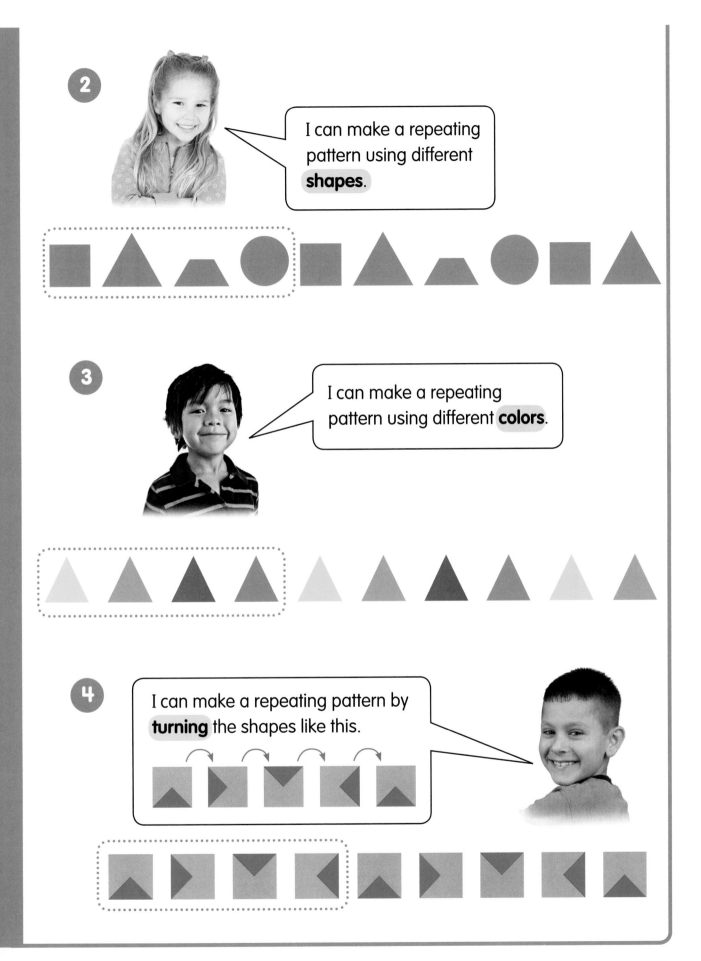

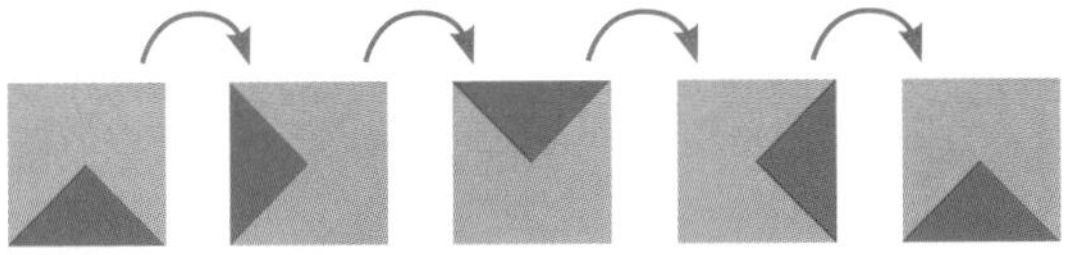

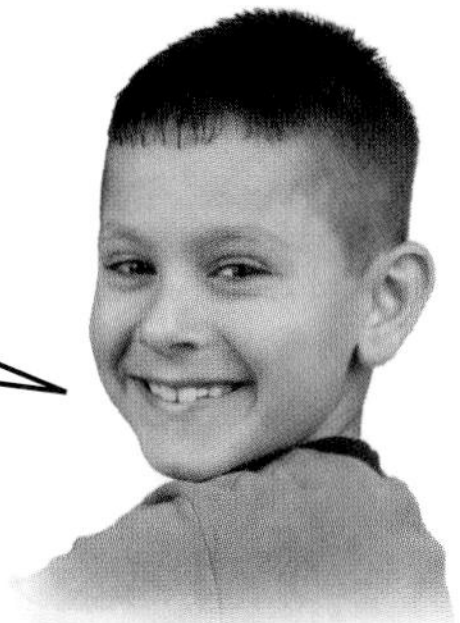

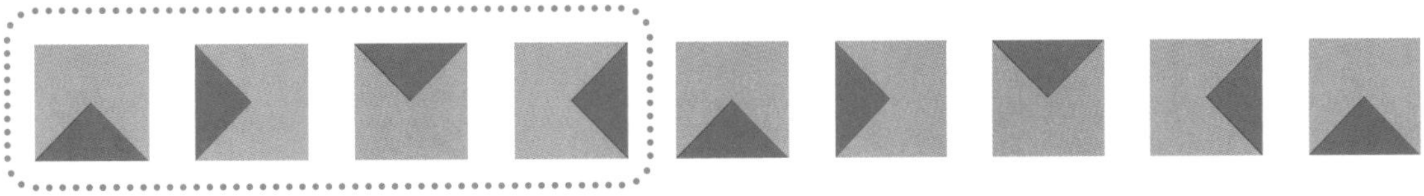

Guided Practice

Study the patterns.
What comes next in each pattern?

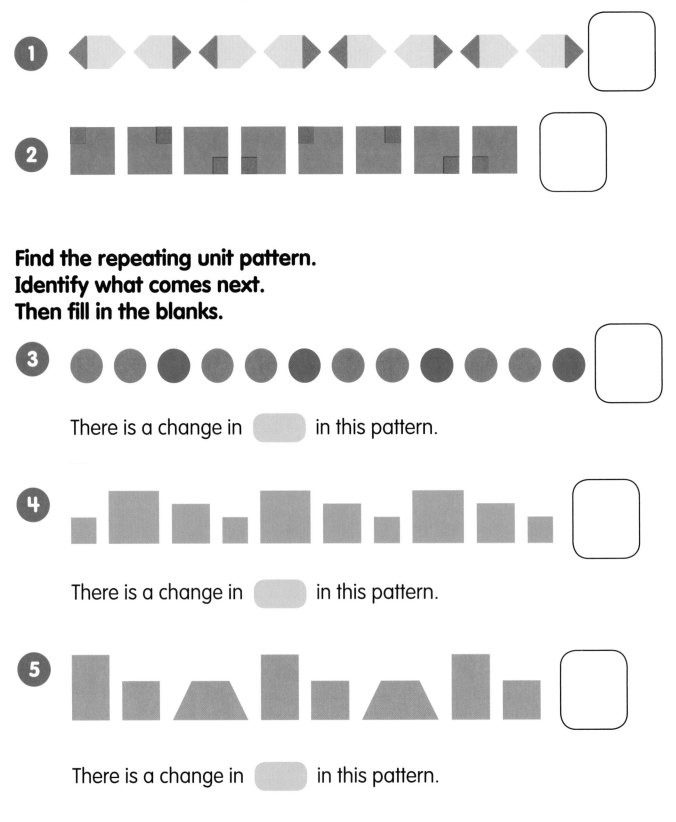

1 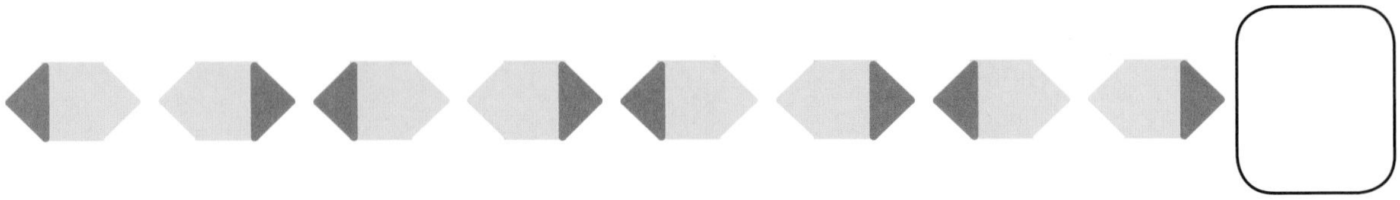

2 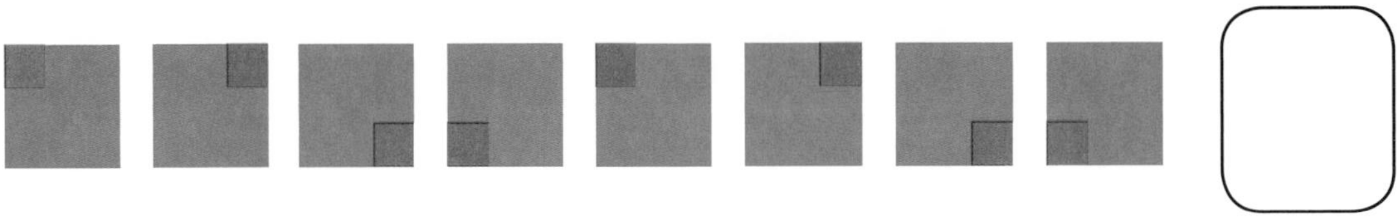

Find the repeating unit pattern.
Identify what comes next.
Then fill in the blanks.

3 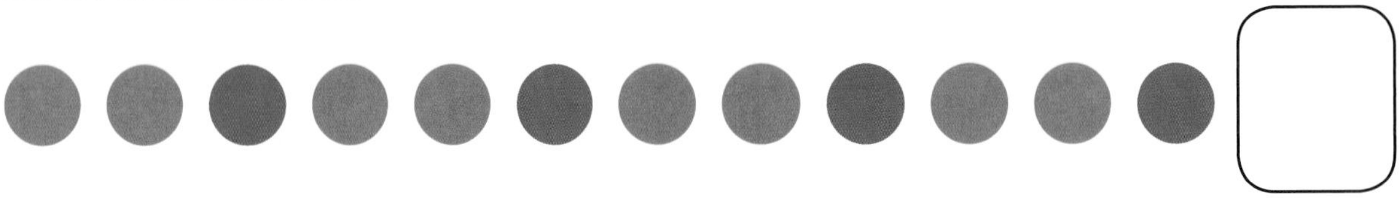

There is a change in ______ in this pattern.

4 

There is a change in ______ in this pattern.

5 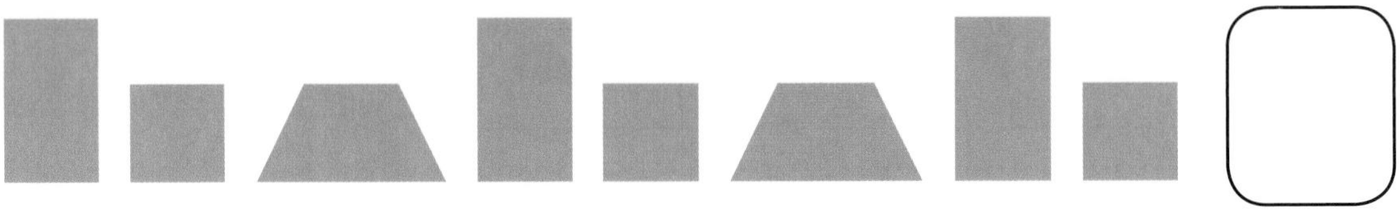

There is a change in ______ in this pattern.

Learn

You can make repeating patterns with plane shapes that change in more than one way.

Look at these patterns.

1 

There is a change in size and color.

2 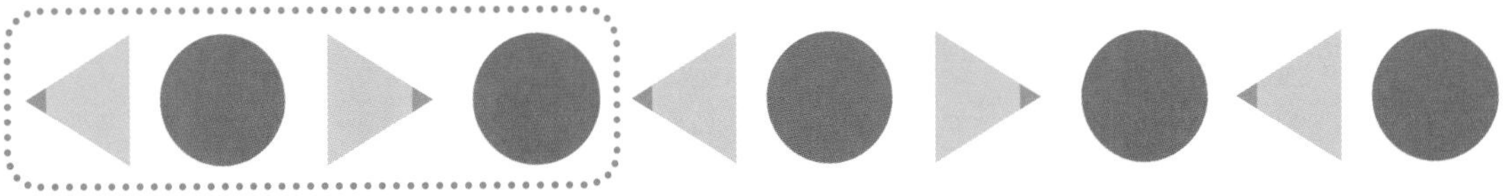

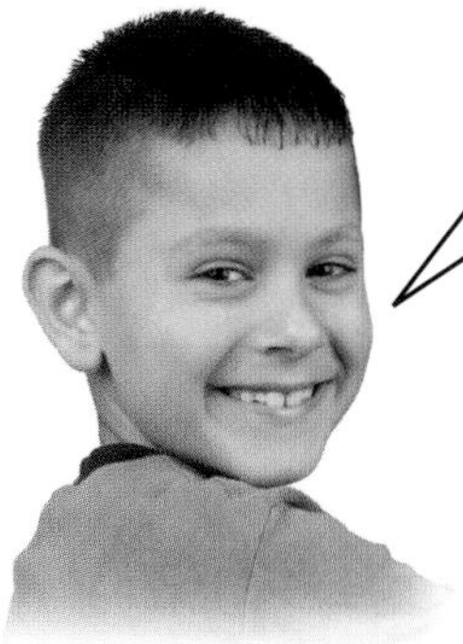

This pattern is made with two shapes!

It is also made by turning the triangle.

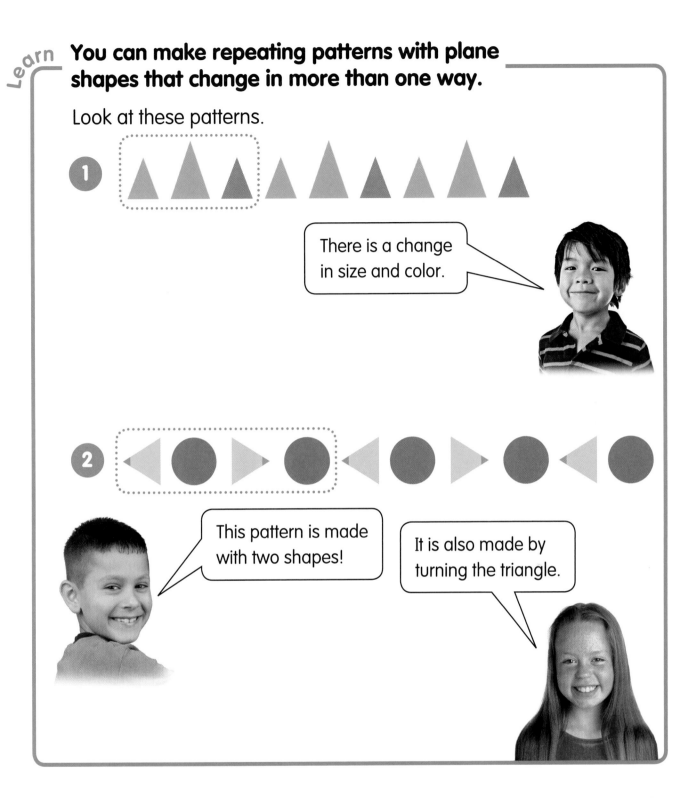

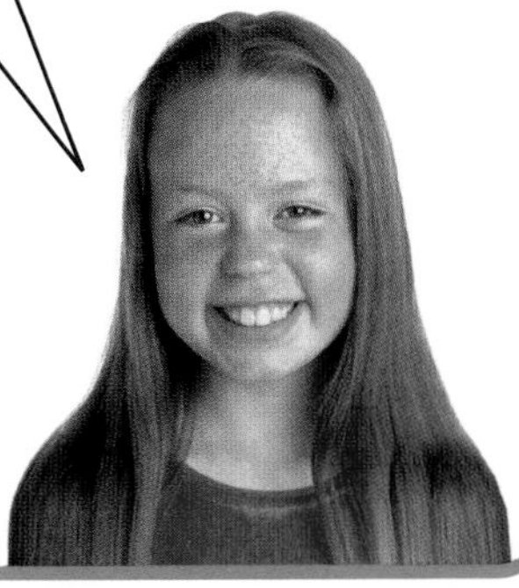

Guided Practice

Study each pattern.
Describe the pattern.
What comes next?

6 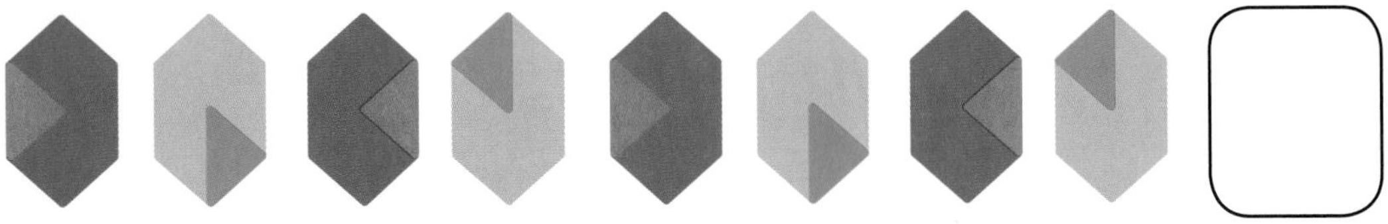

7 

8 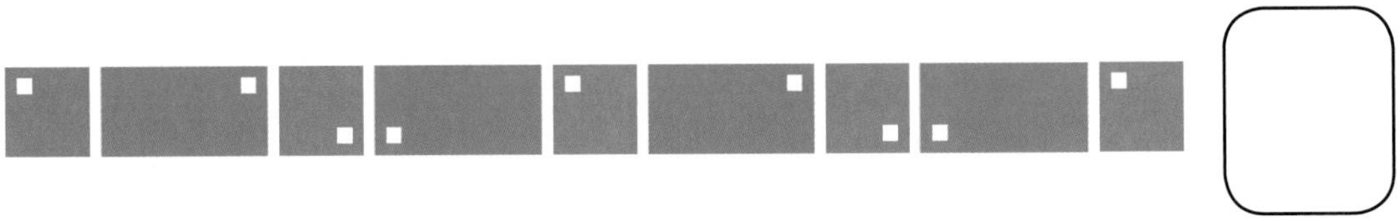

9 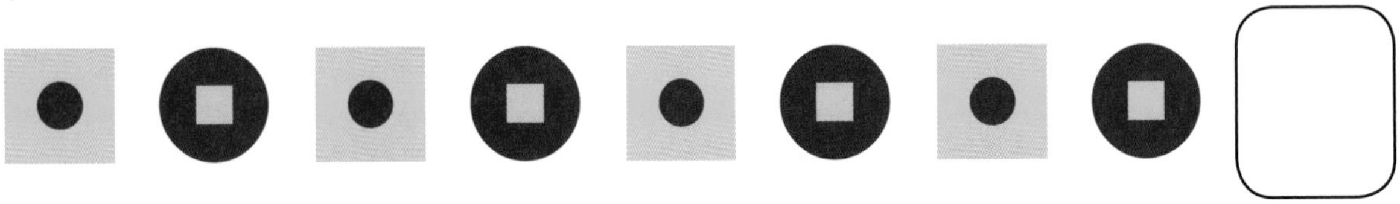

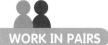

Hands-On Activity

WORK IN PAIRS

Use scissors, crayons, glue, string, 3 strips of paper, a plastic clothes hanger, and these shape cut-outs.

STEP 1 Trace the cut-outs onto the paper.

STEP 2 Color and cut out the shapes.

STEP 3 Arrange the cut-outs to make three different patterns.

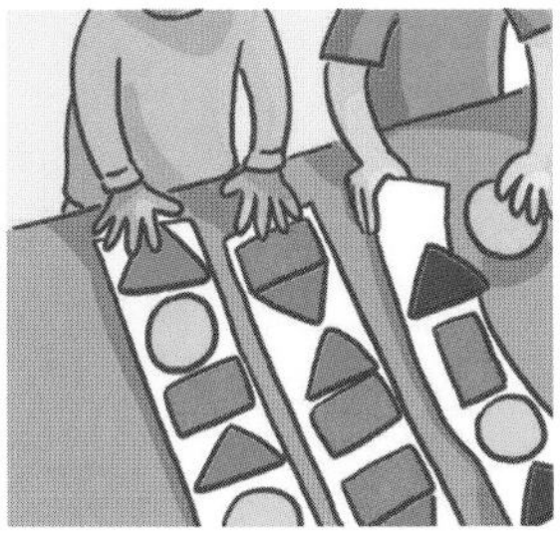

STEP 4 Glue the patterns on the strips of paper.

STEP 5 Tie the three strips of paper to the clothes hanger.

Now you have your own pattern mobile!

Learn You can make repeating patterns with solid shapes.

I can make a repeating pattern using different **sizes**.

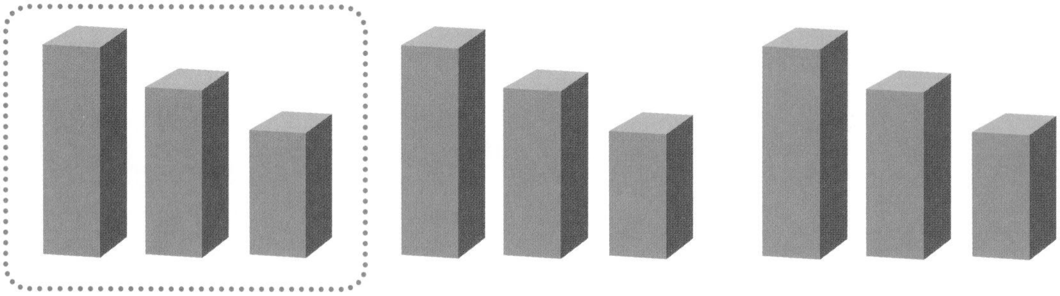

Pattern unit

I can make a repeating pattern using different **shapes**.

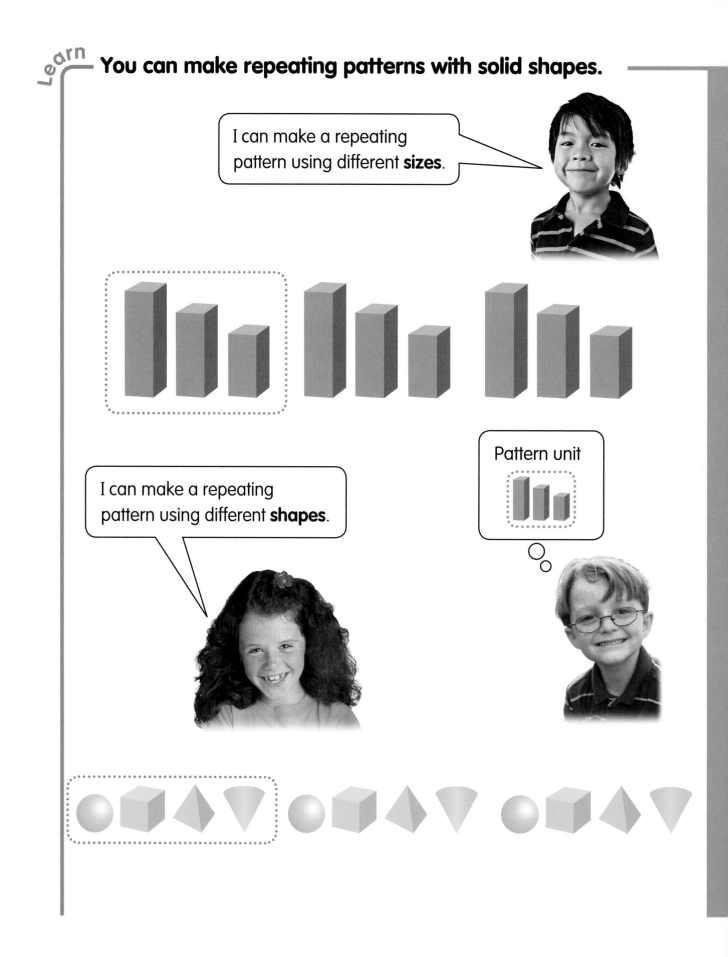

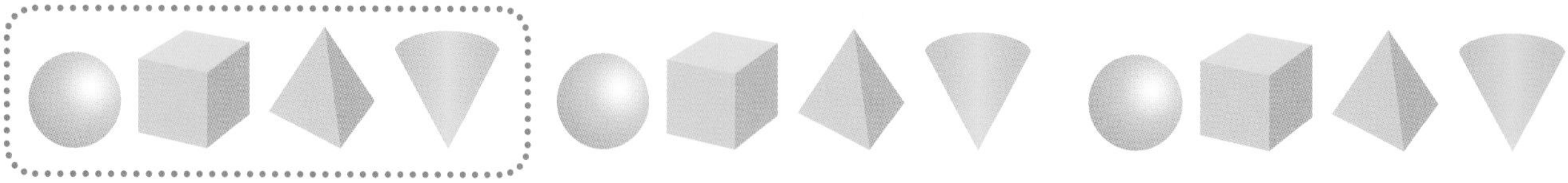

I can make a repeating pattern using different **colors.**

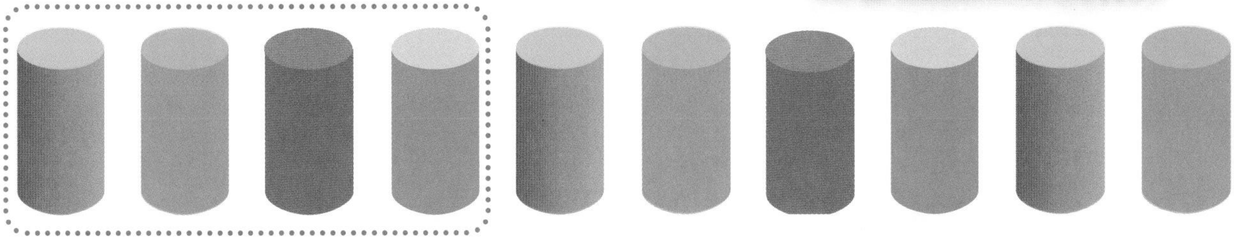

I can make a repeating pattern by **turning** the shapes.

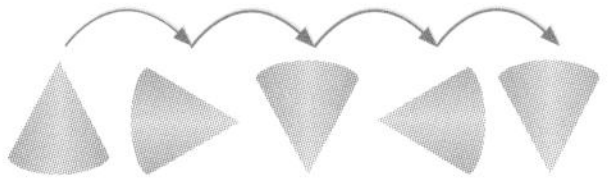

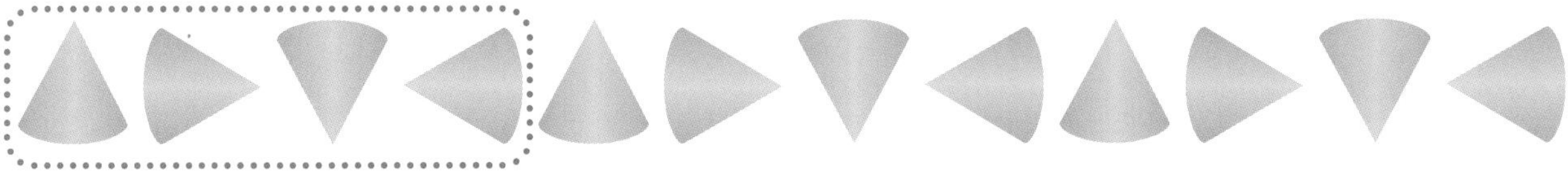

Guided Practice

Choose the shape that comes next in each pattern.

10 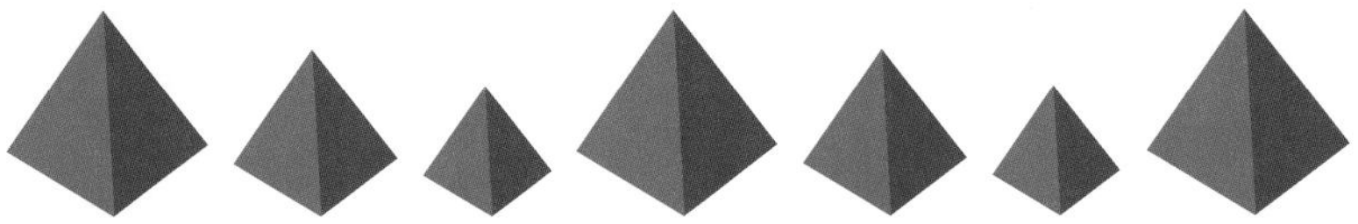 

11 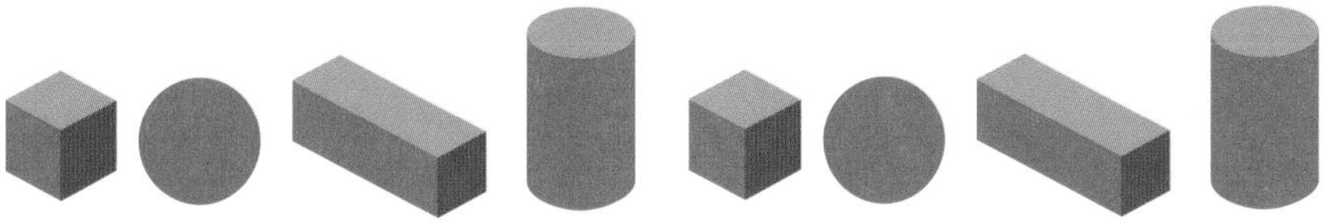 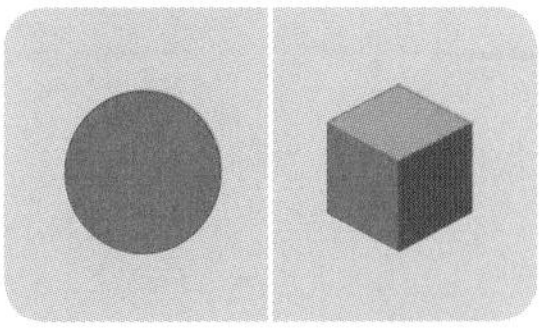

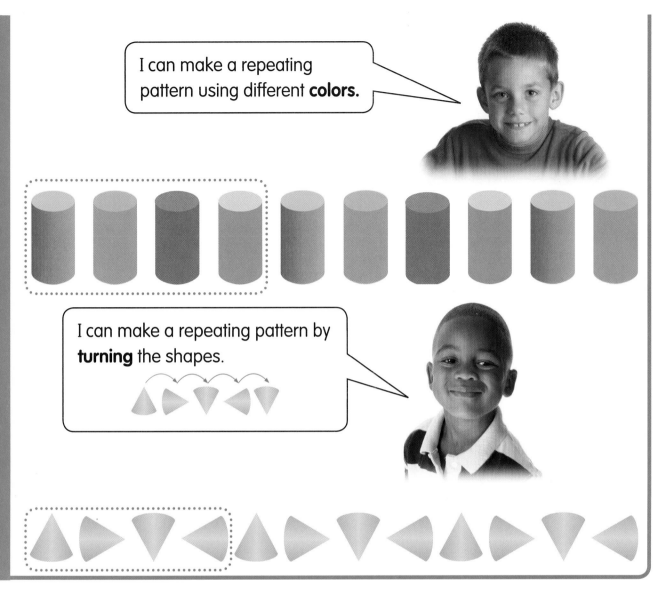

Learn **You can make repeating patterns with solid shapes that change in more than one way.**

Look at these patterns.

There is a change is size and color.

This pattern is made with four different solid shapes!

It is also made by turning the shapes.

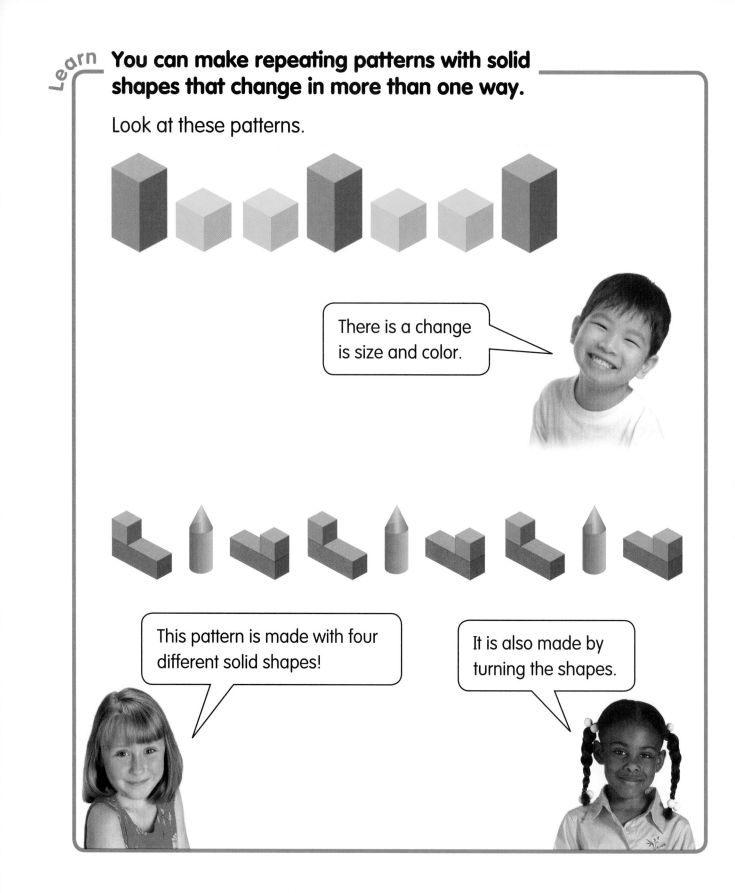

Guided Practice

Look at each pattern.
Choose what comes next.

12 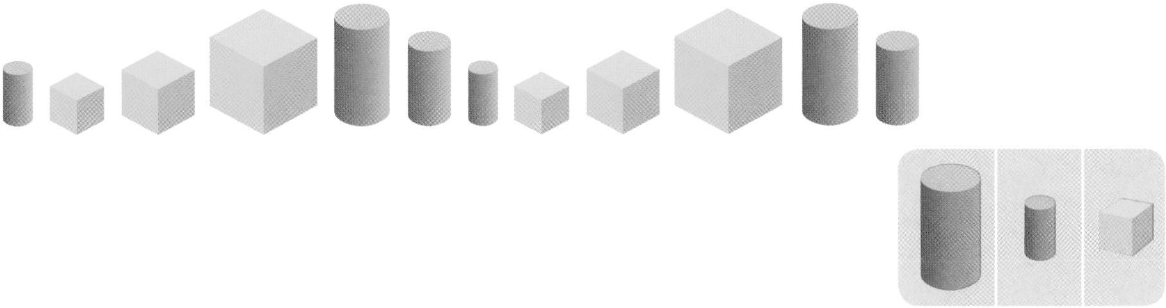

13 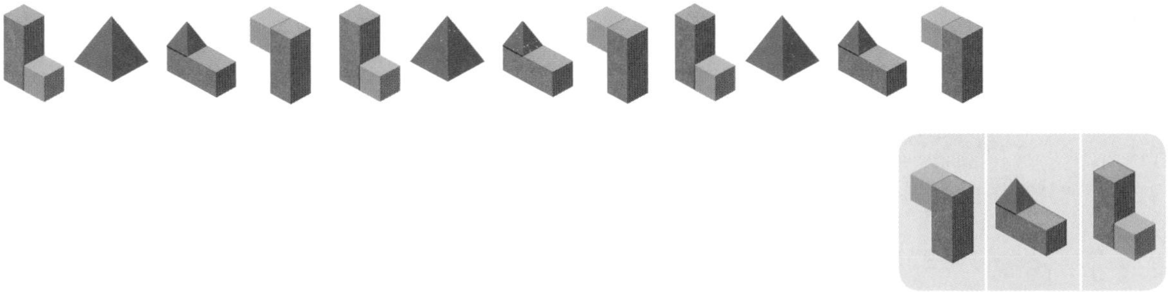

Let's Practice

Look at each pattern.
Choose what comes next.

1 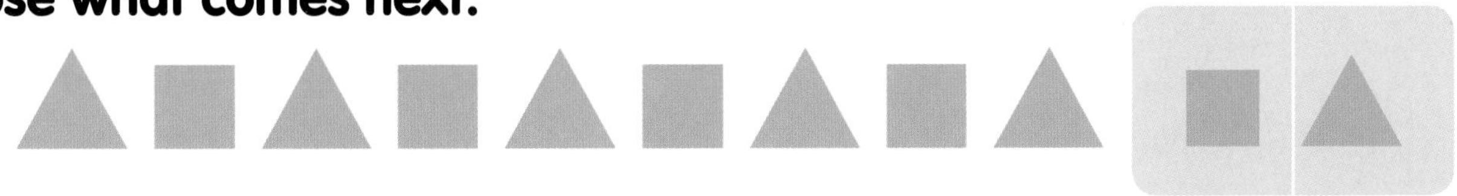

2 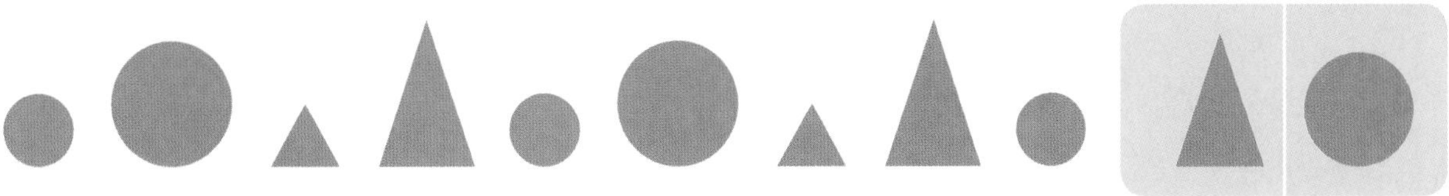

3 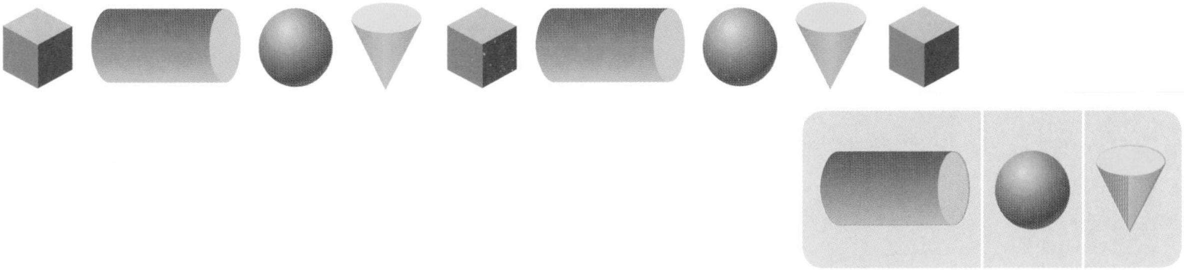

Look at each pattern.
What shape comes next?

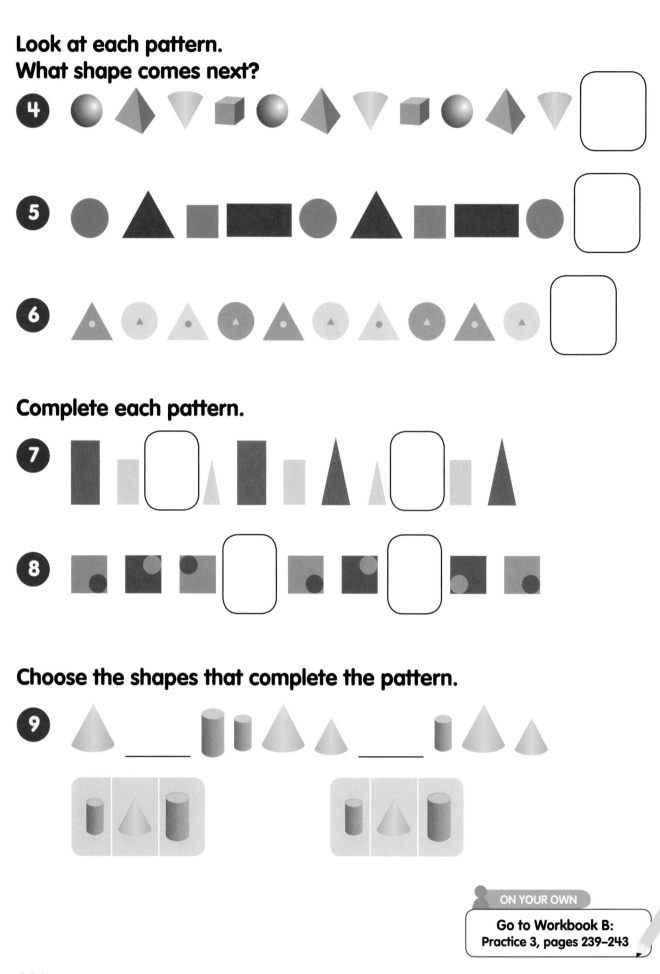

4 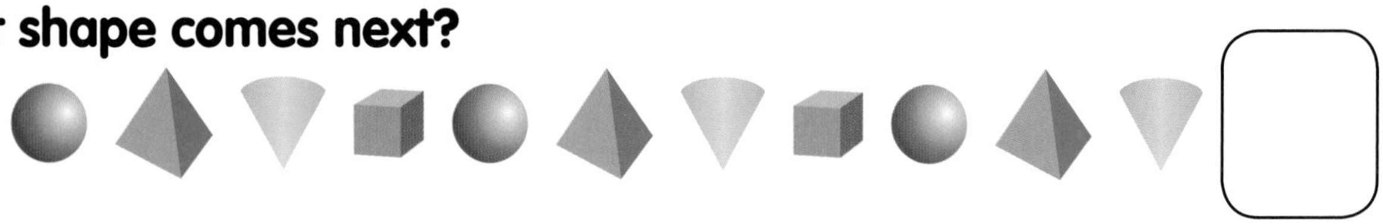

5 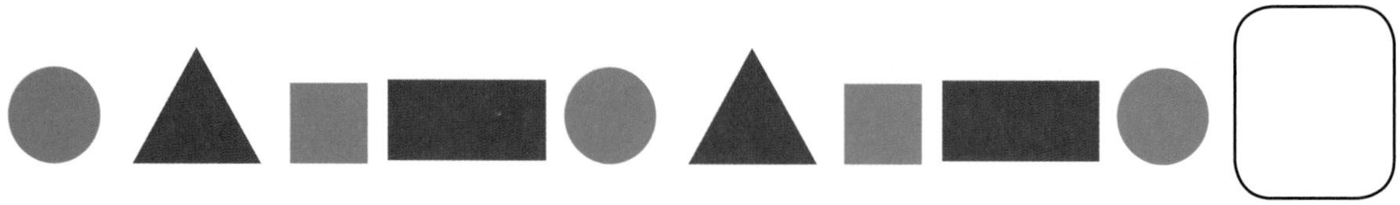

6 

Complete each pattern.

7 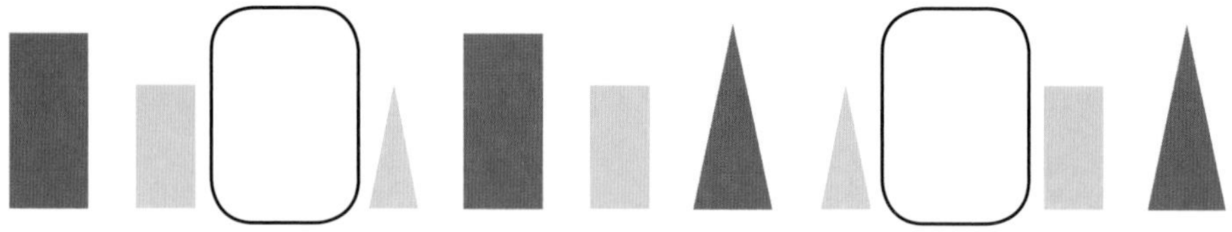

8 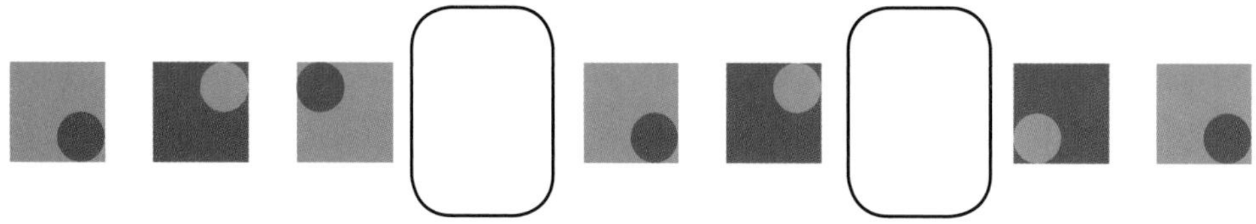

Choose the shapes that complete the pattern.

9 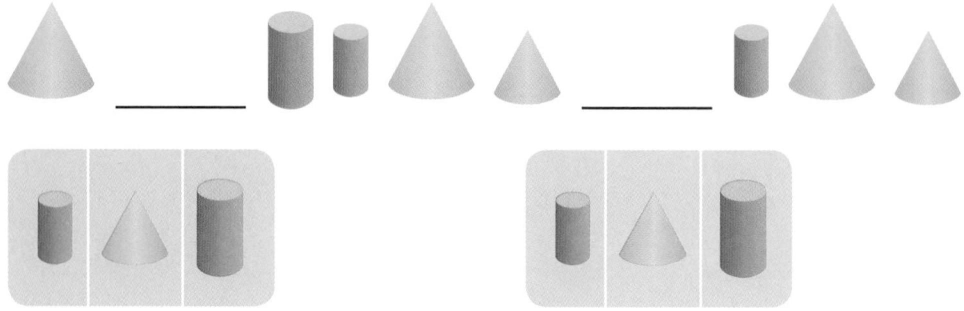

ON YOUR OWN

Go to Workbook B:
Practice 3, pages 239–243

CRITICAL THINKING SKILLS

Put On Your Thinking Cap!

PROBLEM SOLVING

This is a tangram.
It is a square made up of seven different shapes.

Put this tangram on a sheet of paper.
Cut along the lines like this:

Now mix up the pieces.

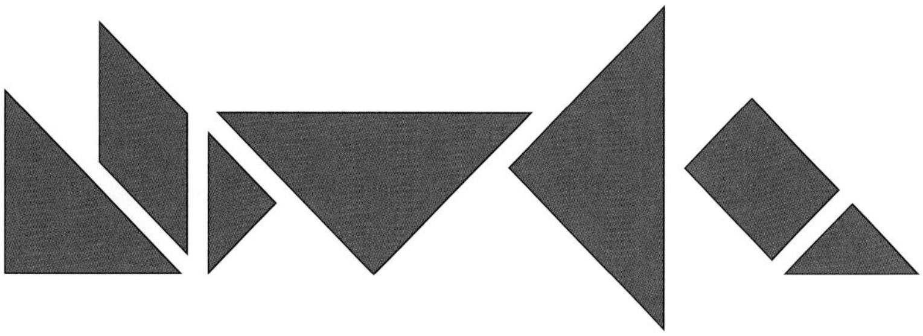

Put them back into the original shape of a square.

ON YOUR OWN

Go to Workbook B:
Put on Your Thinking Cap!
page 244

Chapter Wrap Up

You have learned...

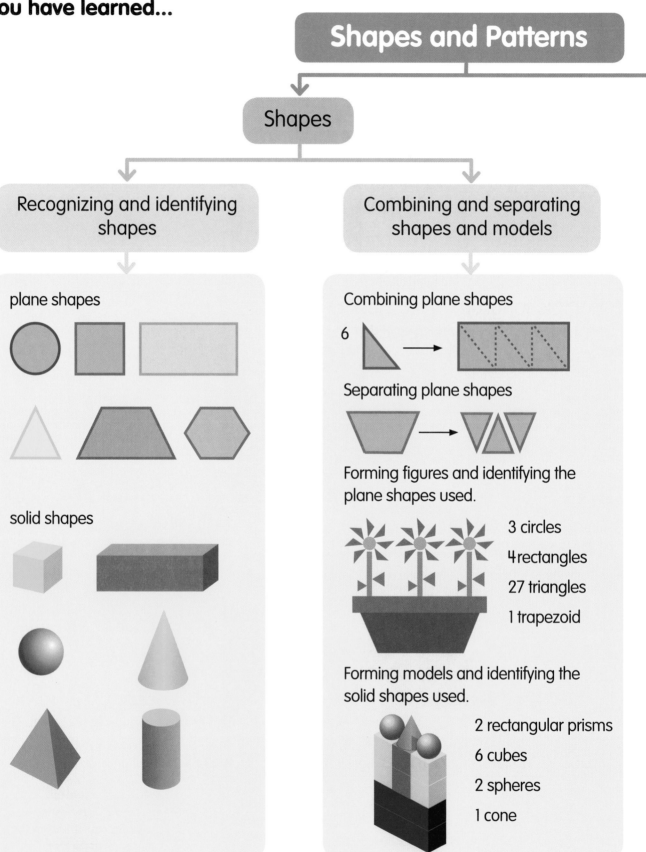

Shapes and Patterns

Shapes

Recognizing and identifying shapes

plane shapes

solid shapes

Combining and separating shapes and models

Combining plane shapes

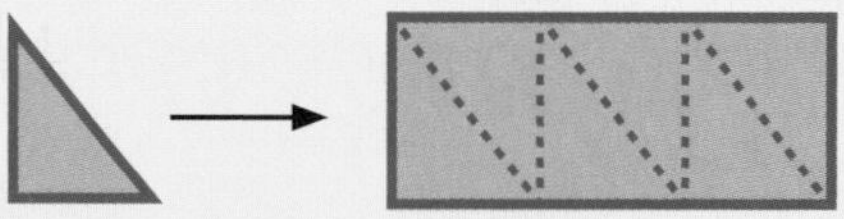

Separating plane shapes

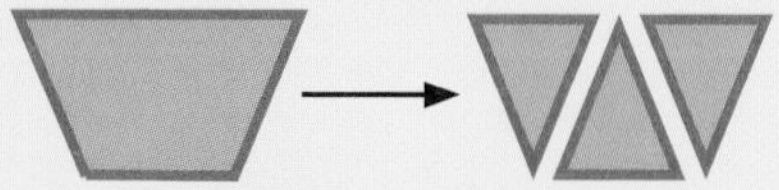

Forming figures and identifying the plane shapes used.

3 circles
4 rectangles
27 triangles
1 trapezoid

Forming models and identifying the solid shapes used.

2 rectangular prisms
6 cubes
2 spheres
1 cone

BIG IDEA

Plane and solid shapes can be identified and classified. They can be separated and combined to make other shapes.

Patterns

Making patterns with plane shapes and solid shapes

change in size

change in shape

change in color

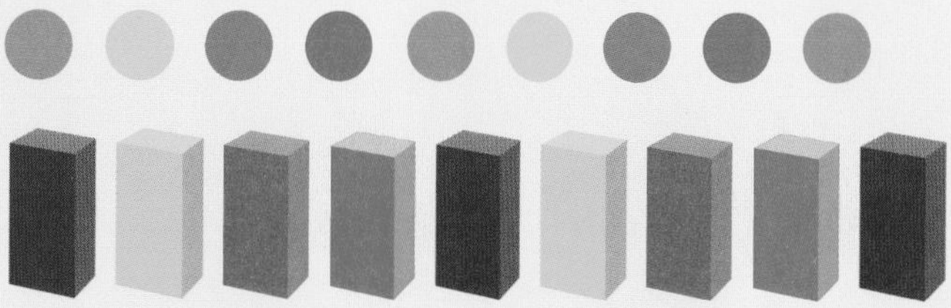

change in shape and color

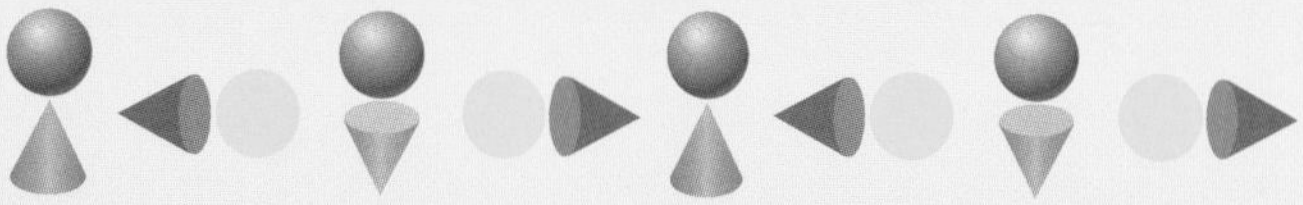

change in shape, size, and turns

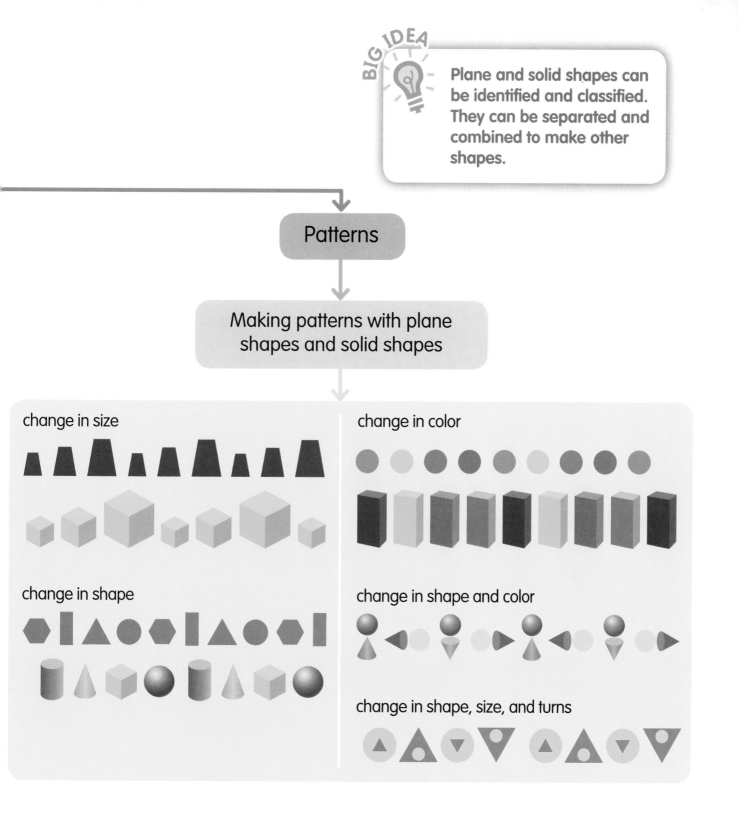

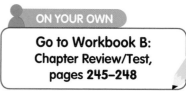

ON YOUR OWN

Go to Workbook B: Chapter Review/Test, pages 245–248

Blank

COMMON CORE

Focus Lessons

LESSON 3.a

Real-World Problems: Money

COMMON CORE

2.MD.8. Solve word problems involving dollar bills, quarters, dimes, nickels, and pennies, using \$ and ¢ symbols appropriately.

Lesson Objective

- Solve word problems using \$ and ¢ symbols.

Learn

You can solve word problems using \$ and ¢.

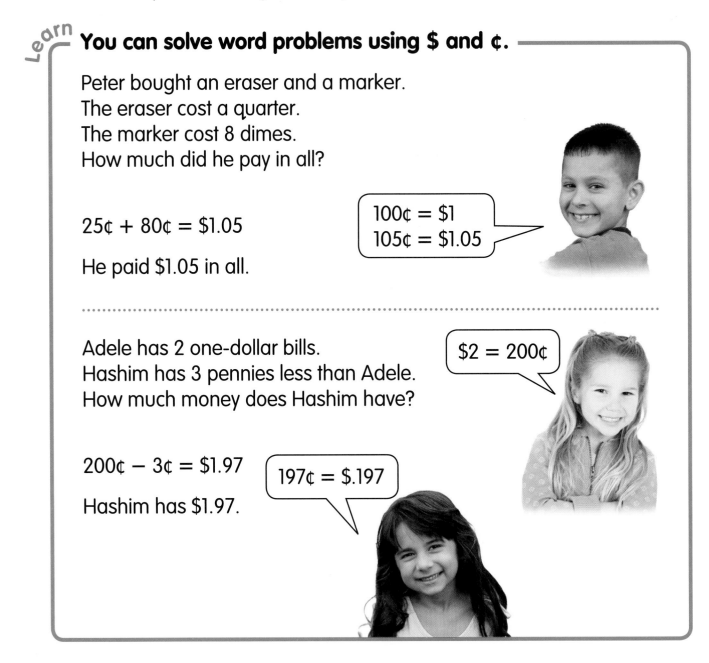

Peter bought an eraser and a marker.
The eraser cost a quarter.
The marker cost 8 dimes.
How much did he pay in all?

25¢ + 80¢ = \$1.05

100¢ = \$1
105¢ = \$1.05

He paid \$1.05 in all.

Adele has 2 one-dollar bills.
Hashim has 3 pennies less than Adele.
How much money does Hashim have?

\$2 = 200¢

200¢ − 3¢ = \$1.97

197¢ = \$.197

Hashim has \$1.97.

Let's Practice

Solve.
Write your answer using $.

These are some things on sale.

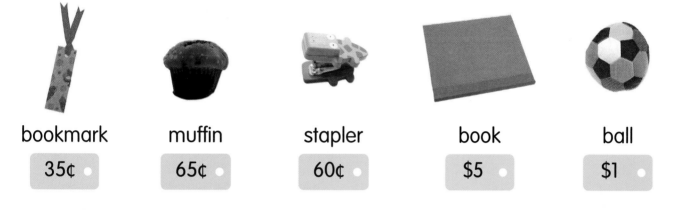

bookmark

35¢

muffin

65¢

stapler

60¢

book

$5

ball

$1

1. Dylan buys a muffin.
   Meena buys a bookmark.
   How much do they spend in all?

2. Rita buys a stapler and a ball.
   How much does she pay in all?

3. Jane has a dollar bill and 2 quarters in her purse.
   She buys a bookmark.
   How much does she have left?

4. Damon has a five-dollar bill.
   He wants to buy a book and a bookmark.
   a. How much more money does he need?
   b. How many nickels does he need to make that amount?

LESSON 4.a

Comparing Inches and Feet

COMMON CORE

2.MD.2. Measure the length of an object twice, using length units of different lengths for the two measurements. Describe how the two measurements relate to the size of the unit chosen.

Hands-On Activity

WORKING TOGETHER

Measure each object in inches. Then measure it again in feet.

	Measure (in.)	Measure (ft)
The width of your teacher's desk		
The height of your chair		
The length of the board		
The height of the bookshelf		
The length of a textbook		

1. Which objects are easier to measure using inches?

2. Which objects are easier to measure using feet?

3. Why are there more inches than feet when you measure the same object?

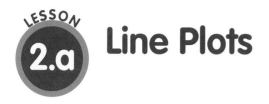

LESSON 2.a

Line Plots

COMMON CORE

2.MD.9. Generate measurement data by measuring lengths of several objects to the nearest whole unit, or by making repeated measurements of the same object. Show the measurements by making a line plot, where the horizontal scale is marked off in whole-number units.

Lesson Objective

- Make a line plot to show data.

Vocabulary

line plot

Learn

You can show data using a line plot.

Ben counts the number of stickers that his friends have.

Stickers Ben's Friends Have

Name	Rick	Jane	Ken	Suki	Tasha	Jamal	Tiva
Number of Stickers	2	3	4	1	3	2	2

Then Ben records his data in a tally chart.
This will make it easier to draw a line plot.

Number of Stickers	**Tally**	**Number of Friends**
1	/	1
2	///	3
3	//	2
4	/	1

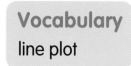

Ben now draws a line plot to show his data.

A **line plot** shows data on a number line.
The ✗ shows how often something happens.

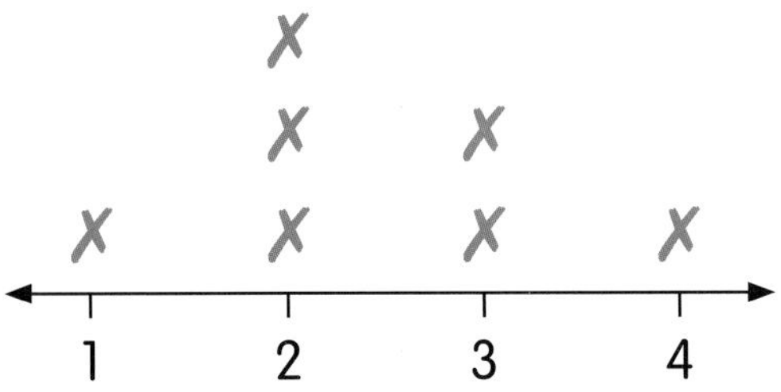

Number of Stickers Ben's Friends Have

Key: Each ✗ stands for 1 friend.

1, 2, 3, and 4 are the numbers of stickers.

One ✗ means 1 friend has 1 sticker.

Three ✗ means 3 friends each have 2 stickers.

How many friends have 3 stickers?

How many friends have 4 stickers?

Hands-On Activity

WORKING TOGETHER

Use an inch ruler to measure the objects in your classroom.

Find four objects on your desk or in your classroom that you think are about 1 to 4 inches long.
Measure the length of each object to the nearest inch.
Record the data in the table.

Object	Measured Length (in.)

Ask two other children for their measurements.
Record all your data in the tally chart.

Length (in.)	Tally	Number of Objects
1		
2		
3		
4		

Then show the data on a line plot.

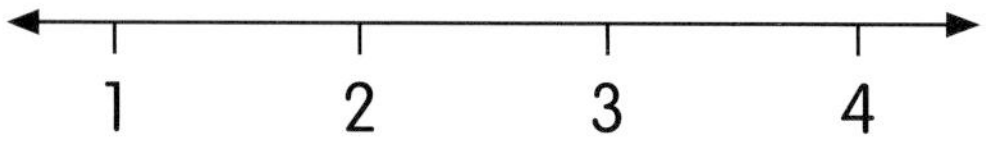

Length of Object (in.)

Key: Each ✗ stands for 1 object.

1. How many objects are 2 inches long? ________

2. How many objects are 4 inches long? ________

3. The most number of objects are ________ inches long.

4. How many objects were measured altogether? ________
   How do you know?

LESSON 1.a

Quadrilaterals and Pentagons

COMMON CORE

2.G.1. Recognize and draw shapes having specified attributes, such as a given number of angles or a given number of equal faces. **Identify triangles, quadrilaterals, pentagons,** hexagons, and cubes.

Lesson Objectives

- Identify quadrilaterals and pentagons.
- Recognize and draw shapes having a given number of angles.

Vocabulary

quadrilateral

pentagon

angle

Learn

Get to know quadrilaterals and pentagons.

These are **quadrilaterals**.

A quadrilateral has four sides.
A rectangle and square are also quadrilaterals.

This is a **pentagon**.

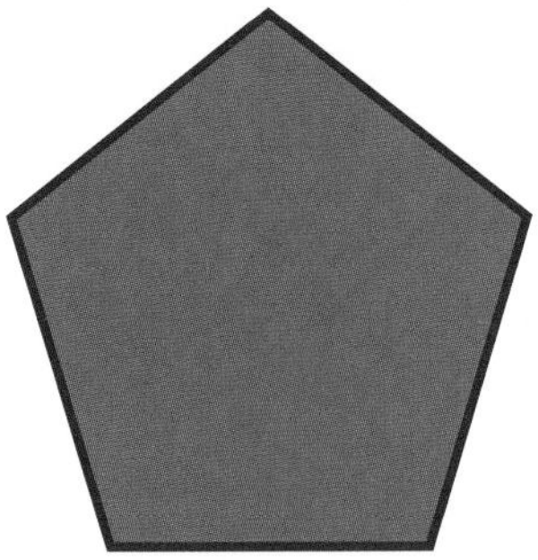

A pentagon has five sides.

Let's Practice

1 Color the quadrilaterals blue and the pentagons green.

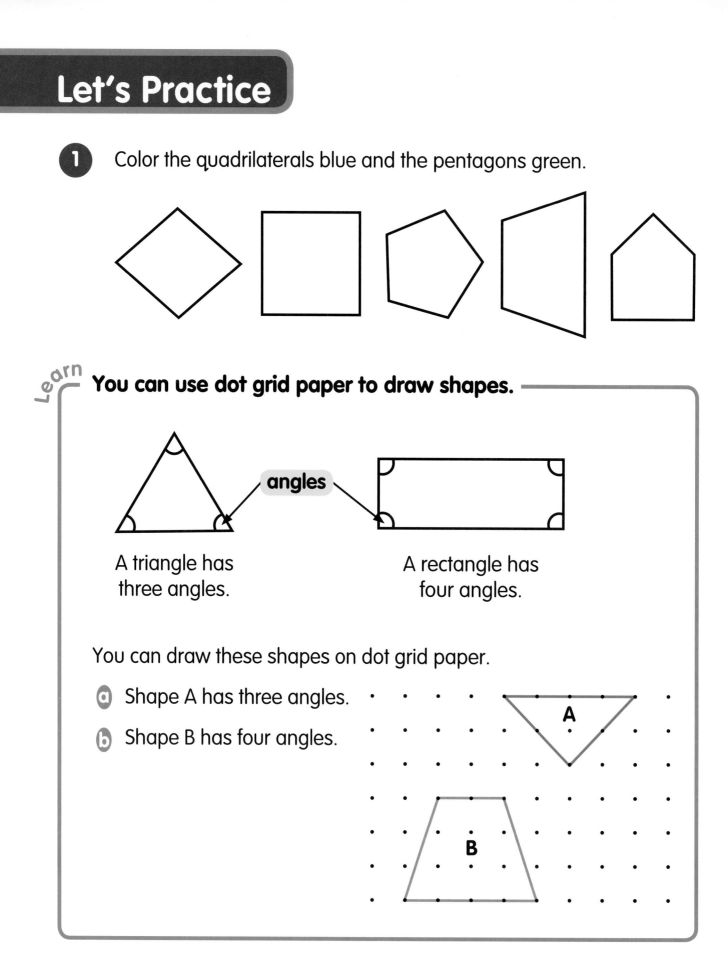

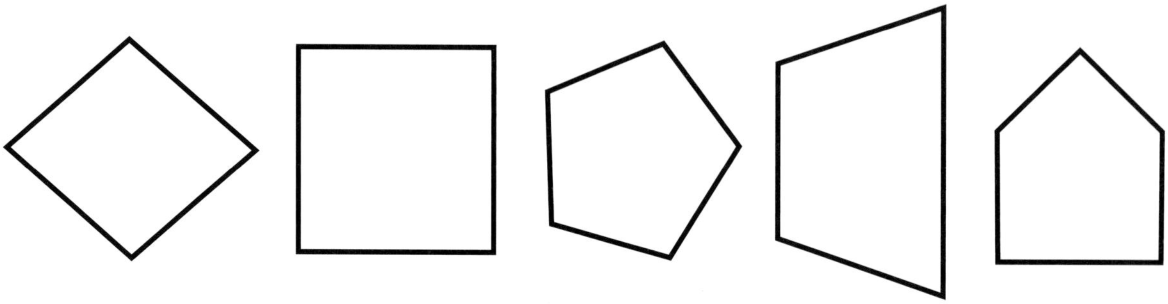

Learn

You can use dot grid paper to draw shapes.

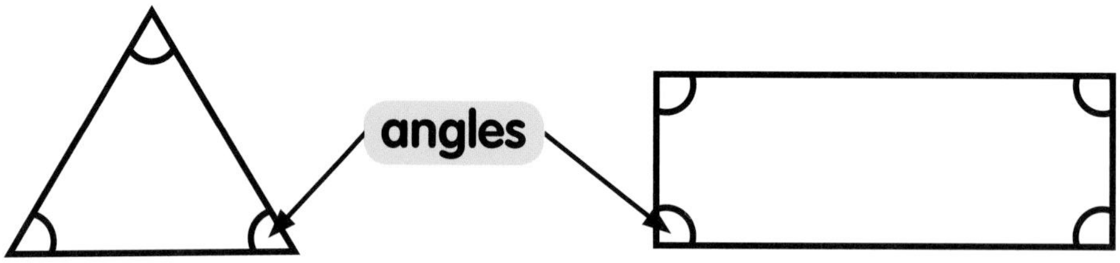

A triangle has three angles.

A rectangle has four angles.

You can draw these shapes on dot grid paper.

a Shape A has three angles.

b Shape B has four angles.

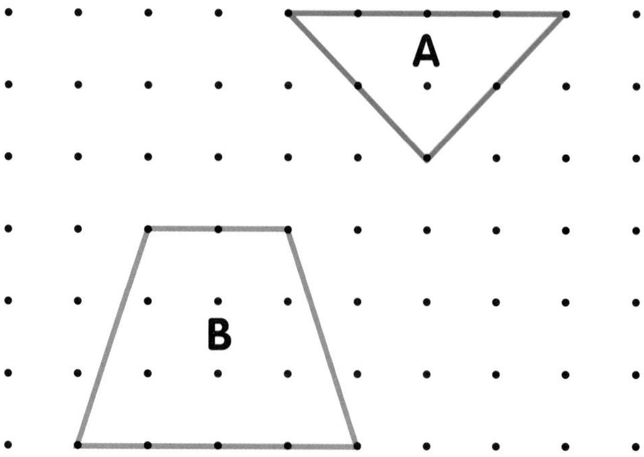

Let's Practice

1 Draw a quadrilateral on the dot grid paper.

2 Copy this pentagon on the dot grid paper.

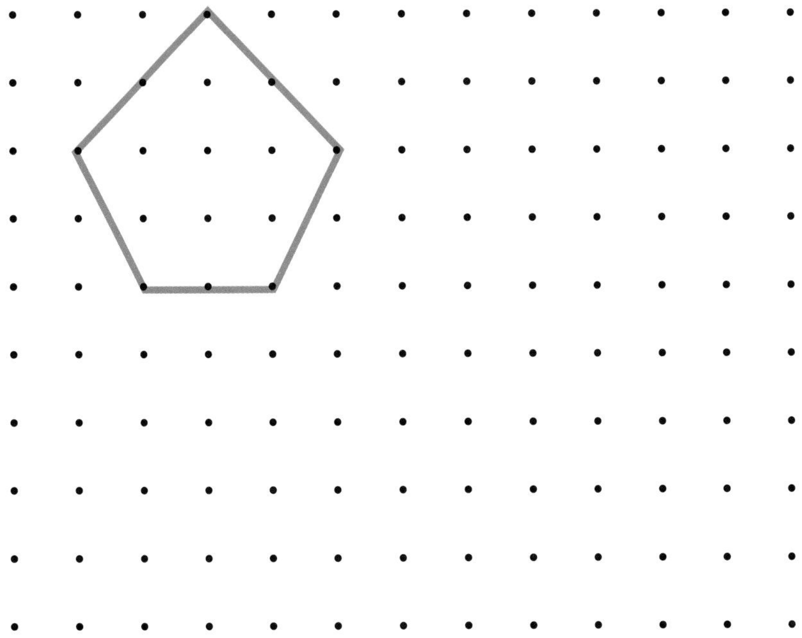

3. Draw a shape with three angles on the dot grid paper.

4. Draw a shape with four angles on the dot grid paper.

LESSON 2.a

Faces of a Cube

COMMON CORE

2.G.1. Recognize and draw **shapes having specified attributes, such as a given number of** angles or a given number of **equal faces. Identify** triangles, quadrilaterals, pentagons, hexagons, and **cubes.**

Lesson Objective

- Identify and count the equal faces on a cube.

Vocabulary

face

Hands-On Activity

WORK IN PAIRS

Each flat surface of a solid is called a **face**.

1 Count the faces on the cube.

a The cube has ________ faces.

b What can you say about the faces?

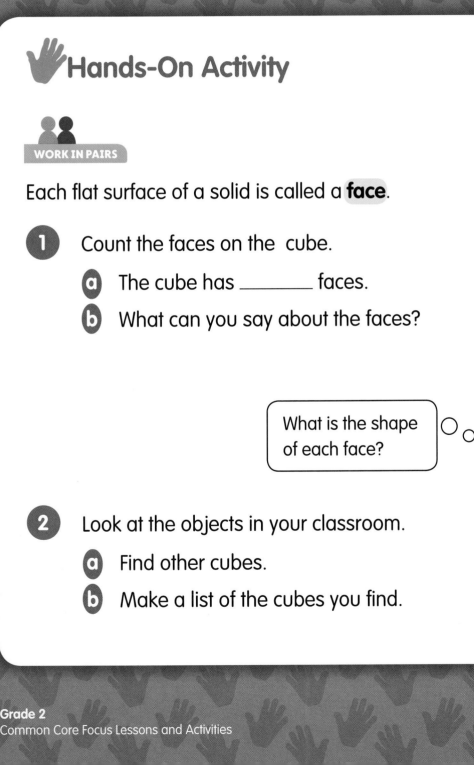

What is the shape of each face?

2 Look at the objects in your classroom.

a Find other cubes.

b Make a list of the cubes you find.

Glossary

A

- **add mentally**

  You can add numbers mentally.

  Find 38 + 8.

  8 = 10 − 2
  38 + 10 = 48
  48 − 2 = 46
  So, 38 + 8 = 46.

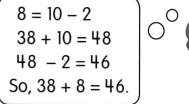

- **about**

  82 is about 80.

- **after**

It is 15 minutes after 7 in the morning.

- **A.M.**

  Use A.M. to talk about time just after midnight to just before noon.
  I get up each day at 7 A.M.

B

- **bar models**

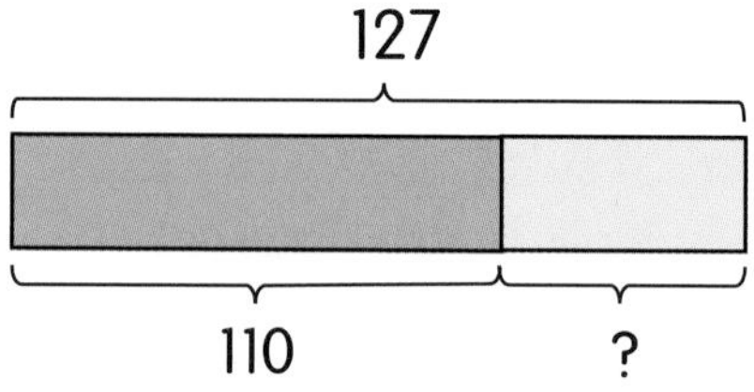

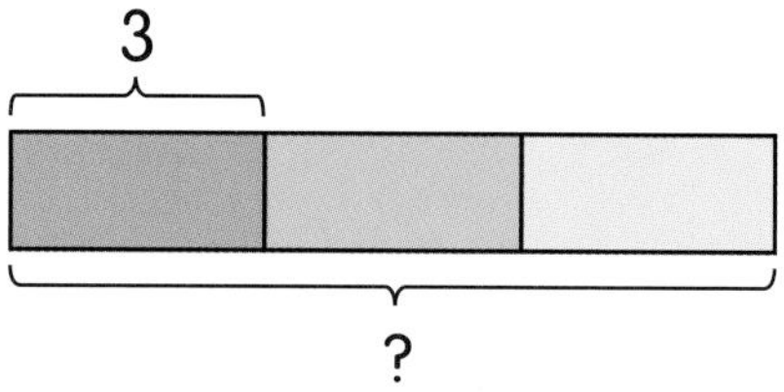

These are examples of bar models.
Use bar models to help you add, subtract, multiply, and divide.

C

- **cent sign (¢)**

10¢

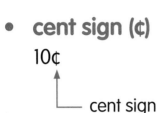

↑ cent sign

- **clock face**

This is a clock face.
The short hand tells the hour.
The long hand tells the minutes after the hour.

- **curve**

Each of these drawings is a curve.

- **curved surface**

This ball has a curved surface.

D

- **decimal point**

A decimal point separates the cents from the dollars.

$10.15

↑ decimal point

- **difference**

Difference is the result when one number is subtracted from another.

50 – 35 = 15

↑ difference

- **dollar sign ($)**

$20.00

↑ dollar sign

- **dot paper**

  A dot paper shows a set of dots in equal rows and equal columns.

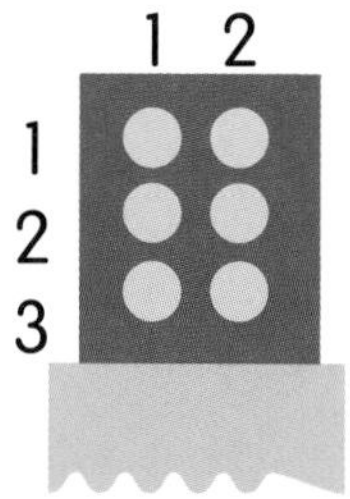

  This is dot paper.
  It shows 3 rows of 2.

E

- **equal parts**

  Each part is the same size.

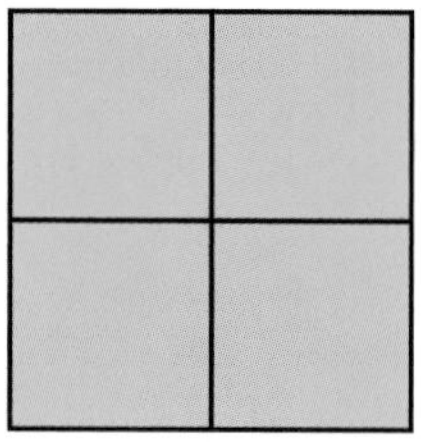

  This square is divided into four equal parts.

- **estimate**

  An estimate is a number close to an exact amount.

  105 + 7 is about 110.

  estimate

F

- **figure**

  You can make a figure by combining different plane shapes.

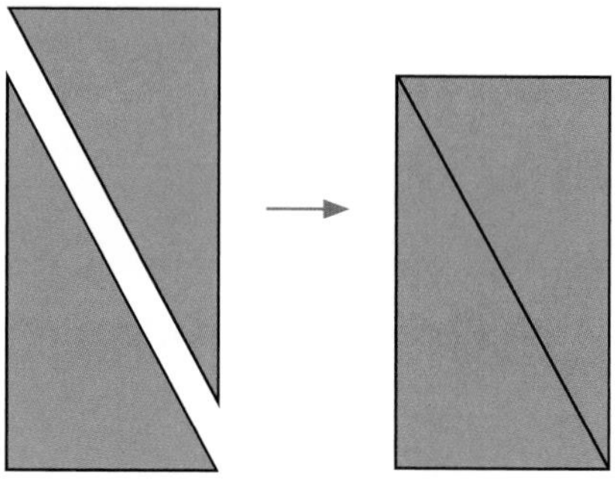

  You can combine two triangles to form a rectangle.

- **flat surface**

  This book has a flat surface.

- **foot (ft)**

  Foot (ft) is a customary measurement of length. Write ft for foot or feet.

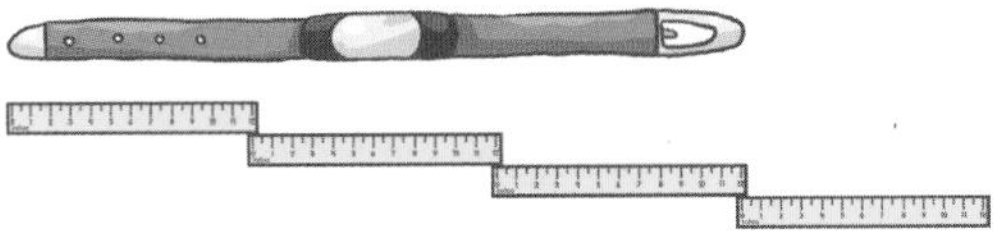

  This belt is 3 feet long.

- **fraction**

  A fraction is a number that names equal parts of a whole.

  $\frac{1}{4}$ is a fraction.

G

- **greater than (>)**

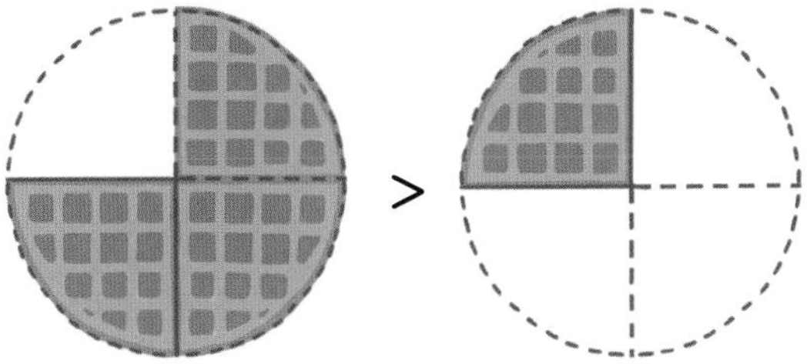

  $\frac{3}{4} > \frac{1}{4}$

  $\frac{3}{4}$ is greater than $\frac{1}{4}$.

H

- **height**

  Height describes how tall something is.

  The height of the stack of books is 9 inches.

- **hexagon**

  A hexagon is a plane shape that has six sides.

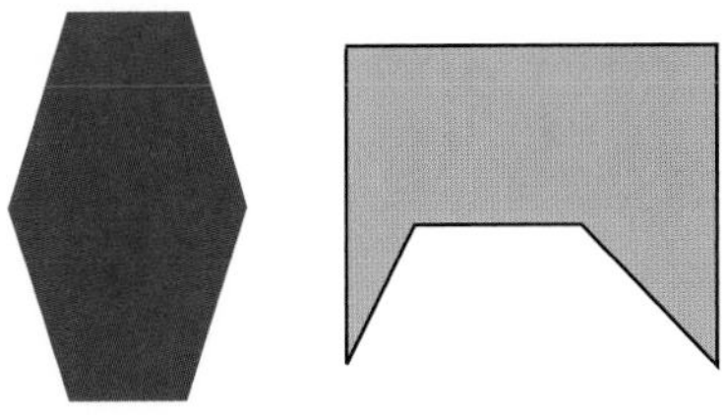

  These are hexagons.

- **hour**

  Hour is a unit of time equal to 60 minutes.

- **hour hand**

  Hour hand is the short hand on a clock.

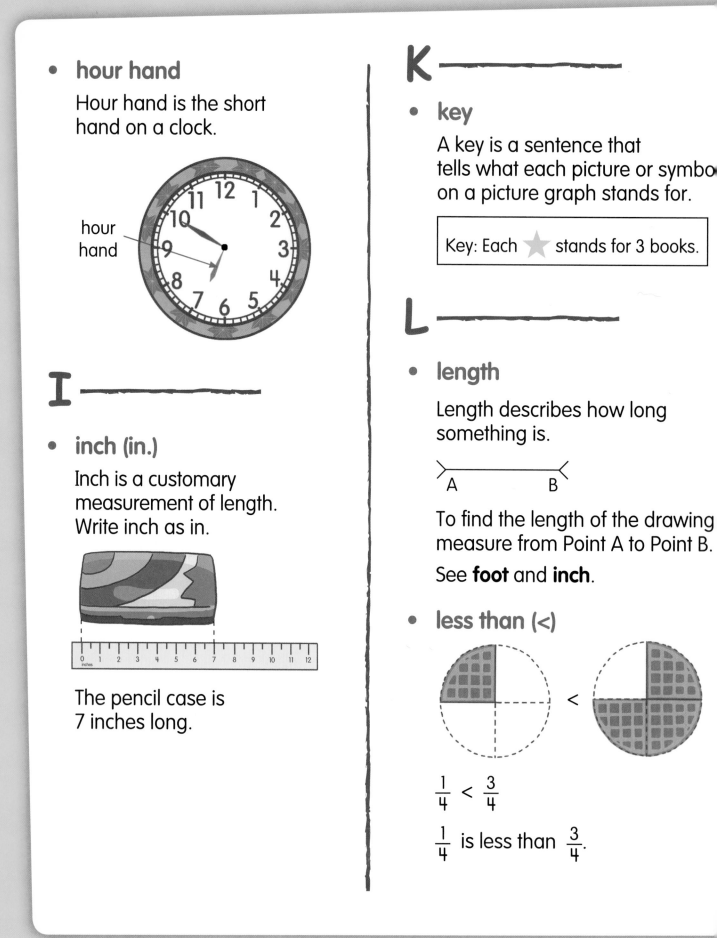

I

- **inch (in.)**

  Inch is a customary measurement of length. Write inch as in.

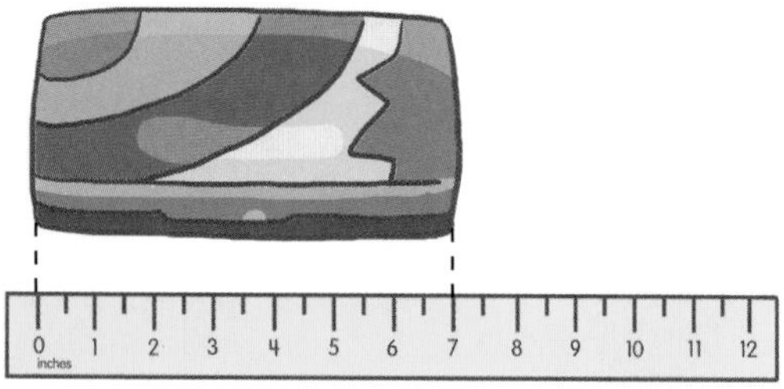

The pencil case is 7 inches long.

K

- **key**

  A key is a sentence that tells what each picture or symbo on a picture graph stands for.

Key: Each ★ stands for 3 books.

L

- **length**

  Length describes how long something is.

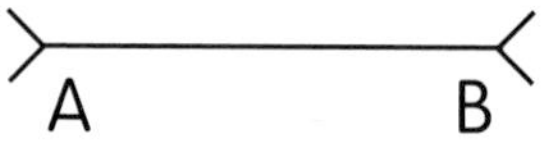

To find the length of the drawing measure from Point A to Point B.

See **foot** and **inch**.

- **less than (<)**

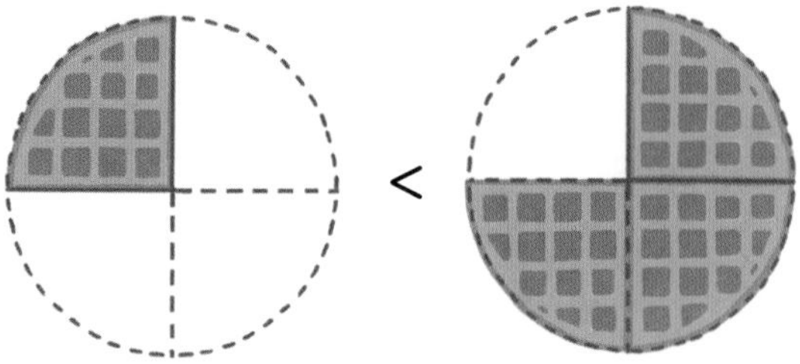

$\frac{1}{4} < \frac{3}{4}$

$\frac{1}{4}$ is less than $\frac{3}{4}$.

- **like fractions**

$\frac{1}{4}$ and $\frac{2}{4}$ are like fractions.

The bottom numbers are the same.

- **longest**

A word used when ordering three objects by length.

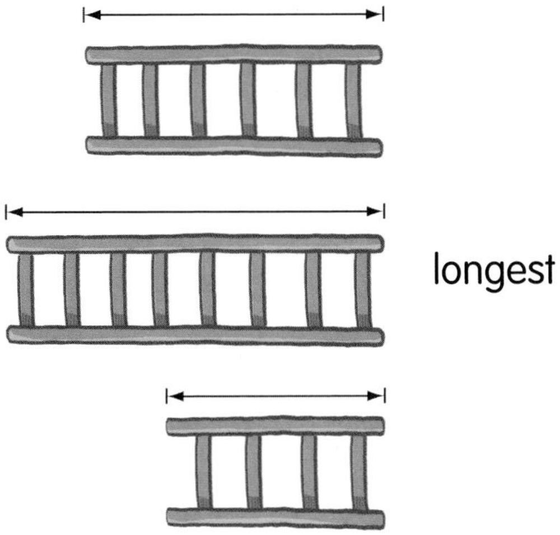

M

- **minute**

Minute is a unit of time. 60 minutes equal 1 hour.

- **minute hand**

Minute hand is the long hand on a clock.

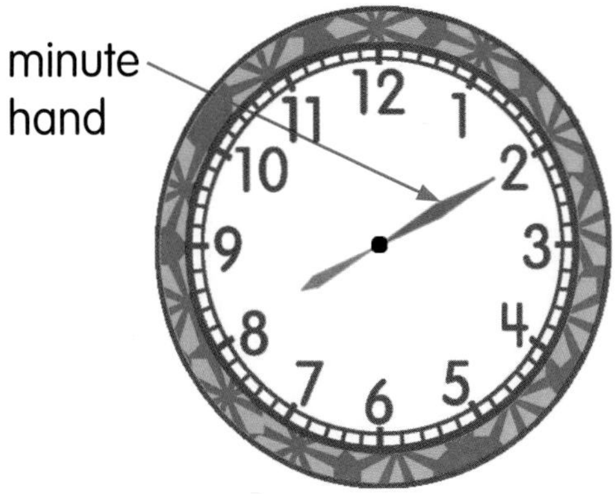

N

- **nearest ten**

44 is 40 when rounded to the nearest ten.

- **number line**

A line that shows numbers in increasing size from left to right.

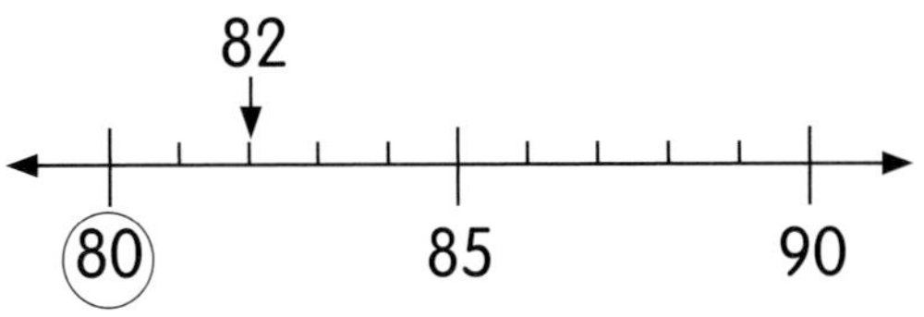

O

- **o'clock**

  O'clock means according to the clock.

It is 8 o'clock.

- **one half**

  One half is one of the parts you get when you divide something into 2 equal parts.

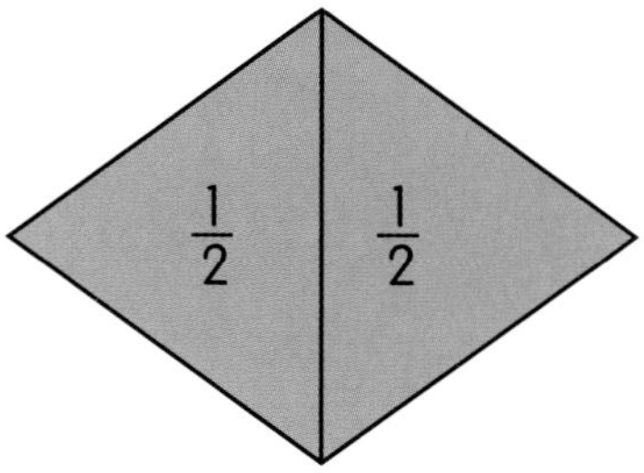

- **one fourth**

  One fourth is one of the parts you get when you divide something into 4 equal parts.

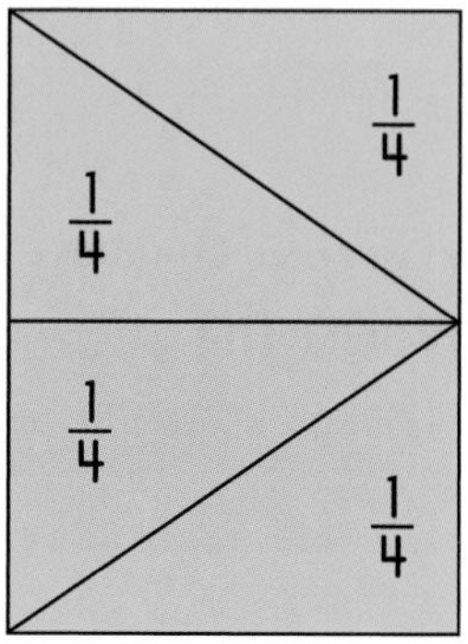

- **one third**

  One third is one of the parts you get when you divide something into 3 equal parts.

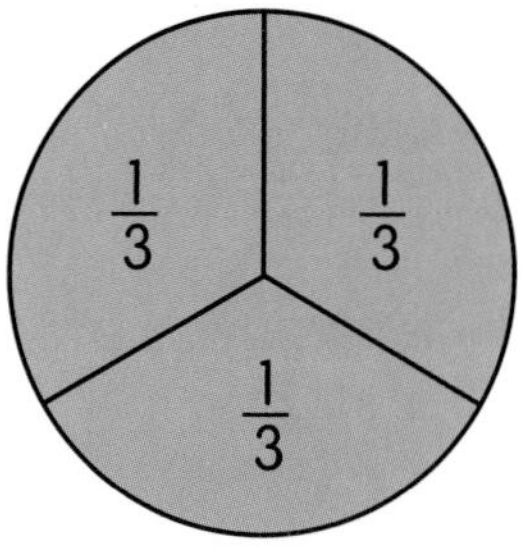

P

- **part of a line**

This drawing is a part of a line.

- **pattern**

  A pattern is something that changes in a regular way.

- **pattern unit**

This is a pattern unit.

- **picture graph**

Groups at the Workshop

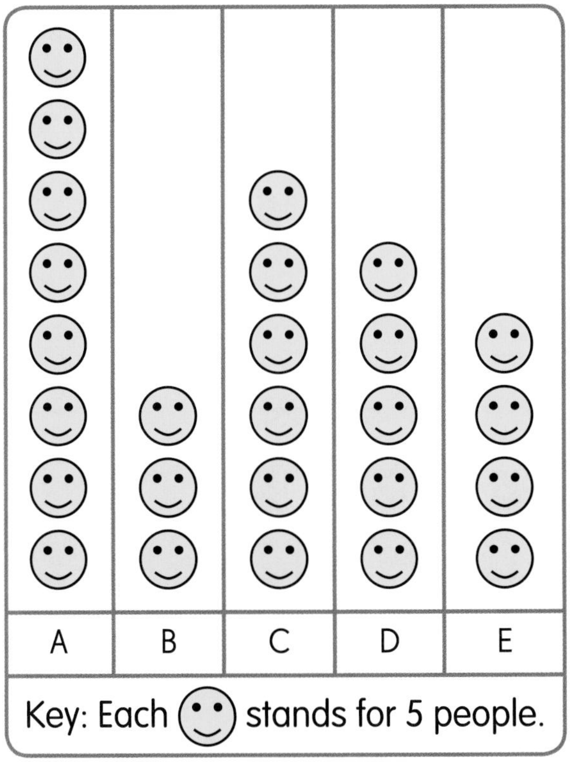

- **P.M.**

  Use P.M. to talk about time just after noon to just before midnight.

  At 7:00 P.M. I watch my favorite T.V. show.

R

- **reasonable**

  You can use rounding to estimate sums and differences and check that answers are reasonable.

  105 + 7 = 112
  105 is about 110.
  7 is about 10.
  105 + 7 is about 120.
  Because 120 is close to the actual sum, which is 112, the answer is reasonable.

  176 – 12 = 164
  176 is about 180.
  12 is about 10.
  176 – 12 is about 170.
  Because 170 is close to the actual difference, which is 164, the answer is reasonable.

- **related multiplication facts**

  3 × 4 = 12
  4 × 3 = 12

  These are related multiplication facts.

- **related multiplication and division facts**

  5 × 3 = 15 15 ÷ 5 = 3
  3 × 5 = 15 15 ÷ 3 = 5

  3 × 3 = 9
  9 ÷ 3 = 3
  These are related multiplication and division facts.

- **repeating pattern**

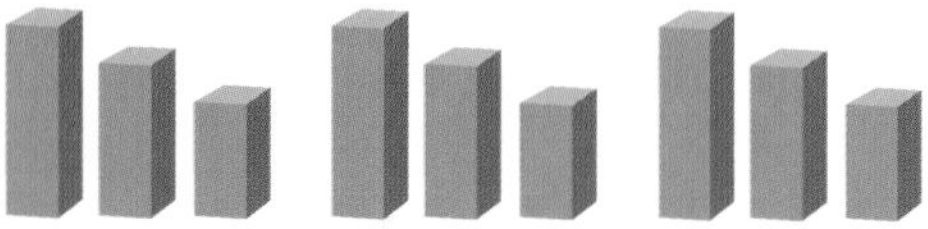

  This is a repeating pattern.

- **roll**

  You can roll objects that have curved surfaces.

- **round**
  See **nearest ten**.

- **ruler**

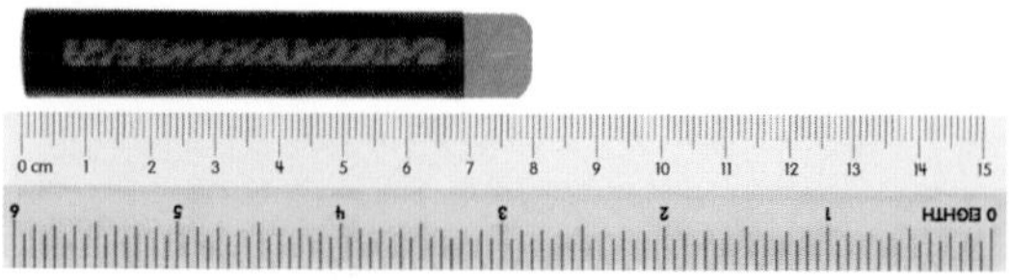

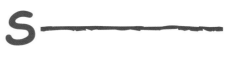

  A ruler is a tool used to measure lengths of objects.

S

- **shapes**

  You can make a repeating pattern using different shapes.

- **shortest**

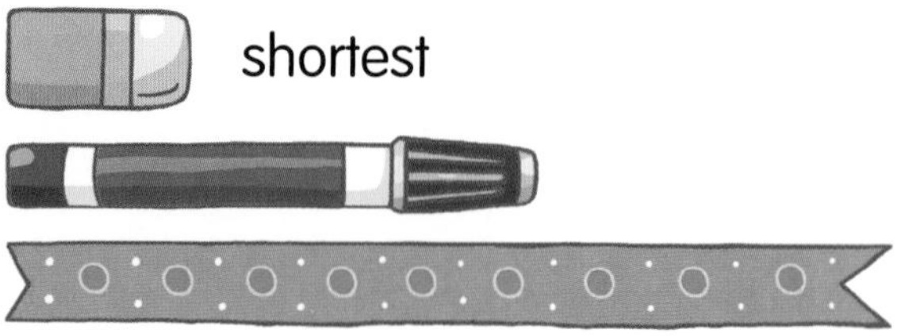

- **skip-count**

  Skip-count by 3s:

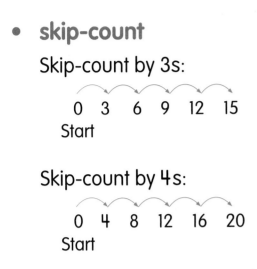

  0 3 6 9 12 15
  Start

  Skip-count by 4s:

  0 4 8 12 16 20
  Start

- **slide**

  You can slide objects that have flat surfaces.

- **stack**

  You can stack objects that have flat surfaces.

- **subtract mentally**

  You can subtract numbers mentally.

  Find 64 − 8.

  64 − 10 = 54
  54 + 2 = 56
  So, 64 − 8 = 56

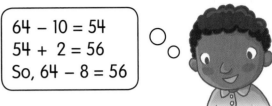

- **sum**

  Sum is the result when numbers are added.

  50 + 35 = 85

  sum (arrow pointing to 85)

- **symbol**

  A symbol is a picture that represents data in a picture graph.

  Key: Each ● stands for 4 days.

  symbol (arrow pointing to ●)

T

- **table**

You can use a table to organize data in rows and columns.

You can use dollars and cents tables to compare amounts of money.

	Dollars	Cents
Anne	15	20

	Dollars	Cents
Adela	15	35

	Dollars	Cents
Maggie	15	50

$15.50 is the greatest amount.
$15.20 is the least amount.

Maggie has the most money.
Anne has the least money.

- **tally chart**

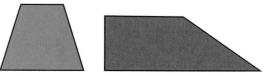

Snowy Days in December			
卌 |	||	||||	卌 |
First Week	Second Week	Third Week	Fourth Week

This is a tally chart.

- **trapezoid**

A trapezoid is a plane shape that has four sides.

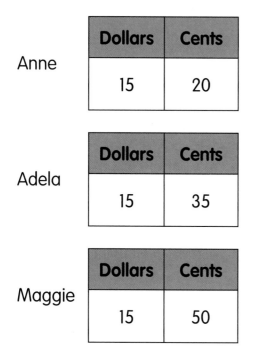

These are trapezoids.

- **turn**

You can turn a shape many times to make a repeating pattern.

U

- **unequal parts**
  Each part is not the same size.

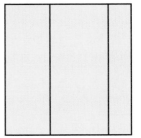

This square is not divided into three equal parts.

- **unit**
  An inch is a unit of measurement.

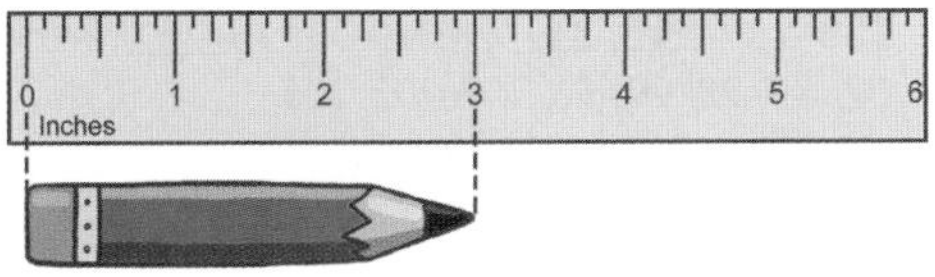

The pencil is 3 inches long.

- **unit fraction**
  A unit fraction names one of the equal parts of a whole.

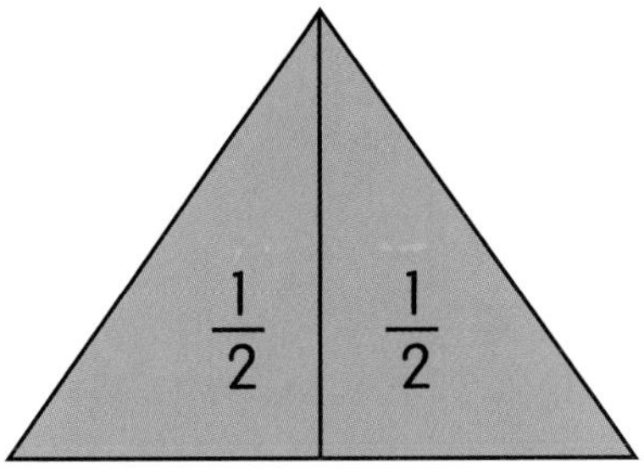

$\frac{1}{2}$ is a unit fraction.

W

- **whole**
  A whole describes an entire figure and is equal to one.

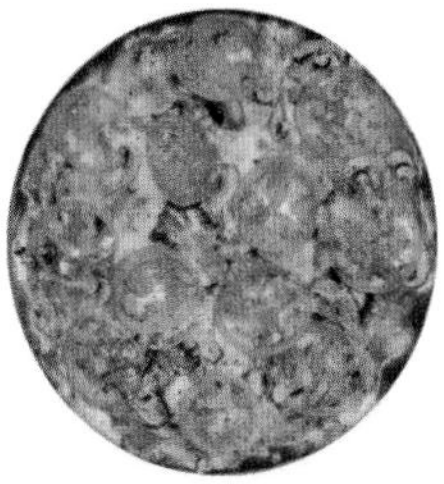

This pizza shows one whole.

- **width**
  Width describes how wide something is.

The mouth of the vase is about 4 inches wide.

Index

A

B

Bar models, **96**
- length, 216–220; 122–126, 206–208, 218; *WB 179–182; WB 89–90, 96, 169–171*
- mass, 253–258; 209–211, 215–216, 218; *WB 213–214; WB 172–173, 181*
- numbers,
  - comparing sets, *See* Set–compare
  - joining sets, *See* Set–join
  - part-part-whole, *See* Part-part-whole
  - taking away sets, *See* Set–take away
- volume, 278–281, 283

Base-ten blocks, *See* Manipulatives

C

Communication
- Math Journal, 65, 70, 107, 132, 169, 175, 206; 16, 27, 38, 146, 200, 204; *WB 18, 91–92, 118, 149–150, 207–208, 228*

Comparing, **18**
- fewest, **231**
- greater than, **18,** 19–23, 33; 72, 83, 85; *WB 13–14, 23, 99*
- greatest, 24, 25–26, 30, 33; 63, 65, 84–89, 99; *WB 23, 43–44, 67, 245; WB 36*
- height, *See* Length
- least, 24, 25–26, 30, 33; 63, 65, 84–89, 99; *WB 23, 43, 67, 245; WB 36, 38*
- length, *See* Length
- less than, **19,** 26–28, 31, 33, 192–195; *WB 13–14, 99, 165–166, 168; WB 24–25, 35, 63–66*
- mass, *See* Mass
- more than, 26, 27–28, 31, 192–195; 52, 62–63, 67, 85, 97–98; *WB 165–166, 168, 25, 35, 63–66*
- most, *WB 24*
- numbers, *See* Place value
- using inequalities, 18–23, 33, 99
- sets, *See* Sets
- width, *See* Length
- volume, *See* Volume

Connecting cubes, *See* Manipulatives

Counters, See Manipulatives

Counting, **6,**
- on by 1s, 10s, and 100s to 1,000, 6–10; *WB 1–6, 16–18, 20, 24, 99*
- counting back, 27–28, 31–33; *WB 16–17, 20, 23, 99*
- counting on, 6–10, 26–30, 31, 33; *WB 1–6, 16–20, 24, 99*
- skip-counting, *See* Multiplication

Cube, *See* Geometry

Cumulative Review, *See* Assessment

D

Difference, *See* Subtraction
- estimate, 35, 37–38, 41; *WB 19–20*

Division, **134**
- basic facts, 134–141; *WB 111–114*
- equal groups, **134,** 135, 140–141, 148; *WB 111, 121*
- inverse operation, *See* Inverse operation
- repeated subtraction, 136, 137–139, 141, 146; *WB 112–114, 117, 121–122, 158*
- related division facts, **179;** 184–189, 193;
- sentence, 134, 135, 137–141, 143–144, 146; 184–188, 192–193, 201–204, 206, 209, 213, 218–219; *WB 111–114, 117–118, 121–122, 124, 145–148, 152, 155–156, 158–159, 161, 163–164; WB 151–154, 166–168, 170–175*
- sharing equally, **134,** 135, 140–141; 201–202, 207–208, 219; *WB 111; WB 165–168*
- using related multiplication facts, 179–185, 188; *WB 145–148*

Dot grid paper, *See* Shapes and Patterns
Dot paper, *See* Manipulatives

Pages listed in regular type refer to Student Book A.
Pages in blue type refer to Student Book B.
Pages listed in *italic* type refer to Workbook (WB) A.
Pages in *blue italic type* refer to Workbook (WB) B.
Pages in **boldface** type show where a term is introduced.

E

Equal
equal sign (=), *throughout. See for example* 6, 12–14, 29, 38–43, 45–51, 53–55
equal to, *throughout. See for example* 6, 12–14, 29, 38–43, 45–51, 53–55, 52

Equal groups, *See* Multiplication *and* Division

Estimating measures
length, *See* Length
mass, *See* Mass
volume, *See* Volume

Exploration,
Let's Explore!, 29–30, 120, 131, 147, 172, 183; 16, 27, 33, 51, 53, 173, 187

F

Fact families, *See* Addition *and* Subtraction

Fractions
and equal parts, 75–79, 81–82, 90–91, 98–99; *WB 45–50*
comparing, 83–89, 97, 99; *WB 51–52, 59*
like fractions
adding, 90, 92–93, 96, 99; *WB 53–55, 62*
subtracting, 93–94, 96, 99; *WB 55–57, 62*
making one whole, 90–91, 98; *WB 59*
ordering, 84–86, 89, 99; *WB 52, 61*
part of a whole, 76; *WB 59*

G

Games, 15, 22, 28, 44, 52, 76, 162–163, 166, 170

Geometric solids, *See* Manipulatives

Geometry
combining shapes, 274–278
corners, 250, 252,
models,
moving solid shapes
rolling, 261–264, 267
sliding, 261–264, 267
stacking, 261–264, 267
patterns, *See* Patterns
plane shapes
circle, 249–252, 271–272, 277, 279, 281; *WB 225*
hexagon, 271, 274, 277, 281; *WB 225*
rectangle, 249–252, 271–272, 276–277, 279–281, 285; *WB 225*
square, 249–252, 271–272, 274, 276–277, 279, 281; *WB 225*
trapezoid, **271,** 272, 274, 277, 279–281; *WB 225*
triangle, 249, 271–272, 274–275, 277, 279–281, 285, 295; *WB 225*
sides, **250**
solid shapes,
cone, **287**, 289
cube, **287**, 289, 291
cylinder, **287**–288, 289, 291
pyramid, **287**–288
rectangular prism, **287**–289, 291
sphere, **287**

Glossary, 284–294, 306–318

H

Hands-On Activity, 100–101, 105, 112, 112, 139, 194, 198, 205, 213, 230, 247, 249, 255, 267, 270

Height, *See* Length

Hundred, **6**

Hundreds, *See* Palce value

Hundreds chart, **173,** *WB 141*

I

Inequality, *See* Comparing–inequalities

Inverse operations,
relate addition and subtraction, 57, 59, 61–66, 68–71, 74–75, 80–81, 85, 87, 90–91, 98; *WB 49, 51–52, 53, 55–57, 59–61, 63–66, 69, 101*
relate multiplication and division, 179–185, 188; 184–189, 193; *WB 145–148, 154–155; 151–154, 158*

J

Join, *See* Set-join

L

Length, **192**
- about, **114,** 116; *WB 70*
- comparing,
  - longer, **197,** 198–199, 211–215; 107–108, 110, 117–121; *WB 166, 169, 172, 188, 235; WB 67–68, 75–76, 81, 83, 85*
  - longest, **197,** 200, 211, 214; 107; *WB, 68, 73*
  - shorter, **197,** 198–200, 211–213; 107–109, 117–118, 120, 128; *WB 166, 170, 172; WB 75–76, 79, 81, 83*
  - shortest, **197**, 200, 211; 107, 118; *WB 170, 188; WB 85*
  - taller, **196,** 200; 110, 128; *WB 169–170; WB 67*
  - tallest, **196,** 200; 110; *WB 170*
  - estimating, 194, 204; *WB 168, 187*
  - height, **193,** 194, 196, 207, 215; 104, 106; *WB 73, 165, 167, 169–170, 185; WB 63*
- tools,
  - centimeter ruler, **201;** *WB 171–178, 188*
  - inch ruler, **113,** 115–117, 119–120; *WB 79–82*
  - meterstick, **192,** 193–200; *WB 165–170, 185*
- units,
  - centimeters (cm), **201,** 202–215, 218–220, 222–223; *WB 171–178, 180–183, 185, 188, 190, 235–236, 246, 248*
  - feet (ft), **100,** 103–110, 122–123, 126–129;*WB 73–78*
  - inches (in.), **100,** 111–121, 124–125, 126, 128–129; *WB 79–86*
  - meters (m), **192,** 193–200, 216–217, 220–221, 221–223; *WB 165–170, 179–180, 185–186, 189*
- width, **193,** 194, 206; *WB 167, 169–170, 186*

Let's Explore, *See* Exploration

Let's Practice, *See* Practice

Lines,
- part of a line, **115,** 115–117, 120, 253–257, 266; *WB 209–244*
- curve, 113, 253–257, 266; *WB 209–244*

M

Manipulatives,
- balance scale, 231–235, 237, 240, 243, 260–261; *WB 191, 194, 196–197, 207, 209*
- base-ten blocks, 6–12, 17–21, 23, 33, 38–40, 42, 44, 46–47, 49–50, 61–63, 67–68, 72–74, 76, 78–80, 84–85; *WB 1, 4–5, 7–9, 21–22, 245–246*
- cards, 9
- centimeter ruler, 201–215, 218–220, 222–223; *WB 171–178*
- classroom objects,
  - counters, 139
  - craftsticks, 139
  - string, 105, 113, 116; *WB 167–168, 172–173; WB 66, 69*
- computer, *See* Technology
- connecting cubes, 92, 96–99; 8
- dot paper, 156–160, 168, 171, 176–178, 187–188; 161–162, 164, 170–173, 179–182, 191–192; *WB 129–132, 137–140, 153–156, 160–161; WB 135–138, 143–146, 154*
- foot ruler, 103–108; *WB 73–78*
- inch ruler, 111–121; *WB 79–88*
- measuring cup, 274–276, 283; *WB 221–224, 229, 232–233, 239, 248*
- measuring scale, 229–234, 236–238, 241, 243–245, 248, 250–252, 260; *WB 191–196, 198–203, 208–212, 248*
- meterstick, 192–200; *WB 165–170, 185*
- number cube, 9

Mass, **228**
- comparing,
  - as heavy as, **229;** *WB 191, 208*
  - heavier than, **235,** 246, 248, 252, 260; *WB 203–204, 211*
  - heaviest, **237,** 239, 245, 247, 260; *WB 191, 203–204, 208, 212*
  - less than, **229;** *WB 191*
  - lighter than, **235,** 240, 246, 248, 252, 260; *WB 203–204, 208*
  - lightest, **237,** 239, 245, 247, 260; *WB 191, 203–204, 211–212*
  - more than, **230;** *WB 191,*

Pages listed in regular type refer to Student Book A.
Pages in blue type refer to Student Book B.
Pages listed in *italic* type refer to Workbook (WB) A.
Pages in *blue italic type* refer to Workbook (WB) B.
Pages in **boldface** type show where a term is introduced.

N

O

Ones, *See* Place value

Operations, *See* Addition, Division, Multiplication, *and* Subtraction

Ordering, *See* Fractions, Length, Mass, Numbers, *and* Volume, Time

P

Part-part-whole, **96,** 97–102, 216–218, 220, 256–258, 261, 278, 280–281, 283; *WB 73–76, 85, 88, 90, 96, 102, 205–206, 213, 225–226, 240–242, 250*

Patterns, **26**
- number
  - creating, 29–30; *WB 18, 20, 23–24*
  - completing, 26–28, 31–32, 89; *WB 17, 19, 23, 100, 102, 105, 128, 141, 160, 143*
  - describing 26, 29, 32, 89; *WB 16*
  - extending, 32
  - skip-counting, *See* Multiplication
- shapes
  - completing, 294, 299, 301–302; *WB 239–242*
  - creating, 292–293, 305
  - describing, 294, 296; *WB 243*
  - repeating, 292–295, 298, 300; *WB 243*
- Picture Graphs, **220**
  - making, 232–234; *WB 183–188, 190*
  - reading, 224–231; *WB 179–182*
  - tally chart, 232, 234; *WB 183, 185, 187, 198*

Place value, **11**
- chart, 11, 15, 38–40, 42; *WB 7–9, 15, 22*
- comparing numbers, **18,** 19–23; *WB 13–14, 23*
- expanded form, **12,** 13–17, 33; *WB 7–10, 21–22, 99, 246*
- hundreds, **9,** 11–31, 38–43, 61–65, 68–69, 71–75, 77, 79–82, 84–87, 90–91; *WB 7–12, 15, 22–23, 25, 31, 35, 39, 45, 49, 53, 57, 65, 69, 99, 243–244*
- identifying, 11–31; *WB 7–20, 22–24*
- ones, 11–31, 38–43, 45, 61–65, 67–69, 71–75, 77–79, 81–82, 84–87, 90–91; *WB 7–12, 15, 22–23, 25, 31, 35, 39, 45, 49, 53, 57, 65, 69, 243–244*
- standard form, **12,** 13–17, 33; *WB 7–10, 21–22m 99*
- tens, 11–31, 38–43, 45, 61–65, 67–69, 71–75, 77–82, 84–87, 90–91; *WB 7–12, 15, 22–23, 25, 31, 35, 39, 45, 49, 53, 57, 65, 69, 99, 243–244*
- thousand, **7;** *WB 2, 21*
- word form, **12,** 13–17, 33; *WB 7–10, 21–22, 247*
- zeros in, 12–14, 16–17, 21–23, 24, 27; *WB 8–11, 13–21*

Plane shapes, *See* Geometry

Practice,
- Guided Practice, *throughout. See for example* 7–9, 12–15,21, 25, 27, 39–41, 43
- Let's Practice, *throughout. See for example* 10, 16–17, 23, 30–31, 41, 45

Prerequisite skills,
- Recall Prior Knowledge, 2–4, 35–37, 57–59, 93–94, 125, 150, 190, 225–226, 263–264, 2–4; 43–44, 74, 101, 131, 160–162, 195–196, 221–222, 249–251, 268–269
- Quick Check, 4–5, 37, 59–60, 95, 126, 151–152, 191, 226–227, 265; 5, 44–45, 74, 102, 133, 163–165, 197, 223, 251–252, 269–270

Problem Solving,
- Put on Your Thinking Cap!, 32, 54, 88–89, 147, 186, 221, 259, 281; 39, 70, 128, 157, 190, 217, 240, 266; *WB 19–20, 43–44, 67–68, 93–94, 119–120, 151–152, 183–184, 209–210, 229–230; WB 41–42, 58, 91–92, 119–120, 151–152, 173–174, 195–196, 221, 244*
  - strategies,
    - act it out, *WB 20, 93, 94, 119, 120, 152, 183; WB 221*
    - before-after, 121; *WB 93, 94*
    - draw a diagram, 89, 121, 127, 137, 259, 281; *WB 20, 93, 94, 119, 120, 152, 210; WB 195–196*
    - guess and check, 221; *WB 43, 44, 67–68, 70, 120; WB 41, 152*
    - look for patterns and relationships, 32, 186; *WB 19, 119; WB 151, 195–196*
    - make a diagram, 190
    - make a list, *WB 44, 68, 230*
    - make suppositions, *WB 184*
    - make a table, *WB 195–196*

Pages listed in regular type refer to Student Book A.
Pages in blue type refer to Student Book B.
Pages listed in *italic* type refer to Workbook (WB) A.
Pages in *blue italic type* refer to Workbook (WB) B.
Pages in **boldface** type show where a term is introduced.

difference, *WB 7–10*
fact family, 57
inverse operations, *See* Inverse operations
mental, *WB 11–14*
models for,
abstract, 98–99, 101–102, 106–108, 111–115, 117–123, 216–220, 278–281, 283; *WB 75–76, 79–85, 87, 89–92, 94–98, 101–103, 105, 112–114, 117, 180–181, 189–190, 205–206, 212–214, 225–227, 240–242, 249, 252; WB 7–10*
concrete, 61–63, 67–68, 72–74, 78–80, 84–85
pictorial, 98–99, 101–102, 106–108, 111–115, 117–123, 216–220, 254, 256–258, 278–281, 283; *WB 75–76, 79–85, 87, 89–92, 94–98, 102–103, 105, 205–206, 213–214, 225–227, 240–242, 249*
hundreds from a 3-digit number; *WB 7–9, 14*
ones from a 2-digit number; *WB 11*
ones from a 3-digit number; *WB 12*
tens from a 3-digit number; *WB 7–9, 13*
place value, *See* place value
real-world problems, *See* Real-world problems
regrouping,
hundreds as tens, 72–77, 79, 81–83; *WB 57–60, 67, 69–72, 101–102, 245, 247*
hundreds, tens, and ones, 78–83; *WB 61–64, 67, 69–72, 101–102, 247*
tens as ones, 67–71, 78, 81–83; *WB 53–56, 67, 69–72, 101–102, 244-245, 247*
repeated, *See* Division
strategies,
comparing sets, *See* Set–compare
part-part-whole, See Part-part-whole
subtract 100 then add the extra tens, 24
subtract the hundreds, 25
subtract the ones, 21
subtract 10 then add the extra ones, 20, 22
subtract the tens, 23
taking away sets, *See* Set–take away
without regrouping up to 3-digit numbers, 61–66; *WB 49–52, 67*
with zeros, 57

Sum, *See* Addition
estimate, 34, 37–38; *WB 15, 19–20, 22*

Surfaces
flat, 258–264, 266; *WB 215*
curved, 258–264, 266; *WB 215*

T

Taking away, *See* Set–take away

Tally chart, *See* Picture Graphs

Technology
Computers, 278

Tens, *See* Place value
Thousand, *See* Place value

Time,
A.M. 142–149 ; *WB 107–110, 121*
elapsed, 150–153, 155; *WB 111–117*
hour hand, *WB 104–106, 111*
minute hand, 133–136; *WB 97–100, 103, 105, 111*
ordering, 145, 149; *WB 110*
P.M., 142–149; *WB 107–110, 121*
reading, 137–141; *WB 101–102, 106*
writing, 137–141; *WB 101–102, 106, 115, 121*

Tools (of measure), See Length, Mass, and Volume

Triangle, See Geometry

U

Units (of measure), *See* Length, Mass, *and* Volume

V

Vocabulary, 6, 11, 18, 38, 42, 61, 103, 109, 127, 134, 153, 156, 192, 196, 201, 228, 235, 240, 266, 273; *WB 21, 45, 69, 95, 121, 153, 185–186, 211, 231*

Volume, **266**
comparing,
as much as, 268; *WB 215*
least, 268, 269, 271–272, 277; *WB 216–220, 231*
less than, 268, 269, 272, 273–274, 277; *WB 215, 231, 248*

Pages listed in regular type refer to Student Book A.
Pages in blue type refer to Student Book B.
Pages listed in *italic* type refer to Workbook (WB) A.
Pages in *blue italic type* refer to Workbook (WB) B.
Pages in **boldface** type show where a term is introduced.

W

Z

Photo Credits

3: ©Jupiter Images, *8:* ©iStockphoto.com/Wessel Du Plooy, *11:* ©Jupiter Images, *13:* ©Stockbyte, *17:* ©iStockphoto.com/Liza McCorkle, *20:* ©iStockphoto.com/Jaimie Duplass, *22:* ©iStockphoto.com/Petre Milevski, *24:* ©iStockphoto.com/Quavondo Nguyen, *28b:* ©iStockphoto.com/Daniel Rodriguez, *32:* ©iStockphoto.com/Sean Locke, *34:* ©iStockphoto.com/Andrew Manley, *35:* ©Stockbyte, *45:* ©iStockphoto.com/Sean Locke, *46:* ©iStockbyte, *49:* ©iStockphoto.com/Quavondo Nguyen, *50t:* ©Jupiter Images, *50b:* ©Stockbyte, *51t:* ©Stockbyte, *51b:* ©Stockbyte, *52:* ©iStockphoto.com/Liza McCorkle, *55t:* ©Stockbyte, *55b:* ©Stockbyte, *56tl:* ©Stockbyte, *56tr:* ©Stockbyte, *57:* ©iStockphoto.com/Andrew Manley, *60:* ©Stockbyte, *62t:* ©iStockphoto.com/Jaimie Duplass, *62b:* ©iStockphoto.com/Tracy Whiteside, *63:* ©iStockphoto.com/Wessel Du Plooy, *66:* ©iStockphoto.com/Marilyn Nieves, *67:* ©iStockphoto.com/Quavondo Nguyen, *68t:* ©Stockbyte, *68b:* ©iStockphoto.com/Andrew Manley, *70:* ©Stockbyte, *71:* ©Jupiter Images, *75:* ©Stockbyte, *76t:* ©iStockphoto.com/Juan Monino, *76b:* ©Stockbyte, *77:* ©iStockphoto.com/Daniel Rodriguez, *79:* ©iStockphoto.com/Sean Locke, *83:* ©iStockphoto.com/En Tien Ou, *85t:* ©Stockbyte, *85m:* ©iStockphoto.com/Tracy Whiteside, *85b:* ©iStockphoto.com/Jaimie Duplass, *92t:* ©iStockphoto.com/Marilyn Nieves, *92b:* ©iStockphoto.com/Liza McCorkle, *93:* ©Stockbyte, *94:* ©Jupiter Images, *112t:* ©Jupiter Images, *112b:* ©iStockphoto.com/Marilyn Nieves, *113:* ©iStockphoto.com/Marilyn Nieves, *115tl:* ©Stockbyte, *115tr:* ©iStockphoto.com/Wessel Du Plooy, *115b:* ©iStockphoto.com/Quavondo Nguyen, *117:* ©Stockbyte, *118:* ©iStockphoto.com/Liza McCorkle *119:* ©iStockphoto.com/Sean Locke, *121:* ©Jupiter Images, *124t:* ©Stockbyte, *124b:* ©iStockphoto.com/Andrew Manley, *125t:* ©Stockbyte, *125b:* ©Stockbyte, *134:* ©Jupiter Images, *137t:* ©Stockbyte, *137b:* ©Jupiter Images,*138t:* ©iStockphoto.com/Liza McCorkle, *138b:* ©Stockbyte, *139:* ©iStockphoto.com/Jaimie Duplass, *142:* @Jupiter Images, *150:* ©iStockphoto.com/Quavondo Nguyen, *151:* ©iStockphoto.com/Sean Locke, *152t:* ©Stockbyte, *152b:* ©iStockphoto.com/Andrew Manley, *159:* ©Stockbyte, *162t:* ©iStockphoto.com/Andrew Manley, *162b:* ©iStockphoto.com/Marilyn Nieves, *166t:* ©Stockbyte, *166b:* ©Stockbyte, *167t:* ©iStockphoto.com/Tracy Whiteside, *167b:* ©iStockphoto.com/Sean Locke, *170:* ©Stockbyte, *171:* ©iStockphoto.com/Daniel Rodiguez, *172:* ©iStockphoho.com/Jaimie Duplass, *173:* ©Stockbyte, *175b:* ©Jupiter Images, *176t:* ©iStockphoto.com/Quavondo Nguyen, *176b:* ©iStockphoto.com/Tracy Whiteside, *179:* ©Jupiter Images,*181t:* ©Stockbyte, *181b:* ©iStockphoto.com/Andrew Manley, *182:* ©iStockphoto.com/Jaimie Duplass, *184t:* ©Stockbyte, *184b:* ©iStockphoto.com/Sean Locke, *185:* ©iStockphoto.com/Daniel Rodriguez, *186:* ©Jupiter Images, *188:* ©Stockbyte, *190:* ©iStockphoto.com/Daniel Rodriguez, *198t:* ©iStockphoto.com/Wessel Du Plooy, *198b:* ©Jupiter Images, *200:* ©iStockphoto.com/Daniel Rodiguez, *201t:* ©iStockphoto.com/Andrew Manley, *201b:* ©Stockbyte, *202t:* ©Stockbyte, *202b:* ©Stockbyte, *205:* ©iStockphoto.com/Marilyn Nieves, *206t:* ©Stockbyte, *206b:* ©Jupiter Images, *207t:* ©iStockphoto.com/Petre Milevski, *207b:* ©iStockphoto.com/Sean Locke, *209:* ©Stockbyte, *210:* ©Stockbyte, *211:* ©iStockphoto.com/Tracy Whiteside, *213t:* ©iStockphoto.com/Jaimie Duplass, *213m:* ©iStockphoto.com/En Tien Ou, *213b:* ©iStockphoto.com/Daniel Rodiguez, *214t:* ©Stockbyte, *214b:* ©iStockphoto.com/Liza McCorkle, *224:* ©Stockbyte, *225:* ©iStockphoto.com/Andrew Manley, *226:* ©iStockphoto.com/Tracy Whiteside, *236r:* ©iStockphoto.com/Marilyn Nieves, *236l:* ©Stockbyte, *238:* ©iStockphoto.com/Liza McCorkle, *249ml:* ©iStockphoto.com/Jon Helgas, *249bl:* ©Dreamstime.com/Jimikuk, *249br:* © Dreamstime.com/Daruda, *251tr:* © Dreamstime.com/Goosey, *253t:* ©iStockphoto.com/Andrew Manley, *253b:* ©Stockbyte, *254:* ©iStockphoto.com/Quavondo Nguyen, *258t:* ©iStockphoto.com/Jaimie Duplass, *258bl:* ©Stockbyte, *258br:* ©iStockphoto.com/Tracy Whiteside, *259t:* ©iStockphoto.com/Quavondo Nguyen, *259bl:* ©iStockphoto.com/Liza McCorke, *259br:* ©iStockphoto.com/Daniel Rodriguez,

264: ©iStockphoto.com/Carlos Alvarez, *271:* ©iStockphoto.com/Sean Locke, *272:* ©iStockphoto.com/Quavondo Nguyen, *280:* ©iStockphoto.com/Liza McCorkle, *282:* ©iStockphoto.com/En Tien Ou, *283:* ©iStockphoto.com/ Liza McCorkle, *287t:* ©Jupiter Images, *287b:* ©iStockphoto.com/ En Tien Ou, *288t:* ©iStockphoto.com/Quavondo Nguyen, *288b:* ©iStockphoto.com/Petre Milevski, *292t:* ©iStockphoto.com/Andrew Manley, *292b:* ©iStockphoto.com/Petre Milevski, *293t:* ©iStockphoto.com/Sean Locke, *293m:* ©iStockphoto.com/Andrew Manley, *293b:* ©iStockphoto.com/ Petre Milevski, *295tr:* ©iStockphoto.com/Andrew Manley, *295bl:* ©iStockphoto.com/ Petre Milevski, *295br:* ©Stockbyte, *298tr:* ©iStockphoto.com/Andrew Manley, *298bl:* ©Stockbyte, *298br:* ©iStockphoto.com/ Liza McCorkle, *299t:* ©iStockphoto.com/ Wessel Du Plooy, *299b:* ©iStockphoto.com/Jaimie Duplass, *300t:* ©iStockphoto.com/En Tien Ou, *300bl:* ©Stockbyte, *300br:* ©Jupiter Images

Blank

Blank